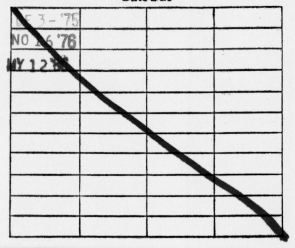

The Warren
REVOLUTION

Reflections on the Consensus Society

L. Brent Bozell

 ARLINGTON HOUSE
New Rochelle, New York

Library of Congress Catalog Card Number 66–23141

SECOND PRINTING, JANUARY 1969

MANUFACTURED IN THE UNITED STATES OF AMERICA

For My Children
I hope the book may
recommend to them
pietas

ACKNOWLEDGMENTS

The credit for this volume belongs, above all, to my wife, Patricia, mostly for reasons that she alone, and for others that not even she, will understand. For the rest I am indebted to my brothers and to William Buckley, Jr., Willmoore Kendall and Frank Meyer without whose encouragement and teaching the argument would not have been made, and certainly not half so well formed. And to Michael Lawrence whose labors and good sense were indispensable in hammering it all together.

. . . the candid citizen must confess that if the policy of the Government upon vital questions affecting the whole people is to be irrevocably fixed by decisions of the Supreme Court, the instant they are made in ordinary litigation between parties in personal actions, the people will have ceased to be their own rulers, having to that extent practically resigned their Government into the hands of that eminent tribunal.

Abraham Lincoln, *First Inaugural Address*

CONTENTS

INTRODUCTION
Crisis in The Consensus Society   15

THE WARREN COURT IN THE DOCK
Brown *v.* Board of Education   41
Pennsylvania *v.* Nelson   58
The Schempp-Murray Cases   70
Wesberry *v.* Sanders   80

THE FACES OF JUDICIAL REVIEW   115

THE TRADITION, I
From Coke to Blackstone   123
Across the Atlantic   137
The "Higher Law"   148

THE TRADITION, II
Independence: The Beginning of an "Irresistible Process"?   159
The Case of Josiah Philips   162
Holmes *v.* Walton   166
Commonwealth *v.* Caton   173
Rutgers *v.* Waddington   179
Trevett *v.* Weeden   185
The Symsbury Case   195
The "Lost" Massachusetts Precedent   197
Some New Hampshire "Occurrences"   199
Bayard *v.* Singleton   203
A Summary   213

E PLURIBUS UNUM

The Problem at Philadelphia   219
The Meaning of the Supremacy Clause, I   227
The Meaning of the Supremacy Clause, II   243
The Meaning of the Supremacy Clause, III   257
Judicial Review Elsewhere in the Constitution   268
Judicial Review at the Constitutional Convention   273
The Federalist   300
1789: The Status Quo Ante   328

Appendix   341

Notes   351

Index   361

INTRODUCTION

CRISIS IN THE CONSENSUS SOCIETY

This book is concerned with how our society makes, or should make, public policy, rather than with what our public policy is, or should become. To be sure, the disintegration of Western Civilization is to be understood primarily in terms of failures in the latter area: regardless of how they have been made, or by whom, the decisions that have determined Western fortunes for the past half century, perhaps for the past half millennium, appear in the reckoning to have been wrong. And the man is irredeemably insensate who, having the capacity to recognize sickness, does not devote a good part of his waking hours to agonizing over the West's sickness and to searching for the keys (which are probably theological) to recuperation and health. But the substantive ills of the West must be diagnosed elsewhere. Our intention is to speak of method, to inquire whether the responsibility for diagnosis and cure, in the public sphere, has been entrusted to the people and to the institutions—the "machinery," to summon the contemporary figure—that are likely to do the best job.

It is probably more a symptom of disintegration than a cause that the method of public policy-making in the United States has undergone a fundamental change in the past decade without the change having been widely commented on, or, by most of us, even noticed. True, the change is not apparent at the stages of policy-making we ordinarily think of as decisive. "We the people" still elect or indirectly appoint our public officials as we have done in the past. Our officials, in turn, enact and administer the laws much as they always have— allowing, of course, for the continuing expansion of the bureaucracy's role, and for the increasing influence of non-governmental "opinion molders." In the total business of governing a society, however, these dimensions are not nearly so important as they must seem to those who move in them. We may recall the famous husband who, challenged to disprove the sociologists' thesis that the woman rules the modern

American family, replied that in *his* family *he* made the decisions on
the major issues—e.g., whether the U.S. should continue to belong to
the United Nations, and what should be done about right-to-work. But
the sociologists' concern, as we know, was not so much to distinguish
between "major" and "minor" decisions as to demonstrate that most
day-to-day decisions are *derivative,* that they are made in the context
of and are therefore largely determined by the family's peculiar character, or ethos—its ethical substructure—which, according to the thesis,
is largely established and defined by the woman.

In dealing with political societies, we properly speak of the society's
ethical substructure as its "constitution." It is in the matter of *constitution-making* that the fundamental change in American public life
has recently occurred.

Before indicating the nature of the change, let us be as clear as we
can about what a "constitution," in the generic sense in which we are
using the term, is. And perhaps the best way of getting at that is to
state what a constitution does, or may do.

In part, it is a scheme under which public authority in a society is
divided up: it sets forth who, in the conduct of public business, shall
have power to do what to whom.

Second, it may establish, or attempt to establish, the boundary lines
of the public business, beyond which no public authority is expected
to venture; that is, it may reserve certain areas of private freedom.

Third, it may grant certain privileges of a public nature—what we
are accustomed to call "civil rights."

And fourth—a function that both underlies the first three and also
extends far beyond them—a constitution embodies an understanding
among the society's members about the *kind* of society it is. What are
the society's purposes? Or does it have any purpose beyond merely sur-
viving? What does it "believe in"? Or does it consider itself to be
"open" and thus, as a society, to believe in nothing? Does it relate, or
seek to relate, its individual members as "equals"? Or according to
various "structures" that have been established by its organic processes?
Is the society expected to serve the interests of its members, or are the
members expected to serve the society's interest? And so on.

Now regardless of which of these roles it performs—whether it dis-
penses authority, or reserves freedom, or grants rights, or reflects a
consensus about the society's underlying character—a constitutional
provision is superior to ordinary acts of government in this respect:
it is a *standard* to which the ordinary governmental act is expected to
conform—conformity being the condition on which the society's mem-

bers have agreed to be governed at all. A constitution, then, is a society's internal treaty of peace. If the peace terms are honored, the society may look forward to tranquility, order, obedience: the expressions of peace. If they are breached, the society may anticipate, according to the gravity of the matter, discord, violence, rebellion: the expressions of war.

Let us probe a little further. Everyone knows that constitutions may be written, as in the United States, or unwritten, as in Great Britain. What is less often noticed is that a society that has a written constitution also has an unwritten one: in a society like ours, that is to say, only *part* of the Constitution is written down. In the United States, moreover, this is true with respect to each of the four constitutional functions we have mentioned.

The division and granting of power, to take the first, is largely taken care of in our written Constitution; but the authority of Cabinet members and of the various bureaucracies is not specified there—and is not less secure, or "constitutional," for the fact it is not specified. Nor, to anticipate our thesis a little, does the written Constitution say anything about our society's *supreme* authority—the one that is meant to construe its *Constitution*. As we shall see, this is a matter that has always been the exclusive concern of our unwritten constitution.

As for reserving freedom, our Bill of Rights does indeed purport to safeguard certain areas, at least against federal intrusion; but there are other private freedoms of constitutional status—the right to marry whom one chooses and the right to move freely about the country are two of them—to which neither the Bill of Rights nor the Constitution proper makes allusion.*

Regarding public privileges, the right to a jury trial is conferred by the written Constitution, as is the right not to be excluded from the franchise because of race or sex; but the right to vote itself, or, to cite an even more recent entry, the right to a free formal education, are assured, if at all, only by our unwritten constitution.†

---

* We do not suggest that these freedoms are absolute under the unwritten constitution, but that it is largely the unwritten constitution, rather than the reservation clauses (the Ninth and Tenth Amendments) of the written one, that determines where the lines are drawn. This may be appreciated by a moment's reflection on how our society handled Mormon polygamy on the one hand, and the supposed danger of sabotage by Japanese-Americans during World War II, on the other.

† Of course such rights may be expressly conferred by written state constitutions or laws; but this fact does not detract from their status as elements of an unwritten *national* consensus.

Finally, the matters that fall under the heading of a society's character or credo are largely the concern, in the United States anyway, of our unwritten constitution. For example, as significant a characteristic of our society as that it is "religious," i.e., that the generality of its members acknowledge God, certainly can not be discovered in the written Constitution proper—nor, for that matter, in the First Amendment which treats the subject in a back-handed fashion, which is to say in language clearly more appropriate for protecting a minority than for affirming the belief of a majority. The written Constitution, however, is not altogether silent on such matters. The "obligation of contracts" clause, for instance, says a lot about what we now call the Protestant ethic, and has played no small role in causing its observance in American public life. Still other matters of this kind are merely hinted at, as the provision limiting the importation of slaves hinted that our society was already developing doubts, although somewhat diffidently, about slavery, and as the equal protection clause later hinted that our beliefs were moving in the direction, not merely of freedom (for that is another matter), but of equality.

But saying this much takes us to a consideration that is even less frequently noticed, with the result that an important element of our political machinery is generally misunderstood. What must be said now is that *some matters—and they are momentous matters—appear to be dealt with, and settled, by our written Constitution, but in point of fact are not settled by it.* Perhaps the best example is the matter of free speech. We have been taught to believe that the constitutional status of freedom of speech in the United States is set forth in the First Amendment. That this is not and could not be true is apparent from the language of the Amendment, which is recognizably unserviceable as a working constitutional directive. To be sure, there is a school of thought that contends the words "Congress shall make *no* law abridging the freedom of speech" were intended by the framers to be taken literally. But sober students have a different understanding of the matter: they know, a priori, that no responsible group of law givers would deprive their society of the means to protect itself against speech that endangered its survival; and they know, a posteriori, that this particular group of law givers did not think of themselves to be doing so, as witness that the Congress that wrote the First Amendment also wrote, a scant five years later, the Alien and Sedition Acts. But if the framers' formulation was not meant to be taken literally, then it was merely metaphorical—an indication that the society for which the framers spoke thought highly of free speech. But if only metaphorical, it is, we repeat—and has proved to be—quite useless as a constitutional standard. Actually, our constitutional rule about freedom of speech, to the extent it has proved capable of being written down at all, is embodied in the "clear and present danger" doctrine which was first put into words by a Supreme Court justice in the twentieth century. Justice Holmes did not, however, invent the rule. He found it, as we still find it today, in a consensus that has been hammered out over the years by legislatures, Presidents, courts; the rule was to be found, in a word, in our *un*written constitution.

The free speech matter is, as we say, merely illustrative. That much the same point must be made about the reach of the commerce clause, the balance of the First Amendment, and parts of the Fifth and the Fourteenth Amendments—to mention a few of our written Constitution's more important provisions—does not require elaboration. It follows that to try to distinguish between our "written" and "unwritten" constitutions—since a provision may appear formally in one, but actually be in the other—is not particularly helpful, and may be misleading. We are better advised to draw the line, for distinctions indeed must be made, between what we shall henceforth call our *fixed* constitution and our *fluid* constitution, it being understood that while all "fixed" provisions are written, not all written provisions are fixed. So let us turn to the differences, which are fundamental, between our fixed and fluid constitutions.

The principal differences arise out of the method by which the two types of constitution are *made*, and thus the method by which they may be *unmade*, or changed. A fixed constitutional provision, under our system, is made by *formal* procedures which have been designed a) to define the proposed provision unambiguously; b) to subject it to open, deliberative debate by the appointed constitution-makers; c) to dispose of the proposal definitively by public tabulation of the constitution-makers' votes. A fluid provision, on the other hand, is made by *informal* procedures which are calculated, precisely, to *avoid* exact definition, deliberative debate, and public vote-taking.

We may spell this out a little. In the case of a fixed provision, our society has in effect convened itself in extraordinary session—either in special constitutional convention or by summoning Congress and the state legislatures to act in that capacity—to consider issuing a binding policy directive to its various public authorities. The task of the session is to determine whether there exists, at this time and place, a sufficiently broad consensus about the desirability of a given policy to warrant placing that policy beyond the reach of the society's ordinary political processes. And the test of sufficiency will be whether a clear statement of the policy, after its meaning and implications have been fully explored and weighed in open debate, can command the support of a "constitutional majority" of the society, as measured by the formal constitution-making machinery set forth in Articles V and VII of the written Constitution. Moreover, and most important of all, the society has made a prior *"moral"* commitment that should the required majority affirm the statement, the decision will thenceforth be binding, not only on its individual members, but on every public authority— *until such time as a contrary-minded constitutional majority has been mobilized and has recorded a new consensus through the same arduous, exacting procedures.* Thus, on July 12, 1909, two-thirds of the Congress proposed an amendment to the Constitution that would permit the levying of a federal tax on incomes; by February 25, 1913, three-quarters of the state legislatures had ratified the proposal, thereby incorporating it into the fixed constitution as the Sixteenth Amendment. And thus it has been understood ever since, no less by the enemies of the federal income tax than by its friends, that the power conferred by the Sixteenth Amendment cannot be withdrawn, or modified, except in compliance with the Amendment procedures stipulated in Article V.

It is quite otherwise with the fluid constitution. Here we are dealing with "provisions" such as our constitutional rule about freedom of speech, that are fashioned gradually, subtly, often imperceptibly, by the society's organic process. There is no moment—no "time and place" —at which the provision may be said to have been framed and adopted; rather, it has *developed*, the product of the society's inner dynamics of experience, growth and change. It may have had, at its point of departure, a "principle" set forth in the written Constitution, such as "freedom of speech," "due process of law," "equal protection of the law"; but except as the framers made clear their expectations as to how the principle was to be applied,* the provision will not become

---

* As we shall see shortly in connection with the *Brown* desegregation case, some provisions of the written Constitution have both fixed and fluid features. The legislative history of the Fourteenth Amendment makes clear, that is, that the equal protection clause was intended to give constitutional status to the concrete guarantees of the Civil Rights Act of 1866, and the clause is, to that extent, a "fixed" provision; it is equally clear from the historical data that any further implications "equal protection" might have had were to be left to organic development, and are thus in the "fluid" category.

effective until the rivalries, the interplay, the give and take among the society's diverse forces and factions, have hammered out a working consensus about the concrete particulars of application.

Nor is it likely, either in the process of its adoption or thereafter, that a fluid provision will, or can, be reduced to a neat formulation that establishes, with equal clarity for everybody, its exact dimensions and implications. *For the distinctive characteristic of a fluid provision is precisely that it carries shadings of meaning, provisos, exceptions, qualifications—a hundred nuances that will permit different interpretations by different people in different situations, and without which general acceptance could not be expected.* Any attempt to spell out the nuances would probably prevent a constitutional consensus from taking shape, and so destroy the possibility of giving *the principle* in question effective constitutional status.

This is why a fluid provision cannot prudently be "put to a vote," why no one seeks to measure the consensus by a mathematical formula. Adoption is accomplished, rather, by an *accumulation* of actions taken over a period of years by various public authorities, as well as by private citizens and groups—actions that may often be in sharp conflict with each other, but which may eventually produce a broad synthesis. Congress and the state legislatures—for example—may indicate a preference for one course of action; the courts may resist, or perhaps try to go the other way; the President may join one side or the other, or possibly bring his weight to bear on behalf of compromise; community practice, meanwhile, is recording its own judgment. And as each participant in the process absorbs the impact of the others' behavior, sufficient veerings and withdrawals may occur to produce a common course along which the society as a whole can be seen to be traveling. Once this has happened one of our constitution's fluid provisions has come into being.

But mark well two aspects of the process that bear heavily on today's problems. The first is that the establishment of this kind of constitutional consensus does not preclude divergences from the fluid provision's principal thrust; rather, as we have noted, the consensus may depend precisely on the recognition and toleration of disparities, of meanderings from the main stream. It is in the very nature of a fluid provision, since it springs from the organic pressures of a diversified society, that it contemplates some front-runners, some laggards, even some die-hards who try still to move in the opposite direction. The American colonies, toward the end of the seventeenth century, were moving toward a general rule of religious toleration, and the emergence of the rule was no less apparent for the fact that Massachusetts, unlike the more enlightened colonies further south, was still hanging witches. The second thing to remember is that the substance and direction of the flow are established, not by the action of one force, but by the *interaction* of many. Thus while the fluid constitution is subject to constant change, the change is always a community undertaking. A fluid constitutional provision is unmade, or revised, in the same fashion it was made—by a shift in the consensus, brought about and registered by the society's organic processes.

The gradual emergence of our national government as a "welfare state" illustrates the making of a fluid provision. Our fixed constitution simply does not deal with the subject of federal welfarism. To be sure, certain passages of the written document—the Preamble, the taxing power, the commerce clause, the due process clause, and the Tenth Amendment—can be and have been read, in net impact, as authorizing welfare measures; but they also can be and have been read as forbidding such measures. Careful commentators on both sides, moreover, have always acknowledged the inconclusiveness of the evidence. Therefore, the existence and scope of the national government's power in this area have necessarily been the product of an *informal* constitutional consensus.

And note that while that consensus, historically, has changed very little from year to year, it has undergone a substantial change over the course of many years. At the turn of the century the notion that Congress is constitutionally competent to "wage war on poverty" would have been laughed out of court. Today it is probably correct to say that our society recognizes a congressional *power* to undertake any welfare measure that can be accomplished by the appropriation and allocation of public funds. The sharpest shift in the consensus occurred, of course, in the nineteen-thirties, and was reflected in a dramatic struggle between the President and Congress on the one hand, and the Supreme Court on the other, with the state governments (though their interests were as deeply involved as any) meekly watching the contest from the sidelines. The mechanics of that shift—for instance as it affected the field of agriculture—are worth remembering. Congress and the President attempted to aid the agricultural community by the imposition of certain production controls, said to be justified under the taxing power. The Supreme Court denied the taxing power was that extensive, and so declared the first AAA unconstitutional. Congress then retaliated with the second AAA—this time, however, advancing its plan under the cover of the commerce clause.

The Court retreated, clearly not because it believed Congress now to be on superior constitutional ground, but because community sentiment, as reflected in part by President Roosevelt's "court-packing" threat, had rallied to the support of New Deal legislation. The Court's capitulation thus *ratified* a revision of the fluid constitutional consensus. This pattern of settlement, moreover, seems sure to be followed in the future: whether the trend towards increased welfarism is sustained or reversed, the American people will continue to make constitutional decisions on such matters through the informal, organic processes of the fluid constitution, rather than by formal, rigid declarations of policy set forth in the fixed constitution.

At this point a general observation may be in order about how constitutions ought to be made. It would appear that certain kinds of problems are more appropriately and successfully handled by the informal procedures of a fluid constitutional provision, while certain other kinds of problems lend themselves more readily to the rigid affirmations of a fixed constitution. There are some matters, that is to say, in which continuing growth and change, and not always in the same direction, or with the same impact on all parts of our society, can be expected. In these matters the *flexibility* of the fluid constitution allows our various governmental structures to absorb and reflect the diverse shifts in community consensus that are going on down below, and may thus be an indispensable condition of stability and order, as well as of maximum freedom. For this reason, such bottom-level and fundamentally ethical decisions as those that determine the kind of economic system the society will sustain, the type of social order it will observe, how it will handle the problem of political orthodoxy and dissent, its approach to religion, the code of personal morality it will sanction—such matters are usually better left to adjudication in the fluid constitution. The fixed constitution, on the other hand, is usually the more appropriate place for allocating the public authority to various branches and levels of government; for providing means of preserving the allocation—e.g., our system of "checks and balances"; for prescribing the conditions of conferring authority—e.g., the qualifications of public officials and the mode of selecting them (which would include the problem of the franchise); for describing certain details of government organization—minutiae such as the date Congress is to convene; and finally for asserting those strictly juridical or "courtroom" rights that are designed to assure individuals, irrespective of changing historical currents, an even-handed administration of justice. To be sure, such matters can become intertwined with bottom-level questions: an allocation of power—of the taxing power, for instance—may affect a society's basic economic structure; the franchise may affect its social structure; a guarantee of juridical rights may affect the underlying balance between orthodoxy and dissent; and so on; and when such complications occur a society will understandably be at sixes and sevens in deciding whether to deal with the problem in its fixed or in its fluid constitution. But on the whole the type of question just mentioned, unlike the bottom-level questions, can be succinctly posed and resolved by a "hard," relatively permanent constitutional consensus; for that reason, the interests of stability, order and maximum freedom are normally better served by a fixed provision.

There is a corollary to all of this. A *mixing* of constitutional categories—a failure to deal with a given matter by the type of provision suited to it—may lead to unhappy consequences.* On the one hand, failure to formalize a hard constitutional consensus by recording it in a fixed provision may permit a simple, transitory majority temporarily to defy the consensus for want of enforcement machinery. Prior to 1940 the President's tenure was limited to two terms by what most Americans thought to be a very hard "consensus." But since the consensus had been sanctioned by tradition only, the two-term rule was, in effect, a fluid constitutional provision. Consequently, Franklin Roosevelt was able to side-step the rule on the approval of a simple majority. A decade later the framers of the Twenty-second Amendment sought to repair the oversight by placing the question of Presidential tenure where a constitutional majority has now formally decided it belongs—in our fixed constitution. On the other hand, attempts to give fixed constitutional status to policies that do not lend themselves to that treatment will be at best futile, and at worst productive of great mischief. The attempt to define a constitutional rule about freedom of speech in the First Amendment settled nothing. The attempt to

---

* We speak here only of the United States; quite different generalizations might apply to other societies. For example, a more religiously homogenous society, like Spain, might find the State's relations with a given religion a proper subject for its fixed constitution. And on the other hand, the political systems of the Continent have never been particularly successful in giving fixed constitutional status to allocations of authority and limitations on the State's power generally. When formal constitution-making came into vogue in Europe in the early part of the nineteenth century, Prince Metternich persuasively argued that only the Anglo-Saxon peoples had sufficient self-restraint to maintain a meaningful distinction between the "state" and "society," and thus to observe fixed constitutional limitations on the State's power.

deal with the country's drinking problem by constitutional fiat in the Eighteenth Amendment led to a breakdown of the public order and was in due course withdrawn by the Twenty-first Amendment.

We are now ready to state the principal thesis of these volumes. It is a) that until a dozen years ago the constitution-makers of the United States by and large observed the distinction between the type of provision that is suited to the country's fixed constitution and the type that is suited to its fluid constitution, with the result that the country for the better part of this 165-year period enjoyed internal peace. The notable exceptions are the Civil War and, less calamitously, the Prohibition Era, when the distinction broke down. And it is b) that during the past twelve years the Supreme Court, with the encouragement of the country's intellectual establishment, has instituted a *third* kind of constitution-making, which is revolutionary both in its method and in its consequences. This new kind of constitution-making, to state the phenomenon broadly, *has sought to transfer the solution of some of the most momentous problems of contemporary public policy from the fluid constitution to the fixed constitution—by judicial decree.* The result is that the internal peace of the country has been gravely disturbed, and the country's potential for peaceful growth in the future seriously jeopardized. This is not the place to document the thesis in detail, but it will be helpful to indicate here some of its configurations.

One of the more remarkable aspects of the American political system is how little our fixed constitution has been altered since the first ten amendments were added on November 3, 1791, and thus how much of the country's growth and development and accommodation to changing times has been accomplished through the organic processes of our fluid constitution. In over a century and a half, the American Constitution has been amended by formal procedures only fourteen times— a record that becomes even more remarkable when we consider the kind of amendments those fourteen were.

One of them, the Twelfth Amendment, merely corrected an oversight in the original document regarding the method of electing the President, and thus made no substantive change in the system.

Another, the Twentieth, was a decision of administrative convenience, bringing Congress' annual meeting date into line with the date of the President's inauguration; it, too, reflected no substantive change in the country's political system.

A third, the Twenty-second, may be said to have affected the Constitution's original allocation of authority by potentially limiting the power of an individual President; but the two-term rule, as we have just remarked, did not so much change the system as recognize that the better way to guard an ancient consensus about how the system should operate was to remove the rule from the fluid into the fixed constitution.

Three other amendments dealt, in their principal effect, with the distribution of power between the national and state governments. The earliest, the Eleventh, reflected a decentralization tendency. The States, as sovereign entities, were not to be subject to suit in the national courts. Two later amendments, the Sixteenth and Seventeenth, reflected the centralization tendencies of the present century. The Sixteenth permitted Congress to levy an income tax without regard to the former rule that direct taxes be assessed in proportion to each State's population. The Seventeenth made senators popular representatives rather than representatives, in effect, of the state governments.

Another group of four, the Fifteenth, the Nineteenth, the Twenty-third and the Twenty-fourth, dealt with the franchise. Note, however, that the first of these four had origins of a very different character from the latter three, with the result that until recently it enjoyed a very different status in our constitutional system. The Fifteenth Amendment was conceived and promoted as an instrument of the Northern radicals' Reconstruction program; it was one of the conditions of peace laid down by the victors in the Civil War. While the Fifteenth's proponents formally observed the prescribed amendment procedures, they did not really command the support of a hard constitutional consensus. The country as a whole in 1870 was little more prepared to welcome Negroes to the franchise than the deep South was in 1960. As a result, the Fifteenth Amendment's status in the fixed constitution was extremely shaky until the present decade. It was honored as much in the breach as in the observance precisely because it lacked the sanction of a bona fide consensus. To be sure, recognition of Negro voting rights steadily increased over the years, but this development proceeded apace with changing social attitudes and economic conditions in various parts of the country—which means that the problem, in reality, was being adjudicated over a period of ninety years by our fluid constitution. Today, at last, a hard constitutional consensus about Negro voting has come into being, an event that was memorialized in 1964 by the adoption of the Twenty-fourth—the anti-poll tax—Amendment.

Now the Twenty-fourth is similar in this respect to the Nineteenth and the Twenty-third which, respectively, forbade the exclusion of women from the franchise, and gave the vote in Presidential elections to residents of the District of Columbia: all three merely formalized a consensus that had already been brought into being by the operation of the society's organic processes. It is not to disparage the suffragette movement or the agitations of disenfranchised Washingtonians, to recognize that their successes had been assured by a prior evolution of attitudes and practices in the country's economic and social structures. The franchise amendments, in a word, show that meaningful provisions of the written Constitution must have the support of a broadly-based consensus—that while the written Constitution can record, it cannot peaceably *produce* a change in the society's underlying ethical substructure.

The Thirteenth and Fourteenth Amendments were also conditions of peace imposed by the winning side in the Civil War. But each of them has peculiar aspects of which we should take careful account. The Thirteenth, unlike the Fifteenth, appears to have had the support of an authentic constitutional consensus at the time it was adopted. To be sure, a hard national consensus concerning the status of slavery had not emerged before the War, and the unwillingness of intransigents on both sides to allow the problem to be "worked out" through the organic processes precipitated the war. But the verdict of the war produced a consensus that Negroes should be free, which was no less authentic for the fact it was hammered out by force of arms. The problem of Negro slavery was thus adjudicated by our fixed constitution—notwithstanding the modern thesis that if wiser heads had prevailed the same result would have been achieved less painfully through the organic processes. Much the same may be said about one aspect of the Fourteenth on which we shall be commenting at some length below; suffice to note here that the Fourteenth's framers viewed certain elemental juridical rights as necessary concomitants of Negro emancipation, and these rights, like the Thirteenth itself, enjoyed fixed constitutional status from the beginning. However, the Amendment's broader implications, as suggested by the due process and equal protection clauses, were left for future implementation to the organic processes of the fluid constitution.*

---

* The process by which the vague, admonitory language of the Fourteenth Amendment has been transformed into effective national law is a lengthy, fascinating and still unfolding chapter of our constitutional history. And of course the developments have not been confined to the area of race relations. The point we make here, which anticipates our discussion of *Brown v. Board*

There are, finally, the Eighteenth Amendment which is the *reductio ad absurdum* example of the kind of problem that should never be thrust into the rigid prescriptions of a fixed constitution, and the Twenty-first which recognized and corrected the error.

For the rest, American constitution-making, up until 1954, proceeded in "fluid" channels. Our fixed constitution survived more or less intact, according to the framers' original plan and apparent expectations. It served us well, not only as a guarantor of stability and peace, but as a firmly grounded launching pad for innovation and relevant response to changing situations and changing times. This is not to say the framers would have felt altogether at home in our mid-twentieth-century American society: a century and a half had brought about profound changes in our insights and our outlooks, in our social, economic, and political organization, even in the substantive values we embraced. But it is to say that the framers, with remarkable shrewdness, seem to have anticipated the areas in which the changes might take place, and to have left those areas open—"flexible"—and unguarded by prescriptive dogma. It is also to say that the framers' successors had by and large recognized the wisdom of keeping things that way. The elastic clauses of the written Constitution remained flexible instruments of government. Our major policy decisions continued to be the product of an interaction—a series of organic tensions —between the wills of all branches of government. Our governors, whether in courts, legislatures or executive mansions, showed a remarkable reluctance to obstruct the flow of the fluid constitution by trying to give fixed constitutional status to policies around which an authentic consensus had not yet formed.

The Supreme Court's new method of constitution-making has exposed the country to a quite different experience during the past twelve years.

We have seen certain matters, of which the race problem is the one that comes most readily to mind, that were in the process of adjudication by the country's varied and intricate organic mechanisms, suddenly subjected to the rigid imperatives of a judge-defined "supreme law."

We have seen matters, like the relationship between church and state, that in the American experience have always defied simplistic,

---

of Education, is that the framers of the Fourteenth were themselves agreed on only a very limited application of their language: it would give constitutional sanction to the Civil Rights Act of 1866. See "Brown *v.* Board of Education," p. 44 et seq.

doctrinaire solutions, suddenly chained to abstract formulas that may be familiar to the rhetoric but are altogether alien to the customs and underlying attitudes of the people.

We have seen matters, like the apportionment of legislative representatives, that have traditionally been handled according to local needs and desires and thus disparately, suddenly laced into a single theory of politics that must be uniformly enforced alike in situations where the theory is helpful according to the community's lights and in those where it is not.

We have seen matters, like our national policy toward political dissidence, that have always been a function of competing concerns—in this case usually a compromise between each man's concern for personal freedom and the society's concern for consensus and self-preservation—suddenly treated as though only one concern were involved—in this case the First Amendment's paradigmatic statement about freedom.

Above all, in every such case, we have seen matters about which a hard constitutional consensus does *not* exist treated as though such a consensus *did* exist: we have been summoned to accord merely *judge*-endorsed policies the same dignity we accord policies that have passed the muster of the Constitution's formal amendment procedures.

This momentous innovation has been accomplished through the quietest of revolutions. The Warren Court, with the approval of much of the country's intellectual leadership, has simply expanded an old judicial function into a new one. From the earliest days of the Republic, the Supreme Court was a major participant in the making of our fluid constitution. Principally through the power of *judicial review*, the Court helped discover and develop working consensuses in areas not covered by the fixed constitution. Its decisions, strictly speaking, adjudicated nothing more than the rights of the litigants in the case at hand: nonetheless they were understood to be affirming a "judicial policy" that would govern similar cases in the future. And since that policy carried the sanction of the Court's considerable prestige as a putatively disinterested party, it is understandable that other policy-makers—Congress, the President, the States—were reluctant to repudiate judicial policy by ignoring or resisting the Court's rulings. The Court's views, to be sure, did not always prevail. But they were always an important factor in determining how the country should be run in those areas governed by the organic processes of the fluid constitution. Today, however, the Court claims not just a participant's role in the making of the fluid constitution, but the *umpire's* role. From its old

job of being *an* expounder of the constitution, it has become *the*
expounder. Its judgments are not simply a *factor*, along with the judgments of other public authorities, in the making of the fluid constitution; the Court now insists that its judgments are final and binding,
not only on the litigants in the case at hand, but on all public
authorities. The only recourse for those who disagree with the Court,
under the new understanding, is to the formal amendment procedures
of the written Constitution. *Thus, a Supreme Court decision has become equivalent to a provision of the fixed Constitution.*

In all respects, that is, save one. Like a fixed provision, it is binding
on all public authorities. Like a fixed provision, it can be changed
only by invoking the arduous amendment machinery of Article V. *The
one respect in which a Court decision differs from other provisions of
the fixed constitution is that it has acquired that status, not by securing
the endorsement of a hard national consensus, but by securing the
certification of a nine-man tribunal.*

¥   The race problem is an instructive instance of how this new method
of constitution-making has affected our society's traditional way of
doing business. Prior to the Civil War there were only two fixed constitutional provisions affecting the relationship between the white and
Negro races. One dealt with the importation of slaves, forbidding
Congress to ban the slave trade prior to 1808, and permitting (but not
requiring) it to do so thereafter.* The other provided that slaves were
to be counted as three-fifths of a white person for the purposes of
apportioning representatives and levying direct taxes. For the rest, the
original framers in effect decided that the problem should be dealt
with by the machinery of what we are calling the fluid constitution:
while later generations might adopt a fixed constitutional provision to

---

* This has been our only experience with an "executory" constitutional
provision. The consensus of 1787 asserted, in effect, that the country had
made up its mind to place the slave trade under the control of the national
government, but that this decision was to take effect at a fixed future date.
Note that this does not mean the framers anticipated the emergence of a *new*
consitutional consensus in 1808, but rather that the forces favoring national
control were already of consensus proportions in 1787, and that the achievement of their goals was merely postponed as part of the ratification strategy.
The curious codicil to Article V, forbidding alteration of the importation provision even by constitutional amendment, is inexplicable except as an acknowledgment that the forces favoring national control would probably have the
votes to write a fixed provision from the first moment the Constitution went
into operation.

govern this or that aspect of the problem, this would require the emergence of a hard constitutional consensus that was not present in 1787. Regarding the fundamental issues of whether slavery should be extended, and whether there should be slavery at all, no such consensus ever took shape through the organic processes; and as we have noted the Civil War occurred because neither side was prepared to wait for the consensus machinery to work out a solution. This judgment is not entirely hindsight. At the moment of crisis, in his first Inaugural Address, Mr. Lincoln made a last plea for submission to the true constitutional morality. The Union had thus far survived, Lincoln thought, because the country had refrained from forcing explosive issues to premature conclusions. It had not resolved its great disputes by submitting them to some final arbiter—whether to a popular majority as reflected by Congress, or to the individual States asserting their sovereign prerogatives, or to the Supreme Court that had recently handed down the Dred Scott decision—but by entrusting them to the consensus machinery that could speak and act for the whole. Lincoln's counsel, however, fell on deaf ears: the country was impatient with the consensus machinery, and the country fought.

The Civil War itself, as we have seen, produced two additions to the fixed constitution: Negroes were to be free—the Thirteenth Amendment; and they were to have the elemental juridical rights enjoyed by white persons—the Fourteenth. But until the adoption of the Twenty-fourth Amendment in 1964, which confirmed the inclusion of Negro voting rights in the fixed constitution, it was impossible to mobilize a hard constitutional consensus around any further rule for governing race relations. This does not mean, of course, that relations between the Negro and white races during these years remained frozen where the Civil War amendments left them; it simply means that all further developments took place under the aegis of the fluid constitution. It does not mean, to take a concrete example, that the implications of the equal protection clause were restricted to the narrow aims of the Fourteenth Amendment's framers. It does mean, however, that the expansion of the concept of equal protection occurred through evolution, through our society's organic processes.

It is worth noting why this evolutionary process, although it moved slowly by the standards of modern civil rights enthusiasts, succeeded both in generating progress and in keeping the peace. The changes that were brought about between the Civil War and 1954 were the end product of many forces, acting through many agents, operating by different methods, often moving in different directions. These changes never eliminated "racial tensions"; on the contrary, it was precisely the organic dynamics of the tension between political, social, economic and moral forces that produced and shaped the changes. Congresses, Presidents, courts, state governments, schools, churches, trade unions, private philanthropies, crusaders, agitators—all made their separate contributions; combined, they produced a relationship between the races that proved to be, in the jargon of today, "viable." They produced solutions that were far from perfect—that differed from place to place and from situation to situation—but solutions that the country, at any given moment, could live with. The reason, at bottom, why the country could live with imperfect solutions was that they were open to further change *as the country's attitudes and practices changed*: the organic processes had produced a *living* law; they had produced rules for governing the relations of the races that closely reflected, and promised to continue to reflect, the going beliefs, practices, capacities, and desires of the people. And so the country, instead of fragmenting from the tensions, paradoxically found successive formulas for unity and peace and future progress, through preservation of the tensions.

Then came *Brown v. Board of Education*. In May, 1954, the country was very far from having made up its mind on the question of segregated schools. It was divided in its practices in this matter because it was still profoundly divided in its beliefs. No hard constitutional consensus had been reached, or was likely to be reached in the foreseeable future. Therefore neither side, neither the "integrationists" nor the "segregationists," insofar as they were then identified as distinct groups, could realistically hope for the adoption of a constitutional amendment—a provision, that is, of the fixed constitution—that would embody its views and make them thenceforth the supreme and uniform law of the land. In this situation, the Supreme Court, visibly moved by the ideology of equality, took matters into its own hands and sought to impose upon the country a uniform solution to the problem of mixing the races in the public schools. The Court not only decided that the Negro plaintiffs in the *Brown* case were entitled to admission to white schools. It also, the following year, ordered a staged desegregation of public schools throughout the land, an order the judicial system itself proceeded to administer. And that was not all: although the claim had been implicit in the logic of the *Brown* opinion, the Warren Court, in 1958, formally proclaimed that its own views about segregated schools—or on any other subject for that matter —were binding on other public authorities in the country's political system. In the Little Rock school case of *Cooper v. Aaron*, the Supreme

Court, for the first time, entered its own explicit claim to judicial supremacy:

> [*Marbury v. Madison*] declared the basic principle that the federal judiciary is supreme in the exposition of the law of the Constitution, and that principle has ever since been respected by this Court and the Country as a permanent and indispensable feature of our constitutional system. It follows that the interpretation of the Fourteenth Amendment, enunciated by this Court in the *Brown* case is the supreme law of the land, and Article VI of the Constitution makes it of binding effect on the States any Thing in the Constitution or Laws of any State to the Contrary notwithstanding.[1]

Thus, as Professor Charles Hyneman has written, "the judges regarded their statement as to what the Constitution means to be identical with the words of the Constitution itself in capacity to impose obligation upon the rest of the nation."[2] Thus the Court abandoned the organic processes of the fluid constitution with respect to this aspect of the race problem, and would do so later on with respect to others. Thus these explosive issues were transferred to the fixed constitution—by judicial fiat. And the country's most learned commentators counseled obedience to the fiat. They asserted there was no alternative to obeying except to amend the Constitution.

With what practical consequences? Our experience with race conflict during the past decade speaks for itself. Before the desegregation decisions withdrew the problem from the organic processes, the country's practices by and large had kept abreast of the country's attitudes; the progress that had been made toward improving race relations was thus progress in depth, progress bound to endure because it was rooted in the consent and behavior of those directly concerned. After the decisions, the possibilities of consensual adjustment and accommodation were greatly diminished because of the wide gap between what was commanded and what was desired; and that gap inevitably became filled with hostility. Before the desegregation decisions, our society could respond relevantly to the concrete challenges that changing times produced: it could develop a living law on the race issue because the law, by definition, was attuned to the lives of the people. After the decisions, the people, Negroes and whites alike, were required to conform their lives to the prescriptions of ideology. Before the desegregation decisions, different sections of the country could deal with the race problem according to the capacities of their own districts which had been destined by history and geography to be disparate. After the decisions, dissimilars were treated as similars, diversity was expunged in favor of a superficial uniformity. Before the desegregation decisions, the country had approached the race issue as part of a multi-dimensional problem: there was not only the matter of giving the Negro his due, but also the matters of preserving the integrity of community life, of maintaining the country's federal political structure, of improving the country's schools, of maintaining the public order, of keeping the country's economic system flourishing, and so on. After the decisions, the issue became single-dimensional: all related problems became subordinate to the goal of satisfying the Negroes' claims.

Nor is this all. Consider the central commitment of American political thought, the idea that just government requires the consent of the governed. What the granting of fixed constitutional status to the Supreme Court's desegregation decisions has done to the concept of consensual government can best be appreciated by recalling the obstacles to *withdrawing* that status. The great anomaly in the Court's new method of constitution-making is that while nine judges can draw up a fixed constitutional provision *without* the authority of a hard constitutional consensus, their decision cannot be reversed *except* on the authority of a hard constitutional consensus. Remember that before the *Brown* case, neither the proponents of the mandatory integration of public schools, nor its opponents, could muster sufficient popular support to overcome the obstacles of Article V and incorporate their point of view in the fixed constitution. But thanks to the proponents' success in enlisting the aid of the Supreme Court in the role of "final arbiter," the opponents must now corral a hard constitutional majority, as reflected by Article V's formal amendment procedures, in order to restore the *status quo ante*. They must either do that, or persuade the Court to change its mind. That is why we may speak today of Judicial Supremacy.

The ultimate concern of these pages is with the *wisdom* of the Supreme Court's new method of constitution-making. We shall be asking in a subsequent volume: Do we wish to make it a permanent feature of our political system? (And let us not suppose, on the strength of what has been said so far, that an answer on the merits must all that surely be, No. Some of our most eminent thinkers have recently advanced powerful arguments in defense of the Court's new role, and we shall want to weigh those arguments carefully.) Or, is it the wiser course to restore consensus rule to the United States? If so, we shall need to acquire a better understanding of the consensus society than most contemporary commentary betrays. We shall also need to know what concrete demands Restoration will make upon us: Where, as a practical matter, do we go from here?

There are, however, some prior concerns that will have occurred to even the most casual witness to the controversy now swirling around the Warren Court. It has become a commonplace to characterize the Court's headline-making decisions of the past decade as political acts of will—to accuse the justices, as we have just done, of having become law-makers, instead of simply law-expounders. Yet there are some who do not accept this judgment, or say they do not. Some of the Court's apologists—although their number, and in any case their reputation for serious commentary, diminishes with each new judicial démarche—vigorously deny that the Warren Court has approached the great constitutional issues of our day in any way different than its predecessors would have done: both the Warren Court's methods and its results, these apologists contend, fall within the traditional pattern of constitutional interpretation and enforcement. What has caused all the commotion, on their showing, is that this particular Supreme Court, in the course of conscientiously performing its work-a-day duties, has stepped on the toes of a number of especially vociferous and intransigent political partisans who have bitterly and unsportsmanly refused to accept verdicts that the Constitution itself commands. As Mr. Joseph Rauh told a Senate committee several years ago: "The Supreme Court is under attack today because its recent decisions emphasizing human dignity and human freedom have gone contrary to the views of segregationist politicians in the South and security-mad politicians in the North."[3] Well, if that is so—if opposition to the Court's recent course can be laid simply to partisan disappointment over the outcome of the cases—then we are all duty-bound to make our separate peaces with the Court, thus helping to put an end to an unseemly sectarian squabble.

✗ Our first concern, then, is with the Supreme Court's recent performance in the field of constitutional law. In the next section we shall examine representative cases in the four areas where the Warren Court's renowned "activism" has been most pronounced: *Brown v. Board of Education*, the original school desegregation decision handed down in 1954; *Pennsylvania v. Nelson*, the Warren Court's earliest (1956) and perhaps its most consequential contribution to the continuing struggle between political dissidence and the public orthodoxy; the *Schempp-Murray* school prayer case, decided in 1963; and *Wesberry v. Sanders*, the 1964 congressional reapportionment case. We

shall see whether the justices have conscientiously tried to apply the
law, as they found it, to the facts before them; whether they have
observed the traditional standards of statutory and constitutional construction; whether they have shown due respect for the canons of
historical research, for the rules of logic, for the demands of candor.
We shall also have occasion to judge whether the Court's reasoning has
proceeded, as charged, from ideological prepossessions, whether it has
juggled evidence, arguments, and precedents to fit conclusions that
were, in reality, pre-ordained. Most readers will not have had access to
the raw data—the official reports of the cases and the relevant historical
material on which the Court relied, or should have relied. Therefore
we shall supply these data on the theory that elaborate analysis may
try the patience of some, but will give to all an opportunity to evaluate
the Court's performance for themselves.

Following the case analyses we shall come to grips with an entirely
different problem. Suppose the case studies convict the Warren Court;
suppose we find the justices guilty, as charged, of an endemic contempt
for the Constitution and the laws, of having pressed the federal judiciary into the service of ideology. What then? Can we only lament the
evil? Must we abide the transgressions on the theory that the Supreme
Court—right or wrong—is the ultimate arbiter of the Constitution's
meaning? Are Congress' hands tied? Are the States'? Is the President,
in the premises, merely Mr. Warren's chief marshal, powerless to interpose an independent judgment? Are we left with no remedy short of
predictably futile campaigns to amend the Constitution—or beyond
feckless pleas that the justices discipline themselves?

These questions, as we indicated earlier, lie at the heart of the
present controversy over the Supreme Court's role in the American
political order. Let us state the problem this way. Does the Supreme
Court have the *authority* to impose its will on the rest of the nation?
Is the Court lawfully entitled to demand obedience from the other
departments of our political system? Most modern commentary assumes
an affirmative answer *ex hypothesi*: What would we do *without* a final
arbiter of the Constitution? What would happen if someone—and who
could be better qualified than the Supreme Court—did *not* have the
"last say" about how our affairs are to be conducted? How else avoid
chaos and anarchy? How else prevent the fragmentation of our society
into as many seats of authority as there are ideas and wills on matters
of public concern? But if the rhetorical approach fails to convince, a
battery of experts is on hand—historians, constitutional lawyers, political scientists—ready to document the answer from an impressive litera-

ture dedicated to demonstrating the *legitimacy* of the doctrine of Judicial Supremacy. The justices of the Supreme Court have the authority to bind the rest of the nation because the founders of our political system granted it to them, and because the participants in the system have ever since recognized it. From the moment Chief Justice Marshall illuminated the framers' intentions about judicial review in *Marbury v. Madison* at the turn of the nineteenth century, the argument goes, the country has acknowledged the Court's power to *settle* constitutional disputes. It has expected the Court to weigh the disagreements between its various public authorities, and then to adjourn them. Chief Justice Hughes was not shooting from the hip, but solemnly affirming the pivotal truth of the American polity when he observed, "The Constitution is what the Supreme Court says it is."

Our second concern, then, is with this far more formidable group of apologists—those who are prepared to concede whatever charges the Warren Court's critics might want to make about the wrongness of individual decisions, but who insist that resistance to them is civil disobedience and therefore reprehensible. We must carefully examine their position. We must discover whether a decision by the Supreme Court is, like the Constitution itself, "the supreme Law of the Land"; whether that proposition was embraced by the Constitution's framers; whether the country's subsequent practices have sanctioned it; whether that, or something else, is what the American doctrine of judicial review, properly understood, implies. The answers are imbedded deep in our history and tradition; they are free neither of complexity—nor, fortunately, of fascination. We shall undertake an extensive search for them, mindful that our thesis deals irreverently with important household gods, persuaded that in our day one cannot properly urge the other departments of government to challenge the claims of judicial supremacy without assuming the burden of proving their lawful authority to do so.

THE WARREN COURT
IN THE DOCK

BROWN *v.* BOARD OF EDUCATION

The *Brown* case of 1954 is famous because of the revolution it precipitated in the field of race relations, but also because of the revolution it is said to have inaugurated in American jurisprudence. Our concern is only with the latter claim, with the charge that the Supreme Court approached the *Brown* case with a visibly different standard of *After (.....)* constitutional construction from that which had ostensibly guided the judiciary department in the past. We shall not tarry to document what that past standard had been: no serious student of the law will deny that prior to *Brown* the avowed role of the courts was to *expound* the law—to tell litigants, in effect, what the words of statutes and constitutions meant. And where the meaning of the words was ambiguous or debatable the courts were expected, as the first step in construction, to try to find out what the *authors* of the words meant by them—to establish by such external evidence as might be available the authors' intentions.

It hardly needs to be said that intention-divining is not one of the exact sciences. Frequently the authors of statutes and constitutions leave no conclusive clues, and may have intended to leave none, as to how they expected their language to be applied to concrete problems. The Sherman Act was clearly an invitation to the courts to formulate criteria for determining the ingredients of conspiratorial "combinations," and for defining "restraint of trade." The commerce clause itself invited the courts, as well as Congress and the States, to join in working out a practical plan for supervising the country's domestic trade. In other constitutional situations, the framers' language may reflect the limited knowledge of an earlier day, and yet be susceptible to interpolations based on technological innovation that plainly do no violence to the framers' intentions: nobody thought, upon the invention of the airplane, that a constitutional amendment was required to give Congress the power to develop an aeronautical weapons system.

There is obviously a difference, however, between interpolating new *knowledge*, and new *opinion*, into a constitutional provision. It is one thing to read the provision that Congress shall "make rules for the government and regulation of the land and naval forces" as meaning that Congress shall "make rules for the government and regulation of the land, naval and *air* forces." But it may be quite another thing to read a prohibition of segregated schools into the equal protection clause. In the one case the framers did not anticipate the Wright brothers and so could not opine or intend anything about an air force—although they manifestly wished Congress to regulate the country's military establishment. In the other, the framers of the Fourteenth Amendment were entirely aware of the phenomenon of public schools, and of segregated public schools, and so presumably did have opinions as to whether or not they should be outlawed. Whether these opinions were sufficiently to the fore in their utterances to establish an "intention" on the part of the Amendment's framers about segregated schools is the problem subsequent interpreters of the Constitution are called upon to solve.

The great constitutional issues of the past, we are saying, arose either from disputes about what a given provision meant in the minds of those who caused its adoption—or, assuming the answer to that question could not be found, from disputes over what to do then. The *first* question to be asked,, according to the canon, was, *What did the framers of the Constitution intend?* To be sure, past courts played loose with the canon in the sense of sometimes paying lip service to it while contriving an appropriate sophistry to circumvent it. For example, the Supreme Court in the late nineteenth century did impute to the framers of the Fourteenth Amendment's due process clause an intention to embrace the economic theories of Manchester. The Warren Court can, therefore, hardly be accused of *inventing* judicial dissimulation. But prior to 1954 the canon itself had avoided official challenge, and was an important factor in creating and sustaining the majesty of the judicial office.

The issue before the Supreme Court in *Brown v. Board of Education of Topeka* was whether the Constitution permits separation of the races in the public schools. Under Kansas law, the Topeka Board of Education is an agent of the State of Kansas; its claim to the right to maintain the kind of schools it pleased was therefore grounded on the Tenth Amendment. *"All powers not delegated to the United States by the Constitution, nor prohibited by it to the States,"* that provision affirms, *"are reserved to the States respectively or to the people."* What the framers of the Tenth Amendment intended with regard to *schools* has never been doubted: power over education—the right to maintain good schools or bad schools, or not to maintain them at all—was among the powers left to the States. But in 1868 the Constitution was amended further. Thereafter the Tenth Amendment had to be read alongside the Fourteenth, so that the question became: Is the provision, *"No State . . . shall deny to any person within its jurisdiction the equal protection of the laws"* a "prohibition" to the States of the power to maintain racially segregated schools? Brown asserted that it is.

Chief Justice Warren opened the Court's discussion of the constitutional issue by asking the correct question—namely, What had the authors of the Fourteenth Amendment *intended* with regard to public education? Much of the argument in the case, he began, had been "devoted to the circumstances surrounding the adoption of the Fourteenth Amendment in 1868." The lawyers on both sides had dealt "exhaustively" with "consideration of the Amendment in Congress, ratification by the States, then existing practices in racial segregation, and the views of proponents and opponents of the Amendment."[1]

The historical inquiry, alas, had proved unrewarding. "This discussion and our own investigation," Warren continued, "convince us that, although these sources cast some light, it is not enough to resolve the problem with which we are faced. At best [sic], they are inconclusive." (To call evidence "inconclusive" that supports the conclusion one is trying to avoid is, of course, accepted practice with lawyers pleading a case. With judges a more fastidious concern for the meaning of words is expected. But let us withhold judgment until we have heard a full report on the Court's "investigation.") The evidence is inconclusive, Warren explained, because the "most avid" supporters of the "post-War Amendments" wanted to "remove all legal distinctions" between Negroes and whites: "their opponents" wanted the Amendments to have "the most limited effect"; while "[w]hat others in Congress and the state legislatures had in mind cannot be determined with any degree of certainty."[2] Gaul, in other words, was divided into three parts: note that in these observations Warren attributes to none of the parties any view whatever concerning *public education.*

An "additional reason" that makes the history of the Amendment inconclusive, Warren went on, is that public education had not really "taken hold" in the South at the time. And while "it is true" that there were plenty of public schools in the North for the framers to evaluate, "the effect of the Amendment on Northern States was gen-

erally ignored in the congressional debates." In other words, the fact
that Congress did not think to inquire how the Amendment might
affect public schools creates doubt as to whether Congress intended
the Amendment to affect public schools! But a more alarming non
sequitur was on its way. "Even in the North," Warren continued, "the
conditions of public education did not approximate those existing
today. The curriculum was usually rudimentary; ungraded schools
were common in rural areas; the school term was but three months a
year in many states; and compulsory school attendance was virtually
unknown. *As a consequence*, it is not surprising that there should be
little in the history of the Fourteenth Amendment relating to its
intended effect on public education."[3]

And that is the extent of Warren's discussion of the "circumstances
surrounding the adoption of the Fourteenth Amendment." In truth,
the Supreme Court had no intention of applying the historical test to
the *Brown* case: Warren had raised the question of the framers' intentions, not with the idea of answering it, but of getting it out of
the way.

The evidence of the framers' intentions is, as we shall show, by no
means inconclusive. There is no reason for uncertainty as to what
the men who wrote and adopted the Fourteenth Amendment had on
their minds. They did not mean to outlaw separation of the races in
the public schools.

The Fourteenth Amendment was a companion piece to the Civil
Rights Act of 1866. Both measures were introduced in the early weeks
of the 39th Congress. The Act was passed in April, 1866; the Amendment was approved in June. The Amendment was designed to give
constitutional sanction to the provisions of the Act, to remove the
danger that a later Congress would repeal the Act. It is not surprising,
therefore, that the most revealing evidence of what Congress meant the
Amendment to accomplish is to be found in the debate on the Act.

The central provision of the Civil Rights Bill, as originally introduced, forbade "discrimination in [observance of] the civil rights and
immunities . . . on account of race."[4] Members of Congress became
disturbed, however, over the phrase "civil rights and immunities."
What rights and immunities did it include? Several feared that the
bill might outlaw segregated schools, or interfere with State anti-
miscegenation laws.

Senator Trumbull of Illinois, who introduced the bill, explained
that the term "civil rights" meant "the right to make and enforce
contracts, to sue and be sued, and to give evidence, to inherit, purchase,
sell, lease, hold and convey real and personal property." That was all.[5]

Representative Wilson of Iowa, chairman of the House Judiciary Committee to which the bill was committed, answered the question in this way: "What do these terms mean? Do they mean that in all things civil, social, political, all citizens, without distinction of race or color shall be equal? By no means can they be so construed. . . . Nor do they mean that . . . their children shall attend the same schools. These are not civil rights or immunities."[6]

Notwithstanding these verbal assurances, Congress thought it wise to spell out its purpose. The words "civil rights and immunities" were eliminated, and the bill was enacted in the following form:

> Citizens of every race and color . . . shall have the same right to make and enforce contracts, to sue, be parties, and give evidence, to inherit, purchase, lease, sell, hold and convey real and personal property and to full and equal benefit of all laws and proceedings for the security of persons and property as is enjoyed by white citizens. . . .[7]

Such was the reach of the Civil Rights Act.

Congress then turned to the task of putting the authority of the Constitution behind the newly recognized Negro rights. The section of the Fourteenth Amendment with which we are concerned—

> No State shall make or enforce any law which shall abridge the privileges and immunities of citizens of the United States; nor shall any State deprive any person of life, liberty, or property without due process of law; nor deny to any person within its jurisdiction the equal protection of the laws

—exhibits a different form from that of the Civil Rights Act; but while the Amendment's approach is negative and its language more general, it was certainly the consensus in Congress that the Amendment covered the same ground as the Act. There were some members of Congress, to be sure, who would have *preferred* a broader measure— Thaddeus Stevens, for example, who complained that the Amendment "does not touch social or political rights." The congressional debates make this point clear: the radicals had to settle for much less than they wanted.

Congress' understanding of the meaning of the Amendment can best be nailed down by taking note of these two facts: 1) *During the entire debate on the proposed Amendment, no proponent of the Amendment once suggested that it would outlaw segregated schools.* 2) *Simultaneously with its consideration of the Fourteenth Amendment, Congress passed a measure—it became law one month after the Amendment was approved, in July, 1866—that established schools in Washington and Georgetown "for the sole use of . . . colored children."*[8]

But while Congress may propose, the States must dispose. By giving the States the last word in the amendment process, Article V of the Constitution emphasizes their permanent role as co-governors of the federal system. How, then, did the States think they were altering the existing Constitution when they ratified the Fourteenth Amendment? Concretely, did they contemplate a surrender of the power, unquestionably theirs under the Tenth Amendment, to provide for racially separate schools?

The Warren opinion is correct. Evidence on the point from the reports and debates of the state legislatures is sparse—practically nonexistent. To be exact, the record divulges one legislator, in Indiana, who thought the Amendment would affect schools.[9] This record, however, does not leave us in the fog of uncertainty alleged by the Warren Court. By all rules of logic, it furnishes powerful circumstantial evidence *against* the possibility that state legislators believed the Fourteenth Amendment called for an overhauling of existing practices and attitudes in the field of education. That is point one.

Point two: there is, in addition, impressive affirmative evidence of the States' intentions—the record of what they actually *did* about segregated schools at the time they were agreeing that no State should deny its citizens the equal protection of its laws. There is, of course, a presumption here—that a State would not deliberately violate its own understanding of a constitutional provision while the ink incorporating that provision into the law of the land was not yet dry. Consider, then, this record of deeds.

Twelve of the 37 states that considered the Fourteenth Amendment—Alabama, Arkansas, Georgia, Kansas, Kentucky, Mississippi, Nevada, North Carolina, Tennessee, Texas, Virginia and West Virginia—enacted legislation requiring or permitting segregated schools during the very legislative session in which they acted upon the Amendment.*[10]

---

* The plaintiffs' brief in the *Brown* case charged that the eight formerly seceded States in this group perpetrated a gigantic fraud—that having ratified the Amendment to gain re-admission to the Union, they promptly broke faith by providing for segregated schools. The charge gives away more than it proves. To be sure, all of the Southern States were at the mercy of the Reconstruction Acts and ratified the Fourteenth Amendment at sword's point—from which it has been cogently argued that the Amendment was illegally adopted. But putting aside the issue of legality, the fact is that the Republican-

Five additional States—California, Indiana, Maryland, Missouri and Pennsylvania—passed laws requiring separate schools within two years after adoption of the Amendment. The laws enacted in California, Missouri and Pennsylvania extended segregation systems that had existed prior to the Civil War; Indiana and Maryland had not previously provided for Negro education.[11]

Four States—Illinois, New Jersey, New York and Ohio—had segregated schools on either a permissive or mandatory basis before the Amendment was adopted, and continued their systems after it was adopted.[12]

One State—Delaware—did not provide for separate schools until 1881, but in practice barred Negroes from State-supported white schools throughout the Reconstruction period.[13]

Here is the score so far: twenty-two States whose deeds unambiguously demonstrate they did not understand the Fourteenth Amendment to require mixed schools. What of the others?

Six States—Maine, Minnesota, New Hampshire, Oregon, Vermont and Wisconsin—had no laws relating to segregated schools, either before the Amendment or in the years following its adoption. Since, in each case, Negroes constituted less than one-third of one percent of the population, these States had no occasion to concern themselves with the problem. Their inaction reveals nothing, one way or the other, about their understanding of the Fourteenth Amendment.

Three States—Iowa, Massachusetts and Rhode Island—had outlawed segregated schools, for one reason or another, *before* the Amendment was proposed;[14] these actions obviously shed no light upon what was intended by their subsequent ratification of the Amendment.

Three States—Connecticut, Michigan and Nebraska—outlawed segregated schools more or less contemporaneously with their ratification of the Amendment.[15] In none of these States, however, is there any evidence from the debates on the school bills suggesting that such legislation was required by the Amendment—or from the debates on the Amendment, suggesting the Amendment would require mixed schools.

In the three remaining States—Florida, Louisiana and South Carolina—it would be foolish to try to generalize about post-war educational

---

controlled state governments in the South that ratified the Amendment—the Negroes and the carpetbaggers and the military governors who were answerable to Washington—also enacted the segregation laws. Whose intentions as to the effect of the Amendment are therefore in doubt? Those of the disenfranchised white Southerners?

policies. Reconstruction conditions in these States were chaotic, even anarchical: state constitutions, laws, governors' addresses, and actual practices on the subject of schools were frequently in conflict; they certainly did not add up to a consistent pattern of state activity. One point, however, does emerge clearly from the historical records: none of the proponents of mixed schools in these three States ever invoked the Fourteenth Amendment as an authority for his position.

To sum up: the contemporary actions of twenty-two States provide clear, positive evidence that the Amendment was not directed against separate schools; the actions of the fifteen remaining States do not shed any light on the question; not a single State can be counted in support of the proposition that the Amendment required mixed schools.

Add to this the fact already noted that schools were simply not discussed in the legislative debates on the Amendment, and the answer to the question the Warren Court pretended to be baffled by is unmistakable. *The States that ratified the Fourteenth Amendment, equally with the Congress that proposed it, had no intention of outlawing separate schools.* They, like the Congress, intended nothing at all about schools.

Let us now return to the Court's opinion in the *Brown* case:

Having declared the framers' intentions unfathomable, the Chief Justice turned to the judicial precedents. How had the Supreme Court interpreted the equal protection clause in past cases involving education? "The doctrine of 'separate but equal' [i.e., that the States may maintain separate public facilities for the white and colored races as long as the facilities are equal]," Warren wrote, "did not make its appearance in this Court until 1896 in the case of *Plessy v. Ferguson,* involving not education but transportation." In the entire history of the Amendment, he pointed out next, "there have been [only] six cases involving the 'separate but equal' doctrine in the field of public education." In the first two of these, decided in 1899 and 1927, "the validity of the doctrine itself was not challenged." In the other four, all decided within the last twenty years, it had been unnecessary "to reexamine the doctrine" since the separate school facilities in question were found to be unequal. And in the last of these four, Warren said finally, "the Court expressly reserved decision" on the applicability of *Plessy v. Ferguson* to public education.[16]

Warren's purpose in this passage was twofold. He had to acknowledge, even if obliquely and grudgingly, what most of his readers were sure to know—that the "separate but equal" doctrine was currently being enforced as the law of the land. And he wanted to show that, even so, the doctrine could be jettisoned without expressly overruling any previous Supreme Court decision. The latter point was designed to accommodate the principle of *stare decisis,* the proposition that stability in the law requires judges to follow their own precedents. Since the Court had not been called upon to weigh the merits of "separate but equal" when it enforced the doctrine in the past, Warren was saying, it had never really *endorsed* the doctrine; consequently, the present Court was free to announce a new doctrine.

But in the process of clearing the way for a new doctrine, Warren had exposed some Supreme Court skeletons that time and previous judicial sleight of hand had managed to inter. The questions fairly leap out of the Chief Justice's argument: if the Supreme Court had never endorsed the "separate but equal" doctrine, under what authority had it been enforcing the doctrine in the past? and if it had not endorsed *that* doctrine, what doctrine, if any, had it endorsed? While Warren did not pursue the matter of precedents any further, we cannot avoid doing so.

The bearing of the separate but equal doctrine on education needs some talking about for this reason: both sides in the *Brown* dispute, the segregationists no less than the integrationists, occupied positions that are, constitutionally, suspect. At the risk of jeopardizing our reputation for social enlightenment, let us weigh the following proposition: The Southern position, that the Fourteenth Amendment ordained equal, but not mixed schools, was wrong; the Amendment's framers did not intend to outlaw unequal schools any more than they intended to outlaw separate schools; the Supreme Court, moreover, did not read the equal protection clause as requiring equal schools until 1938, seventy years after the Amendment was adopted.

How can it be maintained that the Amendment's authors endorsed the "separate but equal" formula for schools? The evidence from the period, as we have seen, indicates they did not intend anything at all about schools. To be sure, some of the state laws and constitutions that required separate schools also provided that Negro and white schools be equal; but there is nothing to suggest that these provisions were enacted with a view to complying with the Fourteenth Amendment. Moreover, the separate Negro schools that were already in existence in 1868 were, in most cases, notoriously inferior in both physical plant and quality of teachers, which are the generally-accepted standards for measuring equality. In the absence of any discussion of the topic during the debates on the Fourteenth Amendment in Congress and the

State legislatures, it is not easy to argue that the Amendment was designed to erase these inequalities. The truth of the matter seems to be—however quaint the notion may strike us today—that Americans in 1868 believed that responsibility for public education rested exclusively with the state and local governments. Undoubtedly, many people of that day, especially after emancipation, held as most of us do now—that Negroes should have the same educational opportunities as whites. But no one seems to have thought this was a right protected by the federal Constitution, or enforceable by the national government.

The Supreme Court itself held this view until quite recently. *Plessy v. Ferguson*, decided in 1896, was, as Warren pointed out, the first Supreme Court case that referred to segregated schools. But the reference, as Warren also pointed out, was not part of the Court's ruling— it was not even an obiter dictum; it was simply an illustration of a principle the Court was applying to another problem. The Court had been asked to pass upon the constitutionality of a Louisiana statute requiring railways to provide "equal but separate accommodations for the white and colored races," and the issue, as the Court saw it, was whether segregation was, in and of itself, repugnant to the Fourteenth Amendment. The Court thought not:

> The object of the amendment was undoubtedly to enforce the absolute equality of the two races before the law, but in the nature of things it could not have been intended to abolish distinctions based upon color, or to enforce social, as distinguished from political equality. . . .[17]

Separation of the races in various situations, the Court went on, had been held to be "within the competency of the state legislatures in the exercise of their police power." Then this illustration:

> The most common instance of this is connected with the establishment of separate schools for white and colored children, which has been held to be a valid exercise of the legislative power even by courts of States where the political rights of the colored race have been longest and most earnestly enforced.[18]

The Court concluded that the railway statute had been a "reasonable" exercise of Louisiana's police power and was

> [no] more obnoxious to the Fourteenth Amendment than the acts of Congress requiring separate schools for colored children in the District of Columbia, the constitutionality of which does not seem to have been questioned, or the corresponding acts of legislatures.[19]

That was the *Plessy* case on education. Nothing was said implying the Fourteenth Amendment had ordained separate but equal schools; only that the constitutionality of separate schools had never been questioned.

Three years later, in *Cumming v. Richmond (Ga.) County Board of Education*, the Supreme Court for the first time was called upon to interpret the Fourteenth Amendment in a school case. Though the *Cumming* case received only footnote treatment in the Warren Court's *Brown* opinion, and has generally been forgotten even within the legal fraternity, it is the authoritative precedent in the field.

And mark well the Court's ruling. The Negro plaintiffs in the *Cumming* case did not complain, as did Brown in 1954, that the Board of Education had denied them access to white schools. They did not complain, as did many Negro plaintiffs during the 'thirties and 'forties, that the Board had provided inferior school facilities for Negroes. They complained that the Board had used public funds, to which Negro taxpayers had contributed their share, to finance a white high school from which Negroes were barred *and had refused to establish any high school for Negroes*—or rather, had established one, but had closed it down. Even so, the Supreme Court rebuffed them.

The Court must have been dominated by racists? It does not seem so. The *Cumming* opinion, which was unanimous, was written by Justice Harlan, a recognized champion of the Negro in his day; Harlan had, in fact, registered a spirited dissent in the *Plessy* case. He was among those who favored giving the broadest possible effect to the Fourteenth Amendment's anti-discrimination provisions, but in the *Cumming* case he affirmed that these provisions did not reach education unless the school laws in question were deliberately designed to discriminate against or penalize a given class of citizens.* Education was the responsibility of the States, Harlan argued: let a State's school laws reflect a legitimate legislative purpose and there can be no grounds for federal intervention, even though unequal treatment may result. When, in the *Cumming* case, the school board closed the Negro school for "economic reasons," the resulting inequality was manifest, but did not, in Harlan's view, affect rights protected by the federal Constitution.

---

* An instance of the kind of discrimination Harlan had in mind came before the Court in 1886 (*Yick Wo v. Hopkins*). A San Francisco ordinance had given municipal authorities arbitrary power to grant or withhold laundry licenses. Chinese launderers could not obtain licenses. The Court found the ordinance to be a covert attempt to keep Chinese out of the trade and struck it down.

> . . . while all admit [the opinion stated] that the benefits and burdens
> of public taxation must be shared by citizens without discrimination
> against any class on account of their race, *the education of the people
> in schools maintained by state taxation is a matter belonging to the
> respective States, and any interference on the part of Federal authority
> with the management of such schools cannot be justified except in the
> case of a clear and unmistakable disregard of rights secured by the
> supreme law of the land. We have here no such case to be determined.*[20]

This, then, was the Court's original construction of the Fourteenth
Amendment's bearing on education: the Amendment did not require
mixed schools, it did not even require equal schools.

The issue next came before the court in 1927. In *Gong Lum v. Rice*
a Chinese girl living in Mississippi wished to attend a white school,
but had been assigned by the local board of education to a Negro
school. Chief Justice Taft, speaking for a unanimous court that included Justices Holmes, Brandeis, and Stone, upheld the board's decision. "The right and power of the State to regulate the method of
providing for the education of its youth at public expense," Taft said,
"is clear. [This] decision is within the discretion of the State in
regulating its public schools and does not conflict with the Fourteenth
Amendment."[21] "Separate but equal" was not mentioned in the opinion: the *Cumming* case was still intact.

The break did not come until eleven years later in the case of
Missouri ex rel Gaines v. Canada. Meanwhile, the Southern States, in
compliance with their own laws and constitutions, had taken long
strides toward equalizing Negro and white school facilities. Graduate
schools were the notable exception—not, perhaps, surprisingly, since
there were few Negro candidates for such schools. Those who were
impatient with the South's social development quite naturally focused
their attention on these schools.

Meanwhile, too, the "Roosevelt Revolution" had occurred. Social
engineers had begun to take charge of the nation's politics, and by
1938 their influence had extended to the Supreme Court. Although
Mr. Roosevelt's court-packing plan had failed, the "strict-construction-
ist" majority that had plagued him through the early days of the New
Deal had been broken: Justice Roberts had switched sides; Van
Devanter and Sutherland were gone; of the strict constructionists, only
Butler and McReynolds remained.

In this context Gaines, a Negro resident citizen of Missouri, called
upon the Supreme Court to compel his admission to the law school
of the University of Missouri. Since the state-supported Negro college

did not have a law school, state authorities had offered to pay Gaines' tuition at a law school in any one of several neighboring, non-segregated state universities. The State Supreme Court had found the arrangement to be in compliance with Missouri's laws and constitution. Gaines claimed it was inadequate under the federal Constitution. The Supreme Court agreed with Gaines—Missouri had not, itself, provided equal facilities for Negroes, and its failure to do so was a violation of the Fourteenth Amendment.

The Court made no attempt to reconcile the *Gaines* decision either with the ideas on schools expressed by the authors of the Fourteenth Amendment, or with previous judicial decisions. The majority blandly announced that "[t]he admissibility of laws separating the races in the enjoyment of privileges afforded by the State rests wholly upon the equality of the privileges which the laws give to the separated groups within the State."[22] Just like that. It was the first time the Supreme Court had applied the separate but equal doctrine to a school case. It was, in one sense, as sharp a break with judicial precedent as the Warren Court's later decision in the *Brown* case. Indeed, *Gaines* probably made *Brown* inevitable, for once the States had been divested of exclusive jurisdiction over their schools, and once the authority to decide what "equal" means had been assumed by the federal courts, separate schools were entirely at the mercy of the social views of federal judges. Let it be noted that Justices Butler and McReynolds dissented in *Gaines,* citing the *Cumming* and *Rice* cases for the proposition that Missouri's school problems were nobody's business but Missouri's.

Between 1938 and 1954 the Supreme Court decided three more cases involving the constitutionality of segregated schools. All of them concerned schools at the graduate level and all of them were resolved in favor of the Negro plaintiffs on the grounds that the separate school facilities under question were not in fact equal. In this fashion—by judicial interpolation—the Fourteenth Amendment had come to require separate but equal schools by the time the *Brown* case came before the Warren Court.

In this background, the Warren Court was certainly entitled to re-examine the separate but equal doctrine—to re-open the question of the Fourteenth Amendment's bearing on education. According to traditional rules of construction, there is one (and only one) justification for abandoning the principle of *stare decisis* on a constitutional issue: If today's judges are convinced that past judges have misinterpreted the design of the Constitution's framers, they have the right

and duty to reverse the current line of decisions and put the law into
accord with the framers' intentions . . . The Warren Court, however,
had re-examined the law with a view—not to restoration—but to still
further innovation. Warren, moreover, frankly acknowledged the
Court's purpose once he got down to the business at hand.

Let us, the Chief Justice said when he had finished paying his
respects to history, try a fresh approach: let us examine "the effect
of segregation itself on public education." Then these alarming words:

> *In approaching this problem, we cannot turn the clock back to 1868*
> *when the Amendment was adopted, or even to 1896 when Plessy v.*
> *Ferguson was written. We must consider public education in the light*
> *of its full development and its present place in American life through-*
> *out the Nation.* Only in this way can it be determined if segregation
> in public schools deprives these plaintiffs of the equal protection of
> the laws.[23]

Only in this way . . . And so Warren lets the cat out of the bag. It
is not the views of the Constitution's framers that matter, but rather
the views of today's justices. The first half of the *Brown* opinion, it
now becomes clear, was merely window dressing. For even if the
framers' intentions *could* have been "determined with . . . certainty,"
Warren is now conceding, that would not have changed the result:
we cannot turn back the clock. A more explicit repudiation of the
underlying assumptions of constitutional government can hardly be
imagined.

Previous courts, as we have noted, had flouted the Constitution. The
Supreme Court had often subordinated the framers' intentions to its
own notions of what is good for society. But the Court's previous trail-
blazings had been cloaked in legal euphemisms that formally, at least,
acknowledged the limitations on the judiciary imposed by constitu-
tionalism. It remained for the Warren Court to cast off the pretense,
to advise the nation plainly of its emancipation from the anachronisms
of an ancient parchment. From then on the *Brown* decision was easy
sailing for the Chief Justice.

Having denied the relevance of past authority, Warren had only to
state the case for mixed schools in a plausible form of words and enter
judgment accordingly. Education, he observed, is indispensable "to
our democratic society." "It is the very foundation of good citizen-
ship . . . it is a principal instrument in awakening the child to cultural
values, in preparing him for . . . professional training . . . in helping
him to adjust normally to his environment. In these days, it is doubtful
that any child may reasonably be expected to succeed in life if he is

denied the opportunity of an education."[24] So much by way of preface. Then: "where the state has undertaken to provide it, [this opportunity] is a right which must be made available to all on equal terms." Does a separate school system provide equal educational opportunities? No: "[to separate Negro children] from others of similar age and qualifications solely because of their race generates a feeling of inferiority as to their status in the community that may affect their hearts and minds in a way unlikely ever to be undone. . . . Separate education facilities are inherently unequal." And, all of this being the case, Brown had indeed been denied "the equal protection of the laws guaranteed by the Fourteenth Amendment."[25]

Warren cited only one legal authority for this conclusion. The Kansas Supreme Court had observed at a prior stage in the Brown case that separation implies inferiority and that "a sense of inferiority affects the motivation of a child to learn." The Kansas court, however, was a strange kind of authority for Warren's decision inasmuch as it had ruled against Brown on the theory that when psychological opinion collides with the law, the latter, in a court of law, must prevail. Warren asserted, nonetheless, that "this finding is amply supported by modern authority." Whereupon he appended the Brown case's famous "footnote 11," which cites a number of psychological and sociological treatises on the point at issue.

As to these treatises, let us not tarry with the points so often made about them—that they are not good treatises, that they were not representative of prevailing thought in their fields, that they are colored by their authors' political predilections: careless or tendentious selection might be demonstrated, but this would not be the first time the Court had been faulted for shoddy scholarship. Let us not waste time, either, on the further point frequently made about the treatises—that they contain, in the very nature of the topic, opinion rather than fact. If it is true that the Supreme Court had full discretionary power to determine whether a local school board had afforded equal treatment to the students in its district—as Warren was plainly asserting through the last half of his opinion—where is the transgression? The ideal method of arriving at such a determination cannot be very different from the one the Warren Court in fact employed. With regard to the tangible factors affecting equality—for example, the physical plant of the schools in question—the Court in the past had relied on the testimony of school construction experts. Now, for enlightenment on the intangible factors—the psychological and sociological ramifications of segregation—the Warren Court went to the psychologists and sociologists. While the judgments of social scientists are, no doubt, often

more "subjective" than expert testimony as to the quality of a classroom, and are thus closer to what is ordinarily thought of as "opinion,"
they are, nonetheless, the best evidence available on a matter having
manifest relevance to the question of equality. No: if the Warren
Court is to be seriously faulted it must be at a prior level and on a far
more fundamental issue. What is wrong, or at least unprecedented, in
the *Brown* approach is the Chief Justice's insistence that the authors
of the Fourteenth Amendment had given the Supreme Court a continuing mandate to read whatever meaning into the phrase "equal
protection of the laws" the Court might deem appropriate.

Let us make sure we understand this contention, for it will be found
to underlie the thinking of most of the defenders of the *Brown* decision; it is also the only hypothesis that lends any color of legality to
the Court's ruling. Warren seems to have been saying that the framers
of the Fourteenth Amendment wrote a *concept* into the Constitution—
equality; and that they deliberately left this concept vague, undefined,
unparticularized—left it, that is to say, to future generations, through
future Supreme Courts, to implement as need might dictate. Under
this theory, the Supreme Court, any Supreme Court in any month of
any year of any decade, is entitled to look at the words, "equal protection of the laws," and read into them any particular meaning for any
particular situation to which the words, taken at face value, appear
to lend themselves. As for segregated schools, the reason the framers
failed to recognize the need to abolish them is that the causes and
consequences of childhood inferiority complexes were imperfectly
understood in the mid-nineteenth century: Senator Trumbull, after
all, had not read Freud. The framers did intend, however, to insure
the equality of the races—and now, in 1954, thanks to the sociologists
and the psychologists, the Supreme Court is at last able to carry out
that general intention. That it took the Court eighty-six years to discover that separate schools make Negroes unequal only shows, according to the hypothesis, that the fulfillment of the framers' intentions
was greatly delayed.

There are two reasons for balking at the continuing mandate theory,
as applied to the *Brown* situation. The first is that it flies into the
teeth of the historical evidence. The framers of the Fourteenth Amendment did *not* look upon the equal protection clause as a blank check
that would be filled out in due course by the Supreme Court. That
kind of argument might have been made about the commerce clause
or the freedom of speech clause where, as we have seen, the framers'
contemporary words and deeds bespoke an expectation that the prob-

lems of application would be worked out in the future. But in the case of the Fourteenth Amendment the framers addressed themselves in the debates both in Congress and in the State legislatures precisely to the question: Which matters are covered by the proposed amendment, and which are not? Schools came in for negligible comment because it had occurred to practically no one that schools would be covered, a fact amply witnessed by what the framers were actually *doing*, at that very moment, about segregated schools.

The second objection is that the theory, if it applies in such a case as *Brown*, reduces to a shambles the whole concept of constitutional government. If the Supreme Court is at liberty to substitute contemporary judgments about the good society for those of the Fourteenth Amendment's framers—and to give those contemporary judgments the force of constitution law—what is the Court, under the pretense of construing the Constitution, *not* at liberty to do? (The argument *reductio ad absurdum* need not be elaborated: there is no project for remaking American society that an imaginative mind cannot trace to some part of the document—remember the Preamble.) But if this is so, if the Court's mandate is plenary, the Constitution is reduced to a clutter of sentiments, a menagerie of well-turned phrases to be trotted out as needed to camouflage the exercise of naked power.

All of this is implicit in Warren's metaphor, "we cannot turn the clock back." The Chief Justice, by using these words, denies—who can doubt it?—the contemporary relevance of the first principle of constitutional government. He may, of course, be right. The problems of today may be too weighty, too complex, to entrust to the judgments of our forebears, notwithstanding the availability of Article V's amendment procedures. It may be, as the advocates of today's "sociological jurisprudence" maintain, that the Supreme Court should be freed from the "dead hand" of the framers—that the Court, as Dean Eugene Rostow of the Yale Law School has written, "should be the proponent and protector of the values which are the premises, goals, needs and ambitions of our culture, as they have been expressed in our living Constitution."[26] Our concern here is not with the merits of the "clock" position, but with the circumstances of its announcement—an event that would have occurred with greater propriety, we think, under the auspices of a more representative gathering of the American community. The *Brown* case raises the question of whether the obsolescence of the Constitution should be unilaterally proclaimed by a tribunal charged and sworn to "support and defend the Constitution of the United States."

PENNSYLVANIA v. NELSON

One day in 1931 Steve Nelson and some twenty associates in the Communist enterprise were called to Party headquarters in New York. "You are being sent to the Soviet Union," Earl Browder informed the group, "for training as professional revolutionaries." For the next eighteen months, Nelson attended the National Lenin Institute in Moscow, learning the skills that would equip him for a highly useful career in the Kremlin's international apparatus. In 1938, following a stint with the Spanish "Loyalists," Nelson was appointed to the National Committee of the Communist Party of the United States. Thereafter, in various places, and at various jobs, Nelson worked openly on behalf of the Communist Party. And sometimes not so openly: in 1943 at Berkeley, California, he passed atom bomb secrets from scientist Joseph Weinberg to an officer of the Soviet consulate in San Francisco. In 1948, Nelson was transferred from California to Pennsylvania where he became chairman of the Communist Party's District 5. It was in that capacity that he was arraigned and, on January 30, 1952, found guilty of violating the Pennsylvania Sedition Act.

Nelson's attorneys challenged the conviction, alleging that Congress, by enacting the Smith Act in 1940, had nullified state sedition laws. The Communist Party thus opened a fight, not merely to free an individual party leader, but to forestall all state prosecutions of subversives. Indeed, by the time *Commonwealth v. Nelson* reached the Pennsylvania Supreme Court, Nelson's own freedom was no longer at stake: On August 20, 1953, he had been convicted in a federal court of violating the Smith Act. The Pennsylvania Supreme Court, to the astonishment of both state and federal authorities,* reversed the state conviction, and the case went to the Supreme Court.

"[All] that is before us for review," Chief Justice Warren stated, at

---

* As an indication of the reaction, see Congressman Smith's letter below.

the beginning of his opinion, "is [whether] the Smith Act of 1940 . . . which prohibits the knowing advocacy of the overthrow of the Government of the United States by force and violence, supersedes the enforceability of the Pennsylvania Sedition Act which proscribes the same conduct."[1] It was distinctly a case of first impression for the Supreme Court. Forty-two States had sedition laws on their books,* some of which had been in force more than a hundred years. These laws had existed side by side with federal statutes on the subject at various periods in the past, and no one had ever seriously questioned their validity. Which is not surprising. For a challenge to these laws involved a challenge to the most fundamental of all States' rights, that of self-defense.

Perhaps the best way of approaching the Warren Court's holding in the *Nelson* case is to ask: How, ideally, *should* the court have handled the issue? Surely, since federal and state laws were allegedly in conflict, the question of constitutional prerogatives was the place to begin. What constitutional powers—if any—belonged to the federal and state governments, respectively, to make and enforce laws against Communist subversion?

The federal power, such an inquiry would quickly conclude, is clear: Congress' express constitutional obligations—to "provide for the common defense" and to "guarantee to every State . . . a republican form of government"—as well as its inherent obligation to preserve the sovereignty of the United States as an independent nation, afford ample authority for laws like the Smith Act. While the States' power is perhaps less obvious, the basis for Pennsylvania's Sedition Act seems equally clear after a moment's glance at the Constitution.

The American States, to begin with, are generally understood to be sovereign bodies, except insofar as they have delegated portions of their sovereignty to the federal government in the Constitution. That is the teaching of the Tenth Amendment. But nowhere in the Constitution do the States renounce, or surrender to the federal government, the attribute of sovereignty here in question, the right of self-protection. On the contrary, lest Congress' powers to provide for the common defense, to raise armies, etc. be construed as *exclusive* powers, the framers reserved in Section 10 of Article I the States' right, without Congress' consent, to "engage in war" with a foreign power

---

* All of them, like Pennsylvania's, were directed primarily against the overthrow of the U.S. government.

in the event of actual or imminently threatened invasion; and in the Second Amendment, the right to maintain armed militias at all times. As regards the mode of self-protection involved here, defense against internal enemies, the framers did not expressly reserve States' rights —presumably because they made no grant of power to the federal government that might be construed to compromise that right. And in any case, there is the Tenth Amendment.

Nor would such an inquiry have found a substantial difference between the States' right to defend their own governments and their right to defend the national government. Obviously, the States would be powerless to defend themselves if the federal government were vanquished by a foreign power, or overthrown by an internal conspiracy. It would seem to follow that Pennsylvania has a legitimate interest in safeguarding the national government as well as its own government.

An inquiry into constitutional powers, therefore, might well lead to this conclusion: both the federal and the state governments have *vested, concurrent* power to protect the federal government against overthrow by force and violence, and the laws of neither can deprive the other of the right to exercise that power.

What conclusion did the Warren Court reach, and how? Alas, the question is simply not discussed in the Chief Justice's opinion. Warren acknowledges "the right of States to enforce their sedition laws at times when the federal government has not occupied the field and is not protecting the entire country from seditious conduct"[2]—presumably a constitutional right. But the opinion does not direct us to the passage in the Constitution that limits this right to the circumstances described.

Pursuing our ideal inquiry further, however, let us concede the possibility of a different finding on the constitutional question. It might be argued that since the federal government has the primary responsibility for defending the nation against sedition, the framers probably intended to make the States' concurrent powers subject to a federal right to annul state sedition laws if the latter should prove repugnant to the national safety. True, no passage of the Constitution specifically authorizes this interpretation;* but neither does any specifically forbid it.

---

* It is hinted at, however, in *The Federalist*, No. 32. But note the stringent test Hamilton prescribed in that essay for determining the federal government's right to assert exclusive jurisdiction: "[Since] the plan of the convention aims only at a partial union or consolidation, the state governments

Under this theory, the first question for a court to ask would be: Has the federal government, *in fact*, exercised its right to exclude the States?—i.e., has Congress expressed an intention to exercise exclusive jurisdiction in the field? If the court could answer this question affirmatively, it might then go on to ask whether Congress' decision to exclude the States was a reasonable one under the circumstances. But first: Did Congress *intend* to do so? Here we may pick up the Warren opinion, for the Chief Justice's argument led off with the question of congressional intent—an issue he plainly regarded as central to the Court's ruling. And this proved to be the occasion for one of the most astonishing analyses in the history of the Supreme Court.

In the course of it, the Chief Justice—

a) cited two cases* in which past courts had ruled that Congress had intended to occupy the field of interstate commerce—about which let us say simply that what Congress might or might not have intended by its commerce laws could not shed the smallest light on what Congress intended by its sedition laws;

---

would clearly retain all the rights of sovereignty which they before had, and which were not, by that act, *exclusively* delegated to the United States. This exclusive delegation, or rather this alienation of state sovereignty, would only exist in three cases: where the Constitution in express terms granted an authority to the union, and in another, prohibited the States from exercising the like authority; and where it granted an authority to the union, to which a similar authority in the States would be absolutely and totally *contradictory* and *repugnant*. [And as for this last case], it is not, however, a mere possibility of inconvenience in the exercise of powers, but an immediate constitutional repugnancy, that can, by implication, alienate and extinguish a pre-existing right of sovereignty." (The emphases are Hamilton's.)

* *Charleston and Western Carolina R. Co. v. Varnville Furniture Co.*, 237 U.S. 597 (1915), which involved conflicting federal and state laws on the question of a common carrier's liability for damages; and *Rice* v. *Santa Fe Elevator Corp.*, 331 U.S. 218 (1947), which dealt with regulations of warehouses.

The dissenting opinion in the *Nelson* case "distinguished" the two cases by pointing out that in *Varnville*, Congress had "expressed a controlling federal policy for this commerce"; and that in *Rice*, Congress had "declared that the authority it conferred 'shall be exclusive with respect to all persons securing a license' under the Act." But "distinguishing" the cases was superfluous; each was an instance of a priori irrelevance. Unless Congress, in drafting the two commerce laws, had relied upon some general rule of construction in order to express its intent, and had relied upon the same rule in drafting the sedition laws—to suggest an imaginary hypothesis that has no support from the facts—what bearing could Congress' intentions in the one field possibly have on its intentions in the other?

b) mentioned the three major pieces of federal anti-Communist legislation then on the books—the Smith Act, the McCarran Act of 1950, and the Communist Control Act of 1954—and briefly described the general scope of each;

c) deduced that "the conclusion is inescapable that Congress has intended to occupy the field of sedition"![3]

Not a single passage of any congressional enactment, indicating an intention to exclude the States, was cited. Nor any statement or speech by a member of Congress during the debates on the bills. Nor a single word from the sponsors of the bills, or from the hearing or reports of the congressional committees that considered the bills. A letter from Congressman Smith of Virginia to the Pennsylvania Attorney General, Frank Truscott, written shortly after the Pennsylvania Supreme Court's decision in the *Nelson* case helps explain why no such evidence was at Warren's disposal (the letter was, of course, available to the Warren Court and was in itself highly relevant evidence):

> As I am the author of the Federal act in question, known as the Smith Act, I am deeply disturbed by the implications of this decision. May I say that when I read this opinion, it was the first intimation I have ever had, either in the preparation of the act, in the hearings before the Judiciary Committee, in the debates in the House, or in any subsequent development, that Congress ever had the faintest notion of nullifying the concurrent jurisdiction of the respective sovereign states to pursue also their own prosecutions of subversive activities. It would be a severe handicap to the successful stamping out of subversive activities if no state authority were permitted to assist in the elimination of this evil, or to protect its own sovereignty. The whole tenor and purpose of the Smith Act was to eliminate subversive activities, and not to assist them, which latter might well be the effect of the [Pennsylvania court's] decision in the *Commonwealth v. Nelson* case.[4]

May we not assume that if Congress had meant to void laws enacted by nearly all of the States of the Union, someone, somewhere, would have indicated that purpose? But this is not all. Not only had Congress failed to drop a hint of the "inescapable" intention attributed to it by Warren; *it had expressly avowed a contrary intent.* After enacting the Smith Act, the federal law that on Warren's showing superseded the Pennsylvania Sedition Act, Congress made it a part of Title 18 of the U.S. Code. Section 3231 of Title 18 provides: *Nothing in this title shall be held to take away or impair the jurisdiction of* *the several States under the laws thereof."** Let us here pay our respects to the dissenting justices in the *Nelson* case† who said this provision was "in and of itself decisive" in establishing Pennsylvania's right to prosecute Nelson.[5]

At this point, our ideal inquiry would have to close.‡ Granting the only hypothesis under which Pennsylvania's conviction of Nelson could be set aside—that the federal government may nullify state sedition laws if Congress determines that the national safety so re-

---

* The Court could not, of course, ignore this provision. Warren dropped a footnote stating that Pennsylvania had made what he called a "subsidiary" argument on the basis of Section 3231. "Section 3231 provides," he pointed out,

'The district courts of the United States shall have original jurisdiction, exclusive of the courts of the several states, of all offenses against the laws of the United States.

'Nothing in this title shall be held to take away or impair the jurisdiction of the courts of the several States under the laws thereof.'

"The office of the second sentence," Warren then commented, "is merely to limit the effect of the jurisdiction grant of the first sentence. There was no intention to resolve particular supersession questions." (350 U.S. 501, note 10.)

It is unclear what this comment was meant to establish. The issue in the *Nelson* case was whether the Smith Act had deprived Pennsylvania courts of jurisdiction to enforce Pennsylvania's Sedition Act. And Warren pointed out that Congress took pains to make clear that Title 18's jurisdictional grant to *federal courts to enforce federal laws* did not impair the jurisdiction of *state courts to enforce state laws*—which is exactly what Pennsylvania was contending! In any event, any possible confusion as to the meaning of Section 3231 had long since been removed. Before the Smith Act was added to Title 18, the Supreme Court interpreted the section to mean that the States may enact and enforce concurrent legislation in the absence of explicit congressional intent to the contrary. (*Sexton v. California*, 189 U.S. 319.) The Congress that passed the Smith Act was presumably aware of this construction.

† Justices Reed, Burton, and Minton.

‡ Although, since Warren had mentioned the McCarran Act, it would, to be sure, have been only proper to add that Congress had also taken pains in that legislation to preclude the inferential invalidation of state sedition laws. The McCarran Act said: "The foregoing provisions of this sub-chapter shall be construed as being in addition to and not in modification of existing criminal statutes." Sec. 1750, USCA 796.

quires—the fact is that Congress did *not* attempt to supersede state laws. What more was there for a court to determine?

But the Warren Court was not yet through. Besides congressional intent, the Chief Justice said, there are two other tests commonly employed in cases of alleged supersession. One is whether "the federal interest is so dominant" in the subject matter under question as "to preclude enforcement of state laws on the same question." The other is whether enforcement of the state laws threatened to interfere with enforcement of the federal laws. Neither of these tests, we repeat, was the legitimate concern of the Supreme Court. It was for Congress, in the first instance, to decide whether "the federal interest is so dominant" that state laws had to go; and it was for Congress, with the advice of the federal law enforcement agencies, to decide whether the state system conflicted with the federal system. Still, let us see how the Warren Court applied the tests.

As for the "dominant interest" test, Warren related that Congress had appropriated money for national defense, and for foreign aid, for the CIA and the FBI, and that it had "proscribed" Communist sedition against government at all levels in order to defend the nation and "to guarantee to each State a republican form of government." So? So "Congress having thus treated seditious conduct as a matter of vital national concern, it is in no sense a local law enforcement problem."[6] Q.E.D. Warren again cited one of the irrelevant commerce cases we mentioned earlier,* and also *Hines v. Davidowitz*[7] in which the Supreme Court, in 1941, had held that the federal Alien Registration Act superseded state alien registration laws. Since this latter case was decided—whether correctly or not, we need not judge—on the grounds that state alien registration laws might jeopardize our foreign relations, it is difficult to see any analogy with the Nelson case.†

There was a case, however, that was very much in point under the "dominant interest" theory; its drawback, from Warren's point of view, was that it pointed toward a quite different conclusion from the one the Chief Justice was driving at. In *Gilbert v. Minnesota*,[8] Minnesota had made conduct that would "interfere with or discourage the enlistment of men" in the U.S. armed forces a criminal offense. Gilbert made an anti-enlistment speech during World War

---

* *Rice v. Santa Fe Elevator Corp.* (See above.)

† Unless Warren was implying that state sedition laws might be offensive to the Soviet Union.

I and was duly convicted in the Minnesota courts. To Gilbert's argument that the federal government has exclusive authority under the Constitution to raise national armies and to deal with any interferences with that function, Justice McKenna, speaking for the Supreme Court, had replied:

> The United States is composed of the States, and the States are constituted of the citizens of the United States, who are also citizens of the States, and it is from these citizens that armies are raised and wars waged, and whether to victory and its benefits, or to defeat and its calamities, *the States as well as the United States are intimately concerned*. . . . [While armies] can only be raised and directed by Congress, [the State] has power to regulate the conduct of its citizens and to restrain the exertion of baleful influences against the promptings of patriotic duty to the detriment of the welfare of the Nation and the State. To do so is not to usurp a National power, it is only to render a service to its people. . . .
>
> We concur, therefore, in the final conclusion of the [Minnesota] court, that *the State is not inhibited from making "the national purposes its own purposes to the extent of exerting its police power to prevent its own citizens from obstructing the accomplishment of such purposes."*[9]

Let us agree, in the light of Congress' express mandate to raise and maintain national armies, that the case for federal supersession in the army-raising field (the *Gilbert* case) was much stronger than in the sedition field (the *Nelson* case). Therefore, the Court's ruling that supersession had *not* occurred in the *Gilbert* case presented serious problems for Warren. One way for the Chief Justice to overcome these problems was to misrepresent that case, which is what he proceeded to do.

Here is the Warren Court's statement on the *Gilbert* case—and note particularly the words within the quotation marks which it attributed to the McKenna Court:

> In the *Gilbert* case, this court . . . treated [the enforcement of the Minnesota statute] not as an act relating to "the raising of armies for the national defense, nor to rules or regulations for the government of those under arms [a constitutionally exclusive federal power] . . . it [was] simply a local police measure. . . ."[10]

In other words, as Warren explained in a footnote, the Minnesota law was simply a measure to protect the local peace against disorder and violence. The casual reader of the majority opinion is thus left

with the impression that the *Gilbert* case was inapposite because it
did not, like the *Nelson* case, involve federal and state statutes on
the same subject.

Now how could McKenna have written the words Warren attributed to him, *and* those we quoted above which show that in upholding Minnesota's jurisdiction the Court treated the Minnesota law
as relating to the raising of armies? The answer is simple. Directly
following the passage that recognized Minnesota's right to make "the
national purposes its own purposes," McKenna had written:

> The statute, indeed, may be supported as a simple extension of the
> police power to preserve the peace of the State. *As counsel for the
> State say,* "The act under consideration does not relate to the raising
> of armies for the national defense . . . it is simply a local police
> measure. . . ."[11]

Thus the words Warren attributed to Justice McKenna had actually
been spoken by the State's Attorney. And McKenna had then gone on
to explain that the statute *could* be upheld, *alternatively,* on the
grounds claimed by the State's Attorney—i.e., even if the primary
grounds for the Court's decision, which McKenna had already discussed, had not existed.

The dissenting justices in the *Nelson* case remarked dryly: "We do
not understand [the *Gilbert*] case as does the majority."[12]

The dissenters' general answer to Warren, under the "dominant
interest" test, is worth noting. "In the responsibility of national and
local governments to protect themselves against sedition," Justice
Reed wrote, "there is no 'dominant interest.' We are citizens of the
United States and of the States wherein we reside and are dependent
upon the strength of both to preserve our rights and liberties. Both
may enact criminal statutes for mutual protection unless Congress
has otherwise provided."[13]

Turning to the majority's third test, Warren asserted that the enforcement of the state sedition acts "presents a serious danger of conflict with the administration of the federal program." Once again, he
cited no evidence that lent support to the assertion, and ignored
readily-available evidence that militated against it. The best the Chief
Justice could manage was to quote a statement by President Roosevelt, made in 1939, and another by J. Edgar Hoover, made in 1940—
both of which were to the effect that local law enforcement agencies
should speedily furnish the FBI with information of subversive ac-

tivities. Neither of the statements contains a word about the necessity or desirability of state governments desisting from enforcing their laws.

Warren also observed, in this connection, that the provisions of some state sedition laws were different from the provisions of federal laws. Specifically, he wrote, some state laws are "vague" and do not have "safeguards" to protect fundamental rights. "Some even purport to punish mere membership in subversive organizations [e.g., the Communist Party] which the federal statutes do not punish. . . ."[14]

We must not be drawn into an argument with Warren on the point he obviously wished to insinuate here: that such state laws were bad laws. For the question he started out asking was: Does the existence of state laws establish a danger of "conflict" or "interference"—Warren used the words interchangeably—with "the federal program?" Not on this kind of evidence, was the answer—unless Warren was saying that in addition to the federal program to punish sedition, there was a *federal program not to punish sedition*, and that the federal program not to punish sedition was what was being interfered with. But that, one must conclude, is exactly what Warren was saying! For in the course of this passage he referred vaguely (and without citation) to an "avowed congressional purpose 'to protect freedom from those who would destroy it, and without infringing upon the freedom of all our people.' "[15] The Chief Justice, in other words, had fought his way back through the jungle of non sequiturs and ended up where the Court's opinion began—with its initial assertion that Congress had intended to occupy the field of sedition.* We have dealt with that contention already.

To return to the "interference test," the clearly competent authority on the question was, of course, the federal agency that is responsible for the enforcement of federal sedition laws. Who was better qualified to say whether the Justice Department's efforts to enforce federal

---

* A year later, Justice Clark, whose genuine concern for bringing the internal conspiracy to bay is demonstrated in other cases, explained what *he* meant by interference with the federal program. Dissenting in the case of *Sweezy v. New Hampshire*, 354 U.S. 234, 269 (1957), which limited state activities in the subversion field still further, Clark lamented: "I had thought that in *Pennsylvania v. Nelson* . . . we had left open for legitimate state control any subversive activity levelled against the interest of the State. I for one had intended to suspend state action only in the field of subversion against the nation and thus avoid a race to the courthouse door between federal and state prosecutors. Cases concerning subversive activities against

laws were being hampered by state laws than the Justice Department? The department, it so happened, filed an amicus curiae brief in the *Nelson* case, on behalf of Pennsylvania, which dealt with the matter as follows:

> The administration of the various state laws has not, in the course of the fifteen years that the federal and state sedition laws have existed side by side, in fact interfered with, embarrassed, or impeded the enforcement of the Smith Act. The significance of this absence of conflict in administration or enforcement of the federal and state sedition laws will be appreciated when it is realized that this period has included the stress of war-time security requirements and the federal investigation and prosecution under the Smith Act of the principal national and regional Communist leaders.[16]

Warren's opinion failed to mention the Justice Department's views. Just as the Court had second-guessed Congress on the question of congressional intent, just so it second-guessed the Justice Department on the question of interference. Nelson thus passed the last of Warren's "tests" with flying colors, and the Court entered judgment in his behalf.

The Supreme Court handed down its opinion in the *Nelson* case on April 2, 1956. By the end of that year, all state prosecutions of subversives had been dropped, and steps were being taken in several states to free those convicted in the past under state anti-subversion statutes.

---

the national Government have such interstate ramifications that individual state action might effectively destroy a prosecution on the national level."

One wonders why Warren found no room for this argument (the best that was available) in writing the majority opinion. But Clark's views are of interest for another reason—namely, the light they shed on the present Supreme Court's concept of the judicial function. Clark, in this passage, is back at his desk in the Attorney General's office. He is making the kind of observation that would be appropriate in a recommendation by the Justice Department for new legislation. The argument he is advancing would properly come into the ken of Clark, the Supreme Court Justice, only if Congress had decided to exclude the States from the sedition field and the reasonableness of that legislative decision had been challenged in appropriate litigation.

As it happened, however—as will be seen in the text—the Justice Department at the time of the *Nelson* case flatly disagreed with the former Attorney General.

And what of Nelson? We saw earlier that when the Pennsylvania case was decided he was also under sentence for violating the Smith Act. On October 10, 1956, *that* conviction was reversed by the Supreme Court.[17] Refusing to discuss the merits of the case, the Chief Justice, again writing the Court's opinion, ordered a new trial for Nelson and his co-defendants on the ground that one witness against them *might* have perjured himself in separate proceedings. Warren found that the "tainted" testimony of this witness had "poisoned the well" in the case against all of the defendants—though the testimony had little bearing, if any, on Nelson's case. Justice Harlan observed, in dissent, that the reversal represented "an unprecedented and dangerous departure from sound principles of judicial administration."

In 1957 the circle was completed: the Department of Justice dropped plans for a new trial of Nelson in the light of the Supreme Court's emasculation of the Smith Act in the *Yates* case.[18] And Steve Nelson, avowed Communist Party functionary and espionage agent, was once again free.

THE SCHEMPP–MURRAY CASES

In the summer of 1962 the Supreme Court decided it was unlawful for children attending New York public schools to say, in their classrooms:

> Almighty God, we acknowledge our dependence upon Thee, and we beg Thy blessings upon us, our parents, our teachers and our country.[1]

A great public furor greeted the decision. This time much of the country seemed to feel the Court had gone too far: as venerable an American institution as baseball, and by some more highly valued, had suddenly fallen under attack—and on the improbable grounds that it was *unconstitutional*. But the country's learned commentators counseled against alarm. What the Court had found objectionable about this particular prayer, they insisted, was that the New York Board of Regents had composed it: the Court had acted only to keep government out of the business of *writing* prayers.* School prayer as such was not in danger.

The commentators, however, were wrong. A year later the storm had largely subsided and the Court spoke again. This time the justices had before them two cases, one brought by a Pennsylvania Unitarian, the other by a Maryland atheist,[2] that involved prayers that some persons believe the Lord Himself composed. And the Court ruled that the Constitution forbids those also to be repeated in the public schoolrooms of the United States.

Once again the average citizen, who was under the impression that eighteenth-century American society was *more* religious than

---

* Actually, the holding in *Engel v. Vitale* was much broader. Justice Black had written in the majority opinion: "each separate government in this country should stay out of the business of writing *or sanctioning* official prayers. . . ."

his own, was perplexed by the holding. Public prayer might be a
fusty relic of a less enlightened age, but it would hardly be the norms
of that former age that would disqualify the practice. Accordingly,
the notion quickly took root, and was carefully nurtured by the
friends of the decision, that the Court had not so much rebuffed public
religion as affirmed traditional standards of individual freedom: the
framers of the Constitution may have contemplated a religious society,
but they did not intend to jam the society's commitment down the
throats of dissenting Unitarians and atheists. All the Court had done,
according to this thesis, was condemn *coercion* in the public sponsor-
ship of devotional exercises—a view with which people could imagine
the framers sympathizing. As a result the nation soon found itself de-
bating the merits of "compulsory" school prayer, and the Court's opposition to it did not seem so surprising after all.

Under the circumstances, we should be quite clear about what the
court really did decide in the *Schempp-Murray* cases, as well as
what its reasoning was. We must, to begin with, distinguish sharply
between the First Amendment's "establishment clause" and its "free
exercise clause." The Amendment provides:

> Congress shall make no law [1] *respecting an establishment of religion,*
> or [2] *prohibiting the free exercise thereof.*

Of course both clauses may be involved in a given case, but they
need not be, and they were not, on the Court's showing, in the
Schempp-Murray cases. There was some talk in the opinion about
the "overlapping" of the two clauses and their "interrelationship"—
but it was only talk. In the final analysis the free excercise clause did
not figure at all since "coercion," the indispensable ingredient of a
denial of free exercise, was not in evidence in either case. The Pennsylvania law, against which Mr. Schempp complained, provided for
recitation of the Lord's Prayer and a reading from the Bible at the
opening of the school day; the Maryland rule, which Mrs. Murray
found offensive, provided only for a Bible reading. *In both cases express provision had been made for excusing pupils who did not wish
to participate in the exercises.*[3] Thus the question of "compulsory"
prayer was never at issue. Nor did either plaintiff attempt to prove
that non-participation could "upset" a child or provoke "psychological disturbances." Mr. Schempp said he feared his children would
be "labeled as 'odd balls' " if they asked to be excused,[4] but neither
trial court heard any evidence on the point, and thus no such evidence

was before the Supreme Court. Given the record before it, then, the
Court could not* and did not find an infringement of the free exercise clause; its holding of unconstitutionality rested squarely on the
establishment clause.

How, then, did the Court extract a prohibition of school prayer
from the words, "Congress shall make no law respecting an establishment of religion . . ."? The majority opinion in *Schempp-Murray* took
the position that an historical inquiry into the clause's meaning would
be tiresome in the light of past decisions, and settled instead for
two *ex cathedra* declarations.

"*First,*" Justice Clark wrote, "*this Court has decisively settled* [that
the establishment clause] *has been made wholly applicable to the
States by the Fourteenth Amendment.*"[5] For proof, he quoted a passage from Justice Roberts' opinion in *Cantwell v. Connecticut*, decided in 1940 (a case, as it happens, that did not involve the establishment clause), and then listed, seriatim, seven subsequent cases.

"*Second,*" Clark said, "*this Court has rejected unequivocally the
contention that the Establishment Clause forbids only governmental
preference of one religion over another.*"[6] Again, instead of argument,
there followed simply a series of citations of recent Supreme Court
decisions, buttressed by excerpts from the two dissenting opinions in
Everson v. Board of Education, the 1948 New Jersey bus case. Justice Jackson had said on that occasion: "The effect of the religious
freedom amendment was to take every form of propagation of religion out of the realm of things which could directly or indirectly
be made public business"; and Justice Rutledge had added: "The
object [of the establishment clause] was broader than separating
church and state in [the] narrow sense [of forbidding preference].
It was to create a complete and permanent separation of the spheres
of religious activity and civil authority by comprehensively forbidding every form of public aid or support for religion."

These latter views, Justice Clark went on, were subsequently un-
derwritten by a majority of the Court in the *McCollum* case (forbidding religious instruction on school premises), the *Zorach* case
(permitting released time for off-premises instruction) and the *Engel*
case (banning the New York Regents' prayer); moreover, "none of
the parties to either [the *Schempp* or *Murray*] case has questioned"

---

* Of course, had it been of a mind to, the Court might have found the free
exercise clause a relevant consideration in determining the rights of students
who *did* want to pray.

them. Therefore, while "others [e.g., constitutional scholars?] continue to question [the] history, logic and efficacy" of the Court's position, Clark concluded, such objections "seem entirely untenable and of value only as academic exercises."[7]

With the only debatable aspects of the case thus disposed of by hypothesis, Clark had no trouble showing that the practices in question were anathema. Prayer and Bible reading, whatever else might be said about them, were "religious exercises, required by the States in violation of the command of the First Amendment that the Government maintain strict neutrality, neither aiding nor opposing religion."[8]

It is allowed to us to devote a moment to "academic exercises." We may begin with the second of Justice Clark's propositions, the one that deals with the original meaning of the establishment clause. And let us agree at the outset that there are three kinds of evidence that might bear on the problem—the *situation* out of which the demand for the provision arose; the *comments* about the provision's meaning made by its authors at the time it was under consideration; and most important, of course, the *text* of the provision. It is hard to imagine relevant data in any other category.

1. The historical background is familiar to most schoolboys. Many of our forebears emigrated to America in order, among other things, to get out from under the official state church that had been established in the old country. Some of the settlers, so they said, were opposed in principle to the idea of an established religion; but most of them quite clearly were not—as witness they promptly established religions of their own preference in the colonies. By the time the Constitution was adopted, however, strong sentiment against the establishment of any church had taken hold in *some* of the States. This happened in Virginia, for example, which disestablished the Church of England in the 1780's and even refused to establish formally, as a substitute, "the Christian religion"; Thomas Jefferson and James Madison, as everyone knows, played leading roles in Virginia disestablishmentarianism. But in other States—five of them to be exact, including powerful Massachusetts—the locally established church held its ground. In this diverse situation, all parts of the country agreed that *a national government should have no power to disturb the existing local arrangements*: congressional power to establish a church would jeopardize Virginia's practice, while a power to disestablish would threaten, e.g., Massachusetts'. Accordingly, control over religion was

excluded from the list of powers delegated to Congress by the original Constitution. Nonetheless, three disestablishment States, persuaded that this negative protection was not enough, requested a constitutional amendment dealing with their particular concerns. Virginia's proposal provided: ". . . *no particular religious sect or society ought to be favored or established, by law, in preference to others.*"[9] North Carolina submitted identical language.[10] The third suggestion, New Hampshire's, asserted simply, "Congress shall make no Laws touching religion. . . ."[11] This, then, was the "situation" in the summer of 1789 when the First Congress considered and approved the establishment clause.

2. James Madison is regarded, rightly, as the principal drafter of the clause. He took on the job of working the various state proposals for amendments into a consolidated bill, and the language he chose for this particular matter was, *"nor shall any national religion be established."*[12] In the course of the debate, Madison's original wording was changed to "no religion shall be established by law,"[13] at which point—evidently perceiving no substantial difference between the first and second versions—Madison advanced this explanation of the proposal:

> . . . he apprehended the meaning of the words to be, that Congress should not establish a religion, and enforce the legal observation of it by law, nor compel men to worship God in any manner contrary to their conscience. Whether the words are necessary or not he did not mean to say [a comment that reflects Madison's oft-forgotten lukewarmness toward the whole idea of a Bill of Rights], but they had been required by some of the State Conventions.[14]

Suffice for these purposes that Madison's understanding of the Amendment was never challenged, either in Congress or by the ratifying state legislatures. The ultimate change in phraseology manifestly did not affect the meaning of "establishment," but merely added an emphasis that would guarantee the integrity of local policy in all of the States.

3. *"Congress shall make no law respecting an establishment of religion."* The language Congress finally approved, given a normal reading of it, produced precisely the results the historical situation called for. The decisive word was "respecting." That word has been read by the Supreme Court for the last fifteen years, and by secularist zealots for longer than that, as though it were equivalent to "tending toward." Yet obviously this is not what "respecting" means. It means

"*having to do with*"; and once we grant that degree of literacy to the framers, it is clear the clause forbade Congress to enact laws either *for* religious establishments or *against* them. The matter was to be left to local discretion. As Justice Story later wrote in his *Commentaries*:

"*The whole power over the subject of religion is left* [by the Amendment] *exclusively to the state governments to be acted upon according to their own sense of justice and the State Constitutions*; and the Catholic and the Protestant, the Calvinist and the Armenian, the Jew and the Infidel may sit down at the common table of the national councils without any inquisition into their faith or mode of worship."[15]

As for the words, "an establishment of religion," there is not the slightest doubt the phrase was a term of art in the eighteenth century, used often by Madison, Jefferson and other political commentators to signify—and never to signify anything else, unless the context clearly indicated otherwise—*a preference of one religion over another*. We may note, as one of a hundred proofs available, the *Encyclopaedia Britannica*'s explanation that the phrase "denotes any special connection with the state, or privileges and responsibilities before the law, possessed by one religious society to the exclusion of others; in a word, establishment is of the nature of a monopoly."[16]

But the reader is now surely entitled to ask: How, if the case is this clear, has the Supreme Court managed to advance and maintain a totally contrary position? Did the Court, in its previous decisions, call attention to evidence we have failed to consider? The answer is, No—the previous decisions reveal no additional data that bear relevantly on the problem. From the *Everson* and *McCollum* decisions, which ushered in the current doctrine, down through the *Engel* case in 1962, the Court dealt with the problem of the establishment clause's history by a) discussing the religious persecutions in Europe from which American settlers fled; b) recalling Virginia's famous struggle against the Anglican establishment, particularly the roles of Madison and Jefferson; c) inferring from Jefferson's, and particularly Madison's, influence on the First Congress that the adoption of the federal establishment clause was merely a replay of the Virginia experience. That has been the sum and substance of the Court's presentation. And with respect to the last point, we say "inferring" with some charity because the argument has been made in the absence of a single item of evidence—and in the teeth of countless pages of evidence to the contrary—that either Jefferson or Madison wished upon, or conceived himself to be wishing upon, the union of thirteen States the arrangement he had recommended to Virginia.*

Before leaving the question of the clause's origins we must take account of the three contentions advanced in this connection by Justice Brennan in a lengthy concurring opinion in the *Schempp-Murray* cases. Brennan, unlike his brethren, did not treat history as entirely irrelevant, and opened his remarks with a burst of candor that may not have pleased the other justices: "*. . . it is true that the Framers' immediate concern was to prevent the setting up of an official federal church. . . .*" "But," he quickly added, "nothing in the text of the Establishment Clause supports the view that [dealing with this concern] was meant to be the full extent of the prohibitions against official involvements in religion."[17] This, surely, is a curious method of adducing the framers' intentions in the absence of *evidence* they had some other prohibitions in mind. Brennan ventured one suggestion—an argument by a Mr. Lardner that the clause's use of the word "religion" instead of "church" was inexplicable except as a proof that government support of religion *per se* was to be condemned.[18] The answer: the framers said "religion" because they meant to prohibit the national establishment not only of a particular religious *sect*—i.e., a "church"; but also of any particular *"religion"* —i.e., as Virginia had done, of "the Christian religion."

Second, Brennan thought that even though Jefferson and Madison may be shown to have been sympathetic to the idea of public school prayer, the "more fruitful inquiry is whether [such prayers] tend to promote the type of interdependence between religion and state which the First Amendment was designed to prevent."[19] We may stop Brennan there: Obviously the "fruitfulness" of the approach is that it assumes an answer to the very question under discussion— namely, What was the First Amendment designed to prevent?

Brennan's third point was that "education, as the Framers knew it . . . was in the main confined to private schools," and for that reason "they gave no distinct consideration to . . . devotional exercises in public institutions."[20] It would have been helpful, however, had Brennan explained why the failure of our Constitution-makers to deal with a given subject is a reason *for* the courts to incorporate that

---

* The Virginia arrangement was, incidentally, a far cry from the Supreme Court's doctrine of "complete and permanent separation of the spheres of religious activity and civil authority." Religious instruction at the State University, for example, was earnestly promoted by Jefferson.

subject into the Constitution, rather than a reason *against* their doing so.

We may turn now to the majority's other proposition, the claim that the establishment clause was made binding on the States by the Fourteenth Amendment. The inquiry need not be extensive. We have no need to probe the general relationship of the Bill of Rights to the Fourteenth Amendment, a question that involves many considerations and would require analysis of forty years of Supreme Court decisions. For even if it were true that the framers of the Fourteenth intended to make all of the rest of the Bill of Rights applicable to the States, there are two decisive reasons why such a conclusion is absurd in the case of the establishment clause.

1. We have seen that the original establishment clause forbade Congress a) to establish a national church, and b) to interfere with existing state arrangements regarding religion. Let us now, following the Supreme Court's theory that the Fourteenth Amendment absorbs the First, place a "State" in the shoes of "Congress," and see what emerges. A State is now forbidden a) to establish a *national* religion! and b) to interfere with a State's—i.e., its *own*—arrangements regarding religion!! Nor are these contradictions produced by mere logic-chopping. The way the Supreme Court has contrived to tie the Bill of Rights into the Fourteenth Amendment in other situations is by arguing that the Fourteenth's framers intended their word "liberty" (as used in the due process clause) to subsume the various "liberties" asserted by the Bill, and as the latter had been protected against federal encroachment, so they would thereafter be protected against state encroachment. But as the late Professor Edward Corwin has pointed out, the establishment clause, unlike, e.g., the right to bear arms, is not in the nature of a "liberty"; rather, it is like the Tenth Amendment, a delineation of the spheres of federal and state power. The only liberty the establishment clause plausibly protects is "freedom from a national church"; but a State is hardly in a position to jeopardize that liberty, if only for reasons of geography.

2. The other point is historical. Attempts to instruct the Court about the intentions of the Fourteenth Amendment's framers frequently must rest on the negative argument that no evidence exists that the restriction on the States in question—for example, that they were not to maintain segregated schools—was on the framers' minds. Here, however, in addition to the negative argument (which happens to be open-go-shut), there is the positive fact that only seven years after the Fourteenth Amendment was ratified, *a serious attempt was*

*made to amend the Constitution by prohibiting state establishments
of religion.* Neither this, the famous "Blaine Amendment,"[21] which
enjoyed President Grant's full endorsement, nor any of the ten other
amendments proposed at that time on the matter of State-church
connections, was approved. Yet the fact that they were proposed and
earnestly debated by the Fourteenth Amendment's contemporaries
surely eliminates the possibility that the Fourteenth was understood
to have accomplished what the Court says it accomplished.

And how had the Supreme Court, as Justice Clark put it, "decisively
settled" this issue to the contrary? It happened, as the inquiring reader
will discover, in the *Everson* and *McCollum* cases, and it happened
without a word of argument.

The Warren Court's efforts to cut off the debate on the historical
meaning of the establishment clause naturally raise the suspicion that
the Court's secularizing objectives are not confined to the elimination
of school prayer. For if the construction of the clause peremptorily
advanced by Justice Clark in *Schempp-Murray* is accepted as "settled" law, no defensible barrier remains to the total secularization of
American public life by judicial order. If the States, as well as Congress must observe a "high and impregnable . . . wall of separation
between church and state," in the language of *Everson* and *McCollum*, or a "strict neutrality" toward religion in the prissier phrase of
Schempp-Murray, then *every public action affecting religious interests constitutes a prima facie case of unconstitutionality.* And should
the Court one day proceed to order—merely by exercising what
amounts to an unlimited discretionary power—the removal of God's
name from coins, public anthems, and the pledge of allegiance, it
would be silly to fault the justices for a "new" usurpation. Critics
may quibble and haggle about whether "neutrality" is better served
by this course or that one—as Justice Stewart did in a feeble dissent
to *Schempp-Murray*—but such arguments must necessarily turn on the
political, sociological, or ideological views of the critics. There remain,
under the *Schempp-Murray* rule, no objective standards on which
to base a judgment that the Court has, as a matter of law, gone too
far.

Do we exaggerate? Consider the formulation the Court announced
in *Schempp-Murray* for applying its "neutrality" principle to concrete cases. "The test [for this and future cases]," according to Clark,
"may be stated as follows: [in order for a given enactment] to with-
stand the strictures of the Establishment Clause, there must be [1] a

secular legislative purpose, and [2] a primary effect that neither advances nor inhibits religion."[22] Now take, as our concrete case, the governmental practice affecting religion that is probably in *least* danger of immediate judicial attack—the tax exemption of church property and income. For a number of years nearly everyone has seen fit to endorse the fiction that the exemption is simply incident to a larger public policy of encouraging charitable and other eleemosynary activities. But let Justice Clark's "test" be applied, and let it be applied candidly: Surely the *"primary effect"* of letting off religious institutions from their taxes is to advance not charity—which is only one of religion's concerns—but *religion*. Or more to the point: Given the validity of the *Schempp-Murray* rule, there can be no legitimate quarrel with the Supreme Court the day it decides to forbid the tax exemption.

There is, of course, an internal reason, having to do with the nature of the subject matter, why the Court's "neutrality" rule is specious—a camouflage for an official policy *against* theistic religion. Christ had the point in mind in observing that those who were not with Him were perforce against Him. It can also be illustrated by the public school teacher's quandary on being asked whether human rights come from a Creator-God, as asserted by the Declaration of Independence. Under the Court's "neutrality" rule, the teacher cannot answer the question by either "Yes" or "No," for this would amount to the government "taking sides." The required reply is, "I don't know"—i.e., *"I cannot say whether it is true or not, because the government cannot take a position on the existence of God."* But that reply, as Professor Charles Rice has remarked, is a far cry from "neutrality": plainly "the teacher is aligning the government on the side of *agnosticism* through his affirmation that, as a matter of state policy, God's existence is unknown or unknowable." Thus "the Supreme Court, while invoking the rhetoric of an impossible 'neutrality,' has neatly replaced our traditional public affirmation of God and His law with a new, non-theistic public creed, demanding of the state a perpetual suspension of judgment on the question, 'Is there a God?' "[23]

We offer no comment, be it noted, on the merits of this new creed. Our only concern has been the "academic" one of whether it is prescribed by the Constitution of the United States.

WESBERRY *v.* SANDERS

"Legislative apportionment," as graceless and forbidding a phrase
as can be found in the Anglo-Saxon idiom, has recently forced its way
into the vocabulary of the average American. A few specially interested parties in our time, most of them in the League of Women
Voters, were previously acquainted with its mysteries, but the Supreme Court has put it on the front pages with a series of rulings
that decreed, in effect, that American legislatures, state and federal, are no longer masters of the organization of their own houses.

Since the country's beginnings, the job of parceling out legislative
representatives had presented a trying (though apparently manage-
able) problem—and understandably. For in the nature of things, population movements precede, and thus tend to render perpetually
obsolete, the dividing up of political areas into election districts. This
natural problem was unavoidably aggravated, moreover, by a fast-
stepping people like ours, imbued with a migratory spirit, ready to
shift its economic commitments at the drop of a hat, above all vulnerable to the lures of an industrializing process that sucked countryside into city overnight. New apportionment arrangements were
frequently delayed still further by the human tendency, not necessarily venal, to postpone for as long as possible the dispossession of
one's own political power. But that last point, to do justice to our
history, must be placed in perspective: resistance to a purely demographic approach to apportionment was not entirely, or even primarily, self-serving. From the very first, the argument was regularly
made, and attentively listened to and heeded in disinterested quarters, that the organization of a stable and realistic representative system cannot be reduced to the simplistic expedient of nose-counting.
A stable and realistic system, the argument went, will try to respect
a variety of factors—first among them, to be sure, the population of a
given area; but also its historical and cultural attachments, its eco-

nomic involvements, its geographic configurations, its sense of identity and community, the sheer accessibility of its prospective representatives, and so on.

And whom had we charged with the delicate and complex assignment of accommodating these frequently competing considerations? Why, legislators of course, and for at least three plausible reasons. Legislators were far more conversant than any other officials with the variables involved in the equation, and so far better equipped to weigh and balance them. But, competence aside, the legislative solution was obviously the most congenial to the premises of republican government: What could be more vital to the integrity of a *representative* system than that the supervision and regulation of the system be entrusted to officials directly responsible to the people, i.e., to their representatives? Finally, not a small consideration, the legislative solution, or so everyone thought, had plainly been prescribed by the Constitution of the United States.

The legislative answer, to be sure, was not fool-proof. In the best of possible worlds this time-chasing and balancing operation would prove to be an onerous, exacting—and, above all, thankless task. From one side there would always be heard plausible claims of under-representation; and from the other, understandable fears of domination by rootless, and hence easily corrupted, urban masses. In the imperfect world we actually live in the results were even less satisfying. From time to time quite absurd disparities in election districts occurred that were difficult to defend on any grounds—just as urban-based "reform" movements occasionally ran rough-shod over the claims of community coherence and stability. And in the former case it was not unknown, even prior to 1962, for the aggrieved party to seek relief in the courts, typically on the argument that the alleged disparity violated Article IV, Section 4, of the Constitution, the so-called Guaranty Clause, which assures to every State "a Republican Form of Government." But the courts' response was always the same: the Guaranty Clause was not designed for judicial enforcement; its provisions involved "political questions" that were the proper concern of the "political branches"; the judiciary department was neither equipped nor authorized to interfere in matters that the Constitution had wisely confided to the "political process." And so, without the world coming to an end, the complainants were left to their own resources—to mobilizing support for state constitutional amendments, referenda, new statutes, whatever—on the theory that the surest guarantee of representative government is the energy, imagination, and patience of the represented people, acting within their duly established constitutional forms.

In *Baker v. Carr*,[1] decided in March, 1962, the Warren Court abruptly scuttled the judiciary's "hands-off" tradition: the apportionment of state legislators, thenceforth, *would* be the business of the judicial department, all of the protests and proofs about legislative prerogatives to the contrary notwithstanding. The Court did not pause to inform the States—in this case, Tennessee—what was expected of them. Justice Brennan, who wrote the principal opinion amid a welter of confusing and conflicting views,* simply asserted the Court's jurisdiction. Brennan's analysis recognizably leaned toward the purely demographic, "one man-one vote," approach; but whether the courts would actually seek to impose that rule on the States, and if so, how strictly, and how fast, and whether to only one or to both branches of their legislatures, was anyone's guess. It was a harbinger of the edict-ringed chaos that would presently ensue that the justices, in *Baker*, could agree to do no more than advise the States that a black-robed Big Brother was looking over their shoulders, and would hold them accountable to something or other at his pleasure.

On what authority? Brennan said that it was the Fourteenth Amendment's equal protection clause that had placed apportionment rights under judicial protection. This démarche had the twofold advantage of outflanking the Court's dug-in position on the Guaranty Clause, and of soaring out of reach of any previous critique of the proposed alternative—the latter for the excellent reason that the applicability of the equal protection clause had occurred to practically no one, least of all to the framers of the Fourteenth Amendment. And then, for purposes of defending the decision in the legal fraternity, Brennan's argument had the further advantage, not present in the case we are about to examine, that the thitherto recognized rights of the States in the premises are not explicitly set forth in the Constitution (such a provision would have struck the framers as a preposterous belaboring of the obvious), but are left to inference from a) the logic of the federal system, b) the implications of the voter-qualifications clause of Article I, Section 2,† and c), of course,

---

* There were six separate opinions in all. Justices Frankfurter and Harlan hotly dissented.

† That clause provides: "The Electors [for the House of Representatives] in each State shall have the Qualifications requisite for Electors of the most numerous Branch of the State Legislature"—an indication, surely, that the framers expected the state legislatures to control the elections of their own members.

the general reservation of state powers guaranteed by the Tenth Amendment.

The next major break came in January, 1964, in *Wesberry v. Sanders*.[2] The *Wesberry* decision carried the Court's re-apportionment crusade well beyond *Baker v. Carr*, in two ways. First, the purely demographic approach, foreshadowed in *Baker*, matured into a strict constitutional imperative. But more significant—for few doubted that the new line of decisions would sooner or later settle into the "one-man-one vote" groove—the Court applied its new rule to *congressional* election districts. Here, indeed, was cause for raised eyebrows. In the *Baker* case, involving the apportionment of state legislators, the Court had taken advantage of an arguably ambiguous constitutional situation to batter away at the country's traditional way of doing things. But with the *Wesberry*-type problem, the Constitution—or, again, so everyone thought—leaves nothing to inference. Article I, Section 4, provides

> The Times, Places and Manner of holding Elections for Senators and Representatives shall be prescribed in each State *by the Legislature thereof; but the Congress may at any time by Law make or alter such Regulations*, except as to the place of choosing Senators.

By common understanding this provision had assigned exclusive authority over such matters as districting arrangements to the political departments. The state legislatures would be expected to draw up congressional election districts in the first instance, according to their own lights; but should complaints arise, like that of the Georgia voters in the *Wesberry* situation,* an appeal would lie—to *Congress*. Moreover, Congress, historically, had been attentive to this supervisory power. In 1842 it began to lay down general instructions to the States, requiring, among other things, that congressional districts be geographically contiguous.[3] Then, in 1872, Congress decided that all representatives should "be elected by districts composed of contiguous territory, and containing as nearly as practicable an equal number of inhabitants."[4] That latter requirement was, of course, precisely the one the Warren Court would seek to impose in 1964; and it remained the law of the land for nearly fifty years. Congress, however, eventually thought better of the equal-number-of-inhabitants formula, or at least

---

* The plaintiffs lived in a congressional district, Georgia's Fifth, which had a population in 1960 of 823,680. The average population of the State's ten districts was 394,312. The least populous of these districts had 272,154 inhabitants.

of the desirability of imposing it as a national rule. The requirement
was dropped, after due consideration, in the Apportionment Act of
1929,[5] evidently because the States were deemed the better judges of
their own needs and circumstances. And that decision remained the
policy of Congress down to the moment of the *Wesberry* case, notwithstanding numerous proposals in the intervening years to reinstate
the old equality rule.*

Thus the Warren Court was faced in the *Wesberry* case not only
with an express constitutional mandate that assigned to other departments of government the very authority it wished to claim for
itself; but also with a record of deeds that whisked away the one
remaining excuse for intervention that judicial activists had been
known to advance on such occasions, namely: that a given department's failure to exercise an authority confided to it "defeats"—so to
speak—the framers' expectations, and thereby creates a constitutional
"gap" which the judiciary must fill.† Under the circumstances, what
was the Court to do?

---

* A review of the legislative history of the 1929 Act is set forth in *Wood
v. Broom,* 287 U.S. 1. The Supreme Court said in that 1932 case: "It was
manifestly the intention of Congress not to re-enact the provision as to
compactness, contiguity, and equality in population with respect to the
districts to be created pursuant to the reapportionment under the Act of
1929. This appears from the terms of the act, and its legislative history shows
that the omission was deliberate. The question was up, and considered."
(287 U.S. 7.) For a review of congressional action on apportionment,
generally, see Justice Harlan's dissent in *Wesberry.*

Let it be noted that here, and in the pages that follow, we take no position
on the *merits* of the "one man-one vote" approach to apportionment. Of
course a few biases may emerge as we proceed, but if they should prove
uncongenial, the reader is by all means invited to substitute some of his
own. The point cannot be made too often that we are not concerned in
this book with the wisdom of policies now up for judgment in the American
commonwealth, but with the method by which, under the reign of the
Warren Court, they are coming to be made.

† This argument should not be mistaken for sound constitutional doctrine.
Most commentators agree that the typical grant of power in the Constitution
is an authorization to the designated body to act, *or not to act,* on the subject
matter described—that decision to be made at the discretion of the designated
body. Thus: if Congress had never seen fit to interfere with the States' apportionment practices, there would still have been no warrant for judicial
interference. Since the grant of power to Congress in Article I, Section 4, is
manifestly permissive, congressional inaction would reasonably be taken to
mean that Congress had weighed the States' performance, and approved.

But suppose State X had *also* failed to take action under Article I, Section

Since neither the grant of authority to the States and Congress, nor the fact of its exercise, could be questioned, the Court had no recourse but to assert that the authority had been excercised *wrongly* —that there was, in other words, off somewhere in the Constitution, an a priori standard for apportioning congressmen which the political departments had been expected to observe, but in practice had refused to observe. But where in the Constitution? Justice Brennan had reached airily for the equal protection clause when confronted with a comparable problem in *Baker v. Carr.* Justice Black, needing in *Wesberry* a tool for bringing Congress to heel as well as the States, had to explore elsewhere. At the outset of the opinion, speaking for a majority of seven,* Black revealed what had turned up:

"We hold that, construed in its historical context, the command of Art. I, Sec. 2, that Representatives be chosen 'by the People of the several States' means that as nearly as is practicable one man's vote in a congressional election is to be worth as much as another's."

Our concern in the next few pages will be not so much to discover whether the Court's assessment of the "historical context" was correct. We shall be concerned primarily with whether the assessment was truthful. The Court's evidence, one can safely predict, will not persuade the reader: the more serious question is whether it conceivably persuaded the Court. Was the majority victimized by shoddy scholarship, or did it knowingly endorse spurious scholarship? We think the *Wesberry* record permits the raising of such a question, indeed compels it. This was not a case, be it noted, in which the relevance of the framers' intentions—the propriety of "turning the clock back" —was disputed. On the contrary, the Court pointedly pinned its entire argument to an alleged discovery about those intentions—about what "the clock" said in 1787. Nor in this instance did intention-divining require a weighing of competing historical data, the proper

---

4—had simply never gotten around to arranging for congressional elections? That is a neat question (and probably academic: X's default would not suggest a flourishing interest in the Union, and would in all likelihood foreshadow a decision to secede) , but the answer would seem to be the same: an appeal would lie, not to the courts, but to Congress. That, in any event, appears to have been the understanding of Madison: see note, p. 107.

* Justice Clark concurred in part, but dissented in part. He approved the "one man-one vote" rule, but preferred to enforce it against the States via the equal protection route. How that approach might be enforced against Congress, should Congress insist upon a different rule, Clark did not explain. Justice Harlan thought the majority's whole performance a disgrace, and went to considerable pains to drive the point home.

balancing of which could be the occasion of disagreement between
reasonable men. As we shall see, the "historical context" the Court
spoke of consisted of a single line of evidence—certain remarks that
had been made at the Constitutional Convention and at the state
ratifying conventions in connection with a plainly visible issue over
which the framers were quarreling. Now: as they appear in Justice
Black's opinion, these remarks make a plausible, if thin, case for the
Court's conclusions, but the moment they are placed in their true
context—i.e., once the issue we mention has been identified—the case
seems to vanish altogether. Moreover, we may rule out the possibility
that the majority was misled by a clumsy researcher, or for some
other reason was unaware of the full context. In addition to weighing
the litigants' arguments and briefs, it is the justices' practice to confer
privately about a case before opinions are written, and in this case
Justice Harlan's brutal dissent permits no doubt that the true nature
of Black's "evidence" was called to the majority's attention. Still, under most circumstances, decorum properly counsels against reflections
on the integrity of our highest court. For this reason we shall reproduce in full the majority's discussion of the "historical context," inviting the reader to judge for himself the obligations of responsible
commentary.

Every American schoolboy hopefully has become acquainted with
the "Great Compromise" of the Constitutional Convention, by virtue
of which the large States and the small States finally came to an
agreement as to the composition of Congress and the method of
choosing its members. He knows that the large States had contended
for a system of proportionate representation that would faithfully
reflect the wealth and population of each State. The Virginia Plan,
which they supported, proposed a national legislature of two branches,
both of which would "be proportioned [either] to the Quotas of
contribution or to the Number of free inhabitants" of each State; the
first branch would be elected "by the people of the several States," the
second by [the members] of the first."[6] He also knows that the smaller
States feared domination by the large ones and consequently urged
retention of equal representation as the only system compatible with
the "sovereignty" of each State. The New Jersey Plan, which these
smaller States supported, envisioned a one-house legislature in which
each State would have one vote and whose members would be chosen
by the various state legislatures.[7] The eventual Compromise, which
is called Great because without it the Convention would surely have

collapsed, borrowed from both plans—as may be seen from its ultimate terms as set forth in Sections 2 and 3 of Article I of the Constitution:

"The House of Representatives," Section 2 provides, *"shall be composed of Members chosen . . . by the People of the several States"* who *"shall be apportioned among the several States according to* [the States'] *respective Numbers."* Thus the Virginia contribution.

"The Senate," Section 3 provides, *"shall be composed of two Senators from each State, chosen by the Legislature thereof . . . and each Senator shall have one vote."* Thus the New Jersey contribution.

Before the Compromise was reached, however, each side had naturally advanced arguments extolling the virtues of its own proposal and decrying the alleged shortcomings of the other's. Thus our schoolboy, should he have happened upon a copy of the Convention records, would not have been surprised to find a number of passages supporting the two Virginia ideas of a) popular elections and b) allocation of representatives among the States on a population basis—just as he would expect to find a number supporting the opposing New Jersey ideas of a) election by state legislatures and b) equal representation from each State. Let us agree, however, that he would be less prepared to discover, in this connection, passages relating to a third, and quite distinct issue—namely, What standards, if any, were to govern the distribution of representatives *inside* a given State. For obviously the Great Compromise questions of whether elections should be popular or legislative, and whether representatives should be apportioned *among* the States according to population, or equally, bore no necessary relation to the question of how representatives should be apportioned *within* each State. This third question, be it noted, was the one involved in the *Wesberry* case.

Justice Black's discussion of the "historical context" of Article I, Section 2, was, in toto, a discussion of the Great Compromise. We shall now see how he defeated a schoolboy's expectations and drew from that material proof that the framers required every man's vote to count equally in the election of a given State's congressmen. The presentation began argumentatively:

"To say that a vote is worth more in one district than in another would not only run counter to our fundamental ideas of democratic government, it would cast aside the principle of a House of Representatives elected 'by the People,' a principle tenaciously fought for and established at the Constitutional Convention." Our comment. The first part of the statement is rhetorical and question-begging: to the extent "our fundamental ideas of democratic government" are a rele-

vant consideration, the Court is presumably trying to discover what those ideas, as they bear on the situation at hand, *are*. As for the "principle" the Court accuses Georgia of having "cast aside," Justice Harlan's icy rejoinder is sufficient: "The fact is . . . that Georgia's 10 Representatives *are* elected 'by the people' of Georgia, just as Representatives from other States are elected 'by the People of the several States.' This is all that the Constitution requires." It is certainly all our schoolboy thought the Constitution required, as well as all the large-State delegations at the Convention had asked for. Black continues:

"*The history of the Constitution, particularly that part of it relating to the adoption of Article I, Section 2, reveals that those who framed the Constitution meant that, no matter what the mechanics of an election, whether statewide or by districts, it was population which was to be the basis of the House of Representatives.*" The statement, while tendentious, is literally consistent with the schoolboy's understanding: "population" was indeed to have been "the basis of the House of Representatives"—in the sense that the number of representatives assigned to each State was to be determined by the State's population. Black thereupon devotes two paragraphs to political developments in America between the Revolution and the Convention, which we reproduce in a footnote,* and which, as the reader may observe, are neither here nor there as regards the *Wesberry* issue. Then:

"*The question of how the [federal] legislature should be constituted precipitated the most bitter controversy of the Convention. One*

---

* "During the Revolutionary War the rebelling colonies were loosely allied in the Continental Congress, a body with authority to do little more than pass resolutions and issue requests for men and supplies. Before the war ended the Congress had proposed and secured the ratification by the States of a somewhat closer association under the Articles of Confederation. Though the Articles established a central government for the United States, as the former colonies were even then called, the States retained most of their sovereignty, like independent nations bound together only by treaties. There were no separate judicial or executive branches: only a Congress consisting of a single house. Like the members of an ancient Greek league, each State, without regard to size or population, was given only one vote in that house. It soon became clear that the Confederation was without adequate power to collect needed revenues or to enforce the rules its Congress adopted. Far-sighted men felt that a closer union was necessary if the States were to be saved from foreign and domestic dangers.

"The result was the Constitutional Convention of 1787, called for 'the sole and express purpose of revising the Articles of Confederation. . . .' When the Convention met in May, this modest purpose was soon abandoned for *principle was uppermost in the minds of many delegates: that, no matter where he lived, each voter should have a voice equal with that of every other in electing members of Congress. In support of this principle, George Mason of Virginia 'argued strongly for an election of the larger branch by the people. It was to be the grand depository of the Govt.' "*

Our attention naturally rivets on the "principle" that Black abruptly alleges to have been "uppermost" in many of the delegates' minds: it is of course the very principle the Court is seeking to vindicate. But then, where we might have expected supporting evidence, we find that the very first authority Black reaches for is a remark made at the Convention that is manifestly unrelated to the "principle."* George Mason was merely advocating, as the passage plainly shows, popular election of the legislature's larger branch.

"James Madison agreed, saying, 'If the power is not immediately derived from the people, in proportion to their numbers, we may make a paper confederacy, but that will be all.' " Madison indeed agreed—with Mason—that there should be popular elections. And he added the further thought that the power conferred by the people should be "in proportion to their numbers"—a point that was addressed, as the surrounding context makes abundantly clear, to the small-State argument that the States should be represented in Congress as sovereign equals.† But this passage carries no hint that Madi-

---

the greater challenge of creating a new and closer form of government than was possible under the Confederation. Soon after the Convention assembled, Edmund Randolph of Virginia presented a plan not merely to amend the Articles of Confederation but to create an entirely new National Government with a National Executive, National Judiciary, and a National Legislature of two Houses, one house to be elected by 'the people,' the second house to be elected by the first."

* If Black had permitted him to continue, however, a hint of Mason's views on that subject would have emerged. The larger branch of the national legislature, Mason had said in the next sentence, "was, so to speak, to be our House of Commons. It ought to know and sympathize with every part of the community; and ought therefore to be taken not only from different parts of the whole republic, but also from different districts of the larger members of it, which had in several instances, particularly in Virginia, different interests and views arising from difference of produce, of habits, etc., etc." (*The Records of the Federal Convention of 1787*, Farrand ed., 1911, 48, 49; hereafter referred to as "Farrand") Which makes it clear that Mason favored a system of representation inside each State that would take pains to reflect, not just population, but the diverse "interests, views, produce and habits, etc., etc." to be found within the State!

† Black took this formulation of Madison's position from the notes of

son was agreeing with Black's "principle" of proportional representation *within* a State, or even thinking of it.

"Repeatedly, delegates rose to make the same point: that it would be unfair, unjust and contrary to common sense to give a small number of people as many Senators or Representatives as were allowed to much larger groups—in short, as James Wilson of Pennsylvania put it, 'equal numbers of people ought to have an equal no. of representatives . . .' and representatives 'of different districts ought clearly to hold the same proportion to each other, as their respective constituents hold to each other.' "

We shall examine in due course the contributions of those delegates who "repeatedly . . . rose . . ."* (Black devotes an impressive footnote to them); meanwhile let us pursue the argument as it unfolds in the text of the opinion. James Wilson's allusion to "different districts"— i.e., presumably, different *congressional* districts—seems to have brought us at last to some evidence that is relevant to the *Wesberry* situation. It will prove rewarding to check those appearances against the Convention records. Wilson's remarks on this occasion directly followed a speech by William Paterson of New Jersey, who had characterized "the proposition for a proportional representation as striking at the existence of the lesser States."[8] And in reply to the large-State contention that "a great individual State contributing much should have more votes than a small one contributing little," Paterson had asked: "If the rateable property of A was to that of B as 40 to 1, ought A for that reason have 40 times as many votes as B?" Wilson thereupon "entered elaborately," the record says,

> into a defense of a proportional representation, stating for his first position that as all authority was derived from the people, equal numbers of people ought to have an equal number of representatives. and different numbers of people different numbers of representatives. This principle had been improperly violated in the Confederation [where each *State* had an equal vote], owing to the urgent circumstances of the time. As to the case of A & B, stated by Mr. Paterson, he observed that in *districts as large as States*, the number of people was the best measure of their comparative wealth. Whether therefore wealth or numbers were to form the ratio it would be the same. Mr. Paterson admitted persons, not property, to be the measure of

---

Robert Yates. Madison's own version of the speech, as we shall see momentarily (p. 92), makes the construction Black places on it somewhat more difficult.

* See pp. 95-104.

suffrage. Are not the citizens of Pennsylvania equal to those of New Jersey? Does it require 150 of the former to balance 50 of the latter? *Representatives of different districts ought clearly to hold the same proportion to each other, as their respective constituents hold to each other.* If the small States will not confederate on this plan, Pennsylvania, and he presumed some other States, would not confederate on any other. . . . If New Jersey will not part with her Sovereignty it is vain to talk of Government.[9]

The full record thus plainly reveals that Wilson was using the word "districts" synonymously with "States," and that the entire argument was a plea for proportional representation *among* the States, not *within* them. And the point here is not only that Black misrepresents Wilson's remarks, but that he has gone out of his way to do so. There seems to be no other explanation for his relegating so many similar remarks to footnote status, without quoting them, while choosing to expose this one, with its convenient implication about congressional "districts," to the opinion's readers.

Following a paragraph purporting to describe the position against which the large-State delegates were contending,* Black goes on:

"The delegates who wanted every man's vote to count alike were sharp in their criticism of giving each State, regardless of population, the same vote in the national legislature. Madison entreated the Convention 'to renounce a principle wch. was confessedly unjust,' and Rufus King of Massachusetts 'was prepared for any event, rather than sit down under a Government founded in a vicious principle of representation, and which must be as shortlived as it would be unjust.' "

Madison, then, is represented as having made yet another plea for the principle that "every man's vote [should] count alike." In fact, this new "entreaty" was simply another version (Madison's own) of

---

* "Some delegates opposed election by the people. The sharpest objection arose out of the fear on the part of small States like Delaware that if population were to be the only basis of representation the populous States like Virginia would elect a large enough number of representatives to wield overwhelming power in the national Government. Arguing that the Convention had no authority to depart from the plan of the Articles of Confederation which gave each State an equal vote in the National Congress, William Paterson of New Jersey said, 'If the sovereignty of the States is to be maintained, the Representatives must be drawn immediately from the States, not from the people: and we have no power to vary the idea of equal sovereignty.' To this end he proposed a single legislative chamber in which each State, as in the Confederation, was to have an equal vote. A number of delegates supported this plan."

the passage Black has cited several paragraphs earlier. Madison's notes say:

> . . . not to divest such *unequal* portions of the people, as composed the several States, of an *equal* voice, would subject the system to the reproaches and evils which have resulted from the vicious represen- tation in Great Britain. He entreated the gentlemen representing the small States to renounce a principle which was confessedly unjust, which could never be admitted, and if admitted must infuse mortality into a Constitution which we wished to last forever."*10

It is hard to imagine a plainer demonstration that Madison was think- ing of apportionment among the States, not within them.

And what of Rufus King, Black's other witness at this juncture? It is quite true that King spoke out against the "vicious principle" of representation by States,† but did this commit him—even in the mat- ter of apportionment among the States—to the principle that "every man's vote [must] count alike?" Black must have known that King was, in fact, *opposed* to basing a State's representation purely on its population. On June 29, the delegates agreed to base the first branch of the legislature on "some equitable ratio of representation";11 then, a week later, they turned to the question of what ratio might be equitable. On that subject King had said

> that the number of inhabitants was not the proper index of ability and wealth; that *property* was the primary object of Society; and that in fixing a ratio this ought not to be excluded from the estimate.12

Black now returns to wheel-spinning. The next two paragraphs‡ recall the emotional context of the Great Compromise and its major

---

* Emphasis in the original.

† As it happens, King on this occasion was not urging proportional repre- sentation in the House, which had already been agreed to, but in the *Senate*. The full passage reads: "[King] was . . . filled with astonishment that if we were convinced that every *man* in America was secured in all his rights, we should be ready to sacrifice this substantial good to the phantom of State sovereignty . . . that when a just Government founded on a fair representa- tion of the *people* of America was within our reach, we should renounce the blessing from an attachment to the ideal freedom and importance of *States*: that should this wonderful illusion continue to prevail, his mind was pre- pared for every event rather than sit down under a Government founded in a vicious principle of representation, and which must be as shortlived as it would be unjust." (I Farrand 489-90.)

‡ "The dispute came near ending the Convention without a Constitution. Both sides seemed for a time to be hopelessly obstinate. Some delegations

terms, and note the Convention's decisions a) to omit wealth as a factor in calculating a State's representation base, b) to have periodic censuses, and c) to treat the prospective Western States like any others. All of which is interesting, perhaps, as lore, but furnishes not the faintest clue to how the Convention proposed to apportion representatives within the States . . . Whereupon the opinion shifts back to argument-by-asseveration—apparently on the theory that any dogmatism repeated often enough and solemnly enough will eventually acquire plausibility:

"It would defeat the principle solemnly embodied in the Great

---

threatened to withdraw from the Convention if they did not get their way. Seeing the controversy growing sharper and emotions rising, the wise and highly respected Benjamin Franklin arose and pleaded with the delegates on both sides to 'part with some of their demands, in order that they may join in some accommodating proposition.' At last those who supported representation of the people in both houses and those who supported it in neither were brought together, some expressing the fear that if they did not reconcile their differences, 'some foreign sword will probably do the work for us.' The deadlock was finally broken when a majority of the States agreed to what has been called the Great Compromise, based on a proposal which had been repeatedly advanced by Roger Sherman and other delegates from Connecticut. It provided on the one hand that each State, including little Delaware and Rhode Island, was to have two Senators. As a further guarantee that these Senators would be considered state emissaries, they were to be elected by the state legislatures, Art. I, Sec. 3, and it was specially provided in Article V that no State should ever be deprived of its equal representation in the Senate. The other side of the compromise was that, as provided in Art. I, Sec. 2, members of the House of Representatives should be chosen "by the People of the Several States" and should be "apportioned among the several States . . . according to their respective numbers." While those who wanted both houses to represent the people had yielded on the Senate, they had not yielded on the House of Representatives. William Samuel Johnson of Connecticut had summed it up well: "in *one* branch the *people*, ought to be represented; in the *other*, the *States.* [Emphasis in the original.]

"The debates at the Convention make at least one fact abundantly clear: that when the delegates agreed that the House should represent 'people' they intended that in allocating Congressmen the number assigned to each State should be determined solely by the number of the State's inhabitants. The Constitution embodied Edmund Randolph's proposal for a periodic census to ensure 'fair representation of the people,' an idea endorsed by Mason as assuring that 'numbers of inhabitants' should always be the measure of representation in the House of Representatives. The Convention also overwhelmingly agreed to a resolution offered by Randolph to base future apportionment squarely on numbers and to delete any reference to wealth. And the delegates defeated a motion made by Elbridge Gerry to limit the number of Representatives from newer Western States so that it would never exceed the number from the original States."

Compromise—equal representation in the House of equal numbers of people—for us to hold that, within the States, legislatures may draw the lines of congressional districts in such a way to give some voters a greater voice in choosing a Congressman than others." But the only "principle" we have seen evidence of is that representation in the House was to be allotted to the States in proportion to their populations.

"The House of Representatives, the Convention agreed, was to represent the people as individuals, and on a basis of complete equality for each voter." "The Convention agreed" to *that?* We are still without evidence that a single delegate embraced that theory of politics; but see below.*

"The delegates were quite aware of what Madison called the 'vicious representation' in Great Britain whereby 'rotten boroughs' with few inhabitants were represented in Parliament on or almost on a par with cities of greater population." We have just seen the true context of Madison's observation which the reader will note has now made, though each time under slightly different guise, its third appearance.

"Wilson urged that people must be represented as individuals so that America would escape the evils of the English system under which one man could send two members to Parliament to represent the borough of Old Sarum while London's million people sent but four." In the passage to which Black refers, Wilson said:

> I should be glad to hear the gentleman from Maryland [Luther Martin] explain himself on the remark of Old Sarum, when compared with the city of London. This he has allowed to be an unjust proportion, as in the one place one man sends two members, and in the other one million are represented by four members. *I would be glad to hear how he applies this to the larger and smaller States in America;* and whether [in England] the borough, as a borough, is represented, or the people of the borough.†[13]

* Pp. 100-104.

† This is the version of Wilson's remarks that appears in the notes of Robert Yates. Madison's account of the same speech made an earlier appearance in the opinion (a separate contribution by Wilson, the casual reader would conclude) as a footnoted citation to Black's claim that "Repeatedly, delegates rose," etc. (see pp. 90, 101). In Madison's version, Wilson's argument takes the form of a little joke at the expense of the small State delegates, and includes language even less convenient to Black's thesis than that of the Yates account, which undoubtedly explains the selection of the latter for more prominent treatment. According to Madison, Wilson said:

And with that (excepting one sentence presently to be mentioned),* Black's attempt to prove that the framers revealed at the Constitutional Convention an intention to distribute representatives proportionately *within* each State rested.

It will be recalled, however, that we postponed examination of some of the testimony—the offerings, to which Black referred in a footnote, of those delegates who "repeatedly . . . rose," etc., presumably to endorse the "principle" that every man's vote should count equally,† yet presumably with such frequency as to render actual quotation of their remarks a burden on the reader. We may now turn

---

"The leading argument of those who contend for equality of votes among the States is that the States, as such being equal, *and being represented not as districts of individuals but in their political and corporate capacities*, are entitled to equality of suffrage. According to this mode of reasoning, the representation of the boroughs in England which has been allowed on all hands to be the rotten part of the [English] Constitution, is perfectly right and proper. They are, like the States, represented in their corporate capacity; like the States, therefore, they are entitled to equal votes, Old Sarum to as many as London. And instead of the injury supposed hitherto to be done to London, the true ground of complaint lies with Old Sarum; for London, instead of two which is her proper share, sends four representatives to Parliament." (1 Farrand 449-50.)

Thus, as Madison heard the argument, Wilson contrasted the small-State idea of "the States . . . being represented . . . in their political and corporate capacities" with his own preference for "*the States . . . being represented . . . as districts of individuals.*" Compare this formulation with Black's assertion, "*Wilson urged that people must be represented as individuals. . . .*" For the purposes of the *Wesberry* case the difference is decisive. We are not suggesting that Wilson's overall position on the question of whether members of the House should represent individual people, or aggregates of individual people, was free of ambiguity; see below, pp. 100-104. We do mean to call attention to Justice Black's apparent disregard of minimal standards of scholarship.

* See p. 107.

† It is hardly debatable that this is the significance Black intended his readers to attach to the footnote. The composition and cadence of the governing paragraph of the text (see pp. 88-90) was unmistakably designed to convey the impression that the footnote documented the paragraph's main thesis, to wit: "*One principle was uppermost in the minds of many delegates: that no matter where he lived, each voter should have a voice equal with that of every other* in electing members of Congress. *In support of this principle,* George Mason . . . *argued.* . . . James Madison *agreed.* . . . Repeatedly, delegates rose *to make the same point*: that it would be unfair, unjust, and contrary to common sense to give a small number of people as many Senators or Representatives as were allowed to much smaller groups"; whereupon, the footnote.

to those intriguing citations; they will, among other things, direct us to a fuller picture than we now have of the Convention's mind. Having deployed his witnesses alphabetically, Black first called upon *Benjamin Franklin*.

The day was June 11, and the Convention was about to take a formal vote on the proposition that "the right of suffrage in the first branch of the national Legislature ought not to be according to the rule established in the Articles of Confederation [i.e., one State, one vote] but according to some equitable ratio of representation."[14] Franklin said he had prepared some remarks which he wished to have read to the delegates. The relevant passage related that he had "originally [hoped] every member of Congress [would] consider himself rather as a representative of the whole than as an Agent for the interests of a particular State . . .

> But as I find this is not to be expected, I now think the number of Representatives should bear some proportion to the number of the Represented; and that the decisions should be by the majority of members, not by the majority of States.*[15]

It hardly needs to be pointed out that Franklin was not concerned with apportionment within the States, but among them.

Elbridge Gerry of Massachusetts is next. The question before the house on June 29 was the self-same proposition Franklin had spoken to nearly three weeks before.† Gerry lamented that the smaller States "were intoxicated with the idea of their *sovereignty*,"‡ a theory, he said, that never had been applicable to the American States. Even during the framing of the Articles of Confederation the theory had come under fire:

---

* By the end of this paper, curiously, Franklin had wandered away from the idea of proportional representation. As a kind of compromise, not thereafter heard of, he proposed that each State contribute equal amounts of "money" and "force" to the Union, and that each send *"an equal number of Delegates"* to Congress, but that decisions be taken "by the majority of individual members" of Congress. As a final fillip, he suggested that should the need arise Congress might ask "the richer and more powerful States . . . voluntarily" to contribute additional "supplies . . . leaving to each State the right" to decide whether and how much further aid was "proper." (1 Farrand 199, 200.)

† The proposal to base the first branch on "some equitable ratio of representation" had been adopted on the earlier occasion, but in the meantime the New Jersey Plan had been submitted, which forced a reconsideration.

‡ Emphasis in the original.

The injustice of allowing each State an equal vote was long insisted on.[16]

That was Gerry's contribution to the subject of how representatives should be distributed within each State.

Alexander Hamilton of New York is summoned twice. The first occasion is his famous a-plague-on-both-your-houses speech of June 18, which lambasted both the Virginia and New Jersey Plans and urged a substitute closer to the British form, which Hamilton said was "the best in the world." On the point that concerns us, Hamilton argued that one "destructive ingredient" in the New Jersey Plan was the

> equality of suffrage which is so much desired by the small States. It is not in human nature that Virginia and the larger States should consent to it, or if they did that they should long abide by it. It shocks too much the ideas of Justice, and every human feeling. Bad principles in a Government, though slow, are sure in their operation, and will gradually destroy it.[17]

Then, during the June 29 debate, he again scoffed at the idea of equal voting rights. All of the States, Hamilton said, restricted the suffrage by property qualifications of one kind or another. How inconsistent, then, for the States, which are mere abstractions, to demand equality for themselves.

> [Inasmuch as the] States are a collection of individual men, which ought we to respect most, the rights of the people composing them or of the artificial beings resulting from the composition? Nothing could be more preposterous or absurd than to sacrifice the former to the latter. It has been said that if the smaller States renounce their *equality*, they renounce at the same time their *liberty*. The truth is it is a contest for power, not for liberty.*[18]

In short, Hamilton's concern for proportional representation, even for purposes of allocating representatives *among* the States, hardly sprang from democratic dogma: he wanted not so much a government that would assure the individual voter an "equal voice" as one that would realistically reflect the country's power structure.

Rufus King's comment has already been noted.†

James Madison of Virginia is called up four times. On June 19 he

---

* Emphasis in the original.
† P. 92, note.

directed attention to the problem of admitting new States from the Western territories:

> If they should come into the Union at all, they would come when they contained but few inhabitants. If they should be entitled to vote according to their proportions of inhabitants, all would be right and safe. Let [these new States] have an equal vote, and a more objectionable minority than ever might give law to the whole.[19]

On June 28 he sought to allay the fear Luther Martin had just expressed that under a system of proportional representation the small States could be "enslaved" by a combination of the larger. Most of Madison's lengthy reply was devoted to an historical demonstration that large powers usually fight each other rather than combine to tyrannize over weaker powers. There are only two passages that Justice Black could conceivably have deemed relevant to our subject. At the beginning Madison said

> he could neither be convinced that the rule [Martin had] contended for was just, nor necessary for the safety of the small States against the large States.[20]

A little later he posed a series of rhetorical questions designed to show that the Virginia proposal merely imitated the current practice in some of the States:

> Why are the Counties of the same States represented in proportion to their numbers? Is it because the representatives are chosen by the people themselves? So will be the representatives in the National Legislature. Is it because the larger have more at stake than the smaller? The case will be the same with the larger and smaller States. Is it because the laws are to operate immediately on their persons and properties? The same is the case [etc.].[21]

On June 30 Madison joined King, Wilson, and others in resisting the concession to the small States that was to constitute the second half of the Great Compromise. If the States were given "an equality of votes in the second branch,"

> the Majority of States might still injure the majority of people, [especially since] the second branch will probably exercise some great powers in which the first will not participate.[22]

On July 5 he was still resisting. In order to make equal voting in the second branch more palatable to the large States, a committee had suggested that all money bills originate in the first branch, with no right of amendment in the second. Madison said the proposal

> could not . . . be deemed any concession . . . and left in force all
> the objections which had prevailed against allowing each State an
> equal voice. He conceived that the Convention was reduced to the
> alternative of either departing from justice in order to conciliate the
> smaller States and the minority of the people of the U.S., or of dis-
> pleasing these by justly gratifying the larger States and the majority
> of the people.[23]

Hugh Williamson of North Carolina is called twice. On June 9, as Madison's notes put it, Williamson "illustrated" the reply Wilson had just given to Paterson on the question of whether Pennsylvania was entitled to more votes than New Jersey*

> by a comparison of the different States to Counties of different sizes
> within the same State, observing that proportional representation
> was admitted to be just in the latter case, and could not therefore be
> fairly contested in the former.[24]

Thus Williamson reproached the small States, as Madison was to do on June 28, for an alleged inconsistency: If it was not objectionable for a State to provide that its political subdivisions were to be represented in the state legislature on a population basis, what could be wrong with the nation treating its own constituent parts, the States, in the same way? Note that the argument was by analogy and was addressed only to the question of apportionment *among* the States. There was no suggestion, moreover, that a State would be *required* to give its Counties a proportional vote in its state legislature, much less that it would have to distribute its quota of congressional representatives according to the county system.

The other contribution by Williamson to which Black directs attention is not entirely intelligible. According to the notes of Robert Yates, Williamson said on June 28:

> If any argument will admit of demonstration, it is that which declares
> that all men have an equal right in society. Against this position, I
> have heard, as yet, no argument, and I wish to hear what could be
> said against it. What is tyranny? Representatives of representatives,
> if you give them the power of taxation. From equals take equals, and

---

* See p. 90.

the remainder is equal. What process is to annihilate smaller States, I know not. But I know it must be tyranny if the smaller States can tax the greater, in order to ease themselves. A general government cannot exercise direct taxation. Money must be raised by duties and imposts, etc. and this will operate equally. It is impossible to tax according to numbers. Can a man over the mountains, where produce is a drug, pay equal with one near the shore?[25]

While these remarks were volunteered in the midst of the Great Compromise debate over representation in Congress, it seems clear that Williamson's concern at the moment was not with apportionment of representatives, but with apportionment of *taxes*. William Paterson's notes on this day* reported the episode thus:

> Mr. Williamson: They talk in vague Terms of the great States combining etc.—Wants to know how it is possible that the large States can oppress the small—The rule to tax the States according to their numbers would be cruel and unjust—it would Create a war.[26]

James Wilson of Pennsylvania is Justice Black's final witness. On June 16 he launched a general attack on the New Jersey Plan which had been submitted the day before. One of the plan's shortcomings, Wilson said, was that

> Congress as a Legislative body does not stand on the people. . . . He would not repeat the remarks he had formerly made on the principles of Representation [i.e., Why should the vote of a Pennsylvania citizen count less than that of a New Jersey citizen?]. He would only say that an inequality in it has ever been a poison contaminating every branch of Government. In Great Britain where this poison has had a full operation, the security of private rights is owning entirely to the purity of her tribunals of Justice, the Judges of which are neither appointed nor paid by a venal Parliament. The political liberty of that Nation, owing to the inequality of representation, is at the mercy of its rulers.[27]

On June 25 the Convention was considering the composition of the second branch of Congress. Wilson opposed equal representation of the States even there.

> The General Government is not an assemblage of States, but of individuals for certain political purposes—it is not meant for the

---

* The other note-takers on June 28, Madison and King, took no notice of the Williamson speech.

States, but for the individuals composing them: the *individuals*
therefore, not the *States* ought to be represented in it. A proportion
in this representation can be preserved in the second as well as in
the first branch; and the election can be made by electors chosen by
the people for that purpose.*28

On the 28th, he reached for the Old Sarum-London tableau to por-
tray the absurdity of the small States' claim to equal representation.
We have already taken note of what he said in that speech.†
On June 30, Wilson again tried to block equal representation of
the States in the Senate:

> Such an equality will enable the minority to control in all cases
> whatsoever the sentiments and interests of the majority. . . . Can
> we forget for whom we are forming a Government? Is it for *men*, or
> for the imaginary beings called *States*? . . . If the [Compromise] should
> be agreed to, we shall leave the U.S. fettered precisely as heretofore—
> with the additional mortification of seeing the good purposes of the
> fair representation of the people in the first branch defeated in [the]
> second.‡29

To sum up, *not one* of the speeches cited by Black was concerned
with the problem of how congressional representatives should be
distributed within the States, the problem with which the *Wesberry*
case was concerned. Every one of the cited passages set forth an
argument supporting the large-State position that representatives
should be apportioned *among* the States according to their populations or by some other "equitable" formula. That is point one.

There is a second point that should be equally well noted: only
one of Black's spokesmen, James Wilson, advanced a rationale for
his position that tended, on occasion, in the direction of the *Wesberry*
holding. Wilson, alone among the framers, now and then took as his
point of departure the political rights and interests of the *individual
voter* which he appears to have regarded as in all respects equal.
Starting from this premise he seems to have been arguing, much as
Black did, that justice required every man's vote to "count" equally in
the election of Congress—a result that would arguably demand attention not only to the method of apportioning congressmen among
the States, but also within them. Moreover—assuming this to have

---

* Emphasis in the original. The record shows that Wilson thereupon
moved an amendment to this effect, "which was not seconded."
† Pp. 94-95, note.
‡ Emphasis in the original.

been his governing premise—Wilson was strikingly consistent in demanding the absolute exclusion of the States as a relevant consideration in the formation of the national government. He thought the States would have an important role to play in the spheres left over to them once the national government had been formed, and so may be regarded as a friend of the federal *system*. But he did not favor a federal *government*: the two governments that composed the federal system, Wilson held, should be totally distinct. He made the point sharply in an aside to his argument on July 25 urging proportional representation: "With respect to the province and objects of the General Government, [the States] should be considered as having no existence."[30] In this approach Wilson was faithful to the original conception of the Virginia Plan, which also made no provision for state power or representation within the national government; and he remained so throughout the Convention. For instance, Wilson fought to the last against the Convention's plan of State-appointed presidential electors, arguing that "as it now stands, the President will not be the man of the people as he ought to be . . ."[31] In short, James Wilson may fairly be regarded as an ideological democrat of the modern genre, and if the Convention *had* considered prescribing a constitutional rule for governing apportionment within the States, it is a reasonable prediction that he would have urged the "one man-one vote" solution.

By contrast, the argument of Wilson's large-State allies (and, on some occasions, Wilson's own statements*) proceeded from the premise that the disparate size of the States, whether they were regarded as corporate entities or as mere aggregates of people, required disparate treatment of them in the national government's scheme of representation. The expression of the argument ranged from Hamilton's tart allusion to the *Realpolitik* of the struggle to Madison's loftier appeal to justice, but the point was essentially the same: it would be unrealistic, unwise, unfair, unsomething, to treat unequals as equals. Virginia ought to have a larger representation in Congress than Maryland because she had, in Madison's phrase, "more at stake"; or, according to a somewhat different emphasis, *Virginians* deserved more representatives than *Marylanders* because there were more of them; but on neither showing did the cogency of the argument depend on Virginia's or Maryland's method of choosing its representatives. In short, whether they tended to view the States as corporate entities or as aggregates of people, the majority of the large-

---

* See pp. 94, 95 note, 100.

State delegates, hardly less than those from the small States, expected a member of the House of Representatives to regard himself, as Franklin said, not as a spokesman for the mass of individual voters, but as "a representative . . . of a particular State."

This approach was in keeping, moreover, with the disposition of the large-State delegates (Wilson excepted) to join the small States in forming a quasi-*federal government*, within a *federal system*—a government that would not only be hedged around by the States, through their reserved powers; but to an important degree would *rest* on the States as integrant elements of its own being. The government that would emerge would be, in its composition, partly national, as witness the popular election of the House of Representatives; but it would be mostly federal, as witness the States' role in choosing senators, the President, and, derivatively, the Supreme Court. And even the House of Representatives would bear the States' imprint: each State would determine the qualifications of its popular electors, would be allowed to include three-fifths of its slaves in calculating its representation base, would be entitled to at least one represenative in the House no matter how far its population fell short of the one member-allotment*—and all of this quite apart from the question of intrastate apportionment. To some extent the great struggle at the Constitutional Convention between the large States and the small States was kindled by disagreements over how much the new government should be national in character and how much federal; but the main action in the battle was fought over the composition of the *federal element*. Should the States be represented as *equals*, which the small States said they were in theory and in right? or as *unequals*, which the large States said they were in fact? The part of the Great Compromise to which Justice Black called attention settled that issue—in favor of the large States, with respect to the House of Representatives. It did not settle, nor was it designed to settle, any other issue.

This is not to deny that James Wilson may have been unhappy with the deal, and may have preferred that his side had negotiated on different terms. It is to deny that Wilson's individual preferences, whatever one may make of them, are the same thing as the Consti-

---

* At the present time the populations of Alaska, Nevada, and Wyoming (226,167; 285,278; and 330,066, respectively, according to the 1960 census) each fall well below the population of the average congressional district (410,481)—hardly comfort for the theory that in electing the House of Representatives every American's vote must count equally.

tution of the United States. It is also to deny—and here we meet the
unstated assumption of Black's dialectic—that the argument the
large-State contingent in fact made (that a union of commonwealths
should be based on relative population, importance, etc.) leads in-
exorably, by a kind of inner logic, to the argument the Warren Court,
and perhaps James Wilson, would like to have seen made (that the
ideology of election democracy should pervade each participating
commonwealth to its furthermost canton). The matter may be put
briefly and in modern terms: Ambassador Goldberg could coher-
ently recommend a larger representation for the United States than
for Zambia in the United Nations General Assembly without at the
same time promising to submit his own job to a plebiscite in which
the vote of every American would count equally.

Is it the fact, then, that at the Constitutional Convention the framers simply never got around to the matter of apportionment within
the States? And are we saying, consequently, that the framers referred the matter, by the implications of their silence, to the comprehensive language of Article I, Section 4, which assigns to the States,
subject to Congress' supervision, the power to prescribe "The Times,
Places and Manner of holding [congressional] Elections?" We may
agree that the language of Section 4 could hardly be more plain-
spoken on the point, and so might stand on its own—but no, the argument about framers' intentions does not depend on inference. Later on in the summer of 1787 the delegates did address themselves
to the subject, explicitly. The exchange was brief, but it did underscore the Convention's clear grasp of the problem, and left not the
slightest doubt as to how the framers expected the problem to be
handled.

On August 6 the Convention, as a committee of the whole, began
debate on an initial draft of the Constitution prepared by the Committee on Detail; by the 9th it had turned to the provision that would
become Section 4: "The Times and Places and the Manner of holding
the Elections of the Members of Each House" the draft said, "shall
be prescribed by the Legislature of each State; but their Provisions
concerning them may, at any Time, be altered by the Legislature of
the United States."* The first clause was quickly agreed to; however—

---

* The earlier history of Section 4 can be related briefly. The question of
how, when, and where elections were to be held did not come up at all in
the Convention's general sessions between May and July 26. The reason,

Mr. Pinckney and Mr. Rutledge moved to strike out the remaining part, *viz.*, "but their provisions concerning them may at any time be altered by the Legislature of the United States." The States, they contended, could and must be relied on in such cases.[32]

Nathaniel Gorham disagreed:

> It would be as improper to take this power from the National Legislature as to restrain the British Parliament from regulating the circumstances of elections, leaving this business to the Counties themselves. . . .[33]

Whereupon Madison rose to give the issue a full airing. Note the attention he gave to the kind of question under dispute in the *Wesberry* case:

> The necessity of a General Government supposes that the State Legislatures will sometimes fail or refuse to consult the common interest at the expense of their local conveniency or prejudices. The policy

---

we may surmise, is that the matter was not deemed sufficiently burdensome to warrant a formal Convention decision prior to the first drafting efforts. The delegates apparently assumed the States would be left in control— though judging from later developments there was probably some sentiment for taking precautions against state abuses. On July 23 the Convention decided to refer its preliminary resolutions to a Committee on Detail with instructions "to prepare and report a Constitution conformable [to the proceedings of the Convention thus far]." On the 24th Messrs. Ellsworth, Gorham, Randolph, Rutledge, and Wilson were appointed to serve on the Committee; on the 26th the Convention adjourned until August 6 to await the Committee's report. The first of its working drafts that dealt with elections suggests that the Committee's initial impulse was to lump together the two questions of the regulation of elections, and the qualifications of electors of the House, in a single provision that would give responsibility for both to the state legislatures "subject to the Control of the Legislature of the United States." It was eventually decided, however, to deal with the two matters separately. The qualifications of the electors would be "the same from Time to Time as those of the Electors, in the several States, of the most numerous Branch of their own Legislatures." The regulation of elections, on the other hand, would be "prescribed by the Legislature of each State; but their Provisions concerning them [might], at any Time, be altered by the Legislature of the United States." The drafts in question, as well as the relevant editing, appear, incidentally, in the handwriting of James Wilson, which might suggest that in addition to acting as the Committee's secretary he was also its most forceful member. (See 2 Farrand 84-175, generally, and especially, for the progress of the drafting of Section 4, pp. 153, 163, 165.)

of referring the appointment of the House of Representatives to the
people, and not to the Legislatures of the States, supposes that the
result will be somewhat influenced by the mode. [The] view of the
question [set forth in the Committee's draft] seems to decide that the
Legislatures of the States ought not to have the uncontrolled right
of regulating the times, places, and manner of holding elections. These
were words of great latitude. It was impossible to foresee all the abuses
that might be made of the discretionary power. Whether the electors
should vote by ballot or viva voce; should assemble at this place or that
place; *should be divided into districts or all meet in one place; should
all vote for all the representatives, or all in a district vote for a number
allotted to the district: these and many other points would depend on
the Legislatures,* and might materially affect the appointments.*

Certain abuses, Madison continued, could be predicted if the States
were left entirely to their own devices:

Whenever the States Legislatures had a favorite measure to carry, they
would take care so as to mould their regulations as to favor the candidates they wished to succeed. Besides, the inequality of the Representation in the Legislatures of particular States would produce a
like inequality in their representation in the National Legislature,
as it was presumable that the Counties having the power in the former
case would secure it to themselves in the latter. *What danger could
there be in giving a controlling power to the National Legislature?*[34]

The States' own interests would be adequately protected by this solution, Madison added, thanks principally to their representation in
the Senate. And then:

Mr. King. If this power be not given to the National Legislature,
their right of judging of the returns of their members may be
frustrated. . . .

Mr. Gouverneur Morris observed that the States might make false
returns, and then make no provisions for new elections.

Mr. Sherman did not know but it might be best to retain the clause,
though he had himself sufficient confidence in the State Legislatures.[35]

That was the end of the debate. "The motion of Mr. Pinckney and

---

* Emphases here and elsewhere in this volume are supplied, unless otherwise indicated.

Mr. Rutledge," Madison's account ends dryly, "did not prevail."[36]

In a word: the Convention faced squarely the danger of such election abuses as rotten boroughs—and decided that as between 1) relying entirely on the States' discretion to avoid the abuses, and 2) granting the States a discretionary power subject to corrective action by Congress, it was the more prudent course to place the final authority with Congress.* As for the further idea that Congress' discretion would be subject, in turn, to some pre-ordained formula which Congress and the state legislatures could be compelled to enforce *by the courts*—there is no hint in the colloquy that it ever crossed the delegates' minds.

Justice Black dealt with the August 6 exchange in a single sentence, the *Wesberry* opinion's last reference to the Convention debates. Immediately following the allusion to James Wilson's comment on Old Sarum (which we now know was addressed to the issue of apportionment *among* the States) Black blandly added, as though he had been dealing with evidence relating to apportionment within the States right along:

"*The delegates referred to rotten borough apportionments in some of the state legislatures as the kind of objectionable governmental action* the Constitution *should not tolerate in the election of congressional representatives.*" And in a footnote he assured the opinion's readers that authority for *that* statement was to be found, generally, in the colloquy we have just examined!

The August 6 colloquy does indeed provide evidence that some, perhaps most, of the delegates regarded "rotten boroughs" as an evil to be resisted—as, if you like, "objectionable"; but the colloquy is hardly evidence of the utopian instinct to govern political societies by pronunciamentoes anathematizing every prospective departure from the ideal—as *unconstitutional*, and thus a proper subject for judical intervention. The mode of the men of Philadelphia was rather,

---

* On the suggestion of George Read of Delaware, the phrasing of the disputed clause was changed prior to its adoption to read: "but regulations, in each of the foregoing cases, may, at any time, be made or altered by the Legislature of the United States." "This was meant," a gloss by Madison explained, "to give the National Legislature a power not only to alter the provisions of the States, but to make regulations in case the States should fail or refuse [to act] altogether." (2 Farrand 252.)

as in this case, to assign responsibility for guarding against anticipated
abuses to an appropriate authority—in this case, by their express decision, to the state legislatures, subject to the supervision of Congress.
Justice Black cannot be faulted for lack of boldness: it would not
have occurred to every jurist, in a final appeal to the Convention debates, to cite as justification for a judicial usurpation of power the
very passages in the debates that make the delegation of that power
to the political departments most clear.

The framers' intentions on this subject were also made clear in the
Federalist Papers, and with a glimpse at the relevant passages we will
have done with the *Wesberry* case. In *Federalist* No. 54, Madison
underlined the distinction between the manner of apportioning representatives among the States, a problem that had been solved by a
"federal rule" set forth in the Constitution, and the manner of selecting the representatives within the States, a problem that was to be
solved otherwise:

> It is a fundamental principle of the proposed Constitution, that as
> the aggregate number of representatives allotted to the several States
> is to be determined by a federal rule, founded on the aggregate
> number of inhabitants; so, the right of choosing this allotted number
> in each State is to be exercised *by such part of the inhabitants as the
> State itself may designate.*[37]

Madison was here defending the Convention's decision to allow
slaves, though non-voters, to be included in a State's representation
base on the grounds that the underlying plan of the Constitution assumed that a *portion* of every State's inhabitants would undoubtedly,
at the State's discretion and for a variety of reasons that differed
from State to State, speak for *all* of its inhabitants in the matter of
electing congressional representatives. The argument, as it happened, referred specifically to voter qualifications as set forth in
Article 1, Section 2 (which is why Congress' supervisory power was
not mentioned), but the "fundamental principle" Madison spoke of
was obviously applicable to the problem of drawing congressional
districts as well; and of course it leaves Justice Black's "one man-one
vote" proposition in considerable disarray.

In *Federalist* No. 59, Hamilton dealt specifically with Section 4
which, he said, "authorizes the national legislature to regulate, *in the
last resort*, the election of its own members." Hamilton's defense of
the provision weighed and flatly rejected the idea of trying to govern

elections by hard, immutable formulas, such as Black's "one man-one vote" rule, that would be engrafted on the Constitution itself:

> It will not be alleged that an election law could have been framed and inserted in the Constitution which would have been applicable to every probable change in the situation of the country; and it will therefore not be denied that a *discretionary power* over elections ought to exist somewhere.

But where? In the national courts? Hamilton continued:

> It will, I presume, be as readily conceded that there were only three ways in which this power could have been reasonably organized— *that it must either have been lodged wholly in the national legislature, or wholly in the state legislatures, or primarily in the latter and ultimately in the former. The last mode has, with reason, been preferred by the Convention.*[38]

The reader has now seen enough* to pass judgment on the *Wesberry* ruling—to decide not merely whether Justice Black and the Court majority that supported him performed as conscientious scholars, but whether they had any intention of performing as conscientious scholars. And the verdict, we suspect the reader will agree, fairly raises the larger question of whether the Warren Court is any longer entitled to the confidence and presumption of good faith which, as schoolboys, we accorded past Supreme Courts as a matter of course.

That the Supreme Court, by virtue of *Wesberry* and the companion rulings on the apportionment of state legislators, has decreed a revolution in American politics hardly needs elaboration. In the state cases, beginning with *Baker v. Carr*, and culminating in the *Reynolds v. Sims* group which in June, 1964, imposed the "one man-one vote" on both branches of all state legislatures,[39] the Court's clumsy, imperious hand has reached into the most intimate political

---

* Black's presentation of the "historical context" concluded with two references of his own to *The Federalist Papers* (not surprisingly, the passages we have just read were not mentioned), an allusion to certain remarks made by delegates to the state ratifying conventions, and, finally, a paragraph from a lecture delivered by James Wilson after the Constitution was adopted. This material is of the same order we have already seen. However, an appendix at the end of this volume sets forth these items, as Black did, and supplies, for the reader's comparison, such extracts from the actual record as may be helpful to understanding their true meaning and context.

concerns of every community in the land—and with as little constitutional justification as in the *Wesberry* case. Moreover, in these state
cases the one excuse for judicial intervention that once made some
sense (but only some, and never *constitutional* sense) is no longer
available. It had been said by the reformers that the courts, alone,
could bring about reapportionment since the state legislators who
owed their jobs to allegedly inequitable districting arrangements
could hardly be expected to change those arrangements on their own
initiative—in a word, that the "rotten borough system" was self-per-
petuating. But in *Lucas v. Forty-Fourth General Assembly*,[40] one of
the cases decided in June 1964, the State of Colorado sought to solve
its apportionment problem by popular referendum, with revealing
consequences. Two proposed constitutional amendments had been
placed on the ballot in 1962, the first authorizing some major changes
in the old system including a requirement that members of the Colorado lower house be elected on a population basis, the second requiring that the "one man-one vote" rule be applied to the Senate as
well as the House. The first plan was approved, the second rejected by
a state-wide plurality of over 2-1; and that verdict was endorsed by
a majority of the voters of every county in the State. Whereupon the
Warren Court struck down the decision of the people of Colorado,
and ordered the imposition of its own, "one man-one vote," rule on
both houses of the legislature. . . . The *Lucas* case, coupled with
Wesberry v. Sanders, removed all doubt about the purposes of the
Warren Court. It was not the elimination of obstructions to popular
government that moved the Court; it was a determination to impose
the ideology of equality on the American political system, notwithstanding the clear purposes of the architects of the system, and irrespective even of the wishes of the people who now live under it.

What to do? In the summer of 1964, several weeks after rulings in
the *Reynolds v. Sims* group had been handed down, the United States
House of Representatives decided that what to do was to restrict the
appellate jurisdiction of the Supreme Court under the regulatory
power conferred on Congress by Article III, Section 2, of the Constitution.* The so-called Tuck bill, which the House passed 218-175,
would have withheld from the Supreme Court jurisdiction over all
state apportionment cases on the grounds that the subject was not

---

* "The Supreme Court shall have appellate jurisdiction," that section
provides, "with such Exceptions and under such Regulations as the Congress
shall make."

and had never been a legitimate concern of that department. Simultaneously, over on the Senate side, the Republican minority leader, Senator Dirksen, proposed a less drastic response. The Dirksen measure, which was approved by a 10-2 vote of the Senate Judiciary Committee, and then attached as a rider to that session's Foreign Aid bill, would have authorized the States to suspend the operation of the Court's decrees until Congress had an opportunity to propose a remedial constitutional amendment. Both measures, after generating considerable support on the Hill, and an uproar in the command posts of the American Establishment, failed.

We need not try to identify all of the reasons for the failure, or to rank them. Suffice it to say that one certainly played an important role, as it has in every modern attempt to restrain or discipline the Supreme Court. It emerged in an editorial by the *Washington Post* addressed to the Dirksen Rider, one of hundreds of similar impassioned remonstrances to which Congress and the American people were subjected during that summer:

> [The Supreme Court's apportionment] rulings have unquestionably become the law of the land. It is not the function of Congress to set aside that law, or to thwart its operation. The spectacle of Congress trying to use its legislative power to deny or temporarily nullify constitutional rights which the Supreme Court has clearly upheld is such a serious encroachment upon the orderly division of powers that even extraordinary measures would be justified to defeat it.
>
> There is much controversy, to be sure, over the soundness of the Constitution's [!] edict that both houses of the state legislatures must be apportioned on the basis of population [etc.]. The next Congress will be free, if it wishes, to propose a constitutional amendment [etc.]; however, Congress should not seek to shortcircuit judicial decisions [etc., etc.].[41]

These advices are what this book is about. Whether they shrill from a *Post* editorial, or are ponderously labored from an academy lecture-platform, or are just "felt" by the average citizen, they have become a more formidable threat to authentic popular government in the United States than any that has heretofore dogged the steps of the Republic. If it is true that a construction of the Constitution by the Supreme Court, no matter how spurious or absurd, no matter how damaging to the organic life of the country, is eo ipso "the law of the land," unchallengeable even by a law made by the people's representatives; if it is true that a "constitutional right" can come into being merely on the Court's say, so that every corrective constitutional amendment can plausibly be represented as an attempt to deprive the people of their previously vested constitutional rights (and thus easily defeated)—then, where, in all candor, are we? If a judicial interpretation of the Constitution is, by definition, the *Constitution*, why then we are in the grips of a judicial despotism. That is the meaning of despotism. An unchallengeable authority can be benign, or malevolent, but it is a despotism if the rest of the commonwealth has no practical alternative to succumbing to its will.

This book was born of an intuition that the founders of this commonwealth, and their successors, did not will such a state of affairs upon us. But intuitions are often disappointed by fact. What *is* the fact? What, we are going to ask, is the role in the government of the American commonwealth that Tradition and Constitution and Practice have assigned, through the institution of judicial review, to the United States Supreme Court?

THE FACES OF JUDICIAL REVIEW

THE FACES OF JUDICIAL REVIEW

I

In the chapters ahead, we shall be examining the origins of judicial review and of the doctrine of judicial supremacy. As every student of the subject knows, one of the great barriers to fruitful conversation in this area is semantical. We are all probably clear in our minds as to what *we* mean by "judicial review," and no doubt what we mean is entirely defensible. The point is that each of us is likely to mean something different, and that the people who have dealt with the subject before us—most definitely including those who introduced the concept to our political system—have meant different things from one another. The result is that the student often finds himself dealing with apples and oranges. Jones, Smith, Quinn, and Moore are all "supporters" of judicial review. Jones regards the power as a curb only on state acts. Smith believes congressional acts are also subject to review, but only certain types of congressional acts. Quinn thinks the Supreme Court can refuse to enforce *any* act of Congress or of the States, but disagrees with Moore's position that the Court's word is "final." And so on.

We are not going to settle the problem by prescription. The best we can do is to get the various possibilities in front of us at an early point in the discussion—to take our bearings, as it were, before the story begins.

In general terms, the power of judicial review means the power of a court to pass judgment on the validity of the acts of *non*-judicial branches of government. It is thus distinct from the power to hear appeals under which a higher court may review the decisions of a lower court. Our problem is to transmute this general concept into the specifics of the American political system: *Assuming the*

115

framers of the Constitution contemplated any kind of judicial review by the Supreme Court—a proposition about which we must try to keep an open mind—*against what authorities was it to be exercised? Regarding what kind of acts? With what effect?* To each of these questions, there are a number of serious answers—serious, in the sense that arguments can be found to support them either in the historical data surrounding the Constitution's adoption, or in the views of later constitutional scholars:*

A. The authorities subject to Supreme Court review.

A1. *Only the States.* Under this theory, judicial review is regarded primarily as a means of enforcing the supremacy of the federal government. One of the prime concerns at the Constitutional Convention, as we shall see, was how to enforce congressional authority against wayward States, a problem that had plagued the central government under the Articles of Confederation. To some at the Convention, who may have thought it unnecessary or unwise to subject *federal* legislation to Supreme Court review, such review of state action seemed to be the only way, short of calling out the troops, of holding the emerging nation together. Many years later Justice Holmes said much the same thing: "I do not think the United States would come to an end if we lost our power to declare an Act of Congress void. I do think the Union would be imperiled if we could not make that declaration as to the laws of the several States."[1]

A2. *Only the other branches of the federal government*—Congress and the President. This theory is the converse of the above, and while most scholars have not deemed it worthy of serious consideration, it is implicit in what the Jeffersonian Republicans actually did in the years immediately following the adoption of the Constitution: on the one hand, for example, they called upon the Supreme Court to invalidate Congress' Alien and Sedition Acts, and on the other, insisted that the final arbiters of the States' powers under the Constitution were the *States themselves.* The Kentucky and Virginia Resolutions reflected the latter position, as did, a few years later, Virginia's vigorous resistance to the Supreme Court's decisions in the *Hunter's Lessee* and *Cohens* cases.[2] And we shall discover later on that the Supremacy Clause of the Constitution itself can be read to support precisely this view of the matter.

A3. *Both the States and the other branches of the federal government.* This is the prevailing view of the matter today, and represents the actual practice of the Supreme Court from a quite early moment.

B. The kinds of acts that are within the *scope* of judicial review.

---

* The analysis that follows is borrowed in some part from Edward S. Corwin, *Court Over Constitution*, 1938, pp. 1-3.

B1. *Only those that constitute an invasion of the judicial power.* For example: an attempt by Congress or a State to circumscribe the right of jury trial; or, in the case of Congress, an attempt to limit the tenure of federal judges. Under this theory of *scope,* judicial review is merely an instrument of self-protection—a weapon available to the judiciary for resisting usurpations of its prerogatives by other branches of government. As we shall see, the Supreme Court did not attempt to review any other kind of congressional act until the Dred Scott case in 1857.

B2. *Only acts that constitute a violation of an allegedly explicit prohibition in the Constitution.* The Constitution has, in this view, two kinds of provisions: the grants of power saying what the federal government *can* do, with the implicit reservation (made explicit by the Tenth Amendment) of all other powers to the States, and the limitations, or prohibitions—certain things that, in any case, the federal government or the States *cannot* do. Under this theory, the Supreme Court may enforce the latter type of provision—an "ex post facto Law" passed by Congress, for example, or one "abridging the freedom of speech"; or, in the case of State legislation, a law "impairing the Obligation of Contracts" or denying "equal protection of the laws." But it may not construe the grants of power— for example, by attempting to set the limits of Congress' power to "regulate Commerce." The distinction is typically advanced by partisans of congressional supremacy, persons who are willing to have the courts enforce the "unambiguous" provisions of the Constitution, but who regard federal legislators as better qualified than judges to construe the document as a whole—better qualified, e.g., for such "political" tasks as establishing the boundary line between federal and state power.

B3. *All acts.* Under this view the Supreme Court may interpret all parts of the Constitution, the grants of power as well as the prohibitions; it does act as an umpire in disputes between the federal government and the States.

C. The *effect* of judicial review.

C1. *The Court's decision settles the law of the particular case as far as the judiciary is concerned.* A ruling of "unconstitutionality," that is to say, does not operate to strike the condemned law from the books so as to prevent future cases from being brought under it; nor is it binding, even with regard to the case in question, on other branches of government that might choose to ignore or resist the decision because of a contrary view of the law. *The Court's ruling thus amounts to a declaration that federal judicial machinery is not available for the enforcement of the challenged law, and a warning that it will not be available in similar cases in the future should a future Court choose to follow the rule of* stare decisis. Let us suppose that X, an avowed Communist, has been convicted under a federal statute outlawing the Communist Party, and that he appeals on the grounds that his First Amendment rights have been violated. The

Supreme Court holds the statute unconstitutional and reverses the conviction. Under this view of the *effect* of judicial review, the Court has said simply that, in its "opinion" of the law, X must be released. The President and Congress, however, are free to act upon a different opinion: the President may order the federal warden to keep X in jail, and instruct his Attorney General to start prosecuting Communists Y and Z under the condemned statute. In so doing, he of course accepts the risk the Supreme Court will stick by its guns and "reverse" Y's and Z's convictions as well, with whatever political consequences this kind of running battle with the judiciary might entail.

C2. *The Court's decision settles the law of the particular case against all concerned, but does not so fix the meaning of the Constitution as to prevent other branches of government from disregarding the decision at a future date.* A judgment of "unconstitutionality," under this theory, *does* operate to strike the condemned law from the books, and *does* require other branches of government to deal with the litigant in the case as though the law were a nullity. However, it does not prevent the other branches from challenging the Court's view of the Constitution by enacting and attempting to enforce new laws in conflict with the decision. Again taking the facts of our Communist case: X would have to be freed; no further prosecutions could be brought under the "void" statute; yet Congress would be perfectly within its rights to register its *own* interpretation of the Constitution by passing a *new* act outlawing the party—thus inviting, or forcing, the Court to dispose of the issue differently the next time around. It will be seen that under both theories C1 and C2, interpreting the Constitution is the business of Congress, the President, and the States, no less than of the Supreme Court; the operative difference is that under 2, "reversal" of a Court decision requires some formal, affirmative action—such as re-enactment of a challenged statute.

C3. *The Court's decision is "final"—not only as to the particular case, but as to the meaning of the Constitutional provision involved.* The judgment is thus binding not only on the litigants, but on other branches of government; and not only in this case, but until such time as the Court indicates its view of the Constitution has changed. In terms of our Communist case, X must be freed and the statute falls; but more: Congress is barred from passing another act outlawing the Communist Party, as long as the Court holds to this interpretation of the First Amendment. "The Constitution," to recall Chief Justice Hughes' apothegm, "is what the Supreme Court says it is."

Such are the possible elements of a "position" on "judicial review." Further possibilities could be developed, of course, with the addition of this or that emphasis, but in the last analysis a position is likely to come down to some combination of theories from the three categories above. For instance, the now-prevailing doctrine of judicial supremacy is a combination of theories A3, B3 and C3.

It will be our task in these chapters to try to discover which combination the founders of the American political system had in mind.

II

A word about the procedure we shall be following. One of the self-evident curiosities of our political system is that judicial review is nowhere provided for in the federal Constitution. There are provisions that can be read to support this or that version of it, but such provisions are open to other interpretations as well; and in any event the question naturally arises in connection with a political system grounded in a written Constitution: How can it be that an institution as important to the system as this one has no more imposing foundation than a dubious inference?

The apologists for judicial review have unavoidably been driven to various kinds of circumstantial evidence. Their arguments down through the years may be divided into three:

1. Judicial review had already been adopted by the American community through tradition and precedent by the time the Constitutional Convention convened, so that there was no need for the framers to provide for it in so many words.

2. The apparently ambiguous language of the Constitution, when read alongside certain evidence from the Convention proceedings, shows that the framers thought themselves to be establishing judicial review in the document itself.

3. Judicial review was practiced by the Supreme Court and tolerated by the community immediately following the adoption of the Constitution, so that it became incorporated in our constitutional system by, as it were, ratification.

The apologists, however, have shown a remarkable talent, as the evidence begins to wear thin on one line of argument, for moving the discussion gently, almost imperceptibly, on to another, with the result that the conclusions reached are frequently more notable for the grandeur of their historical sweep than for dialectical precision. We are going to deny ourselves this rhetorical luxury. We shall be examining the three arguments separately, asking what light each of them, on its own, sheds on the root question: *Does judicial review have the prescriptive sanction of constitutional authority? and if so, what kind of judicial review has that sanction?*

We begin with the contention that judicial review was so firmly imbedded in the American tradition prior to 1787 that the framers of the Constitution could assume it would be part of the new government without mentioning it. The following section deals with that part of the tradition that precedes the War of Independence.

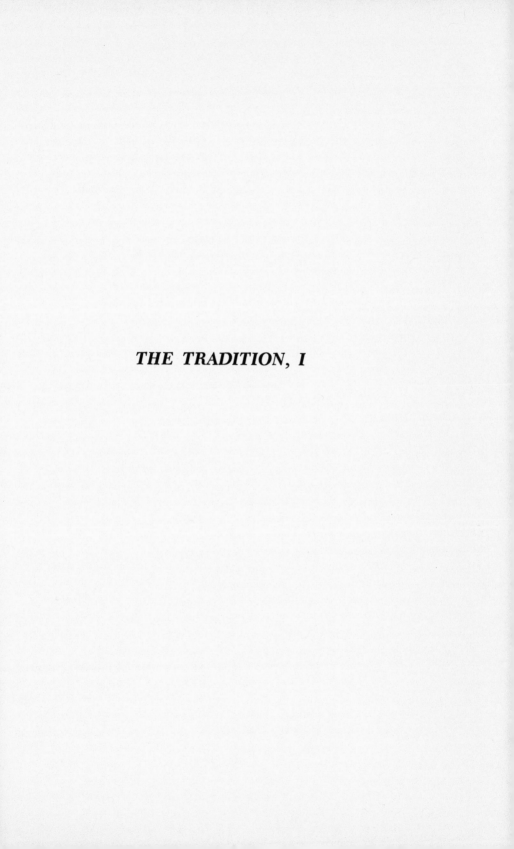

THE TRADITION, I

FROM COKE TO BLACKSTONE

. . . in his dictum in Bonham's case [Lord Coke] furnished a form of words which . . . became the most important single source of the notion of judicial review.

Edward S. Corwin, *The "Higher Law" Back-*
ground of American Constitutional Law

No respectable history of the American doctrine of judicial review begins in America. It is an axiom with legal scholars that the
development is traceable to England—that the American colonists'
exposure to English jurisprudence had "conditioned" them in one degree or another to the idea of judges setting aside acts of legislatures
by the time they had achieved independence. Thus, the argument
runs, when the moment came to create a new political system, the institution of judicial review sprang more or less effortlessly from the
roots of tradition: all the friends of the institution had to do was
loosen up the soil a bit, and a great tree was bound to grow.

One of the difficulties with the axiom, on the face of it, is that
judicial review was *not* part of the English tradition—at least not
part of the dominant tradition. Notoriously, such a power was not
recognized in the English political system during the eighteenth century, nor is it recognized in England today where parliamentary supremacy is still universally acknowledged. On the face of it, then,
the scholars' appeal must be to a *minority* tradition: the search for
precedents must be a search for *rejected* precedents that in one way
or another managed to influence English and colonial political
thought after their formal ejection from the law of the British realm.

This search invariably begins and ends with the ideas of the seventeenth-century jurist and statesman, Sir Edward Coke. The trail can

123

be narrowed down still further. Coke's fame as the father of judicial review rests on his opinion in a single case, *Dr. Bonham's Case*, and, at that, on a single sentence of that opinion—an "aside" that did not figure at all in the reasoning that led to the decision. Moreover, *Dr. Bonham's Case* never became a "leading case" in English history; in addition to its early elimination from the accepted line of legal precedents, Coke's own biographers did not deem the opinion to be of any special interest to history. One of the extended accounts of his life does not mention the case at all, the other lists it in passing without discussion, as one of the five cases Coke's opponents cited against him when he was removed from the bench.[1]

Nevertheless, Coke's Bonham doctrine and its fascinating path through history are worth examining in detail. For it is not to be denied that by tracing the influence of Edward Coke, and the allegedly related influence of natural law theory, we shall have in front of us all of the relevant data for making an informed judgment about the status of judicial review in the American colonies before independence.*

---

* Some writers have pointed to the activities of the British Privy Council during colonial times, alongside the Coke and natural law traditions, as an important influence on the development of the American institution of judicial review. (See, e.g., Charles G. Haines, *American Doctrine of Judicial Supremacy*, 2nd. Ed., 1932, pp. 44-56; Alfred H. Kelly and Winfred Harbison, *The American Constitution*, 1955, pp. 50-55.) We need not tarry long with this suggestion. In the first place, the Privy Council's function of disallowing acts of colonial legislatures was, by everyone's agreement, essentially *legislative* in nature, rather than judicial. If the function anticipated anything in subsequent American thought, it was the congressional "negative" proposed by Madison and others at the Constitutional Convention as a check on state legislation. The criteria for disallowance were, as often as not, considerations of policy or expedience; and while parliamentary statutes and the English common law were often cited as reasons for disallowance, the Council's attitude in applying these standards was hardly that of a judicial court: "The general adoption of the English common law by the colonies," Haines concedes in this connection, "was usually disapproved by the home government on the ground that it interfered with the necessary control over colonial laws." (Op. cit., p. 48.) Moreover, there was no appeal whatever to the "higher law" notions often associated with the practice of *judicial* review.

In the second place, the Privy Council manifestly functioned as an administrative agency of *Empire* for controlling a subject people. This is the only instance we can recall where the machinery of colonialism has been cited as a precedent for the institution of judicial review.

Yet, at first blush, there appears to be one exception to the rule that acts of disallowance were legislative in nature. The colonial legislation involved

Coke's role in English legal and political history is difficult to categorize, if only because a highly variegated public career placed him at one time or another on every side of the main political issue of his day—the post-Tudor power struggle between Parliament and the King. He was born in 1552 at a time when the late Tudor monarchs and Parliament were managing to bury their inherent rivalry under the rubric of "dual sovereignty." During Coke's lifetime this concept came under fire, on the one hand from the Stuarts who began asserting certain Crown prerogatives in the name of divine right, and on the other, by members of Parliament who insisted on the ultimate

---

in the case of *Winthrop v. Lechmere* (1727) —i.e., two Connecticut statutes on intestacy that had disregarded the English law of primogeniture—came before the Privy Council on appeal by the defeated litigant in the Connecticut courts, rather than by the usual practice of automatically submitting new colonial legislation to the Council for review. The Council invalidated the statutes, as well as four colonial court decrees issued pursuant to them. As to whether the disposition of the case actually amounted to something resembling judicial review, we may summon the judgment of Mr. Brinton Coxe, probably the most energetic of the precedent-seekers for judicial review, yet among the most judicious: "If the king proceeding judicially in council ever [voided] a challenged act of a colonial legislature [as is sometimes asserted of the *Winthrop* case]," he observes, "an English model existed in the [eighteenth] century for the American judicial competency. . . . If, however, an order in council . . . could exercise the prerogative legislatively, judicially, and executively at the same time, then *Winthrop v. Lechmere* furnishes no exception to the rule that the king proceeded legislatively in [invalidating] colonial acts." Whereupon Coxe concludes that the *Winthrop* order "was actually of a mixed nature. . . . That part of it was judicial which [reversed the four court decrees—and was thus analogous, we may interpose, to the Council's decree in *Frost v. Leighton* (see "Across the Atlantic," below)]. *That part of it was legislative which declared the two acts of the colonial legislature to be null and void."* (Brinton Coxe, *Judicial Power and Unconstitutional Legislation*, 1893, p. 212.)

In short, the apologists have little ground to stand on in this matter, and their discussion typically dissolves into some variant of Haines' observation that the Council was, in any event, a precedent-maker for judicial review in that "the colonists became accustomed to referring their causes to a supreme tribunal for final adjudication." (Ibid., p. 56.) Yet a little earlier, in countering the "objection" that the Privy Council was never cited as a precedent by "those who were responsible for the adoption of the American practice of judicial review," Haines had observed that this was "not surprising [since] the colonists were as a rule not content" with the idea of submitting the conduct of their affairs to the Council's review. (Ibid., p. 52.) Indeed they were not. The institution was highly unpopular in the colonies and thus was among the least likely candidates for imitation by the founders of the new Republic.

supremacy—even as against the King—of the common law. By all accounts the greatest lawyer of his day, Coke brought to bear on this
contest considerable learning and a powerful intellect—as well as (say
his critics) an immense ambition unencumbered by moral scruples.
Whether he was a purposeful shaper of the struggle, or merely exploited it for his own ends, is one of the unresolved questions of
Coke's life. Suffice it to say that he was *in* the struggle in an important way and from every direction.

In the beginning, Coke was a loyal servant of royal interests. From
1594 to 1606 he served as Attorney General, first under Elizabeth,
then James I, and it was in that capacity of crown prosecutor that he
earned a reputation he has never lived down for harshness and
cruelty.* Then, for a ten-year period, he moved to the bench, first as
Chief Justice of the Common Pleas, and later on—in a kind of kick
upstairs—as Chief Justice of the King's Bench. These were a stormy
ten years that found him in constant battle with members of his own
court, with other courts—and above all, according to his modern ad-
mirers, with the King. Whether Coke's wrangling with James was
really a fight for "principle," or merely a matter of Coke's pushing
his personal claims to power need not concern us. But it is of considerable interest what this "principle," if principle it was, might have
been. For this was the period of the *Bonham* case where Coke
seemed to be putting the courts *above Parliament*. That case suggests a tantalizing question: Were Coke's repeated run-ins with the
Crown his way of helping out the parliamentary cause? or, conceivably, did he entertain the idea of carving out an independent domain
for the judiciary—of making judges a "third force" in the great power
struggle with a role similar in some respects to that of our own Supreme Court? Some scholars have toyed with this latter theory,[2] but
they have been unable to adduce corroborative evidence for it; and,
in any event, if such a scheme was ever in the back of Coke's mind,

---

* Sir Walter Raleigh was one of his "victims." Elizabethan sensibilities are
said to have been greatly offended during that gentle courtier's trial when,
at one point, Coke snarled at the prisoner, "Thou hast an English face, but
a Spanish heart!" The modern animus against Coke on this score has to do
largely with his having introduced into Star Chamber proceedings a new,
and even for that day, quite tyrannical version of the law of criminal libel;
later, mainly through his own written works—e.g., his "report" of the *Case
de Libellis Famosis*—Coke's views, as prosecutor, were incorporated into the
common law. For an account of this episode see Louis B. Boudin, *Government by Judiciary*, I, 487-89.

it died with the sudden collapse of his judicial career. In 1616 he was summarily removed from all of his offices and forced to answer charges that his opinions in a number of cases, including *Bonham's*, had been "extravagant."

In the third and last phase of his career, Coke settled firmly into the parliamentary groove. From 1620 to 1628 he was a member of Parliament and took a leading role in framing the stirring Petition of Right against Charles I. During this period, Coke emerged as the great expounder of Magna Carta and allied himself unmistakably with the partisans of parliamentary supremacy. Thereafter he wrote his famous *Institutes* in which the far-reaching claims of Parliament achieved one of their most striking expressions. This final phase of Coke's life is of great relevance, as we shall see, in evaluating the importance Coke himself attached to the celebrated sentence in *Dr. Bonham's Case.*

Turning now to that case, the relevant facts are these:[3] The Royal College of Physicians in London had been given a royal patent by Henry VII allowing the College to levy a fine on anyone found practicing medicine without its license; half of the fine was to go to the King, the other half to the College. Later on, Parliament confirmed the patent, adding the provision that the President of the College could send non-licensed practitioners to jail. Dr. Bonham failed the College examinations and was denied a license, but he proceeded to practice anyway at the University of Cambridge, claiming the Royal College had no jurisdiction over him. The College disagreed and had him imprisoned, though without the concurrence of the President of the College. Dr. Bonham sued the College for false imprisonment, alleging many grounds. One of the issues that developed at the trial was whether the Royal College's dual role under the patent—its right both to determine the crime and to benefit from the punishment—defied the common law maxim that no man can be judge in his own cause. In this connection Coke wrote his famous lines:

> And it appears in our books, that in many cases the common law will control acts of Parliament, and sometimes adjudge them to be utterly void; for when an act of Parliament is against common right or reason, or repugnant or impossible to be performed, the common law will control it and adjudge such act to be void.

There are three points that need to be made about this passage. First, *Coke's statement of the previous law*—"it appears in our books

. . ."—*was false.* As authority for his contention, Coke cited five cases, the obvious implication being that these were instances in which a court had nullified an act of Parliament for one of the reasons stated in Coke's formula. The fact is that *none* of the decisions nullified an act of Parliament; nor did any of them claim the power to do so; nor is there any reference at all in these cases to a controlling "common right or reason"—the key element in the formula.

Brief mention of two of the cases will show how Coke managed to palm them off as precedents. In *Tregor's Case,* Coke wrote, quoting Year Book 8, Edward III, p. 30: "[Judge] Herle saith some statutes are made *against law and right,* which those who made them *perceiving,* would not put into execution."[4] The italics are ours, and it will be noted that except for these five words Judge Herle said nothing more than that legislators sometimes make bad laws which they allow to become dead letters. We emphasize the five words because they are not to be found in the Year Book report, but were shamelessly put into Judge Herle's mouth *by Coke himself* in order to make his "precedent"!*

In the case known as *Cessavit 42,* Coke discovered an instance in which a court had, indeed, disregarded an act of Parliament—whether because the judges were unaware of the statute or chose to ignore it, the original report of the case does not show. Much less does the report suggest that the judges presumed to declare the statute *void.* But Coke managed to turn the case into a precedent—once again by doctoring the original account with some words of his own: "because it would be against common right and reason," Coke added to the original, "the common law adjudges the said act of Parliament as to that point void."†[5]

---

* What is more, Herle had explained in the balance of the *Tregor* opinion that the statute in front of him did *not* fall into the category he had mentioned, and had gone on to interpret it according to ordinary rules of construction.

† We limit our discussion to two of Coke's cases because in the other three (two of them happily involve the same situation) , the substance of the matter is to be found only at the end of a tortuous journey through medieval jargon and antiquated legal concepts. As a merciful alternative, we may call upon the judgment of Theodore Plucknett, who taught legal history for a number of years at Harvard and later at the University of London, and in 1926 wrote the authoritative monograph on *Dr. Bonham's Case* and its aftermath. (40 *Harv. L. Rev.* 30) . It is not unfair to say that Professor Plucknett wrote as an admirer of Coke and his Bonham doctrine, and in endeavoring to make out the best possible case for both, stretched the evidence as far as

The second point is that the famous passage was irrelevant to the *Bonham* case. The lines were gratuitous; they did not belong in the argument, even in the terms of Coke's own analysis, and they in no way affected the final outcome. The decision turned on many points, but the one that concerns us is how Coke handled the contention that the Royal College could not be both a party and judge in the same case. He resolved this issue by an interpretation of the statute. He said, in effect, that the act (and the royal patent) had not given the College the powers it claimed over unlicensed practitioners—as distinguished from incompetent ones; and anyway that the College had not observed the proper procedures in exercising its powers.[6] *He did not, that is to say, declare the statute invalid; and therefore, under the rule of* stare decisis, *that part of the opinion asserting the court's hypothetical power to invalidate legislative acts could not acquire the status of a "legal precedent."*

(and sometimes farther than, see p. 138) it would go. Yet, after a lengthy discussion of Coke's five precedents, he was forced to this summary:

"*Tregor's Case* proves nothing; *Cessavit 42,* on the other hand, is a strong precedent in his favor; *Annuitie 41* [better known as *The Case of the Seals*] would have looked strong also, although it is, in fact, of doubtful import; while *Strowd's Case* [and its companion, an anonymous case, are] valueless." (Ibid., p. 44-5.)

Our comment: We have seen how "strong" *Cessavit 42* was. One wonders why Plucknett summoned this adjective, having said at an earlier point in the monograph with regard to that case: "There is no such judgment [as Coke said there was] in the report; the statute is not held void; it is just ignored. To this fact Coke has really added an explanation and a theory all his own. . . ." (Ibid., p. 36.) As to the reason *The Case of the Seals* "looked" good to Coke, Plucknett had earlier explained (and a little lamely, we think) that "it was printed clearly and intelligibly in a famous and authoritative folio, with all the pomp and circumstance of Law-French and black-letter." (Ibid., p. 41.) However, what was "printed," he goes on to say (and why not as recognizably for Coke as for Plucknett?) was "not a judgment, but what [the court reporter believed] to be the 'opinion' of the court on this one point that happened to interest him. . . ." (Ibid., p. 40.) And as to the "opinion" on this interesting point, Plucknett further explained "[it did] not necessarily mean more than that the reporter believed that the court inclined to one side rather than the other. *Judgment* [was] *not reported and may never have taken place.*" (Ibid., p. 39.)

Despite its shortcomings as a "decision," *The Case of the Seals* will eventually be of interest to us because of the apt illustration it affords of a statute deemed "impossible to be performed." This concept—though obviously its significance is largely theoretical—constitutes a recognized limitation on the English doctrine of legislative supremacy. (See p. 134.)

The third point is that Coke himself explicitly repudiated his supposed Bonham doctrine in later years. For one thing, there is his answer to the charge of "extravagance" brought against him in 1616 in which he protested that the views expressed in *Bonham* were not necessarily his own, but simply reflected the state of the law as he had been led to understand it: "But I did not mean to declare my opinion even as *obiter*. All I did was to report the argument, and the cases cited in the argument . . ."[7] For another, as we have seen, his parliamentary career was devoted to establishing that body's claims, under the aegis of Magna Carta, to supreme authority. But the decisive evidence is to be found in what must be regarded as Coke's final word on the subject—his *Institutes*. The point could not be put more emphatically: "Of the power and jurisdiction of Parliament for the making of laws in proceeding by bill, it is so transcendent and absolute, as it cannot be confined either for causes or for persons within any bounds." "A parliament," he went on, "brings *judges*, officers and all good men into good order. . . ."*[8]

So much for Edward Coke's personal role in siring the doctrine of judicial review. How, then, did the *Bonham* dictum fare in subsequent English cases? There are only two—one decided shortly after *Bonham*, the other in the century following—in which it received sympathetic treatment. In *Day v. Savadge* (1614) Lord Hobart wrote, evidently with Coke in mind:

> . . . even an act of Parliament made against Natural equity, as to make a man Judge in his own Cause, is void in itself for *Jura naturae sunt immutabilia* and they are *leges legum*.[9]

---

* Some writers have sought to reduce the force of this passage by observing that in those days Parliament exercised some of the powers of an equity court as well as strictly legislative powers; therefore, the argument runs, when Coke affirmed "parliamentary" supremacy, he was not necessarily affirming "legislative" supremacy as we understand the concept. (See E. S. Corwin, *The "Higher Law" Background of American Constitutional Law*, 42 *Harv. L. Rev.* 149, 378.) Very well; but what does the argument prove for these purposes except that Coke's Parliament had even *broader* powers than a "supreme" legislature would possess today? Parliamentary "judges" and Parliamentary "legislators" were, after all, the same men. The fact remains that in Coke's mature judgment, as distinct from his Bonham doctrine, there is no power *beyond* Parliament—i.e., no separate judicial power—competent to second-guess law makers as to what they can and cannot do.

But Hobart's remark, like Coke's, was dictum: the question in the case was whether Parliament had given the City of London authority to collect certain wharf charges, and Hobart managed to answer it without invalidating any statute. Moreover, Hobart's remark, even as dictum, covered far less ground than Coke's since it was expressly confined to the case of the man who had been made judge of his own cause.

The other case, *City of London v. Wood* (1701), raised the same issue. In this instance, however, no act of Parliament was even called into question; the problem was caused by a municipal by-law that allowed the city courts of London to adjudicate fines assessed by the City. Nevertheless, Lord Holt worked into his opinion the remark:

> And what my Lord Coke says in *Dr. Bonham's Case,* in his 8 Co., is far from any extravagancy, for it is a very reasonable and true saying, that if an act of Parliament should ordain that the same person should be party and judge, or, which is the same thing, judge in his own case, it would be a void act of Parliament; for it is impossible that one should be judge and party. . . .[10]

This interjection is doubly curious in the light of Holt's careful explanation at an earlier point in the opinion that the crucial difference between a by-law and an act of Parliament was that *"a by-law is liable to have its validity brought into question, but an act of Parliament is not."*[11] And at another point he commented: "though it may do several things that look pretty odd . . . *an act of Parliament can do no wrong."*[12] Scholars generally agree that from the point of view of consistency Holt's effort in this instance was a disaster. (The ambivalence might have been due to a personal sympathy on his part with Coke's attempt to limit Parliament's authority, coupled with an awareness that a King had lost his crown a scant thirteen years earlier for attempting that very thing.) But the point for our purposes is that Lord Holt's comment simply joined those of Lord Hobart and Lord Coke as yet another dictum. And that was as far as the Bonham doctrine ever got in England.

What we have been dealing with, then, is not—in the legal sense—even a "rejected" precedent, but a theory that never became a precedent, though three judges thought well of it. The Law of England during this period stayed right on course. In 1653 a Captain Streater tried to get a writ of habeas corpus on the grounds that a parliamentary order under which he was arrested was contrary to the "law of the land." The court's answer indicates the set of the constitutional sea: "Mr. Streater, one must be above another, and the inferior must submit to the superior. . . . If the Parliament should do one thing, and we do the contrary here, things would run around. We must submit to the legislative power. . . ."[13]

And yet we cannot leave the matter there. Another English case decided during this same period bears heavily on our subject— though hardly in the way some of the American precedent-seekers would have us believe. *Godden v. Hales*[14] (1686) is indeed an instance, as several apologists for judicial review have pointed out, of an English court deliberately and unmistakably challenging the supremacy of Parliament. It is the only such instance, we may add, in English history. Yet the case is justly celebrated, not as a legal precedent for judicial review (it was expressly overruled several years after the decision), but as a *political* event of the first magnitude, one that figured directly in the deposition of a King, and the estabishment of a new order that, among other things, permanently silenced the pretensions of English judges. For *Godden v. Hales* was one of the immediate causes of the Glorious Revolution. The story surrounding this remarkable case is worth telling—the unsavory political machinations that made it possible, as well as its eventual consequences; for it is poignant testimony to the strength of the English tradition of legislative supremacy even at the moment it was under sharpest attack.

To begin with, *Godden v. Hales* did *not* involve Lord Coke's Bonham doctrine. The issue raised by Coke, and by Hobart and Holt after him, was whether judges had the right to nullify an act of Parliament as contrary to "common right and reason" or some equivalent expression of the natural law. The issue in *Godden v. Hales* was whether the King, in the name of a royal prerogative, had the right to disregard an act of Parliament. The issue, therefore, was not judicial supremacy but royal, or executive, supremacy; and as the issue actually arose in the case, the question was not whether an act of Parliament was "constitutional," but whether an act of the King defying a prior act of Parliament was "constitutional."

The royal prerogative in question was the King's dispensation power under which James II asserted the right to appoint Roman Catholics to public service who had refused to take an oath of allegiance to the Church of England as required by Parliament's Test Oath Act of 1673. James' decision to resist this discriminatory requirement was a ticklish business: Parliament's supremacy was generally acknowledged by this time; moreover, James' brother, Charles

II, had solemnly assured Parliament that the religious test would never be brought into question. The strategy James settled on, under the circumstances, was to get the common law courts to acknowledge the dispensation power. To this end he made preparations for a "test case"—for this account of which we are indebted to Lord Macaulay.[15]

James' first move was to make a private canvass of the judges who would sit on the case. Four of them made clear at the outset that they were not prepared to go along—and it is "remarkable," says Macaulay, "that all of the four were violent Tories and that among them were men who had accompanied Jeffries on the bloody circuit and who had been consenting to the death of Cornish and Elizabeth Gaunt." Jones, the Chief Justice of the Common Pleas, and perhaps the most servile of the royal sycophants, was a case in point. As Macaulay tells the story: "He was plainly told that he must either give up his opinion or his place. 'For my place,' [Jones answered,] 'I care little. I am old and worn out in the service of the Crown: but I am mortified to find that Your Majesty thinks me capable of giving a judgment which none but an ignorant or a dishonest man could give.' 'I am determined,' said the King, 'to have twelve Judges who will all be of my mind in this matter.' 'Your Majesty,' answered Jones, 'may find twelve judges of your mind, but hardly twelve lawyers.' " Whereupon James dismissed the recalcitrant judges and appointed others more open to royal persuasion.

The King had similar troubles with his lawyers. The royal Solicitor General, Heneage Finch, refused to take the case and was summarily turned out of office. The Attorney General, Sawyer, proved equally fastidious—despite the fact, Macaulay says, that he was "stained with . . . blood." James thus had to summon Thomas Powis, an obscure barrister, to defend the prerogative. The King now had to find a "defendant." A Catholic, Sir Edward Hales, was persuaded to accept a military command, on the understanding that he would refuse to take the oath to the established church on the grounds of the royal dispensation. Finally, since Parliament had provided that the penalty for failing to take the oath was payable to any informer of the violation, James arranged for a menial servant to "inform" against Hales and bring suit. The stage for the test case was now set.

The plaintiff, defendant, and King's Counsel all performed their roles according to the script with the result that a momentous constitutional issue was squarely before the court: Could a royal dispensation prevail over an act of Parliament? The packed court also did its duty, even, we are told by Macaulay, to the extent of having a "dissenter"—thus to demonstrate, one supposes, that the decision had been reached after full and vigorous debate. The majority held "that the Kings of England were absolute sovereigns; that the laws were the King's laws; that the King had a power to dispense with any of the laws of government as he saw necessity for it; that he was the sole judge of that necessity; that no Act of Parliament could take away that power. . . ."[16]

James had won his test case, but two years later he lost his throne. Parliament retaliated with the revolution of 1688 which established the supremacy of the legislative authority once and for all in England. And some while later, in the first year of William and Mary, Parliament formally reversed *Godden v. Hales,* declaring that the decision had been erroneous when it was made.[17] It may be said, therefore, that by allowing itself to become the Crown's pawn in the last great battle with Parliament, the English judiciary forever dashed whatever dreams Coke and others might have had for making the judiciary an effective force in English politics. This first and only attempt by English judges to challenge the authority of Parliament was not only crushed, but contributed to a general political readjustment that has kept English courts, as well as English kings, in subordination down to the present day.

Before leaving the English doctrine of legislative supremacy, a more precise statement of it is in order. The doctrine acquired definitive formulation in Blackstone's *Commentaries,* first published in 1765—the famous Tenth Rule (for construing statutes) being the relevant passage for our purposes.[18] This "Rule" calls for close scrutiny, not only because it discloses the strength of the English commitment to legislative supremacy in the eighteenth century, but also because such qualifications of the doctrine as Blackstone allowed played an important role in the early judicial history of the United States.

Blackstone began by stating the qualifications: *"Acts of Parliament that are impossible to be performed are of no validity; and if there arise out of them collaterally any absurd consequences, manifestly contradictory to common reason, they are, with regard to those collateral consequences void."*

What did Blackstone mean by "impossible to be performed?" He had in mind, he said, the dilemma posed by the fifteenth century *Case of the Seals* to which we alluded earlier. Our footnote comment (p. 129) observed only that that case was probably never brought to judgment; we may now note one of the substantive issues involved, a jolly metaphysical problem that won Blackstone's attention and has delighted legal scholarship generally for four hundred years. It seems that certain abbots at the time had the habit of committing their monasteries to legal obligations without the approval of the other monks of the house. This an abbot could do by stamping the relevant deed with his personal seal. And it was not unknown for the monks to disown the obligation later on, on the grounds that the house as a whole had not been consulted. To deal with such situations, Parlia-ment provided that all monasteries should have a "common seal" and that this seal "shall be in the keeping of the prior (who is under the abbot) and four others, the wisest of the house; and that any deed sealed with the common seal which is not in such custody shall be void." Parliament's solution, however, presented certain logical diffi-culties. As the reporter of the case described the dilemma: "the seal being in [his subordinates'] custody, the abbot cannot seal anything with it, [but] when it is in the abbot's hands, it is *ipso facto* out of their custody." The statute was therefore deemed "void," the reporter said, for it was "impertinent to be observed."* That kind of thing.

What did Blackstone mean by "collaterally . . . absurd conse-quences?" Suppose, he explained, that Parliament "in general words" gave a man the power to try all cases that arose in his manor; and suppose further that a case arose in which this man was himself a party. In that event, the act should not be "construed" literally "be-cause it is unreasonable that any man should determine his own quarrel." Blackstone made perfectly clear, however, that in the un-likely event Parliament should *deliberately* provide for this "unrea-sonable" consequence—i.e., in "evident and express words"—"*there is no court that has power to defeat the legislature.*"

"I know," Blackstone said in the best known lines of this passage, that this rule has been "laid down more largely" to the effect that "acts of Parliament contrary to reason are void." This was an allusion to Coke. But the cases usually cited to support that broader doctrine, Blackstone went on, do not actually prove what is claimed for them. And then the true gospel: " . . . *if the Parliament will positively enact a thing to be done which is unreasonable, I know of no power that*

---

* *Impartinent destre observe.* Our account of the case follows Plucknett's translation from the Abridgement of Statham, op. cit., p. 73, in which *impartinent* is literally rendered: "impertinent." The traditional translation is Blackstone's "impossible."

can control it: * [to say] *that where the main object of a statute is unreasonable the judges are at liberty to reject it* [is] *to set the judicial power above that of the legislature, which would be subversive of all government.*"

---

* During the American Revolution Blackstone changed this clause to read: "I know of no power in the ordinary forms of the Constitution that is vested with authority to control it." The change was evidently made to allow for the right of revolution. Manifestly, it works no alteration on the basic idea of the judiciary's subordination to the legislature.

ACROSS THE ATLANTIC

The death of Coke's Bonham doctrine in England would not, of course, necessarily prevent its appearance and survival elsewhere. The apologists, indeed, say that is precisely what happened—that Coke's doctrine took hold in the American colonies even as it was being buried in England, and that it thrived there as a significant undercurrent in colonial political and legal thought and practice, destined to be brought to the surface in the great upheaval of 1776. Our own finding, of course, has been that the doctrine not so much "died" in England as that it was still-born, and that therefore there was not much to keep alive. Still, we must give the apologists a hearing on this further point.

Professor Corwin writes that the doctrine found "its way into the [English] Digests and Abridgments of the time, [and in] these works, as well as the Reports, it passed to America to join there the arsenal of weapons being accumulated against Parliament's claims to sovereignty."*[1] Professor Plucknett's monograph tells us that "Coke's influence was obvious" in the eventual growth of "the practice of judicial invalidation of acts of unconstitutionality, which had begun in colonial days. . . ."[2] Professor Haines, discussing the Bonham doctrine's role in America, advises: "It was not uncommon for colonial lawyers and colonial courts to regard natural law and the ancient principles of the common law as superior to ordinary legislative acts."[3] And so on. Whatever the formulation, the reader is left to understand that the *general thesis* about the influence of the Bonham doctrine in colonial times is beyond doubt—that, while there may be a difference of opinion among scholars about this or that detail, the main argument is not open to question.

---

* Professor Corwin's observation, on the face of it, does not mean much. The Dred Scott decision is also preserved in our records, as are many other very dead cases.

(And this is a danger signal to which we must become alert: the apologists frequently resort to general statements of this kind, not, one suspects, because they deem the evidence too voluminous or too complex to fit into a tidy bill of particulars; but because a tidy bill of particulars—especially when examined closely—might look a good deal less impressive than the general statement. The particulars are mentioned, to be sure, but they are typically stated under some variation of the "for example" formula, or spotted here and there through an extended narrative—either method giving the impression that the possibilities of documentation are infinite.) In this instance, the apologists' argument rest on the following items:

1. The Massachusetts case of *Giddings v. Brown,* decided in 1657.
2. The Massachusetts case of *Frost v. Leighton,* decided in 1739.
3. A case allegedly heard before "a county court in Virginia" in 1766.
4. The Virginia case of *Robin v. Hardaway,* decided in 1772.
5. The arguments of James Otis against the Writs of Assistance.
6. Certain arguments advanced in Massachusetts against the Stamp Act.
7. An exchange of letters between Justice William Cushing and John Adams.
8. The remark of "a New York man."

In *Giddings v. Brown,* Professor Plucknett writes, "we have the first clear example of an act of legislature being invalidated by the judiciary in America."[4] A town meeting, he explains, "voted £100 toward providing a house for Mr. Cobbett, a minister, and the . . . case arose out of Brown's refusal to pay. [The Magistrate] Symonds held that 'it is against a fundamental law in nature to be compelled to pay that which others do give.'" According to Professor Haines, the "suit was instituted . . . to compel the payment of a tax"—and then a similar reference to fundamental law.[5] Both accounts are misleading, in part as to the facts, but principally with regard to the case's contemporary legal significance. Here is what actually happened.[6]

In 1655 a town meeting of Ipswich, Massachusetts, decided to build its new minister a house. However, a heated debate arose as to whether the £100 deemed necessary for the job should be raised through assessment or voluntary contributions. The dispute was allowed to ride for several years, apparently in the hope that the money would come in voluntarily. When it did not, the town elders (whether they were authorized to act by a vote of the town meeting is not altogether clear) ordered Brown, the town constable, to "distrain" the goods of the holdouts to the extent of their fair share of the £100.

Giddings was one of the holdouts; accordingly, Brown made off with
Giddings' pewter dishes. Giddings sued Brown to get back the dishes.
So much for the "act of legislature" that we are told was involved
in this case.

As for the decision, Magistrate Symonds did not seem remotely
aware that in deciding for Giddings he was joining Lord Coke in
challenging the doctrine of legislative supremacy. The town meeting's
action was not, as he saw it, "legislation." The case was simply one
of alleged trespass, to be decided according to the general law of
Massachusetts. But since the colonial legislature had not spoken on
the precise issue, Symonds was required to turn to a 1636 instruction
of the Massachusetts General Court. The General Court had directed
the legislature at that time to draft a code of laws "agreeable to the
word of God," and had added that until the legislature had done so,
magistrates were to proceed "as near to the law of God as they can."
With his duty thus laid out for him, Symonds appealed to Scripture:
"The fundamental law which God and nature has given to the people
cannot be infringed. . . . in this case the goods of one man were
given to another without the former's consent. . . . Is it not to take
from Peter and give it to Paul?"

It seems fair to say, then, that Magistrate Symonds was only trying
to serve Massachusetts Theocracy and did not intend to fire a broad-
side into the principle of legislative supremacy. Let us concede,
however, that his decision was open to another interpretation—i.e.,
that the town meeting's device for bringing holdouts to account was,
nominally, a "legislative" act and could be so regarded by a court.
That, indeed, was the reasoning of Symonds' judicial superiors. *And
on appeal, the decision was reversed by the General Court of Massachusetts.*

Under the circumstances, it is hard to see on what theory the apologists list this case as a precedent. If the point is that the "climate of
opinion" in the seventeenth century was congenial to Coke's Bonham
doctrine, they cannot direct us to evidence of any such thing, either
in the facts of the case or in Magistrate Symonds' opinion. If, on the
other hand, the point is the superficial one that a "case" can be found
in which a "legislative" act was overturned by a judge, they surely
ought to direct us, as with any other "precedent," to the final judgment in the case—which in this instance *upheld* the "legislative" authority.

Frost v. Leighton[7] is on our list only because Professor Haines put
it there, having prefaced his discussion of the case with the comment:

"at times the colonial courts did not hesitate to deny effect to an order of the King or to resist an act of Parliament deemed contrary to their rights as English subjects."[8]

The essential facts are that Leighton, a crown agent, cut down some trees on land belonging to Frost for the purpose of supplying the Royal Navy with masts and spars, asserting the right to do so under a royal license. Frost sued in trespass and, on a procedural point of no importance to us, the Massachusetts court awarded damages of £200. The judgment was affirmed by the Superior Court of Judicature, and the question then became: Was Leighton entitled to appeal the judgment to the Privy Council in London?

The Massachusetts Superior Court said "No" on the grounds of a charter provision limiting appeals to cases involving £300 or more. Leighton took the case to London anyway, and obtained a decree from the Privy Council ordering restoration of the money. The Massachusetts Court then refused to carry out the decree *on the grounds that it was not authorized under Massachusetts law to execute any court's judgment except its own*; it added that under the circumstances Leighton was advised to institute a new action for recovery of the money in a lower court. Leighton apparently felt this was not worth his trouble, and that was the end of the case.

As to the bearing of the case on judicial review, we may note the following:

1. The Privy Council was, among its other functions, a *court* of last resort for the American colonies, and it entered the *Frost* case in just this capacity. Thus what the Massachusetts Court did was to refuse to carry out an order of a superior court, as, in our day, a state court might refuse to execute a judgment of the federal Supreme Court. This was an act of insubordination—and the case is justly famous in American history as an instance of colonial rebelliousness; but disobedience of the Privy Council was not disobedience of a legislature and so had nothing at all to do with Coke's doctrine of judicial "review."

2. Nor can the decision be viewed as an instance of judges presuming to invalidate an *executive* act. Haines apparently regarded the Privy Council's decree as, in some sense, an executive measure since it was issued in the form of the King's order. But even under that superficial interpretation, it remains that the Massachusetts Court did not challenge the *validity* of the decree, but simply pleaded its own inability under Massachusetts law to carry it out.

3. Far from appealing to a "higher law" (Coke's "common right or reason"; Haines' "rights [of] English subjects"), the Court's rea-

soning was precisely that its hands were tied by the *positive law*, i.e., the *legislation*, of the colony.

The "Virginia county court case," which has no official name, is solemnly listed as a precedent for judicial review by nearly all of the apologists on the authority of a passage from John McMaster's *History of the People of the United States* (1900). "One day in February, 1766," McMaster writes, "the clerk and other officers of the Court of Hustings for Northampton County, Virginia, appeared before the bench and moved for an opinion on two questions: Was the law of Parliament imposing stamp duties in America binding on Virginia? Would they, as officers of the law, incur any penalty by not using the stamped paper? The judges were unanimously of the opinion that the law did not bind, affect, or concern the inhabitants of Virginia 'inasmuch as they conceived the said act to be unconstitutional.' "[9]

A search of the Northampton County records yields no additional information—except to identify the "other officers" who requested the opinion as justices of the peace. The three-sentence entry in the record book is wholly silent both as to the events that may have occasioned the request, and as to the judges' reasoning. Still, the circumstances are not difficult to surmise and assess.

First, this was not a "case" at all in the sense of a formal adjudication of the rights of contesting parties that would, in due course, be tested on appeal to a higher court. It was, on the face of it, merely an advisory opinion sought by lower court officials who apparently wished to cooperate with the local resistance to the Stamp Act, but who wished to avoid personal penalties for doing so—i.e., precisely the kind of "guidance" Massachusetts officials had solicited from their Attorney General and other legal authorities a few months earlier.*
Second, the Northampton judges' advice that the act was "unconstitutional" could not have been regarded, even by the most tendentious legal opinion of the time, as a considered statement of the prevailing law. We shall see in a moment that legal experts in Massachusetts, the most agitated of the colonies, let their imaginations run free in search of "authority" for disregarding the Stamp Act, and could find none—not even in Coke, not even in the broad terms of Magna Carta. These county judges, then, must be credited with a brave gesture (made a little easier, perhaps, by the remoteness of Northampton from the seat of British authority in Williamsburg), for no other court in the land, however insignificant, would ever place itself

---

* See p. 144.

in opposition to Parliament. But it seems fair to construe their action not as a serious attempt to expound the law, but as a demonstration of official solidarity with the popular rebellion against the Stamp Act.

Our knowledge of *Robin v. Hardaway*, also decided on the eve of Revolution (1772), comes from Thomas Jefferson.[10] The case involved an attempt to sell certain Indian descendants as slaves, a right the slave traders asserted on the basis of a Virginia statute passed in 1692. In the course of the argument, the Indians' lawyer ventured the theory: "All acts of the legislature apparently contrary to natural right and justice are, in our laws, and must be in the nature of things, considered as void. The laws of nature are the laws of God, whose authority can be superseded by no power on earth. A legislature must not obstruct our obedience to Him. . . ." And he cited as authority *Dr. Bonham's Case*, and *Day vs. Savadge*. What the judges thought of this argument, however, we are not told. The court disposed of the case on the very different grounds that the obnoxious slave statute *had already been repealed by the Virginia legislature.*

We come now to James Otis and his famous argument against the Writs of Assistance in 1761—the moment, Professor Haines once wrote, when "the doctrine of Coke was perhaps definitely and positively introduced into the law of the colonies."*[11]

Otis said: "No acts of Parliament can establish such a writ; though it should be made in the very words of the petition, it would be void. An act against the constitution is void."[12]

---

* This estimate appears in the first edition of Haines' *American Doctrine of Judicial Supremacy* (1914). Haines evidently thought better of such gross exaggerations the second time around, for this and other judgments are considerably toned down in the 1932 edition. As witness what the second edition says of the Otis matter: "It was the resistance to English authority which culminated in the American Revolution, that rendered the conception of fundamental law and of individual natural rights popular and encouraged judges to regard it as their peculiar duty to guard and defend the superior laws. The doctrine that there were superior laws to which all legislation must conform was eloquently defended by James Otis." (p. 59.) But the changes were not made before a good number of students, in an era in which Haines was regarded as the leading authority on the subject, had absorbed his extravagances as gospel.

Though other scholars, as well as Haines, now advance more modest claims for the Otis episode, it is cited by practically everybody and is regarded as perhaps the chief colonial precedent for the doctrine of judicial review.

The fame of Otis' comment is doubtless due in part to the enthusiastic romanticizing of the event by John Adams, who is our main source as to what happened. As a young man Adams was present at the trial and, according to his biographer, "took some slight notes of the argument" on the basis of which "in his old age he proved the indelible impression which it had made on him by writing out the vivid story."[13] "Then and there," Adams was to comment, "the child Independence was born."[14]

Otis' act of defiance is indeed a notable event in American history, but we must try to view it in proper perspective—especially as it bears on the alleged entry of Coke's Bonham doctrine into colonial law.

In the first place, a minor point, Otis' claim that Parliament was incompetent to pass laws "against the constitution" was an oratorical flourish—an aside to his main argument. Otis' principal contention was that the writ should not be enforced *because Parliament had not authorized it*. The link between that main argument and the flourish was formed by these words: "but had this writ been in any book whatever, it would have been illegal."[15]

The major point, however, is that Otis *was not the court*; he was a *lawyer* in the case; *and his side was defeated*. Far from admitting Coke's Bonham doctrine into the law of the colonies, the Massachusetts court rejected Otis' whole argument and upheld the writ,[16] leaving that disappointed barrister to take his theories elsewhere.

This Otis proceeded to do in a pamphlet published in 1764 called *The Rights of the British Colonies Asserted and Proved* in which he eloquently developed his courtroom flourish and, among other things, expressly enlisted the support of Coke.

The next item consists of several expressions of opinion recorded in Massachusetts at the time of the Stamp Act controversy. Early in 1765, it will be recalled, Parliament levied a series of heavy excise taxes in the form of revenue stamps which were to be placed on a variety of legal and commercial documents, as well as on certain items offered for sale such as playing cards and newspapers. Indignation ran high all along the seaboard, and in Massachusetts particularly the protests assumed a revolutionary character—a development not unconnected, one supposes, with the influence of Otis' pamphlet which appeared the year before. Whether or not he had Otis in mind, Lieutenant Governor Hutchinson wrote on September 12, 1765, ". . . friends to liberty take the advantage of a maxim they find in Lord Coke that an Act of Parliament against Magna Carta or the peculiar rights of Englishmen is *ipso facto* void." "This [attitude]," he added darkly, "taken in the latitude the people are often disposed to take it, must be fatal to all government. . . ."[17]

Later on in the month, a popular demonstration forced the resignation of the only officer in the colony authorized to sell the stamps, and this raised a neat question: On what *grounds* should the colonists' defiance proceed? Should the stamp requirement be ignored for the convenient reason no stamps were to be had? or should an appeal be made to "principle"? Hutchinson later recorded that by the end of September both arguments were in the air, but that "the prevailing reason, at this time, is that the act of Parliament is against the Magna Carta and the natural rights of Englishmen, and therefore according to Lord Coke null and void."[18]

The popular view of the matter, however, was evidently not shared by the legal authorities. In February, 1766, Massachusetts' Justice William Cushing wrote Hutchinson about the problem of how the courts were to proceed with legal papers that had not been stamped. Cushing's letter related that several months earlier Attorney General Gridley had thought that in the absence of stamps the courts could not proceed at all on civil matters, but that Gridley later changed his view and was at that moment searching the books for some authority for his new position. "What [Gridley] has found," Cushing said, "I know not, and am doubtful whether he can find any [authority] in point." Cushing then ventured his own opinion that the popular notion that "an Act of Parliament against natural equity is void" would not be regarded as applicable to this case, and therefore that the courts ought to proceed with their business on grounds of necessity: "If we admit evidence unstamped *ex necessitate*, query if it can be said we do wrong."[19]

The seventh item is an exchange of letters between the same Justice Cushing and John Adams. While the incident is manifestly insignificant, it bears a close look as an illustration of how this field of history has been victimized by faulty scholarship. For two distinquished scholars, Professor Corwin and Professor Plucknett, have managed, each in his own way, to make highly misleading use of the exchange.

First Plucknett. After relating Justice Cushing's opinion as to how Massachusetts courts should proceed in the absence of stamps (the passage we noted in the previous item), Plucknett wrote in his very next sentence: "As the months went by Cushing's opinions became more settled, and we find him writing to John Adams, 'I can tell the

Grand Jury the nullity of acts of Parliament, but must leave you to prove it by the more powerful arguments of the *jus gladii divinum*, a power not peculiar to kings and ministers;' to which Adams replied, 'You have my hearty concurrence in telling the jury the nullity of acts of Parliament, whether we can prove it by the *jus gladii*, or not. I am determined to die of that opinion, let the *jus gladii* say what it will.' "[20]

Now Corwin. Directly following a reference to the "Virginia county court" case we discussed above, he writes: "As late as 1776, Chief Justice William Cushing of Massachusetts, who was later one of Washington's first appointees to the Supreme Court of the United States, was congratulated by Adams for telling a jury of the nullity of Acts of Parliament."[21]

Each of these accounts is attributed to the same source, a passage from John Adams' *Life and Works*[22]—and each has an element of truth in it. *Corwin's date*, 1776, is correct—so that Plucknett's matter of "months" becomes *ten years*, and the bottom thus drops out of his implication that Massachusetts popular opinion as to the nullity of the Stamp Act under the Bonham doctrine was soon certified by the colony's legal authorities. On the other hand, *Plucknett's account of what the letters actually said* is correct—so that Corwin's suggestion that a steady growth of Coke's influence finally culminated in an eminent jurist's formal charge to a Grand Jury, and that this action was applauded by a future American President, is seen to rest on nothing more than an agreement between the two men that such a charge *might* be made, but that its importance would be academic since matters had come to war.

Cushing was saying—if we may paraphrase the correspondence—that the dispute between the colonies and Parliament was now to be settled by the sword; and Adams answered that however the battle went, he would continue to believe the colonies were in the right.

The last item. "As late as 1759," Professor Corwin writes, "we find a New York man referring quite incidentally to 'a judicial power of declaring them [the laws] void.' "[23] Professor Plucknett had the same "man" in mind in a footnote he attached to the assertion we saw earlier to the effect that "judicial invalidation" of legislative acts began in colonial times. The note reads portentously enough: "See Colden's protest, July 5, 1759, in New York Historical Society Collections."[24]

Which shows how far the apologists have been willing to travel to find "precedents." Nobody knows who Mr. Colden was, nor what his qualifications were for commenting on the laws, nor what might have prompted him to interject his observation about them "quite incidentally" into a totally unrelated discussion.[25] What we have here is, as the source suggests, a collector's item—an anachronism that might indeed be treasured by the keepers-of-the-books of the New York Historical Society. Might we not expect legal scholars to treat such "evidence" more circumspectly?

In any case, so ends the list.

We are able to see a little better now the kind of argument we are dealing with. The quality of the evidence just reviewed shows pretty clearly that the apologists' theory about the Bonham doctrine's influence on colonial thinking did not emerge from the data. Pretty clearly it happened the other way 'round: the theory came *first*, as part of the notion that judicial review has ancient roots—*then* the search for corroboration began. In time it was carried into every nook and cranny of colonial history: every court decision, the arguments of lawyers, books, newspapers, pamphlets—indeed anyone qualified as a precedent-maker who managed in the course of 150 years to get his views committed to paper. And with what result? Two court decisions that on close examination give no support whatever to the theory, a county court "case" whose support for the theory is dubious even supposing that what transpired in the courtroom constituted a case; the arguments of two lawyers, one expressly rejected by the court, the other ignored; occasional reference to Coke's doctrine in Massachusetts' revolutionary agitation; the comment of a New York man.

Nor does it help the apologists' showing to observe that many colonial cases were never officially reported. Our knowledge of the colonial cases, to be sure, is frequently traceable to private reports: someone witnessed or got wind of a case that interested him, and wrote about it. But this only corroborates the argument we are advancing: we may be reasonably confident that any case that really broke the rule of legislative supremacy would have been deemed sufficiently interesting for word of it to have gotten around.

One final point: the recognized authority on jurisprudence on this side of the Atlantic, as in England, was *Blackstone*, whose *Commentaries* were extremely popular in the Colonies, among laymen as well as lawyers.*

---

* Edmund Burke told Parliament in 1775 that he understood that nearly as many copies of the *Commentaries* had been sold in America as in England. (William Crosskey, *Politics and the Constitution*, II, 1326-7, n. 3.)

In short, we are not impressed with the apologists' case, and conclude: *the doctrine of legislative supremacy as asserted by Coke himself in his later days, and then by Blackstone, was as secure in colonial America as it was in England; the Bonham doctrine as an element of the going legal tradition was equally moribund on both sides of the Atlantic.*

This is not to deny, we may note in passing, the Bonham doctrine's usefulness in the colonies as *a weapon of revolution*; and one wishes the apologists had confined their argument to this point. Every revolution has a variety of weapons; but in societies with a deeply engrained constitutional sense, the logic of rebellion demands that legalistic appeals to "authority," if necessary even contrived ones, be included in the arsenal. The revolutionary leaders must be able to point to some portion of tradition—to "precedents"—to justify and dignify their defiance of the established order. It is not unpatriotic to acknowledge that our own revolutionary leaders in the decade and a half preceding the final rupture (the only period in which the Bonham doctrine figured at all in colonial history) were on the lookout for just such ammunition. A number of possibilities were available. There were the Rights of Englishmen as asserted by Magna Carta, for instance—an appeal that had a strong claim to historical legitimacy. And there, also ready for summons, was the imposing figure of Sir Edward Coke. Coke was already a famous and highly regarded name among colonists familiar with English history—*not* because of his Bonham opinion, but because of his memorable exposition of Magna Carta and his *defense* of Parliament in its seventeenth-century row with the King. To enlist Coke in the American struggle *against* Parliament was thus a polemical coup of the first order—a temptation the embattled colonial leaders were not likely to resist. Understandably, then, our James Otises tried to make political capital out of Coke's Bonham phase; but this is obviously a quite different thing from saying that the Bonham doctrine had a serious hold on the colonies' legal and political tradition.

Of course it is possible that what was a mere weapon of revolution before 1776 would take its place among the accepted legal doctrines of the new country once independence had been achieved. Our only point for the moment is that the Bonham tradition was not such as to make that evolution automatic, or even easy.

THE "HIGHER LAW"

The thesis that Coke's Bonham doctrine significantly affected American political thought almost invariably keeps company with a second and broader thesis; namely, that whatever happened in colonial courts, the colonists' profound commitment to the concept of *natural law* (Coke's "common right or reason") was bound, in itself, to create conditions favorable to the development of judicial review. The notion of a "fundamental law" superior to any man-made laws, the argument runs, was destined sooner or later to produce an institution—i.e., an independent judiciary—with the power to test positive laws—i.e., the acts of legislatures—against this higher standard. Not surprisingly, then, judicial review apologists attach great significance to the fact that certain political writers who were understood to espouse natural law, or "the law of nature"—notably the Englishman Locke and the Frenchman Vattel—were widely read in pre-revolutionary America.

Now: there is no question about the popularity in the colonies of expounders of "the law of nature," especially of John Locke. Nor, again, about the fullness of our forebears' belief in the existence of a "higher law"— a belief that had been in the main stream of Western political thought for two thousand years. Yet it takes a good deal of doing to hold up the natural law tradition of the West, and most especially the rendition of it by Locke and his eighteenth-century contemporaries, as a precursor of judicial review.

Natural law, as a Western idea, arguably has roots in Greek philosphy. It seems to be suggested by Plato's "World of Ideas"; Aristotle recognized "natural justice"—"that which everywhere has the same force and does not exist by peoples' thinking this or that";[1] with the Stoics, a kind of natural law became the source of all personal morality as well as a sure guide for human happiness. But Greek thinkers never suggested that the political organization of a society ought to provide for a special institutional safeguard for the natural law—that it ought to have law "judges," as distinct from law "makers," with the former having the job of passing upon the work of the latter.

Such a notion was equally foreign to Roman thought. A version of natural law theory was familiar to the Romans: Cicero, for instance, wrote of a "true law . . . harmonious with nature, diffused among all, constant, eternal . . . binding all nations through all time. . . ."[2] But Cicero's point was that it is a "sacred obligation"—for lawmakers— "not to attempt to legislate in contradiction to this law."[3] (And Cicero's main point, it seems, was that Roman positive law was, in fact, a faithful reflection of the law of nature, a belief that was to lead, in Eric Voegelin's phrase, to the "divinization" of Roman society under the Emperors.)

The idea of a higher law emanating from God is, of course, integral to the World View of the Christian Church, and from the earliest moments of the Christian ascendancy the Fathers insisted that temporal magistrates conduct the affairs of state in accord with this law. The high drama of St. Ambrose requiring Theodosius to do public penance for the massacre of the Thessalonians in 390 reveals the early strength of the Christian idea of holding Caesar accountable to the law of God. To be sure, direct ecclesiastical control of state affairs in due course gave way, under force of circumstances, and the influence of theology, to a duality in the existential order—a sharp division of the temporal and spiritual spheres. But even under the Augustinian concept of "two cities," the standards of earthly rulership were to be found in the laws of the heavenly city; the "happy emperor" of Civitatis Dei became the model and the ideal of the Christian prince.

Throughout the Middle Ages, the great political thinkers—Gratian, John of Salisbury, Alexander of Hales, St. Isidore of Seville, Albertus Magnus, William of Occam, and, of course, St. Thomas—grappled with derivative problems: What are the sources of natural law? What is its specific content? How is it transmitted to the human mind? Important divergences emerged from these speculations, but the points of agreement were far more significant than the differences: a fundamental law reflecting God's will and the nature of his creation does exist; somehow it is apperceivable by man; the makers of this world's positive laws are obliged to observe it. The commitment of medieval political thought to the concept of limited government was thus emphatic and unambiguous; and it thoroughly dominated Western tradition down to Machiavelli.

But to say that government is "limited" in the Christian tradition is not to say anything about judicial review. Medieval thinkers, like the Greeks and the Romans before them, did not distinguish between the authority to make laws and the authority to interpret and enforce them. The Christian doctors addressed themselves to the prince, and the prince was at once the law-maker and the law-enforcer. And later—as can be seen in the teachings of Bracton and Sir John Fortescue—when parliaments came to participate in law-making, the natural law's command was deemed to be addressed to *them*. A separate institution for judging the acts of law-makers, in other words, was unheard of in the Western tradition;* nor was it in any way implied by the philosophy of the tradition.

Such was the natural law tradition handed down to John Locke. Whether Locke really accepted the tradition (as opposed to merely giving lip-service to it) is, as contemporary Locke scholars have amply demonstrated,[4] open to considerable question. But there seems to be little doubt that he led earlier readers of his *Second Treatise on Civil Government* to believe that he did; and there is certainly no doubt that he invoked what he chose to call "the law of nature" as the source of the inalienable right to self-preservation that he said had belonged to men in the state of nature—and thus as the authority for his contentions about the origins and proper conduct of civil society.

Civil societies, or "commonwealths," according to Locke's theory of the "social compact," came into being in order to protect the individual's "natural" right to life, liberty, and property—or, in the single term that subsumes these three, and is repeatedly summoned by Locke to emphasize the meaning he wishes to attach to them: the individual's right to *"self-preservation"*—which right, Locke maintains, was in jeopardy as long as man lived in the state of nature. Governments, therefore, are "naturally" and thus properly charged with the

---

* The administration of Canon Law is a special case. At first glance it might seem that the right sometimes asserted by canonical courts to invalidate lay laws that conflicted with "ecclesiastical liberties" is a precedent for our civil tradition of judicial review. Indeed, such an argument is made by Mr. Coxe, op. cit., pp. 121-163. The point need not be labored, however, that there was no rivalry here between "legislative" and "judicial" authority. The rivalry was between the spiritual and temporal spheres, and involved an assertion by the spiritual authority of ultimate power to determine the extent of its prerogatives. In any event, it is stretching things a bit to suppose that the founders of the American Republic were anxious to imitate a device for protecting the ecclesiastical privileges of the Roman Catholic Church.

responsibility to guard and promote the right of self-preservation, together with the responsibility to preserve the society itself—and with no other responsibilities. It is in this sense that Locke meant that the power of government is inherently limited by bounds prescribed by "nature."

For our purposes, however, the critical question remains to be asked—namely, How, as Locke saw it, are these "natural" limitations on the power of government to be *enforced*? How is the commonwealth to organize itself, and how conduct its affairs, so as to make sure that "the law of nature" is faithfully observed? Let us follow closely Locke's reply, which is unambiguous:

> [T]he first and fundamental positive law of all commonwealths is the establishing of *the legislative power;* [just] as the first and fundamental natural law, which is to govern even the legislative itself, is the preservation of the society, and (as far as will consist with the public good) of every person in it. *This legislative is not only the supreme power of the commonwealth, but sacred and unalterable in the hands where the community have once placed it;* nor can any edict of anybody else, in what form soever conceived, or by what power soever backed, have the force and obligation of a law, which has not its sanction from that legislative which the public has chosen and appointed.[5]

There is much more of the same in this passage, which, however, close to its end, hints at one qualification:

> [Nor can] any domestic subordinate power discharge any member of the society from his obedience to the legislative, *acting pursuant to their trust. . . .*[6]

That hint Locke in due course elaborates:

> Though . . . there can be but one supreme power, which is the legislative, to which all the rest are and must be subordinate, yet the legislative being only a *fiduciary* power to act for certain ends, *there remains still in the people a supreme power to remove or alter the*

---

* Which does not mean, on Locke's showing, that the entire "legislative power" is always to be placed in the hands of "the legislature." I.e., he envisions situations in which "the executive" will have "a share" in the legislative power (151); and still others, it seems, in which all of the legislative and executive power will be combined in a single person (153). At no point, be it noted, does he suggest that *judges* might share in "the legislative power."

*legislative when they find the legislative act contrary to the trust
reposed in them*; [the people in such a case may] rid themselves of
those who invade this fundamental, sacred, and unalterable law of
self-preservation for which they entered into society.[7]

But this limitation on the legislative power, which is the only one he
recognizes, turns out to be Locke's way of saying that the moment
legislators betray their trust, *government ceases to exist*:

> . . . the community may be said [in the sense just mentioned] to be
> always the supreme power, *but not as considered under any form of
> government,* because this power of the people can never take place
> till the government be dissolved.
>
>   *In all cases whilst the government subsists, the legislative is the
> supreme power. . . .*[8]

We may now compare Locke's teaching on this point with that of
the natural law tradition. To the question, How are the natural limits
on the power of government to be enforced? the answer of medieval
thinkers had been: the law-maker—the prince—*must restrain himself,*
and be prepared to answer to God for failure to do so. Locke's answer was: the law-maker—which after 1688 meant Parliament—*must
restrain itself,* and be prepared to answer to the people for failure to
do so. Thus the prospects of a judicial role in this area were every
bit as barren under Locke's system as they had been in the traditional practice and teaching. To the extent that Locke acknowledged
a "higher law," *it was a law that was to be recognized and articulated
by the legislative branch of government, and ultimately by the people.* To be sure, there was a role for judges in Locke's system—as enforcers of the positive law. But Locke did not *separate* the judicial
power from the legislative power: he did not call for an "independent" judiciary. And as for the further possibility that the judiciary
might interpose its own understanding of the "higher law" *between*
the people and their chosen representatives, the idea is as thoroughly
repugnant to Locke's thought as any that can be imagined.

To put the same point in a framework with which we are already
familiar: legal historians are in the habit of contrasting Locke's es-
pousal of "the law of nature" with Blackstone's insistence on legislative supremacy, and this intimation of a clash between Locke and
Blackstone, we are now saying, is obviously and grossly misleading.
Locke was writing as a political theorist, Blackstone as a lawyer. As
a political theorist, Locke was concerned primarily with the *source*
of political authority—with the locus of sovereignty—which he con-

tended was "the law of nature" as apperceived by a consensus of the community. Secondarily, he was concerned with how authority was to be exercised, and his answer was that the legislative power must be the supreme authority of government, an authority that would cease to be supreme only when government ceased. Blackstone went at the problem the other way around. He was primarily concerned with describing the English political and legal system, and thus stressed the point that the way the system operated, Parliament had the final say. Secondarily, he was interested in the philosophy behind the system; and accordingly, the opening pages of his *Commentaries* set forth in a more or less perfunctory manner the traditional natural law doctrine. In short, to pit the concept of a "law of nature" as expounded by Locke *against* the concept of legislative supremacy as expounded by Blackstone is to thoroughly misunderstand both Locke and Blackstone. And to suggest, without a shred of supporting evidence, that Locke's readers so misunderstood his teaching on this question is to play an extremely fast game with history.

Similarly with the readers of Emmerich Vattel whose *Law of Nations* was published in 1758. Vattel subscribed to a more-or-less traditional view of natural law, but contributed the notion that such a law ought to be embodied in a written constitution. Echoing Cicero, he said this fundamental law "must be sacred" to legislators, from which it followed that they were not at liberty to change the constitution. But on the question of what was to be done in the event legislators did, in fact, violate the fundamental law, or were thought to have done so, Vattel was at one with Locke: "If there arise in the State disputes over the fundamental laws, over the public administration, or over the rights of the various powers which have a share in it, it belongs to the Nation alone to decide them, and to settle them according to its political constitution." The recourse, in other words, was to the people, i.e., not to judges. "It would be dangerous to commit the interests of the citizens to the mere arbitrary will of those who ought to distribute justice," Vattel wrote at another point. And at still another: "The legislature should assist the understanding of the judges, force their prejudices and inclinations, and subject their wills to simple, fixed and certain rules."[9]

We have been talking so far about what the natural law writers said and were understood to be saying about the institutional arrangements for putting natural law doctrine into practice. A word is in order about what their non-American readers actually *did* in response to this teaching. The underlying question here, let us remember, is whether natural law theory is likely to have moved colonial political thought in the direction of judicial review; it is thus not impertinent to ask: Did it move *anyone else* in that direction? In England, the answer is plain enough. Locke achieved his great popularity as an apologist for the parliamentary revolution of 1688. Thereafter, letting the post hoc, propter hoc chips fall where they may, it can be said that the more Englishmen read Locke, the more solidly England became committed to the notion of legislative supremacy as it was to be defined by Blackstone.

And in France, the other great market for natural law literature? Here the answer was even more dramatic. In 1789 France took her great plunge back into the state of nature as Vattel, Rousseau, and Voltaire and his fellow Encyclopedists had urged, ripping off all institutional inhibitions save those the natural law writers had said were suitable to nakedness. And when the time came for putting clothes back on, what was the lady wearing? The new Republic's constitution proclaimed unambiguously *the doctrine of legislative supremacy*—a theory that has dominated French republicanism ever since, or at least until the advent of de Gaulle. As for judges, the Constitution of 1791 took special pains to remind them of their places: "The tribunals cannot interfere with the exercise of the legislative power, *nor* [here is the specific denial of the right of judicial review] suspend the execution of the laws, nor encroach upon administrative functions, nor cite any administrators to appear before them on account of their functions."*

---

* Article 16. Certain of the apologists, e.g., Brinton Coxe, and evidently following him, Professor Haines, have suggested that this strong language is the result of a peculiar *French* enmity to the judicial power arising out of unpleasant experiences under the Monarchy. Coxe cites three instances in which the Parliament of Paris (actually a judicial court) took sides in political quarrels between various claimants to the regency during the minorities of Louises XII, XIV, and XV. (Op. cit., pp. 79, 80.) These are indeed curious pickings. In the first place, no "laws" were involved with which the "judiciary" might be said to have interfered—only the testaments of Kings. In the second place, the old French parliaments were understood to have extrajudicial powers—i.e., "political" powers—as well as judicial ones, and the Parliament of Paris was clearly acting in its extrajudicial capacity during these power struggles. In the third place, it is not particularly convincing to suggest, in the absence of supporting evidence, that French Jacobins were moved to circumscribe the republican judicial power because of the nasty things its predecessor had done to this or that faction of the House of

We may summarize:

1. There is no necessary connection between natural law and judicial review. The former, that is to say, does not imply anything one way or the other about the latter, either dialectically or in the experience of the Western tradition.

2. Natural law doctrine, as it was actually handed down to the American colonies, expressly denied the connection: the great natural law teachers read by the colonists were also exponents of legislative supremacy.

3. The principal non-American readers of the natural law teachers, the English and the French, also denied the connection by establishing systems of government based on legislative supremacy.

Now it does not follow that American thinking, for reasons of its own, could not have embarked on a radically different course. It does follow, however, that should American thinking eventually take this different course, it would do so not *because* of the influence of Locke, et al, but *in spite of* that influence. We make this point about the influence of natural law doctrine for the same reason we made a similar point about the influence of Coke's Bonham dictum—to put to rest the idea that judicial review was part of America's pre-independence inheritance, needing only the toll of the Liberty Bell to come into its own.

This idea is part of the broader theory that judicial review had taken such a firm hold on American political thought by 1787 that the framers of the Constitution could suppose it would be incorporated in the new government without their mentioning it. Our answer, so far, is that down to 1776, there is no evidence at all to support the theory. Whether the events of the ensuing eleven years dealt more kindly with it, is the question to which we now turn.

Bourbon. We repeat: the reasonable explanation as to why French republicans adopted the principle of legislative supremacy is that their ideological tutors, who were also to some extent the ideological tutors of American republicans, told them to.

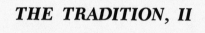

THE TRADITION, II

INDEPENDENCE: THE BEGINNING OF AN "IRRESISTIBLE PROCESS"?

> By 1775 the principle [of judicial review] had taken
> such a firm hold on the minds of lawyers and judges that
> decisions were rendered in rapid succession [which]
> maintained the authority of courts, as guardians of a
> fundamental law, to pass upon the acts of coordinate
> departments. This authority was steadily asserted after
> the colonies became states, and by an irresistible pro-
> cess was made one of the prime features of the new
> federal system established by the Constitution of 1787.
>
> Charles G. Haines, *The American
> Doctrine of Judicial Supremacy*[1]

The argument that judicial review came into its own in the eleven
years between the Declaration of Independence and the framing of
the Constitution rests primarily, in all of the apologists' accounts,
upon the decisions of the state courts during that interval. The court
decisions are, indeed, the only plausible authority for the argument—
although, as we shall see, a "rapid succession" of cases becomes
"nine" when one actually stops to count them, and those nine turn
out to constitute something less than an inexorable historical force
destined to impose judicial review on the Men of Philadelphia.

Before taking up the cases, however, we will do well to look
briefly at the state constitutions under which they arose. We have
seen something of the political system, especially with regard to the
judicial power, that prevailed in the American colonies under English rule. So it is not amiss to ask: What governments did the colonists
establish once they were free to conduct their own affairs?

159

The answer is simple, uniform, uncontestable. *Every one of the new state constitutions fully embraced the principle of legislative supremacy handed down from Blackstone's England.* Professor Corwin has conceded the point, observing that the Virginia constitution of 1776 "may serve as a model." "The legislative department," he writes, [was] mightily exalted, that of the executive correspondingly depressed. . . . judges [though being allowed to hold their offices "during good behavior"] were the legislature's appointees, and judicial review [was] nowhere hinted."[2] But that isn't all. While it did not occur to the framers of the state constitutions to allow judges to interfere with the legislative power, there were evidently no corollary misgivings about legislatures interfering with the judicial power. Legislative appointment of judges, often for a short term, was one opening; another was the woolly character of "separation of powers" provisions. Moreover, legislatures were frequently left free to revise judicial proceedings and to authorize appeals on their own motion; they even took upon themselves the right of interpreting the law for individual cases.[3]

But while judicial review was clearly excluded in the post-Independence scheme of things, three States adopted institutions that are said to have adumbrated its future development.[4] The Pennsylvania and Vermont constitutions established what was called a "Council of Censors." Every seven years, according to the Pennsylvania provision, two persons were to be chosen by ballot from each city and county "to inquire whether the constitution [had] been preserved inviolate" and also "whether the legislative and executive branches of government [had] performed their duty as guardians of the people." If they chose, the censors could "recommend to the legislature the repealing of such laws as [they deemed] contrary to . . . the constitution." They could also call a special convention "if there [appeared] to them an absolute necessity of amending . . . the constitution."[5] The Vermont provision was a verbatim copy of the Pennsylvania scheme except for certain election details.

What we have here, obviously, is not a precursor of judicial review at all, but a provision for popular democracy according to the teachings of Locke and Vattel. The idea that the people are the ultimate custodians of every constitution is now, in Pennsylvania and Vermont, to be implemented by an ingenious device for periodic popular checks on the legislature. Note, however, that nobody is given power to *invalidate* legislative acts. The censors can "recommend" certain things; or they can try to amend the constitution by a popular convention, if they think that will help; but as with Locke and Vattel, no power is available to *coerce* legislators except the threat to turn them out of office. The check on legislative power, in other words, remains *outside* of government, and the essential ingredient of judicial review theory—that a power superior to the legislature exists *inside* of government—is as far away as ever.

The New York framers had a different idea.[6] Fearing, so they wrote, that "laws inconsistent with the spirit of this constitution" might be "hastily and inadvisedly passed," the New Yorkers created a "Council of Revision," composed of the governor and two supreme court judges with power to review bills during the process of legislation. If the Council deemed the bill "improper," the latter could become law only if the legislature overruled the Council by a two-thirds vote. The idea, of course, was a direct ancestor of the presidential veto power. The governor and judges of New York, like the President today, were to participate in the legislative process. But the legislature, qua legislature, had the last say; and in New York, as elsewhere, there was no governmental power *beyond* the legislative process to question that last say.

So much for the kind of governments the new States created. We may now turn to the "irresistible process" by which state judges are supposed to have engrafted judicial review on the American political system—notwithstanding the provisions of state constitutions.* Most of the apologists, it is fair to say, have had the good sense to omit some of these judicial "precedents" from their lists; but so that the reader may judge the evidence for himself, we shall look into every contender.

---

* The anomaly here is obvious: if it is true that state courts during this period invalidated legislative acts as contrary to state constitutions, they could have done so only by *exceeding their powers*—i.e. "unconstitutionally."

THE CASE OF JOSIAH PHILIPS

In 1803 Judge St. George Tucker, who may well qualify as the first of the apologists, wrote in his edition of Blackstone:

> In May 1778, an act [was] passed in Virginia to attaint one Josiah Philips unless he should render himself to justice within a limited time; he was taken after the time had expired and was brought before the general court [according] to the directions of the act. *But the court refused to pass the sentence and he was put upon trial according to the ordinary course of law.* This is a decisive proof of the importance . . . of the independence of the judiciary; a dependent judiciary might have executed the law, whilst they execrated the principles upon which it was founded.[1]

Judge Tucker, then, had discovered a remarkable event: a state court, well before the end of the Revolutionary War, had refused to obey a legislature. Whether the judges had disobeyed because they deplored bills of attainder, or because they deemed such measures prohibited (as they certainly were) by Virginia's 1776 Declaration of Rights,[2] Tucker did not say, and did not have to say in order to qualify the decision as a clearcut instance of judicial review. Moreover, the *Philips* case appeared for many years to be the first such case on record, and thus once occupied an illustrious niche in the apologists' showcase.

Before turning to what actually happened in the case, we should remark the *kind* of judicial review, in terms of the schema set forth in an earlier chapter,* that Judge Tucker and subsequent apologists put on display. Note, first, that the bill of attainder involved in the *Philips* case was ad hominem legislation that sought to arraign and convict a man without judicial trial, and was therefore a direct invasion of judicial prerogatives. Thus with regard to the *scope* of ju-

---

* See "The Faces of Judicial Review."

dicial review, the judges are not represented as having asserted a broad right to keep other branches of government in line (B2 or B3 in the schema), but the more modest right of self-defense (B1). Note, second, with regard to the *effect* of the decision, the court is not alleged to have "voided" the law (C2), much less to have instructed the legislature not to enact such laws in the future (C3) ; on Tucker's showing, it simply refused to enforce the law (C1).

But while these observations may be helpful in grasping the very limited view of judicial review held by Judge Tucker and other early exponents of the power, they are neither here nor there under the true facts of the *Philips* case, which turn out to be these:

Josiah Philips was a notorious brigand who had allied himself during the Revolutionary War with the British. After the outbreak of hostilities, Philips' band of marauders had holed up in the Dismal Swamp and from that excellent cover conducted hit-and-run raids against the countryside. The operation was so successful that the Virginia legislature, with the approval of Governor Patrick Henry, finally resorted to a bill of attainder. Thomas Jefferson drew up the bill which gave the marauders until "the last day of June [1778]" to give themselves up; otherwise, they would "stand and be convicted and attainted of high treason." As things worked out, however, the state authorities caught up with Philips on June 11th—*before the attainder was to go into effect.* He was charged with highway robbery, and thereupon tried, convicted and sentenced to death under the common law robbery charge. So much is established by the court records.

Edmund Randolph, who was Virginia's Attorney General at the time, was apparently responsible for ignoring the attainder. According to Jefferson, Randolph explained after the trial that "he had thought it best to make no use of the Act of Attainder, and to take no measure under it." Randolph's reason, we may surmise, was the obvious one that the attainder, since its time limit had not expired, did not apply. But whatever our surmise about why the attainder was dropped, the fact remains it was dropped, and not by the court but by the attorneys who prosecuted the case. *The legislation the judges are said to have disobeyed was thus never before them.*

Now all of this has been known since 1914 when some primary research unearthed the real story.[3] Useful myths die hard, however, and the case is still paraded in some of the literature—typically as evidence of what the case's contemporaries, and thus what the framers of the federal Constitution, *thought* the case stood for. For example,

Professor Haines judiciously observes that rejection of this precedent "fails to give due weight to the influence on legal thinking of
incorrect facts and incorrect assumptions when such facts and assumptions are believed to be true."[4] Fair enough, but it would have
been good of Professor Haines to have indicated what those "incorrect facts and assumptions" might have been. For we know the real
story on that point, too.

One day in 1788, ten years after he had helped send Josiah Philips
to his death, Edmund Randolph, now one of the framers of the proposed federal Constitution, rose to address the Virginia ratifying convention. With passion riding on every word, Randolph argued that
the Constitution was needed because the cause of human rights was
in disarray throughout the country—as witness, said he, something
that happened not so long ago right here in Virginia.

> . . . an example so horrid that if I conceived my country would passively
> permit a repetition of it, dear as it is to me, I would seek means of
> expatriating myself from it. A man who was then a citizen was
> deprived of his life thus: from a mere reliance on general reports
> [a Member informed the House of Delegates] that a certain man
> [Josiah Philips] had committed several crimes and was running at
> large perpetrating other crimes. He therefore moved for leave to
> attaint him. . . . Without being confronted with his accusers and
> witnesses, without the privilege of calling for evidence in his behalf,
> [Philips] was sentenced to death, and was afterwards actually executed.
> Was this arbitrary deprivation of life, the dearest gift of God to man,
> consistent with the genius of republican government? . . . with the
> spirit of freedom? This, sir, has made the deepest impression on my
> heart, and I cannot contemplate it without horror.[5]

Randolph, of course, knew better than anyone else how the case
had been resolved—although a truthful account, we may agree, would
have considerably dampened the effect of his verbal pyrotechnics.
But the point for our purposes is not that Randolph distorted, but
that he got away with the ruse. His opponents knew no more about
the facts than he evidently supposed they did, and were trapped into
defending both the bill of attainder and Philips' alleged execution under it! After all, Patrick Henry retorted, Josiah was no "Socrates."
"He was an enemy to the human name. Those who declare war
against the human race may be struck out of existence as soon as
they are apprehended. *He was not executed according to those beau-
tiful legal ceremonies which are pointed out by the laws in criminal
cases.* The enormities of his crimes did not entitle him to it." The

debate went on for some while in this vein—Benjamin Harrison, John Marshall, George Nicholas all got into it—but apparently no one knew the facts well enough to call Randolph's bluff.[6]

In short, we have a *third* version of the case. Having seen 1) the apologists' version—that the good judges refused to enforce the attainder; and then 2) the true version—that the attainder was inapplicable under its own terms; we now learn 3) that ten years after the event most of the great men of Virginia were under the impression the bill of attainder actually got poor Josiah! So Professor Haines may be right in thinking that some of the framers misunderstood the case. But they hardly understood it as an instance of judicial review. They understood it as an instance of legislative extremism—an act of tyranny according to Randolph, a justifiable war measure according to Henry—in which, as was expected in those days, the judiciary dutifully acquiesced.

HOLMES *v.* WALTON

The modern textbook writers, Professors Kelly and Harbison, are among those who have given up on the *Philips* case. Accordingly, they wrote in 1955: "The first well-authenticated instance, after Independence, of a state court's holding a law void occurred in New Jersey in 1780." "*Holmes v. Walton*," the professors went on to explain, "involved the validity of a legislative act of 1778 providing for six man juries in cases arising out of confiscation of enemy goods. The New Jersey constitution of 1776 had guaranteed the right of jury trial in perpetuity, and the court held the act in question void as in conflict with this provision, since traditionally common-law juries had been composed of twelve men."[1]

The Kelly-Harbison version of *Holmes v. Walton* is, then, impressive authority from the point of view of judicial review partisans. There is, however, an even more impressive version. The traditional account, as originally set forth in Professor Austin Scott's nineteenth-century monograph,[2] and generally followed thereafter, has it that the New Jersey court not only voided the 1778 act, but forced the legislature into a tacit acknowledgment of its right to do so. Haines has described the legslature's surrender in this way: "The next session of the legislature [following the decision] ratified the action of the court by passing a law requiring justices, on the demand of either party, to grant a jury of twelve men."[3]

Putting this latter version in the perspective of our schema: it is clear that the chief issue allegedly at stake—the right to a certain kind of jury trial—involved judicial prerogatives, and so establishes *Holmes v. Walton* as merely a B1 case with regard to the *scope* of the power the court is supposed to have exercised. But with regard to the *effect* of the decision, we have an alleged instance of the sweeping C3 power—a claim that New Jersey, several years before the federal Constitution was adopted, went the full distance in recognizing the judiciary's supremacy over other branches of government.

Let us again see what really happened—or at least what *seems* to have happened according to the best evidence available. This will not be easy going. For one thing, there is no extant record of the court's opinion in *Holmes v. Walton*, nor, indeed, any indication that an opinion was ever written—a fact Louis Boudin deems sufficient in itself to discredit the apologists' claims.* We must therefore reconstruct the case from the pleadings, which are preserved, and from the state of the law at the time. For another thing, the jury problem, which is the only issue out of many involved in the case that concerns us (whether the court had any particular interest in it is one of the things we do not know in the absence of an opinion), sprang from a complex relationship between several laws and customs. To minimize the confusion, let us get those elements of the law in front of us at the outset:

1. The New Jersey constitution of 1776 provided that "the inestimable Right of Trial by Jury shall remain confirmed, as a Part of the Law of this Colony, without Repeal forever"; and to underline the importance they attached to the matter, the New Jersey framers specified that legislators were to take a special oath never to violate this guarantee. The constitution said nothing about the *number* of jurors that might be required.[4]

2. The practice in New Jersey at that time (and for many years thereafter) was to have six-man juries for cases involving claims of six pounds or less, and twelve-man juries for larger claims.[5]

3. In 1775 the colonial legislature had enacted a "Small Causes Act" which outlined the procedures for certain small claims trials—

---

* Boudin's approach to these problems is typically apodictical, often bellicose; but passion with this colorful barrister-scholar seldom interfered with logic. *Holmes v. Walton* "is not a case," he wrote in 1932, "where the papers have been lost. On the contrary, the files of the Supreme Court of New Jersey contain two packages of papers . . . containing all sorts of unimportant matter, such as depositions, etc., *but no opinion.* Nor is there any indication anywhere, either among these papers or in the docket of the Supreme Court, which also has been preserved, indicating that an opinion was ever written. To anyone really interested in discovering the truth of the matter, this alone should be sufficient proof that there was no such opinion. It should be remembered that if the claims advanced on behalf of *Holmes v. Walton* be true it was the first instance [declaring] an act of legislation unconstitutional by a state court in this country. Clearly, therefore, no court would have made such a decision without writing an opinion; and no opinion of this kind, if written, could have been lost, when all of the papers in the case, including a lot of unimportant trash, have been carefully preserved, for nearly one hundred and fifty years." Op cit., p. 545.

and, in addition, expressly provided for a six-man jury in such trials.[6] After 1776, when the colony of New Jersey became the State of New Jersey, the Small Causes Act was extended by a constitutional provision stating that all colonial laws not "incompatible" with the constitution should continue in force.[7]

4. In 1778 the legislature enacted a war measure aimed at trading with the enemy. The basic idea was a variant of the "citizen's arrest," and this was the thing that set Holmes against Walton. The act provided that if A suspected B of smuggling goods across the British lines, A could seize the contraband, take it to a Justice of the Peace, and on proving B's guilt, keep the goods himself. And on the matter that directly concerns us—the provision the apologists assert was declared unconstitutional—the act directed the Justice of the Peace, in the event either party should demand a jury, "*to grant the same*, and to proceed in all *other* respects" according to the procedures set forth in the Small Causes Act of 1775.[8]

We underscore part of the above provision to show that the authors of the 1778 act distinguished between 1) the right to jury trial, which they apparently recognized *tout court*, and 2) "other" procedures, which were to be copied from the Small Causes Act. The provision appears to have been composed in haste, but what the legislators had in mind seems fairly plain. They wanted to provide for a kind of summary justice in the contraband cases—hence the use of the speedier small claims procedures, regardless of the amount actually involved. At the same time, they were aware of what the constitution said about juries, to say nothing of their own recently taken oaths on the subject—hence the recognition of *that* right *without* qualification, and thus without running the risk of creating a constitutional problem. And it would follow under this legislative scheme that the *number* of jurors in a contraband case, like any other—since this is the way the constitution left that problem—would be determined by the prevailing common law practice: twelve men for large amounts, six for small ones. Let us agree that this is not the only interpretation of the act, but that it is the natural one.*

---

* Messrs. Boudin and Crosskey go further. A different interpretation, they say in effect—e.g., to read "other respects" as including the matter of the number of jurors—is completely out of the question since it would involve twisting the natural meaning of the language to produce a deliberate violation of the constitution on the part of the legislature. (See Boudin, op. cit., pp. 543-48, and Crosskey, op. cit., pp. 948-51.) The gentlemen are right, of course, as a matter of legal presumption. But we are interested at this point

Now Holmes, in our case, was the alleged smuggler, and Walton, a major in the New Jersey militia, seized the smuggled goods. The contraband in question amounted to something like $27,000—obviously a long way from the small claim category. Holmes was thus entitled to demand a twelve-man jury under our reading of the trading-with-the-enemy act, and apparently did so. But the Justice of the Peace, probably because he read the act carelessly, thought that small claims procedures governed the matter, and granted a jury of only six. The verdict went against Holmes, and Holmes then appealed to the state Supreme Court. The Supreme Court reversed. The question is: On what grounds?

The apologists' version of the case, we may remember, is that the Supreme Court reversed on the grounds that the provision of the 1778 Act, which the Justice of the Peace relied on in assigning only six jurors to the case, was unconstitutional. Is that view warranted? Is it even plausible? In the absence of an opinion, we must consult circumstantial evidence—a task, fortunately, that will not prove arduous since the only clue the records provide is the Bill of Exceptions to the Justice of the Peace's ruling which Holmes filed with the Supreme Court when he took his appeal.

The first thing the Bill reveals is that the jury issue was but one of eight grounds on which a reversal was requested; and as a matter of fact, in the order of listing—and of importance?—it was seventh among the eight. The sixth ground, for example, protested that "the said Elisha Walton did at his own expense and without the consent of [the defendants] treat with a strong liquor the jury sworn to try this cause. . . ." In short, the Supreme Court may have reversed for any of seven different reasons *having nothing at all to do with the jury issue*.

Let us assume, however, that the complaint about the number of jurors turned out, in the Supreme Court's view, to be the crucial one. On this point Holmes charged that the jury had "consisted of six men only when *by the laws of the land* [not, be it noted, "by the constitution"] it should have consisted of twelve." Later, in a statement of "Additional Reasons" for a reversal, Holmes expanded the charge: the six man jury was a) "contrary to law," b) "contrary to the constitution," and c)—a catch-all category—"contrary to the constitution,

---

in what the legislature *in fact* intended; and though the possibility is remote in this instance for the reasons noted, it was not unknown at that time for legislatures to violate constitutions, and to do so with their eyes open.

practices and laws of the land." Thus, while Holmes eventually reached for every possibility in sight, it never occurred to him to allege that *the legislation in question was unconstitutional*. As we might have expected, Holmes' point was simply that the Justice of the Peace had misinterpreted the act of 1788, and—since the constitution was also involved—that his mistake had amounted to a violation of *both* the act *and* the constitution.

We may now pass an informed judgment on the apologists' view of *Holmes v. Walton*. We are asked to believe that the New Jersey Supreme Court defied the theretofore unbroken tradition of legislative supremacy, and declared a statute void, even though

—the court evidently did not find the case worthy of a written opinion;

—the question of the statute's validity was never raised by the parties;

—the court could have raised the question on its own motion only by perversely insisting on an unnatural reading of the statute—something that even a modern, "judicial review" court would be unlikely to do, given the generally acknowledged rule that courts must always do their best to save a statute.

And this is to ask us to believe too much. It seems clear that what really happened was a commonplace, undoubtedly as familiar to the jurisprudence of the 1780's as of our own time: a higher court simply rebuffed a lower court for not knowing enough about the law, and did not deem the matter of sufficient difficulty or importance to bother writing an opinion about it.

But if the truth is all that simple, the reader is entitled to ask: How did the legend get started that the New Jersey Supreme Court, in *Holmes*, laid down a challenge to legislative supremacy? The answer lies, apparently, in the following episode. Shortly after the case was decided, the New Jersey Assembly received a petition "from sixty inhabitants of the county of Monmouth." The petition is represented in the Assembly records, as "complaining that the justices of the Supreme Court have set aside some of the laws as unconstitutional, and made void the proceedings of the magistrates, though strictly agreeable to the said laws, to the encouragement of the disaffected and great loss to the loyal citizens of the state."[9] We shall never know for sure why the petition was framed in such terms, but it is not hard to guess. Monmouth County was where the *Holmes* case arose, and the "sixty inhabitants," as Professor Crosskey surmises, were "probably men interested in the forfeitures that had been upset [and] were

therefore desirous of presenting the New Jersey Supreme Court's action in the light most likely to discredit it. . . ."[10] Now, as we shall see
in some of the other cases, the surest way of getting a court in trouble
with a legislature, in those days, was to represent the court as having
disobeyed the legislature. And that must have seemed easy enough
to do in the *Holmes* case inasmuch as the Supreme Court had not
given its reasons for disallowing the forfeiture.

The origin of the legend is thus accounted for. It remains to inquire
how much currency the legend had at the time; for we are concerned
not only with the truth about these cases, but also with the possibility
that the framers of the federal Constitution were substantially influenced by false stories about them. We know that the *Holmes* legend flowered after 1899, when Professor Scott's monograph appeared;
but what of the 1780's?

There is one piece of evidence on this point. A speech Gouverneur
Morris delivered in 1775 seems to prove that the false version of
Holmes v. Walton got at least as far as the neighboring state of Pennsylvania. Morris' purpose in the speech was to dissuade the Pennsylvania legislature from enacting certain legislation he deemed unconstitutional. Warning his colleagues of the possible consequences of
the action they proposed, Morris remarked that "a law was once
passed in New Jersey, which the judges pronounced to be unconstitutional, and therefore void." "Surely, no good citizen," he went on,
"can wish to see this point decided in the tribunals of Pennsylvania."[11]

Morris probably had the *Holmes* case—or, rather, the *Holmes* legend—in mind. Moreover, the memory of it may still have been with
him two years later at the Philadelphia Convention. But the important point, surely, for our purposes, is that this could not have been
a *fond* memory, or one that Morris was likely to parlay into an argument *for* a federal power of judicial review. For Morris obviously did
not approve of the New Jersey court's alleged action, and indeed
had geared his speech to the Pennsylvania legislature to the assumption that his colleagues would take exactly the same view of the matter.

Finally: even supposing the *Holmes* legend got around widely—
and, aside from the Morris episode, there is no evidence it did—there
is little chance the delegates to the federal Constitutional Convention were themselves misled. For one of the New Jersey delegates to
the convention, David Brearly, had been Chief Justice of the New
Jersey Supreme Court when the *Holmes* case was decided. Let us
assume the delegates, one day, got to talking about *Holmes v. Walton*,

as a "precedent" for judicial review. May we not also assume Judge
Brearly set them right about it?*

---

* The reader may wonder what basis there is to the apologists' further
contention, noted earlier, that the New Jersey legislature capitulated to the
Supreme Court after *Holmes v. Walton* had been decided. Of course the
contention depends entirely on the supposition which we may now call a
fantasy, that there was something to capitulate *to*. Nonetheless, the legislative
sequel to the *Holmes* case is not without value in assessing the nature of the
relationship during this period between courts and legislatures.

The tendency of the apologists' view, it will be recalled, holds 1) that
the *Holmes* court ruled that six-man juries were unconstitutional in New
Jersey, even though they had been authorized by certain prior legislation,
and 2) that post-*Holmes* legislation, in effect, ratified the court's ruling,
and thus implicitly acknowledged the court's authority to sit as final arbiter
of the state constitution's meaning. We may test that view by the following
sequence of events:

In the summer of 1779, a Justice of the Peace ruled that a contraband case
involving $27,000 (*Holmes v. Walton*) was governed by the Small Causes
Act, and thus must be heard by a six-man jury.

In December 1779, a month or so after the Supreme Court heard the
argument on the *Holmes* appeal, but before it handed down its decision, the
legislature passed an act expressly empowering justices of the peace in contraband cases to call juries of twelve men inasmuch as "Causes of Considerable Value may [arise in these situations] wherein it may be prudent
to have the judgment of a greater number than six jurors."

In September 1780, the Supreme Court reversed the Justice of the Peace's
ruling in *Holmes v. Walton*.

In December 1780, the legislature passed a new act, *requiring* Justices of
the Peace to grant twelve-man juries in contraband cases whenever they were
requested.

In June 1782, the legislature enacted a comprehensive substitute for all
previous contraband laws, providing, among other things, that juries were to
consist of twelve men in large claim cases, regardless of the parties' wishes.

In the same month the legislature revised the Small Causes Act, expressly
reaffirming that claims involving less than six pounds were to be tried by a
six-man jury including contraband claims. This provision remained in force
and was consistently followed by the Supreme Court until 1844 when New
Jersey adopted a new constitution.

In a word, the legislature seems to have been attempting during this period
to remove certain ambiguities created by overlapping and possibly contradictory statutes and customs, with the idea of codifying a comprehensive
body of law. Whether it had the *Holmes* case in mind at any point in the
process is not altogether clear. But if it did, the sequence of events suggests—
not as the apologists would have it—that the legislature followed the courts;
but that the courts followed the legislature. The sequence also demonstrates
that the apologists' main contention here—that the Supreme Court forced
the legislature to abandon six-man juries on constitutional grounds—is the
purest hokum.

COMMONWEALTH *v.* CATON

"[It is my duty] to protect one branch of the legislature, and, consequently, the whole community, against the usurpations of the other; and, whenever the proper occasion occurs, I shall feel the duty, and fearlessly perform it. Whenever traitors shall be fairly convicted . . . if one branch of the legislature, without the concurrence of the other, shall attempt to rescue the offenders from the sentence of the law, I shall not hesitate, sitting in this place, to say to the General Court,* *Fiat justicia ruat coelum* [that is: Let justice be done, though the heavens fall!].

"Nay more, if the whole legislature, an event to be deprecated, should attempt to overleap the bounds prescribed to them by the people, I, in administering the public justice of the country, will meet the united powers at my seat in this tribunal; and, pointing to the Constitution, will say to them, here is the limit of your authority, and hither shall you go, but no further."

Our hero is Judge George Wythe, as portrayed in a collection of early Virginia cases published in 1827 under the sonorously archival title, "Call's Reports." The occasion when "the united powers" were thus defied, notwithstanding the risk of cosmological retribution: the 1782 case of *Commonwealth v. Caton.* Judge Wythe's intrepidity, moreover, appears to have been contagious, for according to the report six of his seven brethren agreed "that the court had power to declare any resolution or pact of the legislature, or of either branch of it, to be unconstitutional and void." And lest the significance of the moment be underestimated, Mr. Call, the reporter, added a personal postscript: "N.B.: It is said that this was the first case in the United States where the question relative to the *nullity* of an unconstitutional law was ever discussed before a judicial tribunal; and the firmness of the judges (particularly of Mr. Wythe) was highly honorable

---

* I.e., the trial court.

to them, and will always be applauded, as having incidentally fixed
a precedent, whereon a general practice, which the people of this
country think essential to their rights and liberty, has been established."[1]

We have seen something already of the apologists' talent for making a feast of the thinnest morsel. It should not be surprising, under
the circumstances, that *Commonwealth v. Caton* is regularly celebrated in the literature as a precedent for judicial review. But neither
should it be surprising that on closer examination there turn out to be
reasons for more discriminating students to seek table elsewhere. For
one thing, the apologists seldom give sufficient attention to the *result*
of the case—as it appears on the face of the report. The court did
not hold the statute in question unconstitutional, although it undoubtedly was; indeed, Judge Wythe, as the court's principal
spokesman, expressly ruled in *favor* of its constitutionality. Rather,
the court held that a *resolution*, passed by one house of the legislature, was "inoperative" on the grounds that the other house had not,
as the dubious statute had required, concurred in the resolution. For
another thing, a reasonably attentive perusal of the report reveals
that the part of it that purports to relate the action taken by the
court is hopelessly garbled—concretely, that it attributes to Judge
Wythe a speech that he almost certainly never gave. Finally, the in-
congruities in Mr. Call's account are so spectacular as to raise questions—which it happens are answerable—about his motives.

But before getting into that, let us see what actually happened in
*Commonwealth v. Caton.** The case can be reconstructed without
difficulty by viewing the chain of events recorded by Call over
against the state of the law at the time, as the latter appears on the
margin of the report.

Caton and two other men were convicted of treason under a Virginia sedition statute enacted in 1776. The statute provided that the
pardoning power in such cases was to be exercised, not by the governor, as had been the custom under British rule, but by joint action of

---

* We shall not stop to ask in this case—nor in three others that follow,
viz., *Rutgers v. Waddington, The Symsbury Case,* and the "lost" Massachusetts case—what kind of judicial review was involved: the "scope" and
"effect" analysis we have employed heretofore is pointless unless the court
has purported, arguably, to exercise *some* version of the power. That condition, as we shall see, is not met here, nor in the three other cases mentioned.

both houses of the legislature.* In June 1782, the Virginia House of
Delegates voted to pardon the Caton defendants, and sent the resolution to the Senate for concurrence. The Senate, however, did not
take action. By October the Senate had still failed to act; whereupon
the attorney general requested the General Court to have the sentence carried out. Caton resisted the motion on the grounds that the
statutory provision, requiring the approval of a pardon by both
houses of the legislature, was unconstitutional. Caton was pretty
clearly right about this, for the Virginia constitution had provided
that in those cases where the legislature chose to deprive the governor of the power, the granting of pardons was to be the exclusive prerogative of the House of Delegates.† But the General Court, evidently
having no stomach for a battle with the legislature, begged off the
issue on grounds of "novelty and difficulty," and passed the case on
to the Court of Appeals. That court, alas, was no braver. Judge
Wythe said of the statute: "there is nothing unconstitutional in it."
The other appellate judges, save one, agreed not to contest the law,
and, accordingly, ordered the General Court to proceed with the
executions.‡

---

* The act read: "The Governor . . . shall in no wise have or exercise a
right of granting pardon to any person or persons convicted in manner
aforesaid, but may suspend the execution until the meeting of the General
Assembly, who shall determine whether such person or persons are proper
objects of mercy, or not, and order accordingly." (4 Call's Reports, p. 5.)

† The constitution said: "[The Governor] shall, with the advice of the
Council of State, have the power of granting reprieves or pardons, except
where the prosecution shall have been carried on by the House of Delegates
[i.e., impeachments], or the law shall otherwise particularly direct; in which
cases, no reprieve or pardon shall be granted, but by resolve of the House of
Delegates." (Va. Const. of 1776, Art. 9.)

‡ There is, besides Call, one other source of information about what the
court did in *Commonwealth v. Caton*. Six days after the decision one of the
judges, Edmund Pendleton, wrote a memorandum on the case to James
Madison, a copy of which is still extant and appears to be authentic. (See
Crosskey, op. cit., pp. 958-60.) Placing Pendleton's notes alongside Call's
account, the following seems to be a true picture of what went on in and out
of chambers. The public decision of the court was 6-2 against the validity
of the House of Delegates' pardon. The dissenting judges were James Mercer
(not to be confused with John F. Mercer of Maryland who during the Constitutional Convention explicitly declared against a judicial power of review)
and Bartholomew Dandridge. Mercer contended that the treason act of 1776
was unconstitutional and therefore void, and was thus the one judge out of
eight who favored exercising the power of judicial review. Dandridge upheld
the pardon on the grounds it was, somehow, consistent with the act of 1776.

Thus Caton and his companions died, even though they had been validly pardoned under the terms of the state constitution. They were victims, certainly in the first instance, of a legislative usurpation; but they were ultimately done in by the judges of the highest court of the State who dutifully—though most ignobly by modern lights—acquiesced in the aggression.

Now, since all of this is plain from the record, the question naturally arises: How account for the Homeric posturing of George Wythe and his brethren, as solemnized by Mr. Call? The answer is it cannot be accounted for by the internal evidence, but must be laid to the intervention of an outside hand. For the *analysis* of the case attributed to Judge Wythe—quite aside from the bellicose rhetoric—bears no relation at all to the situation that was actually before the court. The passages of Wythe's "opinion" that we saw earlier clearly intimate that the aggressor in the situation was the *House of Delegates*, and that the main issue before the court was the constitutionality of its pardoning resolution. And that is the picture of the case that emerges from the opinion as a whole. Elsewhere Wythe asserts: "Every view of the subject . . . repels the construction of the House of Delegates." And again: "The pretensions of the House of Delegates cannot be sustained." Still again: the Senate and the general community must be protected against "the usurping branch of the legislature," which service Judge Wythe, "pointing to the constitution," was going to perform. But Wythe *could* not have held this view of the case because: a) the House of Delegates made no "pretensions": it merely voted to pardon some people, as both the constitution and the 1776 statute had expressly authorized it to do; b) the House cast no separate "construction" on the law: on the contrary, the House and Senate appear to have been in complete agreement as to what the law required, as witness that the House forwarded its pardoning resolution to the Senate for approval as the 1776 act had

---

The judges voting against the pardon appear to have agreed with Wythe that the treason act and the House's resolution were inconsistent, and that the former, since it was valid, prevailed. The question of whether the court, theoretically, had the *power* to declare a statute unconstitutional was evidently discussed, as Call maintains, but did not figure significantly in the decision. On this issue, five judges, including Pendleton, refused to commit themselves. Of the other three, Peter Lyons expressly declared against the power; Mercer and Wythe declared for it, although the latter, we repeat, declined to exercise the power, and thus emerges as the affair's most conspicuous poltroon.

prescribed—and, according to Wythe, had validly prescribed; and c) the only legislative measure open to the charge of unconstitutionality was that act of 1776, which, we repeat, the majority of the court, along with everyone else except the unfortunate defendants, said *was* constitutional.

What, then, may be conjectured about the outside hand? And another question: How account for its presence having passed largely unnoticed by students of constitutional law? *Commonwealth v. Caton* appears in the literature over the laconic note, "4 Call 5." This is the case's "citation," the approved shorthand for directing interested readers to a primary source—in this instance to page 5 of what would appear to be the fourth volume of certain official court reports that were published under the name (for such was once the fashion) of the court reporter. All too often, however, a citation serves a quite different function: it tends to authenticate; it may *discourage* further investigation precisely because of the assumption it creates as to what the investigation is likely to turn up. As here, for example, where one might expect the obscurities of *Comonwealth v. Caton* to be confirmed by the original records, but where, in fact, the original records illuminate a great deal. For Mr. Call's fourth volume turns out to be —not like the first three, a collection of recorded cases—but a series of Call's own reconstructions of old Virginia cases that had *never* been recorded. He had done the job, he explained in the volume's preface, "with great labor and expense from the notes and memoranda of the judges and lawyers, who attended the courts, and a diligent examination of the records."[2] This means, in the case of *Commonwealth v. Caton*, that the job was done 45 years after the events in question took place—at a time, it turns out, when all of the participants were dead.[3] Moreover, the unveiling occurred at just the moment when the emerging institution of judicial review was under bitterest attack. In Virginia, Ohio, and elsewhere, legislatures with strong popular endorsement were in open rebellion against the activities of John Marshall's Supreme Court—and proponents of judicial review were thus very much in need of historical precedents. That Call himself was an enthusiastic champion of judicial review is evident, of course, from the tendentious "N.B." he appended to the *Caton* report. It is clear, then, that Call had both opportunity and motive for allowing his imagination to roam freely in assembling the material for this particular "reconstruction." And what of Wythe's special role? The dead judge, it appears, had been a kind of mentor to Call; it was to Wythe, "to whom I owe the little knowledge I possess," that Call dedicated the first volume of his "Reports."[4] Under the circumstances, Call probably believed the majestic effusions of the Caton speech would be a fitting memorial to his fallen master.*

To be sure, these conjectures invite an objection. Why, if Call was attempting hanky panky, did he do such a poor job of covering his tracks? But there is a short answer. The job was as good as it had to be. Perhaps because gross hyperbole has a way of conferring verisimilitude (in our day we speak of "the Big Lie"), perhaps because of his audience's disposition to listen—it remains that Call's version of *Commonwealth v. Caton* survived virtually unchallenged, for nearly a century and a half, as a proof that judicial review was *in vogue* in post-Independence America. Call's achievement is all the more remarkable, of course, for the fact that the case actually furnished a vivid documentation of the opposite state of affairs. Contrary to the representations of latter-day historians, legislatures did not, during this period, violate constitutions as a matter of course; but when they did, *Commonwealth v. Caton* indicates they could—as a matter of course—count on the cooperation of the courts.

---

* Another "case" reported in Call's fourth volume, which reveals Wythe in a rather more pusillanimous role, may have suggested the need for rehabilitation. "The Case of the Judges" could not easily have been misrepresented since it had received widespread newspaper coverage at the time (1778), and even as late as 1827, apparently, was a well remembered event. The case actually took the form of a "Respectful Remonstrance" to the legislature in which Wythe, Pendleton, and others petitioned the legislature to reconsider certain of its actions of which the judges took a dim view. Professor Crosskey's account of what happened is adequate to our point: "In that 'Remonstrance,' [as] Call reports it . . . the Virginia judges did not say to their legislature: 'Hither shall you go, but no further!' They displayed, instead, the greatest diffidence that the legislature would heed their view. And, as a matter of fact, the legislature did not. So, in the end, as Call's report makes clear, the Virginia judges were obliged to meet the legislature's views; and this, though the case involved, or was supposed to involve, a legislative invasion of the judiciary's own 'prerogatives.'" Crosskey, op. cit., p. 957.

RUTGERS v. WADDINGTON

We have come at last to a case where, mercifully, neither the facts nor what the court did with them is in dispute. The Court's decision was committed to a written opinion at the time it was handed down; it was thereupon published in pamphlet form and widely distributed throughout the country—all as befits one of the most famous cases of the era. Indeed, the importance of the case in American history—as contrasted with its usefulness as a "precedent" for judicial review—is such that it occupies a place of prominence in the apologists' showcase second only to that of *Trevett v. Weeden.**

Rutgers v. Waddington, decided in 1784,[1] raised the momentous question of whether the individual States or the central government was supreme under the Articles of Confederation. The issue, concretely, was whether an act of a state legislature could be annulled by the Treaty of Peace with England, just ratified by the Continental Congress. The New York court that heard the case was hardly in an enviable position: it could not declare *for* the treaty without calling into question the supremacy of its own legislature, and it could not declare *against* the treaty without running the risk that the British would regard the action as a breach of faith and seize upon it as an excuse for resuming hostilities against their former colonies. Understandably, the court strove mightily to have it both ways—and to a remarkable degree succeeded. It refused to invalidate the statute, declaring in the most sweeping terms imaginable its capacity to do such a thing, and then proceeded to "interpret" the statute in a way that saved the Treaty of Peace. Even so—to anticipate our story— the court did not quite pull it off: despite the court's earnest protestations to the contrary, some New Yorkers thought the judges had tampered with the legislative authority, and, accordingly, took it out of their hides.

---

* See below.

179

The statute in question, enacted early in 1783, had given New York patriots who fled their "places of abode" during the British invasion the right to bring an action for trespass against Tories who afterwards occupied the abandoned property under the authority of the British military. Elizabeth Rutgers had owned a malt house and a brewery in New York City, and had abandoned both when the British conquered the city in 1778. Joshua Waddington, a British subject, had thereupon received from the British commander a license to operate the premises; and this use of the property, Miss Rutgers claimed, had cost her, all in all, £8000. Waddington, with no less a personage than Alexander Hamilton as his chief counsel, resisted the claim on the grounds a) that the British commander had been authorized to license the property by "the law of nations"—which law, he said, determined an occupying army's rights in wartime; and b) that the Treaty of Peace signed by Great Britain and the United States in September 1783 had contained a mutual renunciation of all financial claims arising out of the war.

The facts of the case are thus simple enough. The court's reasoning, however, is a little more difficult to follow. It will be easier to understand the argument—and, more important, the considerations that governed the court's approach—if we pause for a moment to inquire how a similar case might be approached today.

A modern court might begin its discussion by remarking that the New York legislature, in attempting to penalize conduct deemed legitimate under the recognized rules of war, had violated international law. But a modern court would probably go on to say that judges are not expected to enforce international law except as it has been incorporated in the jurisdiction's positive law—and therefore that the conflict between international law and the state statute in this case was insufficient grounds for invalidating the statute. The Treaty of Peace, however, was something else again. For the treaty, implicitly at least, did incorporate the relevant international law into the positive law of the United States—by providing for a mutual release from wartime claims. That is, the treaty provided that the nationals of neither side were to be penalized for doing what was approved by the rules of war. Our modern court would therefore conclude that a justiciable conflict existed between a national act (the Treaty) and a state act (the statute), and that since the national power must prevail over a local power, the Treaty must be held to have repealed the statute.

There were compelling reasons why the Mayor's Court of New

York City, in 1784, could not take this view of the case. While nearly everyone at the time accepted the idea that the individual States were subsumed in a "Confederation," and were, in some sense, subordinate to it, this was not a relationship to be defined by the *courts*. New York might have to bow to the central government, but she would do so under the authority of her legislators, who were supreme, and not by the order of her judges who were not. That was the understanding of the situation that governed public opinion, and the judges of the Mayor's Court were well aware that they would defy it only at their own considerable peril. On the other hand, the integrity of the Treaty was a matter of the greatest *practical* urgency. During that first year of peace, the danger was never far from American minds that the British were on the lookout for a pretext for resuming the war. The court's fears along this line were plainly evident: ". . . we hold [the Treaty] to be sacred and shall never, as far as we have power, suffer it to be violated or questioned. It is the great charter of America—it has formally and forever released us from foreign domination. . . ."[2]

The unavoidable strategy of the court, therefore, was to make the saving of the Treaty the *legislature's own doing*.

The first step in this strategy was to renounce any intention of challenging the omnipotence of the legislature:

> *The supremacy of the legislature need not be called into question;* if they think fit positively to enact a law, *there is no power which can control them.* When the main object of such a law is clearly expressed, and the intention manifest, the judges are not at liberty, although it appears to them to be unreasonable, to reject it; for this were to set the judicial above the legislative, which would be subversive of all government.
>
> But when a law is expressed in general words, and some collateral matter, which happens to arise from those general words, is unreasonable, there the judges are in decency to conclude, that the consequences were not foreseen by the legislature; and therefore they are at liberty to expound the statute by equity, and only *quod hoc* to disregard it.
>
> *When the judicial make these distinctions, they do not control the legislature; they endeavor to give their intention its proper respect.*[3]

Here, then, was the orthodox doctrine of legislative supremacy— even down to a plagiarism of phraseology. Recognizably, the court's language was copied nearly verbatim from Blackstone's "Tenth Rule" for construing statutes.* And this explicit acknowledgment of

---

* See p. 134.

the legislature's supreme authority was manifestly designed, we repeat, to disabuse anyone of the suspicion that the court might be laying pretensions to the power of judicial review. Having taken that precaution, the court went on to its second step—namely, an application of "these general remarks to the particular case under . . . consideration."

The second step was not, however, what we might have expected —to invoke the Peace Treaty as the "unforeseen circumstance" the legislature had not taken into account when it passed the statute. Blackstone, himself, might have deemed this solution a proper application of his rule, but the court apparently felt that to hold that the New York legislature's real "intention" had emerged when the central government signed its peace treaty would look too much like acknowledging the authority of the central government to *repeal* acts of state legislatures—would not appear, that is to say, to be giving the legislature's intention "its proper respect." Accordingly, the second step was to reject the possibility that such a repeal had occurred. "There is not a tittle in the Treaty," the court said flatly, "to which the statute is repugnant."[4] The possibility of conflict between the two, the court then disingenuously explained, would arise only on the assumption the legislature was less solicitous about the *"law of nations"* than the makers of the Treaty were. And that is not an assumption, the court said, climbing onto its third step, we will lightly make.

Thus the decisive question, on the court's showing, became: *Did the New York legislature intend to repeal the law of nations* when it passed the 1783 act? With studied deference, the court refused to impute any such design to the legislature in the absence of express words to that effect. The judges concluded that the legislature did, indeed, mean to respect the law of nations, and consequently that it did not intend to give Elizabeth Rutgers a cause of action that would be repugnant to that "law."

Now this last step was, of course, a subterfuge. There was no reason to suppose the New York legislature had been unaware of the recognized rules of war when it passed the 1783 act, and its decision to disregard them did not require, under the usual standards of statute-drafting, an express acknowledgment. The court could not seriously have expected from the legislature a formal announcement that New York would no longer be bound by the law of nations!

The point is not, of course, that the judges of the Mayor's Court were bad lawyers; on the contrary, the opinion as a whole was a remarkably sophisticated and imaginative piece of work. The judges' evasions simply show the importance they attached to preserving the appearances of legislative supremacy, once they had decided, *pro bono publico*, that the Treaty must be saved.

It remains to remark briefly the aftermath of *Rutgers v. Waddington*. For, alas, the court's analytical gymnastics were not appreciated by those they were designed to appease. Two weeks after the court announced its decision, a popular protest meeting was called in New York. That meeting produced a formal "Address to the People" in which the Mayor's Court was assailed for having "assumed and exercised a power to set aside an act of the State." If such a power were conceded to the courts, the protest went on, it "would be destructive of liberty.... The duty of courts of justice in our government from the very nature of their institution, is to *declare* laws, not to *alter* them."[5]

A month later the legislature itself took action. The decision of the Mayor's Court, a formal resolution charged, "is, in tendency, subversive of all law and good order, and leads directly to anarchy and confusion...."[6] Some of the legislators were not content with mere censure, and sought to have the Mayor and the City Recorder, both of whom had been judges in the case, removed from office. While matters never went this far, and the removal motion was defeated, there could be no mistaking the popular mood.

Alexander Hamilton, for example, got the word loud and clear, and concluded that Waddington's success in the Mayor's Court was certain to be reversed on appeal. Accordingly, Hamilton persuaded Miss Rutgers to settle out of Court and thus saved his own client from victimization by the public furor.*

In the light of the foregoing, it is difficult to understand why so many apologists for judicial review have insisted on including *Rutgers v. Waddington* in their list of "precedents." As far as the *law* of the case is concerned it is, clearly, a precedent *against* judicial review. As one of the more careful apologists, Brinton Coxe, has acknowledged: "[The court] felt compelled to lay down the law of

---

* Hamilton later commented: ". . . *the suit of Rutgers v. Waddington . . . was terminated by a compromise, according to the advice of defendant's counsel, owing to the apprehension of an unfavorable issue in the Supreme Court; and this, notwithstanding the defendant was a British subject.*" Hamilton's *Works*, V, 227. For an account of the public reaction to *Rutgers v. Waddington*, see the introduction to Henry B. Dawson's pamphlet, *Elizabeth Rutgers v. Joshua Waddington*, 1866.

legislation in terms fully securing the supremacy of the legislature
and the subordination of the judiciary . . . If, [as the court main-
tained], Blackstone's doctrine was the law of New York, no court
could ever reject a statute in order to save the constitution, although
the latter was written. . . . [It] is, therefore, correct to say that according to the law of the opinion, no [New York] court could decide a
questioned statute unconstitutional and hold it therefore void."[7]

It is true that when the time came to apply the law to the facts,
the court stretched Blackstone's doctrine to the point of meaningless-
ness. We must therefore match Mr. Coxe's concession with one of
our own—namely that despite its vigorous defense of the legislature's
supreme authority, and despite its refusal to challenge the statute in
question head on, the Mayor's Court did disregard the statute. But
to concede that, is not to concede very much in the way of "precedents." The court's subterfuge in *Rutgers v. Waddington* can no
more be considered as "authority" for judges surreptitiously disregarding statutes than the Warren Court's misrepresentation of constitutional history in *Brown v. Board of Education* can be considered
authority for judges indulging in shoddy scholarship.

And to the extent that *Rutgers v. Waddington* reveals the climate
of contemporary public opinion, once again we might have expected
the apologists to give the case a wide berth. Let us recall the apologists' theory as to why judicial review was not mentioned in the federal Constitution—namely, that the practice of courts supervising legislatures had become so familiar and acceptable to the American people that the framers assumed it would continue unmolested, notwithstanding the absence of express safeguards. *Rutgers v. Waddington*
is not particularly good evidence for that theory. The main lesson
of the case, in which Alexander Hamilton would have been the first
to instruct his colleagues in Philadelphia, was that judges who chose
to second-guess legislators would have to look after their jobs.

TREVETT v. WEEDEN

A chapter on judicial review in Professor Herman Pritchett's recent book, *The American Constitution*, sums up the period we are examining as follows:

> There were some nine cases decided in eight States between 1776 and 1789 which purported to declare state legislative acts unconstitutional. . . . The best known is *Trevett v. Weeden* (1786) in which a Rhode Island Court invalidated an act of the State Assembly requiring the acceptance of paper money as legal tender.[1]

We have selected Professor Pritchett's comment more or less at random as a representative account not only of what the pre-Constitution state courts, in general, are alleged to have been up to, but more particularly of the supposed facts and historical significance of the *Trevett* case. On the latter point the received view is accurate enough: *Trevett v. Weeden* is undoubtedly the "best known" of the nine, a characterization that would have been equally valid at the time of the Constitutional Convention, thanks to an account of the case written by one of the lawyers, James Varnum, and later published in a widely read pamphlet.

Varnum's purpose at the trial, as Weeden's counsel, was to persuade the court to disregard an act of the legislature; his pamphlet's purpose was to relate the extent to which he had succeeded—and thus may well have been tendentious. The Varnum pamphlet, moreover, is practically our only source of information about the case. There was no official court report that might have clarified some of the ambiguities in Varnum's account, and that, better still, would have been free of the suspicion of bias. Besides Varnum, our only source is a brief newspaper report of the court's action.

The case arose out of an attempt by the Rhode Island legislature in the spring and summer of 1786 to introduce paper money into the

State—a series of measures designed to inflate the currency as an aid to the debtor classes. The initial legislation, enacted in May, provided for the issuance of paper notes, and required that they be accepted on a par with silver and gold in all commercial transactions, including the payment of past contractual obligations. Understandably, the measure ran into stiff resistance by the business community and creditors in general. As a result, in June, the legislature decided to put teeth into the law, and imposed a $100 penalty for refusal to accept the paper bills, half of the fine to go to the State and half to the debtor. "Experience," Varnum relates, "soon evinced the inadequacy of this measure"—evidently because of the reluctance of the courts to give speedy relief—and in August the legislature, specially convened for the purpose, struck a third time. On this occasion it provided that all claims under the law should be tried before special courts, and that the trials should proceed "without any jury . . . according to the laws of the land." The decisions handed down in these summary proceedings, moreover, were to be final and conclusive . . . from which there shall be no appeal."[2]

This third law was indeed destined to run into trouble, for at least two reasons. First, and most important as Varnum tells the story, it eliminated juries. While Rhode Island had no written constitution at the time, the customs and usage of the people unquestionably included the right of jury trial. Moreover, everyone thought that the State's "fundamental law" had been stated by its colonial charter, which, in turn, had subsumed the jury provisions of Magna Carta and English common law. And there was the further complication of the jury issue, which the reader may have noticed, that the August provision required that trials be conducted *both* without a jury *and* according to the laws of the land—an apparent contradiction in the light of the latter's affirmation of the right to a jury.

The second problem was the denial of the right of appeal. This provision, as it happened, was of no practical consequence in *Trevett v. Weeden* since the plaintiff took his complaint directly to the Superior Court of Judicature,* which thereupon constituted itself the "special court." But the informer, under the provision, could just as well have taken his complaint to one of the county courts of common pleas; in that event, as Varnum put it, the action of the lower court would have been "uncontrollable by the supreme judicial court of the State."[3]

Within a month after the August act was passed, a test case came

---

* As the Rhode Island Supreme Court was designated.

before the Superior Court. John Trevett had tried to buy meat with
paper bills. John Weeden, a butcher, had refused to accept the paper, whereupon Trevett had filed a complaint with the Superior
Court. Chief Justice Mumford issued an "information"—i.e., a formal
statement of the charges—and convened a special court to hear the
charges. The following day, September 26:

> The Court delivered the unanimous opinion of the judges that the
> information was not cognizable before them.[4]

This passage—which amounted to an assertion by the court that it
had no jurisdiction—is all that Varnum communicates on the critical question of what the court actually said and did during the trial.
We may thus take it as representing the entirety of the official judgment. The only other clue to the court's opinion is to be found in a
brief account of the case published in the Newport *Mercury* on October 2, and reprinted elsewhere by other newspapers:

> Judge Howell, in a fine, sensible and judicious speech, assigned the
> reasons which induced him to be of the opinion that the information
> was not cognizable by the Court—declared himself independent as a
> judge—the penal law to be repugnant and unconstitutional—and there-
> fore gave it as his opinion that the Court could not take cognizance
> of the information: Judge Devol was of the same opinion. Judge
> Tillinghast took notice of the expressions of the act, 'without trial by
> jury, according to the laws of the land'—and on that ground gave his
> judgment the same way. Judge Hazard voted against taking cognizance.
> The Chief Justice declared the judgment of the Court without giving
> his opinion.

The legal significance of the court's action is a matter to be explored with some care. For the moment, however, let us focus on the
practical consequences of what the court did. Unavoidably the impression went out to the community that the court had declined to
enforce the legislature's latest paper money law. Within a week the
judges were haled before the legislature to give an accounting. The
legislative summons angrily demanded that the judges "assign their
reasons" for declaring "an act of the supreme legislature of this State
to be unconstitutional, and so absolutely void." The court's decision,
the summons went on, is "unprecedented in this State and may tend
directly to abolish the legislative authority."[5]

The court's first response was to plead sickness on the part of two
of the judges, and the legislature agreed to a postponement of the
hearing. But by late October, with its health evidently restored, the

court was ready to appear. It seems the judges had used the respite to agree upon a strategy—and upon Judge Howell as their principal spokesman. Once again it is lawyer Varnum who supplies our knowledge of what was said at the hearing, a fact that lends considerable significance to Howell's vigorous post-trial denial that the court had declared a law "unconstitutional," as charged by the legislative summons.

Judge Howell began by observing, disingenuously, that the legislature's summons could be interpreted in two lights. Either "the House might be considered as [having called upon the judges] to assist in matters of legislation"—i.e., Howell explained, to act in their capacity as "legal counselors for the State . . . in framing new or repealing former laws." Or—the other possibility as Howell saw it, and the one that of course he knew squared with reality—the summons might be read as an order that the judges "render the reasons for their judicial determination" in *Trevett v. Weeden* on the theory that they were "accountable to the legislature for their judgment."

On the assumption the judges were there merely as the legislature's "legal counselors," Howell went on, he and his brethren were perfectly willing to talk; they were eager, he said, "to render every kind of assistance." Whereupon Howell proceeded to speak "upwards from six hours," according to Varnum, expounding a "variety of conclusive arguments [proving the legislation] was unconstitutional, had not the force of law, and could not be executed." In this first phase of his presentation, in other words, Howell advised the legislature *it should not have enacted the law in the first place, and ought now to repeal it.*

Howell then turned to his second possible reason for the summons—namely, that the judges were being asked to disclose the reasons for their decision in *Trevett v. Weeden.* In this connection, he made two points. The first was that the judges were not bound to divulge and justify the reasoning behind the decision inasmuch as the reasoning had not been made part of the record. "Whatever might have been the opinion of the judges, they spoke by their records, which admitted of no addition or diminution. [The individual judges] might have been influenced respectively by different reasons [for which] they were accountable only to God and their own conscience."* The second point, and the crucial one for our purposes,

---

* Thus Judge Howell was able to avoid an explicit commitment on the main theoretical issue the case raised—namely, whether the court would have been answerable to the legislature if it had expressly cited Rhode Island's

was that the legislature's summons, in any event, *had been issued on a false premise.* Varnum relates this, the core of the court's defense, as follows:

> Here it was observed, that the legislature had assumed the fact, in their summons to the judges, which was not justified or warranted by the records. The plea of the defendants, *in a matter of mere surplusage,* mentions the Act of the General Assembly as "unconstitutional, and so void"; but the judgment of the Court simply is, "that the information is not cognizable before them." *Hence it appears that the plea has been mistaken for the judgment.*[6]

Not surprisingly, Judge Howell's elaborate rationalization failed to appease the legislature. True, he had proved incontestably that the court had not entered a judgment of unconstitutionality, or sought to invalidate the legislation, or anything of the sort. And since Howell had not even hinted that the court possessed such a power, the doctrine of legislative supremacy was not really at issue. Yet the hard, practical fact remained that the court had not enforced an act of the legislature dealing with the hottest of political questions; it had sought, moreover, to obscure that hard fact in a maze of technicalities. No American legislature in the year 1786 was prepared to be dealt with in so cavalier a fashion. Accordingly, the Rhode Island legislature formally declared it was not "satisfied with the reasons given by the judges in support of their judgment."[7] Thereupon the legislators sought to dismiss the judges from their offices—a motion that was defeated when the State's Attorney General ruled such a remedy was not available except on a charge of criminality.[8]

Six months later, however, the legislature had its revenge. When

---

traditional respect for the right of jury trial as its reason for declining jurisdiction in the *Trevett* case. By implication Howell tacitly agreed the court *would* be answerable under such circumstances, for he relied entirely in the passage we have just seen on the court's right to confine its explanations to matters of record. Another passage Varnum attributes to Howell is to the same effect: "It would be out of the power, therefore, of the General Assembly to determine upon the propriety of the Court's judgment [when the court has not given] a particular explanation." Let us agree on Howell's probable motives: he made the implicit concession in order to appease the legislature; yet he declined to make the point expressly because he was reluctant to give away, on behalf of the court, more than the immediate political situation required. We must remember that Howell and his associates were playing an extremely close game; on the one hand they wished to assert a measure of judicial independence; on the other, they wished to keep their jobs.

the judges' terms expired the following spring, only the Chief Justice—the one member of the bench who had not declared his opinion in the case—was chosen by the legislature for another term. The other four were replaced by jurists who, the legislators presumably felt, would be more likely to remember their places.

The paper money laws, incidentally, remained on the books until they were superseded by Rhode Island's adherence to the federal Constitution in 1791. And the fact they were regularly enforced during this period by the courts—notwithstanding *Trevett v. Weeden*—ought to be sufficient answer to the question of who had the "last say" in pre-1787 American history, the judiciary or the legislature.

So much for what happened in *Trevett v. Weeden*. We must now examine the legal situation a little more closely in order to determine what, exactly, the case is "precedent" *for*. Three points need to be made in this connection.

First, with regard to the *scope* of the judicial power, it is clear that *Trevett v. Weeden* is, at best, a B1 case. No matter how their treatment of the law is to be interpreted, that is to say, the *Trevett* judges could not have been asserting anything more than a judicial right of self-defense. For the law they were dealing with constituted *a direct assault on established judicial procedures*: it abrogated the right of jury trial; it created special jurisdictions and procedures for the trial of certain cases; and it denied to the State's highest court the right to hear appeals. Moreover, these latter provisions were probably understood, and may well have been intended, as a deliberate slap at the Superior Court of Judicature.

Now: one of the reasons *Trevett v. Weeden* is accorded so much historical significance is precisely that legal scholars have regularly misrepresented this aspect of the case. Somewhere along the line the notion took hold in the literature that the *Trevett* court challenged the Rhode Island legislature's right to *issue paper money*, and thus asserted, in effect, a broad power to review *all* legislative acts. And most modern writers, it seems, have not done their own homework well enough to discover the error. Thus, Professor Pritchett's description of the case, noted at the beginning of this chapter. Thus also the Kelly-Harbison version: "[The Rhode Island court] voided a paper-money force act as contrary to the property guarantees of the old charter. . . ."[9] We have seen of course that the paper money issue, and the question of property rights were not even *before* the court, and we are saying that if legal writers had only apprised themselves of what *Trevett v. Weeden* was *about*, they would have gone a long way toward putting its "precedent" value in proper perspective.

Second, with regard to the *effect* the judges intended their decision to have, *Trevett* is clearly a C1 case. This is the point that Judge Howell took such pains to make in his speech before the legislature. By claiming it "could not take cognizance of the information," Howell explained, the court had merely asserted its inability—for reasons he was unwilling to disclose—to *execute* the law. The court had not purported, that is to say, to judge the law "unconstitutional," or "void," and thus to strike it from the books—which would have made *Trevett* a C2 case. Anyone who takes that view of the decision, Howell said, has "mistaken the plea . . . for the judgment." Much less did the *Trevett* judges anticipate the modern (C3) view that a judicial ruling in such a case is "final"—i.e., that the legislature is forever bound to abide by the court's decision.

It is perhaps more significant still that Varnum, on his own showing, did not even *ask* the court to reach beyond the C1 theory. For if courts were thought to have the power to declare laws void, we may be sure that Varnum, as Weeden's lawyer, would have urged the court to exercise it in this case. Yet a close reading of Varnun's argument shows that while he, indeed, gave it as the defendant's opinion that the law was "unconstitutional and void," he did not ask *the court* to make that declaration. Rather, he advised the court that judges "*cannot admit* any act of the legislative as law, which is against the Constitution"; and again, that "if the General Assembly attempts to make laws contrary [to the constitution], the court *cannot receive them*."[10]

And if to the modernist all of this seems like nit-picking, we must say once again that the distinctions insisted upon here are critical in assessing the *kind* of judicial review—assuming they envisioned it at all—that the framers of the federal constitution had in mind. Was it the modern kind, wherein courts allegedly have the power to *invalidate* legislation—and are thus, in effect, *superior* to legislatures? There is no hint by any of the participants in *Trevett v. Weeden*—including the attorneys who attacked the law—of that kind of power.* Or was it the more modest claim that judges may refuse to cooperate in the enforcement of certain legislative acts—on the understanding that the

---

* The only suggestion the court actually exercised such a power appeared, as we have seen, in the legislature's summons—i.e., in the form of an *accusation* aginst the court. This fact calls to mind the "Monmouth Petition" in *Holmes v. Walton* (pp. 170-171) and the various "protests" following *Rutgers v. Waddington* (pp. 183-184), two earlier occasions on which incorrect charges, plainly designed by the court's enemies to discredit it, provide the sole basis of the apologists' case.

refusal constitutes an invitation to the legislature to change its mind, but is in no sense *binding* on the legislature? That view of the matter, given the far superior political weaponry at the legislature's command, unavoidably leaves courts *inferior* to legislatures, and is the very most, we are saying, that can be extracted from *Trevett v. Weeden.*

Third, there remains the possibility—indeed, it may strike the reader as a strong probability—that *Trevett v. Weeden* did not involve *any* kind of judicial review. Let us remember that our analysis, up until now, has assumed something we do not know—namely, that the *reason* the *Trevett* judges refused to execute the law was they deemed it "unconstitutional," a violation of the Rhode Island tradition regarding jury trials. And on that assumption, we concluded that *Trevett v. Weeden* was a B1, C1 case of judicial review. But is the assumption really tenable? The main burden of Judge Howell's speech before the legislature, after all, was that the judges *had not, and were not going to, reveal the reason they decided the case as they did.*

It is true that a substantial portion of Varnum's brief was devoted to the constitutional argument—which means the court was adequately exposed to that argument before handing down its decision. It is also true that the Newport *Mercury* reported that two of the five judges, Howell and Devol, *thought* the law was unconstitutional—which may mean, but also may not mean, they actually decided the case on that basis. It is true, finally, that Judge Howell vigorously "counseled" the legislature, subsequent to the decision, on the constitutional point.

But consider now the evidence that supports a different hypothesis, namely: *the judges reasoned, not that they should not enforce the law because of its unconstitutionality, but that they could not enforce it inasmuch as the legislature had simultaneously commanded two contradictories—that trials be conducted without juries,* and *according to the laws of the land.*

1. Most writers appear not to have noticed that Varnum also devoted a substantial portion of his brief to this contention. He began the argument by citing from Bacon's *Abridgment* the traditional exception to the doctrine of legislative supremacy—recognized, as we have seen, by Blackstone—that "if a statute . . . be *repugnant* or *impossible to be performed*, the common law shall control it, and judge it to be void." The rule applies to this case, Varnum went on, because judges could not both try a man *without* a jury, and at the same time try him "according to the laws of the land," when those very laws

guarantee a trial *with* a jury. Contraries cannot coexist in the law, and they certainly cannot be executed at the same time. *"This act therefore is impossible to be executed."*[10] In other words, according to Varnum, *Trevett v. Weeden* was a latter-day "Case of the Seals" in which a metaphysical impossibility had deprived the court of the power to assume jurisdiction.

2. Judge Tillinghast was expressly represented by the Newport *Mercury* account as having given his judgment on this ground, and on no other. Judges Howell and Devol were both represented as believing the act to be "repugnant" as well as unconstitutional. Judge Hazard, according to the account, gave his judgment on "jurisdictional" grounds. Thus the views of all of the judges, as recorded by the newspaper story, are consistent with the "repugnancy-impossibility" hypothesis.*

3. This hypothesis also tallies, as the other does not, with our two accounts of what the court's actual judgment was. Varnum reported the court "was *unable* to take cognizance of the information." The *Mercury*, implying that Howell's view represented the formal judgment, reported the court *"could not* take cognizance of the information."

Our own view, then, is that it is more likely that the case was decided on "repugnancy" and "impossibility" grounds than on constitutional grounds. And if this is true, it follows that *Trevett v. Weeden* is not justly celebrated as a legal landmark—as a precedent for any kind of judicial review—but only for the political ruckus that developed in the aftermath. As a legal proposition, it stands wholly within the orthodoxy of Blackstone.

Let us, however, not insist on this interpretation, for we do not want to lose sight of the main issue here. It cannot be stated often

---

* Professor Crosskey reasons otherwise. The phrase " 'without trial by jury' was more specific than 'according to the laws of the land,' " he argues. Therefore, "upon elementary principles of construction, it should have prevailed *pro tanto* over the more general phrase. . . ." Crosskey doubts, under the circumstances, that even Judge Tillinghast decided the case on "repugnancy" grounds—the newspaper account to the contrary notwithstanding. (Op. cit., p. 966, note.) We are unconvinced. To argue that judges undoubtedly did thus and so because, under strict legal canons, they *should* have done thus and so is probably the most perilous method of argument open to legal historians. This is especially true when both the internal and external evidence in the case in question suggests the judges had more pressing matters on their minds than "elementary principles of construction."

enough that what we are trying to discover from these state cases is whether the framers of the federal Constitution had any reason to believe the institution of judicial review was so well established in America that they had no cause to make provision for it in the document they drafted in Philadelphia. What we have seen in the *Trevett* case is that a court *may* have gone so far—may, that is, on the reading of the case most favorable to the apologists—as to refuse to execute an act of the legislature that constituted a clear invasion of the judicial sphere. Far from acquiescing in this modest assertion of judicial independence, the legislature haled the judges before it, sought to humiliate them publicly, and, as soon as the law allowed, took away their jobs. If the framers knew about *Trevett v. Weeden*— and we may be reasonably sure all of them did—and if their purpose in Philadelphia was to entrust to the national courts the interpretation and enforcement of the new Constitution, may we not assume that they would have taken some pains to define that role, and to provide some measure of protection against the kind of reprisals that occurred in Rhode Island?

THE SYMSBURY CASE

Why the *Symsbury Case*[1] is included on the traditional list of "precedents" for judicial review will always be a mystery. No one is sure who first put it there, let alone why. The occasional apologist who discusses it in any detail does so with evident embarrassment, perplexed, apparently, that he has been unable to demonstrate the judicial review "point" that was presumably seen by the discoverer of the precedent.

It can briefly be shown that the case did not remotely involve any kind of judicial review.

In 1670, the Governor and Company of the colony of Connecticut granted a tract of land to the "Proprietors of the Town of Symsbury." In 1686, the General Assembly of the colony granted to the "Proprietors of the Towns of Hartford and Windsor" all of the land "west of Symsbury" up to a certain river. The exact location of Symsbury's westerly limits, however, were imprecisely defined in the 1670 grant; hence the dispute between property owners under the two grants that gave rise to the *Symsbury Case* in 1785.

In 1727, meanwhile, the General Assembly had confirmed a new survey of the area that located the boundary between the towns somewhat east of the line that Symsbury property owners claimed had been established by the 1670 grant. Thus the problem before the court in the *Symsbury Case* was twofold. First—Who was right about the location of the 1670 grant? The court said the Symsbury people were. And second—What was the legal effect of the 1727 survey? Had it merely established the municipal boundaries of the two towns, or had it also determined the proprietary interests conveyed under the original grants? The court said that only the former result had been intended, and thus that the claims of the Symsbury property owners were valid:

The act of the General Assembly, confirming [the 1727 survey] operated to restrict and limit the western extent of the jurisdiction of the town of Symsbury, but could not legally operate to curtail the line before granted to the proprietors of the town of Symsbury without their consent.[2]

And that is all there is to the *Symsbury Case*. To suggest that the court's judgment as to the "legal operation" of the 1727 survey constituted an invalidation of the 1727 act, and thus an instance of judicial review, is, on the face of it, absurd.

Professor Crosskey has added: "Even to talk of judicial review in the conditions which obtained in Connecticut, in 1784-85, is nonsense; for the Connecticut legislature was itself, at that time, the highest judicial tribunal in the State, with full power to reverse the Symsbury decision or any other judicial decision if it saw fit to do so.[3]

THE "LOST" MASSACHUSETTS PRECEDENT

In 1788, one J. B. Cutting, who is otherwise unknown, wrote a letter to Thomas Jefferson, enclosing a newspaper reference to the *Case of the Judges*—the Virginia "Remonstrance" episode we mentioned earlier in connection with *Commonwealth v. Caton.** Cutting professed not to know much about the *Case of the Judges*, but ventured "to applaud the integrity of judges who thus fulfilled their oaths and their duties." Then he added:

> I hope you will not think me too local or envious when I mention that a similar instance has occurred in Massachusetts, where . . . the judges of the Supreme Court solemnly determined that the . . . statute [in question] was unconstitutional. In the very next session there was a formal and unanimous repeal of the law, which perhaps, was unnecessary.[1]

It is not easy to explain how Mr. Cutting's Massachusetts case has remained on the traditional list of judicial review precedents. For no serious scholar believes the case ever existed. The information set forth in the curious letter to Jefferson has never been confirmed by any source.† Moreover, seventy years ago, a noted authority on early Massachusetts legal history conducted an exhaustive investigation of the matter, and conclusively demonstrated in a major article for the *Harvard Law Review* that the case was mythical.[2] Even Profes-

---

* See p. 178, note.

† The letter is remarkable for several reasons, the most apparent being Cutting's inability to understand the press notice he so warmly commended to Jefferson. As we have seen, the court's "Remonstrance" in the 1788 *Case of the Judges,* which the press notice reported, was a respectful plea to the legislature to repeal an act the judges thought was unconstitutional. This was Cutting's "similar instance" in which a court "solemnly determined that [a] statute was unconstitutional"!

sor Haines, whose talents for building legal mansions out of the slenderest straws in the wind are already familiar to us, grudgingly concedes the improbability of Cutting's claim: "[The] absolute supremacy of the Massachusetts Legislature after the renunciation of allegiance to the British Crown makes it unlikely that such a decision . . . could have been rendered relative to a law contrary to the State Constitution.[3]

Still, the case appears on Haines' "list," and on almost everybody else's. Often it is referred to as the "lost Massachusetts precedent" on the theory, apparently, that someday someone may manage to rehabilitate Mr. Cutting. However, we may judge as the real reason for the case's survival the indisputable fact that nine "precedents" are more impressive than merely eight.*

---

* Several writers have speculated as to what might have been on Cutting's mind when he wrote the Jefferson letter. Professor Crosskey surmises that Cutting had read an account of the New Hampshire "case" (which we examine in the next chapter) "in some Massachusetts paper" and carelessly mistook it for a report of a Massachusetts case. Mr. Goodell thought Cutting had in mind the Massachusetts case of *Brattle v. Hinckley,* which, he said, decided that a state law had been superseded by the Treaty of Peace with Great Britain. Professor Haines, for one, follows this theory. Mr. Boudin, however, has shown that if Cutting was thinking of *Brattle v. Hinckley* he totally misunderstood the facts; for when that case was finally decided, the last vestige of the constitutional issue had been removed by the pleadings. Crosskey, op. cit., p. 962; Haines, op. cit., p. 121; Goodell, op. cit., p. 424; Boudin, op. cit., p. 555 et seq.

SOME NEW HAMPSHIRE "OCCURRENCES"

Professor William Crosskey, as must already be evident, has done his homework on these cases, and what is more, has shown himself disposed to frame conclusions in rigorous keeping with the facts. We are therefore bound to treat with respect his judgment that "this New Hampshire decision, or decisions [is] the strongest precedent, and, indeed . . . the only strong precedent, for judicial review, in the traditional list."[1] Crosskey's verdict is the more remarkable for the fact that most precedent-seekers do not bother to discuss the case; Professor Haines, for example, leaves it off his list altogether. Our own view is that while "the strongest precedent" may be an apt characterization, "strong precedent" certainly is not, for reasons that will readily emerge.

Crosskey's main piece of evidence is an item that appeared in the *New Hampshire Spy* on June 30, 1787, asserting—as Crosskey puts it—that the so-called "Ten-Pound Act was *treated* by the New Hampshire courts as 'unconstitutional and therefore not binding upon them.' "[2]

When had New Hampshire courts dealt in this fashion with an act of legislature? No one really knows. Crosskey believes it must have been "sometime during the fall of 1786."[3]

What was the name of the case, or cases, in question? Nobody knows that either—or, for that matter, whether there *was* a "case," in the sense of actual litigation.

What courts were involved? The *Spy* story refers to the "Inferior Court"—apparently that of Rockingham County—but even this matter is open to some question.

Let us, however, hear out Crosskey's attempt to piece together the available evidence. In November 1785, he relates, the New Hampshire legislature enacted the "Ten-Pound Act" which directed that certain civil actions involving less than ten pounds should be tried without a jury. Beginning in June, 1786, serious attempts were made in the legislature to repeal the act on constitutional grounds. These grounds were plainly sound, for the New Hampshire constitution had guaranteed the right of jury trial in all civil cases in which that procedure had been "used and practiced" in the past; and the prior practice had placed the minimum claim for which a jury trial might be demanded, not at ten pounds, but at forty shillings. For a while the repeal efforts seemed on the verge of success, but by the end of the summer of 1786 nothing had been done.[4]

There follows a two-months' hiatus in the evidence Crosskey puts forward. But during this period something apparently happened in one of the New Hampshire courts, having to do with a prosecution under the act—an event, or events, that appear to have stirred a group of New Hampshire citizens. For in December, 1786, according to the *Spy* account of the following June, "petitions were preferred to the assembly either to support the law and impeach the obstinate justices of the Inferior Court, or relieve the subject from execution." Evidently the assembly did not respond directly to the petition: the records of the House of Representatives do show, however, that a vote was taken on Christmas Day that reaffirmed the constitutionality of the act, 44-14.[5]

Another evidentiary gap, this one covering six months, pushes the story ahead to the last week of June, 1787. At this point matters moved quickly to a climax. On June 26, a motion was presented to the House to impeach the judges of the Inferior Court of Common Pleas of Rockingham County for refusing to execute a law. On the 27th, a committee appointed to consider the motion advised that the judges were "not Impeachable for Maladministration as their conduct [was] justified by the constitution of this State." The committee's report was approved 35-21. Also on the 27th, the House voted to draft a bill to repeal the Ten-Pound Act. On the 28th, the Ten-Pound Act was repealed.[6]

"A brief notice of these New Hampshire occurrences," Crosskey remarks, "appeared in several of the Philadelphia papers while the Federal convention was in session." What is more, both of New Hampshire's delegates to the Convention lived in Rockingham County, and so were presumably in a position to give their colleagues a first-hand report. Therefore "it is not to be doubted that . . . some, at least, of the members of the federal Convention knew the facts of these New Hampshire cases"—and knew, most particularly, of the nearly successful attempt to impeach the judges. Meaning? Meaning, in Crosskey's view, that "the men of the Convention" had still further evidence of "*the need of stipulating the right of judicial review in the Constitution and protecting the Supreme Court in the exercise of that right, if they meant that body to have it.*"[7]

Even on Crosskey's showing, then, the New Hampshire occurrences did not amount to much. The case* he believes he found was, with regard to its *scope*, of the B1 variety: the court is represented as having merely protected judicial prerogatives, in this case the right of jury trial. As to *effect*, it could have been no more than a C1 case: we are told the judges simply "treated" the case as "not binding upon them" because of the constitutional conflict. And for that degree of "obstinacy" they were very nearly impeached, although they were certainly standing on firm constitutional ground. This is the most favorable interpretation, we repeat, that is open to the apologists. Is it, however, the one the evidence actually recommends? Consider the following:

There was no contemporary "report" of the alleged case or cases. Not only was there no official report, *the story did not even get into the newspapers* until six to eight months after the "case" is alleged to have been decided. Yet we have seen in our review of the *Rutgers* and *Trevett* cases that when a court, in those times, decided to challenge a legislature, it was News. The absence of contemporary commentary is all the more remarkable in the light of the controversy then swirling around the act the court is supposed to have challenged; the Ten-Pound Act, we may be sure, was very much in the public eye, as witness the long legislative squabble that preceded its repeal. Consider, too, that when the newspapers finally got around to reporting the story, there was no mention of a "case," as such, no mention of who the litigants might have been, no mention of what the court actually "said" in its opinion. Yet one supposes that the *Spy's* reporter would have sought out such information, and could easily have tracked it down, had it existed.

In short, it seems reasonable to suppose that there never was a "case," and that the Rockingham court's intransigence—of which there is evidence aplenty—*consisted precisely in refusing to let such a case take shape*. What Crosskey's data really suggest is that during the fall of 1786 there was an indictment, or perhaps several indictments, to which the Ten-Pound Act applied, but which the Rockingham

---

* Or cases—Crosskey adduces from the foregoing facts that there may have been more than one.

court did not allow to come to trial. What pretext the court used—
that its docket was full, that the issue was still moot before the legislature—is anyone's guess. In any event, the court's delays undoubtedly looked like "obstinacy" to the legislative faction, and its
supporters, that had secured the passage of the act the year before;
whence the pressures on the court in December, 1786, to take action.
Just as likely, the other side of the controversy—the repeal faction—
not only approved the court's feet-dragging, but encouraged it. And
we may imagine the court was persuaded to cooperate with this
faction, in part because it objected to the act, but also because de-
laying tactics could be useful in mobilizing sufficient popular sentiment to force the act's repeal. And when, the following June, the
showdown between the two factions came, the court's recalcitrance
and the merits of the Ten-Pound Act were brought to a vote as, in
effect, a single issue. In this ultimate test of strength, the repeal
faction had the votes to win on both counts.

What this view of the evidence suggests, of course, is that the controversy over the Ten-Pound Act was, all along, essentially a struggle
within the legislative process in which the judges of an inferior court
played a cat's-paw role for one of the contending parties. And if this
is true, the New Hampshire occurrences not only fail to add up to a
judicial review "case"—of any kind; they provide still further evidence
of the quite humble place of the judicary in the political systems of
the American Confederacy.

BAYARD *v.* SINGLETON

We come now to a North Carolina case, the last of the nine and yet the first whose presence on the list is readily understandable.* There is no dispute about the facts of the Newbern case, as *Bayard v. Singleton* was known at the time.†[1] There is no questioning, either, the legal significance of the court's decision: it purported to set aside, on grounds of unconstitutionality, an act of the North Carolina legislature that invaded judicial prerogatives. There is little doubt, moreover, that the decision became known to at least some members of the federal Constitutional Convention while it was still in session. In short, the case appears to have impressive strengths as a judicial review "precedent." All the same these appearances should be run through several tests.

First, what are the circumstances in which the Newbern ruling was handed down? what did the judges actually decide? why did they rule as they did? and still more important, to what extent did their action, as a practical matter, place them in *opposition* to the legislature? Second, we should look closely at the chronology of the affair to see whether, and how, the case might have influenced the proceedings at Philadelphia. Finally, we must pose the question the over-all purpose of this inquiry naturally calls for: Was the Newbern case a part of a continuing tradition of judicial review that began

---

* Curiously, the case occupies a far less prominent place in the literature than some of the others we have seen. The late date of the decision is probably responsible. On the face of it, there are formidable obstacles to arguing that a case that was decided at the very moment the Constitutional Convention was convening, at a place some three weeks removed from Philadelphia (by Professor Crosskey's calculations, who assumes that the news was dispatched by the fastest communications), had a significant bearing on the Convention's deliberations.

† Because of the town where the case arose. The court that heard the case was North Carolina's highest court, then known as the "Court of Conference."

with Lord Coke and culminated in the Constitution of 1787—a part of Professor Haines' "irresistible process"? Or was it, rather, an anachronism in American legal history which—in one quite remarkable aspect of the case—anticipated a *new* tradition that was to take hold, not at the Constitutional Convention, but at a considerably later moment?

To begin with, *Bayard v. Singleton* was the B1 case to end all B1 cases. The integrity of the judicial process was at stake, not only because the North Carolina legislature had tried to deny the established right of jury trial in a certain type of case, but because it had tried, in effect, to deny the courts the right to hear such cases at all. The legislature had enacted the law in question in 1785 as an adjunct of North Carolina's war policy of confiscating Tory property. It provided that in the event a wartime confiscation should be challenged in a subsequent legal action, the defendant had merely to file an affidavit with the court asserting the disputed property had been obtained "under a sale from a commissioner of forfeited estates."[2] Whereupon the court was required to dismiss the suit on motion, without looking into the merits of the case. The court did not even have the right, it would seem from the language of the statute, to inquire into the truth of the affidavit. Here, then, was an instance where a legislature sought to accomplish a deprivation of legal rights, clearly guaranteed by the state constitution, by the simple expedient of denying litigants access to the judicial process.

The act was put to the test in the summer of 1786, when Mr. and Mrs. Bayard brought suit to recover some family property in Newbern that had been confiscated during the war. Singleton, the beneficiary of the forfeiture, replied by filing the stipulated affidavit, together with a motion to dismiss the suit. Instead of immediately granting the motion, however, the court entertained "long arguments . . . on constitutional points." At the close of the argument, according to the official report, one of the judges ventured the remark that North Carolina had, after all, divided its political system "into separate and distinct branches [with] several and distinct powers, and prescribing their several limits and boundaries." And the reporter added: "This he said without disclosing a single sentiment upon the cause of the proceeding, or the law introduced in support of it."[3]

That was all the court did with the case at that time, but it was enough to get the judges haled before the legislature the following winter to answer charges of insubordination. For the court was clearly dragging its heels with regard to enforcing the summary judgment provisions of the act. A legislative committee found the judges guilty on the facts, but the legislature itself decided against punitive action on the grounds the court's conduct did not amount to malpractice.[4] But then the legislature took an even more significant step. Earlier in the session, the same faction, apparently, that generated the proceedings against the judges, had proposed a formal instruction to the courts requiring them, in effect, to treat the constitution and legislative enactments as equally authoritative. Now if this resolution had passed, it would have amounted to an implicit legislative order to grant Singleton's motion to dismiss. Yet the legislature decisively rejected the proposal, 58-24.[5] Thus what had begun as a legislative attempt to intimidate the court probably ended up encouraging the court. The judges very likely concluded from what had happened that a majority of the legislature was itself unhappy about the summary judgment act, but was not yet willing to risk the political consequences of trying to repeal it—was not, that is, totally adverse to transferrng that unpleasant task to another branch of the government.

Nonetheless, the judges proceeded warily when they again took up the case the following May. The court's first move was to try to persuade Singleton to *consent* to a jury trial on the grounds that, otherwise, his title would never be secure, inasmuch as the summary judgment act was bound to be repealed "sooner or later."[6] Singleton, however, stuck to his guns. Another compromise solution was then proposed, but it too was rejected. Whereupon, in the reporter's words: "after every reasonable endeavor had been used in vain for avoiding a disagreeable difference between the Legislature and the judicial powers of the State, at length with much apparent reluctance, but with great deliberation and firmness" the court declared that the act of 1785 must "stand as abrogated and without any effect."[7]

In the end, however, the court's differences with the legislature proved far less "disagreeable" than the reporter had feared. For the jury that was then sworn promptly decided *for* Singleton, thus enabling the court to uphold the forfeiture after all. In sum, the court seems never to have really crossed the legislature on any policy issues: on the one hand, the court invalidated the summary judgment provision, which was apparently becoming an embarrassment to the legislature—as witness both what had happened during the legislative session the previous winter, and the court reporter's remark that the provision was due to be repealed "sooner or later"; and on the other, the court upheld the legislature's anti-Tory confiscation policy. It is for this reason that Professor Crosskey calls the court's theoretical challenge to the legislative power "something of a flash in the pan."[8]

Still, a signal event occurred in Newbern, North Carolina, in the late spring of 1787, and we must resist any temptation to play it down. For all the mitigating circumstances, it remains that a judicial court formally proclaimed that a legislative act must, for constitutional reasons, *"stand as abrogated."* This was a form of words never before uttered from a judicial bench in America, or for that matter in the Anglo-Saxon world. What is more, the words implied a far deeper doctrinal breach, vis-à-vis the rule of legislative supremacy, than even that which had been urged theretofore by the avant garde of the judicial power, for example, by Mr. Varnum in the *Trevett* case. For the Newbern judges were saying, not merely that they could not *enforce* the law—which would have made *Bayard v. Singleton* a C1 case as to its *effect*; rather, they seem to have been advancing the C2 theory that the law was, *by force of the court's judgment,* "abrogated"—that is, "abolished," "repealed," "stricken from the books." Whether the legislature actually understood the court to be asserting the power of annulment, and so consciously acquiesced in it, we do not know; but we do know that although the decision caused considerable public ferment in North Carolina during the summer of 1787, the legislature never got around to making the formal remonstrance that was presumably indicated by the canons of legislative supremacy.

Much has been written about what happened when news of the Newbern case reached Philadelphia.[9] We may summarize the speculation as follows: The court announced its decision sometime during the last ten days of May, 1787. Given the various transportation possibilities, the news could have arrived in Philadelphia by mid-June, and it probably got there sometime in July. It most certainly had arrived by August 12, when one of the North Carolina delegates, Richard Dobbs Spaight, wrote home an indignant letter denouncing the decision. The relevant question for our purposes, of course, is whether the decision actually influenced the Convention—and more particularly whether it helped persuade the framers they could ease the power of judicial review into the system of government they were creating without expressly providing for it. The question is necessarily speculative, but such circumstantial evidence as can be adduced does not leave the answer much in doubt. And that answer must be in the negative.

In the first place, no reference at all to the case appears in the records of the Convention's proceedings, or in the contemporary Philadelphia newspapers. This suggests that if anyone knew about the case outside of the North Carolina delegation, it did not create much of a stir. But second, if word did get around—in informal discussion, say—the initiative was more than likely taken by Richard Dobbs Spaight, who we know felt rather strongly on the subject. What Spaight, who was later to become North Carolina's governor, had to say about the case to his Philadelphia colleagues can be imagined from the letter he wrote on August 12 to James Iredell, Bayard's lawyer in the Newbern proceedings. "The late determination of our judges at Newbern," Spaight told Iredell,

> must produce the most serious reflections in the breast of every thinking man, and of every well-wisher to his country. . . . I do not pretend to vindicate the [summary judgment] law; it is immaterial what law they have declared void; it is their usurpation of the authority to do it, that I complain of, as I do most positively deny that they have any such power. . . . Besides, it would have been absurd, and contrary to the practice of all the world, had the Constitution vested such powers in [the court], as they would have operated as an absolute negative on the proceedings of the Legislature, which no judiciary ought ever to possess. [Should the judges be granted that authority], the State . . . would be subject to the will of three individuals, who united in their own persons the legislative and judiciary powers, which no monarch in Europe enjoys, and which would be more despotic than the Roman Decemvirate, and equally as insufferable.[10]

Spaight's letter suggests a third point. Had Spaight understood his Philadelphia colleagues to be writing into the federal Constitution an authority he deemed "more despotic than the Roman Decemvirate," may we not be reasonably sure that he would have risen at some juncture during the convention proceedings to enter an objection? According to the records, he never spoke on the subject.

Fourth, even if Spaight's colleagues took a view of the Newbern case different from Spaight's own—that is, even if they approved the decision*—they could not have been unmindful of the danger to the

---

* As they may possibly have been encouraged to do by North Carolina's other delegate, William R. Davie, who was, at one point, Iredell's co-counsel in the Newbern case. However, there is no record of Davie having discussed the case at the Convention.

court implicit in Spaight's attitude—namely, that some heads were likely to roll down in North Carolina, just as comparable provocations in other States had set in motion vigorous legislative reprisals. Which would have been another reason, had the framers intended to institute judicial review, to have provided some safeguards. While we know that the North Carolina legislature eventually let the matter drop, no such assurance was available to the men in Philadelphia in the summer of 1787.

And fifth: there *is*, after all, a hard chronological obstacle to supposing the Newbern case had the influence some of the apologists attribute to it. For while the news arrived before the Convention was over, it probably did not arrive before the speeches were delivered and the decisions made that, in the apologists' view, show the framers intended to institute judicial review. These matters are treated at greater length elsewhere,* but we may note two items here. For instance, the one and only occasion on which a delegate referred to the alleged state precedents for judicial review occurred on June 4 in a speech by Elbridge Gerry, well ahead of the earliest moment when news of the North Carolina decision might have reached Philadelphia. More importantly, the Supremacy Clause, (which is the sine qua non of the apologists' appeal to the text of the Constitution) had already been considered and *adopted*, as part of the Convention's working draft, by July 17. This does not leave much time, even if we accept the July arrival estimate, for the Newbern case to have figured in the decision, and it excludes the possibility altogether if, as seems reasonable to us, the news arrived close to the moment in the second week of August when Spaight struck off his heated protest to Iredell.

Returning now to the Newbern case itself, let us try to answer the third question posed at the beginning of this chapter. Does *Bayard v. Singleton* fall neatly into place as the capstone of a continuing tradition of judicial review, as the apologists suggest? or were the participants at Newbern, in effect, staking out new ground?

The short answer to the question is, of course, that there *was* no previous tradition. We have devoted considerable attention to the point, and have seen that while the idea that judges might question legislative acts was "in the air" prior to 1787,—e.g., in the *Rutgers* and *Trevett* cases, and maybe in New Hampshire—that is just where it stayed when the time came for handing down formal opinions.

---

* See "Judicial Review at the Constitutional Convention," below.

Another way of answering the question is to ask how the participants themselves treated the case. Did the judges suppose they were
doing what just any old court might do under the circumstances?
Had the attorneys, as attorneys always do when they can, referred
the court to an impressive line of precedents and other authorities
for the course they were recommending? What kind of *argument*
finally persuaded the court to take the action it did? Unfortunately,
the court's opinion was apparently truncated by the official reporter
and is thus only slightly helpful. As it stands, the report mentions
two arguments. First, there was the reasoning, *reductio ad absurdum*,
that if the legislators were conceded the power to disregard the constitution as they had done in 1785, there would be no logical reason
why they should not also make "themselves the legislators of the
State for life" and hand their authority "down to their heirs male
forever."[11] And then the further sophistry that since the legislators
could not change the constitution without "destroy[ing] their own
[claim to] existence," the constitution stood "in full force."[12] The report makes no reference, be it noted, to any previous cases or authorities, American or English.

Now we may agree that more serious arguments than these probably moved the judges—arguments the reporter may have thought
better of publicly attributing to the court. And for clues to what they
might have been, we may summon Mr. James Iredell, whom we have
already met as the recipient of Richard Dobbs Spaight's letter from
Philadelphia. Iredell was then a prominent North Carolina attorney,
and would later be appointed to the United States Supreme Court;
but he figures in our story as chief counsel to Bayard in the Newbern
proceedings.

Iredell's remarks at the trial have not been preserved, but we may
agree with Brinton Coxe that "what must have been said" on that
occasion can be gathered from Iredell's reply to the Spaight letter,
written on August 26, 1787, and from a public letter he published
the previous summer while the case was still under consideration.[13]
These documents have one thing in common with the reporter's official record: they reveal not the slightest interest, on Iredell's part,
in some "tradition" allegedly sired by Sir Edward Coke; or in the
supposed "natural" duty of judges to enforce a "higher law" against
irreverent legislators; or in the practice of other American or English
jurisdictions, to say nothing of the North Carolina courts. Yet he
surely would have cited any or all of these authorities—for he was
not an unlearned man—if he could have done so responsibly and persuasively. On the contrary, Iredell approached his task as though it

presented a *new* question, and proceeded to deal with it by the naked force of logic. The point is not that the logic was unanswerable, but that it was a logic without appeal to authority, a logic consciously tailored to what Iredell believed to be a new and unique *American* situation.

Our own editorial intrusions in the argument are designed merely to clarify; the emphases throughout are Iredell's:

When the United States became independent, "we were not ignorant of the theory *of the necessity of the Legislature being absolute in all cases,* because it was the great ground of the British pretensions. [However], when we were at liberty to form a government as we thought best . . . we decisively gave our sentiments against it. . . ."

How "decisively"?

We created a legislature whose powers are "limited and defined [by a] Constitution: our Legislature is a *creature* of the Constitution. (I hope this is an expression not prosecutable.) "

But there was nothing "decisive" about that, as Iredell's little joke about "prosecution" made all too clear. The question remained: Who was to have the last word in *interpreting* and *enforcing* the constitution? Under Great Britain's unwritten constitution, that power had been left tacitly to Parliament itself, and the written constitutions of North Carolina and the other American States had said not a word to the contrary. Iredell evidently recognized that the argument was, so far, question-begging, for he promptly moved to different ground:

All may agree "the Assembly have not a *right* to violate the Constitution" and we must therefore ask: What remedy is available "if they *in fact* do so"? "The great argument [of the legislative supremists]"—and now Iredell prepares to take on the contentions of Locke and Vattel—is that there are three remedies:

1. "A humble petition [by the people] that the law may be repealed."
2. Dismissal of the offending legislators in the next election.
3. "Universal resistance of the people"—that is, revolution.

To which Iredell replied:

1. The idea of petitioning the legislature to enforce the constitution is denigrating to a free people: "are we to petition [the legislators] that they will be graciously pleased not to be our tyrants?"

2. The next election is not an adequate guarantee of redress: "a new election . . . would only secure the views of a majority; where-

as every citizen . . . should have a surer pledge for his constitutional rights than the wisdom and activity of any occasional majority."

3. And revolution is a "dreadful expedient indeed." Moreover, revolutions do not occur except where there is *"universal oppression"*; meanwhile, "a thousand injuries may be suffered, and many hundreds ruined. . . . Suppose a law is passed by which I am ruined. Have I interest enough to overturn the government of my country?"

Having thus disposed of the "usual" remedies as either insufferable or inadequate to safeguard the integrity of the constitution, Iredell ventured to ask, with a marked diffidence in tone, "whether the judicial authority hath any power to interfere. . . ." By way of answer he proposed a syllogism: judges have the duty "to decide [cases] according to the *laws of the State*"; but "the Constitution is a *law of the State*"—not only that, it is a law "superior" to any other of the State; therefore if a case should arise involving the "law" of the Constitution, the judges must decide the case in conformity with this "superior" law—even if in so doing they must disregard an "inferior" law of the legislature. This does not mean "the judges are appointed arbiters . . . as it were [to decide] whether the Assembly have or have not violated the Constitution"; it means merely that when both types of "laws" are "necessarily brought in judgment before them, they must, unavoidably, determine one way or another."

The judges, then, did have the power to interfere; it was a matter of logical necessity. Still, *ought* they to exercise the power, given the possibilities of "abuse"? One answer Iredell gave is that judges can abuse their power in any event: "every Act of Assembly may occasionally come under their judgment in one shape or another, and *those acts may be wilfully misconstrued as well as the Constitution.*" The other answer—which Iredell appears to have felt safer with— is that they would not dare to abuse it. While North Carolina judges had tenure, "their salaries are precarious . . . they [are] only nominally independent in point of station, when the Assembly may every session determine how much they shall have to subsist upon."

A final point for which Iredell saw no need to supply emphasis, but which might bear remarking in our time: "In all doubtful cases, to be short, the Act [of Legislature] ought to be supported: it should be unconstitutional beyond any dispute before it is pronounced such."

So much for the arguments of Mr. Iredell. The reader may be temped to dismiss them as old stuff. He has probably become acquainted with them as part of his growing up from teachers who typically treat them as *very* "old stuff." And if his interests happen to have carried him into a study of constitutional law, he will certainly have read them for himself—from the pen of Chief Justice Marshall in *Marbury v. Madison*, who, it is true, treated them as "old stuff" even in 1803. But before dismissing the matter thus lightly, he is entitled to ask his teachers the names of those contemporaries of Iredell who were speaking, or writing, as he was at the time the Constitution was framed—or, for that matter, the name of just one such man. For our part, we credit James Iredell of North Carolina with having written the first systematic exegesis of an American doctrine of judicial review, and find him to be, so to speak, the John the Baptist of that institution whose voice, in 1787, was crying in a deep wilderness.

A SUMMARY

We are now in a position to enter some general judgments on the "rapid succession" of state cases between 1776 and 1787 that are said to have made the already "firm" principle of judicial review an all-but-inevitable feature of the federal Constitution.

I. We began with nine possible contenders. Close examination of these nine clearly eliminated six of them. The *Case of Josiah Philips, Holmes v. Walton, Commonwealth v. Caton, Rutgers v. Waddington,* the *Symsbury Case,* and the "lost" Massachusetts case cannot possibly be regarded by responsible scholarship as "precedents" for any kind of judicial review. This leaves *Trevett v. Weeden,* the New Hampshire case, and *Bayard v. Singleton* as the only cases worth talking about. The *Trevett* case is a dubious precedent for judicial invalidation of legislative acts, if only because the judges in the case stoutly denied they had done any such thing and could point to their record to prove it. The New Hampshire case is dubious too, if only because of the strong probability there never was such a case. *Bayard v. Singleton* is dubious, if only because it was decided too late to have influenced the framers.

II. *Each of the cases worth talking about raised a B1 question with regard to the scope of the judicial power. In each instance, that is to say, the courts were called upon to defend the integrity of the judicial process.* In two of the cases (assuming the New Hampshire "occurrences" amounted to a case), the issue at stake was the right to a jury trial, and in the third, the right to have any trial at all. On the previous pages we observed how three courts struggled with that kind of brazen challenge to judicial prerogatives, and we saw that they did so with great hesitation and understandable fear. Now, as we try to summarize the state of affairs in 1787, it is even more important to note that no case prior to the framing of the federal Constitution so much as hinted that the scope of the judicial power of review extended beyond that kind of challenge—no suggestion at all, that is, that the courts were competent to arbitrate the meaning of a state constitution as a whole.

III. With regard to the *effect* of judicial review, two of the three cases worth talking about—*Bayard v. Singleton* is the exception—are C1 cases. No court save the Newbern judges presumed to go further than to decline to *enforce* the law in question. There was no talk of "voiding" or "invalidating" legislation; no suggestion that the law under dispute had ceased to be a law. And while the Newbern judges did purport to strike the summary judgment act from the books, even there, we must remember, it took two parties to *effect* the nullification: the legislature had to acquiesce in the judges' ruling in order for the power of nullification to be recognized. But since there was no opportunity to ascertain the North Carolina legislature's reaction to the Newbern ruling before the Philadelphia convention adjourned, it may therefore be said: *there is not a single case to support the proposition that a judicial power* to nullify *an act of legislature was recognized in the American States prior to the framing of the federal Constitution.* And if there was no real C2 case, there was most emphatically no C3 case embodying the modern notion that the court's word in such matters is "final"—the definitive interpretation of the constitution, and binding as such on all.

IV. Each of the real cases involved a clear-cut legislative violation of the constitution. No one, that is to say, can accuse the pre-1787 courts in the United States of writing their own opinions into a constitution, of helping a "living" Constitution "grow"—as is often said approvingly about our modern courts. In each case the law in question was a flagrant usurpation of power and plainly violated the state constitution. That such self-evident transgressions were a *pre-condition* for judicial review, not even James Iredell had the slightest doubt.

V. Whenever the courts made so bold as to question a legislative act, even within the narrow limits we have remarked, an angry, indignant and vengeful reaction set in—both in the legislature and in the general community—and in every case the reaction was of such proportions that the judges had good reason to fear for their jobs. Moreover, this kind of reaction occurred even in cases—e.g., *Holmes v. Walton* and *Rutgers v. Waddington*—where the court did not actually question the legislature's authority, but was merely reputed to have done so. The American people's extreme sensitivity to this kind of thing is therefore beyond dispute, and we may say flatly, well known to the framers of the federal Constitution.

A final word before leaving the pre-Constitutional "tradition" of judicial review. We have been examining in the previous pages the experience of the American people with the idea of judicial review before 1787—the extent of the experience, the kind of experience it was, how the people received it—and we have been hoping such data would give us a picture of the idea's status in the American community at the time the federal Constitution was drafted. That hope can be fulfilled, however, only if we remember that the matters we have been dealing with represent only a small corner of the picture. The rest of the picture can be seen only if we stop to ponder what the American community was thinking and saying and doing during those eleven years when it was *not* occupied by the handful of episodes we have had under consideration. We can hardly get a reliable "feel" of the pre-Constitutional era, that is to say, without considering the constitutions that were not adopted, the laws that were not enacted, the court decisions that were not handed down, the lawyers' arguments that were not heard, the speeches that were not delivered, the books and pamphlets that were not written—challenging the doctrine of legislative supremacy the American States had inherited from Great Britain. And once we have thought a bit about that, we shall finally be in a position to evaluate the claim that something resembling our modern theories of judicial review and judicial supremacy was firmly embedded in the pre-Constitutional American tradition. Perhaps then we will be able to appreciate how outrageous that suggestion really is—and how irresponsible the legal scholarship that has endorsed it.

E PLURIBUS UNUM

THE PROBLEM AT PHILADELPHIA

It would be fatuous for a chronicler of modern history to account for the League of Nations as the natural outgrowth of an ancient search by the Great Powers for means of settling their disputes by international arbitration and collective sanctions. For the going historical pattern—the "tradition"—was of just the opposite tendency. The events of 1919 might put the historian in mind of certain aberrational precedents, like Prince Metternich's variously motivated Council of Europe. But he would know that since the High Middle Ages, since the collapse of Christendom conceived as an organic community beholden to an authority beyond itself, the idea of a supernational order had no significant place in the main stream of Western political thought. And he would know that, in practice, the omens for such a development were even less favorable: with each passing decade of the modern era, the law of nations had become increasingly indistinguishable from the law of the jungle.

It would be equally fatuous for our historian, situated now as an observer of the proceedings at Versailles, to have pronounced—in the name of the going tradition—that no such peace enforcement machinery as that proposed by Woodrow Wilson could conceivably be adopted by the assembled diplomats. For historians know that traditions *can* be broken—even abruptly broken—provided there are plain and urgent reasons for doing so. Men are creative beings, potentially: they have wit and will. They are not entirely creatures of habit, or prisoners of their pasts. They are capable of responding to new challenges relevantly, of giving to new problems apt solutions; and the unprecedented dimensions of the Great War just finished had undoubtedly posed a new kind of problem. A search for means of avoiding comparable catastrophes in the future was thus not only conceivable but likely; predictably, the Powers would be willing to turn over new ground.

What is more—and here is the key element of the kind of historical phenomenon we are considering—such a break with tradition would not be brought about casually or haphazardly: men prolong traditions *silently*, but they usually sever them with a bang. The innovators normally respond to the motivating cause consciously, deliberately—and, openly. So it was with the founding of the League of Nations. A tradition was being broken, and no one was left in doubt— neither the negotiators at Versailles nor the world that watched their work—that those first modern probings toward collective security heralded a new era in international diplomacy.

We make these observations, surely not controversial ones, to give some perspective to the apologists' second major thesis about the origins of judicial review. That thesis, we may recall, asserts that the framers of the federal Constitution thought themselves to be providing for judicial review in the document they drew up at Philadelphia. Yet we have seen in the previous pages that American opinion and practice down to the summer of 1787 was distinctly hostile to judicial review—that the American "tradition" emphatically affirmed the principle of *legislative* supremacy. So we are saying now, simply, that incorporation of judicial review into the new national charter would necessarily constitute a sharp break with the going tradition, and that therefore we should expect the framers to have taken the step consciously, deliberately, openly. Or, to put this more concretely: we ought to be able to determine whether, in fact, a break occurred, and if so, to assess its dimensions, by a) identifying the exact nature of the challenge that might have prompted the framers to depart from the tradition of legislative supremacy; and b) consulting the public records—the various "draft plans" the delegates considered, the speeches they delivered, the provisions they finally agreed upon—to see how the Convention actually responded to that challenge. The framers were neither fools who might have made revolutionary changes in the American political system unawares, nor conspirators who might have tried to do so surreptitiously. And even if the Convention delegates had been disposed to "pull a fast one," there is no chance at all—given the high level of political sophistication of the times, and the open procedures they themselves stipulated for ratifying the Constitution—that they could have succeeded.

The challenge the framers confronted has been memorialized in our national motto, *E Pluribus Unum*. We have long described ourselves as one nation composed of many nations; but it was the framers' task to bring that arrangement into being. This was the mission

that had brought them to Philadelphia. Full local autonomy—
which is to say the autonomy of the individual state legislatures—had
proved to be an inconvenience of such magnitude as to jeopardize
the new country's nationhood. As a result, most of the leading men
of the country understood that the principle of *local* legislative supremacy, where *"national"* interests were at stake, would have to give
way. What it was to give way *to* was, quite naturally, the overriding
issue at the Constitutional Convention.

The problem would have been relatively simple, if the goal had
been merely national unity: the judicial, executive, and legislative
powers then exercised by the several States could have been consolidated in a central government on the pattern of the old state constitutions. That solution, among other things, would have raised the
prevailing principle of legislative supremacy to a super-State level;
and the problem of keeping the individual States in line with "national" policy, which had so grievously beset the Union under the
Articles of Confederation, would thereafter be settled by force
majeure. But as Madison and others who tended toward such nationalist solutions had to be reminded over and over again during the
summer of 1787, the task of the Convention was not only to create
the *unum*, but also to preserve the *plures*. The supremacy of the
Union had to be established, but not at the expense of eliminating
the States as self-governing political entities. The challenge to the
framers, then, was to pierce the dilemma of dual sovereignty—to find
a formula for keeping wayward States in line with the policy of the
Union while at the same time protecting the States against the danger
of tyranny by a Union government. This was not a challenge written
in blood, like that of the Great War; but it was no less stark on that
account. The framers well appreciated that the ingenuity and skill
and political understanding they brought to bear on the dilemma
would largely determine the future liberty and contentment of the
American commonwealth.

To the modern mind, which tends to mechanistic rather than organic solutions to political problems, there may seem to be a quite
obvious response to the challenge described above. What was needed
to adjudicate potential disputes between the States and the central
government was, plainly, an "umpire." And many of us today, including some of our brightest citizens, think of the federal Supreme Court
as having been given, and as now performing, precisely that role.
Thus it may be of some value, before examining the very different
way in which the framers in fact met the challenge, to note that the

members of the Constitutional Convention undoubtedly considered
the umpire idea as their sessions were getting under way—and rejected
it. We do not know with whom the idea originated. On May 23, 1787,
an anonymous pamphlet appeared in Philadelphia under the title
"Fragments on the Confederation of the American States," which
proposed a number of reforms to the Articles of Confederation; the
most important proposal was the idea of an "Equalizing Court."
Twelve days later (ten days after the Convention began its business)
the proposal was published in the *Freeman's Journal* of Philadelphia,
and from there was quickly picked up by other newspapers throughout
the States.[1]

The "Equalizing Court," the pamphlet said, was to be "an umpire
between Congress and the States." The Court was to have three
judges, each representing a "division" or grouping of States—the
grouping presumably to be determined in a way that would assure
fair representation of diverse sectional interests; and the judges themselves were to be chosen by lot, for life terms, from a list of nominees
submitted by the state legislatures in each grouping. The jurisdiction
was to be narrow, but of the highest order: it would hear appeals by
Congress against a State—alleging disobedience of valid congressional acts; and by a State against Congress—alleging the enactment
of unauthorized Union laws. Congress and the States were to be the
actual parties in such litigation. The Court's decision, most important
of all, was to be "final" and "binding."

Save for a procedural technicality (the fact that today the States
and the federal government are seldom the official parties in litigation between them), it will be seen that the Equalizing Court's "umpiring" duties implied a role very similar to that which the framers,
on the modern accounting, are supposed to have assigned to the Supreme Court.* We remark on the proposal to make clear that the
generation of 1787 was quite capable of imagining such a solution
to the problem of federalism, and had no difficulty finding an appropriate formula for enunciating it. Moreover, in view of the wide-

---

* To be sure, the proposed "Equalizing Court" and the Supreme Court
would differ in the manner by which their members were chosen; thus it
might be argued that the former would have been beholden to the States
while the latter has naturally considered itself a spokesman for the federal
government. We submit, however, that the method of appointment, as a
factor in determining a court's bias, is greatly overrated. Despite some opinion
to the contrary, there is little convincing evidence that the Constitution's
scheme for appointing Supreme Court judges has prejudiced them in favor
of the federal government, that the justices have deemed themselves, in

spread publicity the proposal received, we may be certain the framers themselves were well aware of it, and so rejected it with their eyes wide open. What is more, they evidently did so out of hand, for there was no discussion of that proposal, or any resembling it, during the Convention proceedings. To the framers, the "umpire" court undoubtedly looked synthetic—a "gimmick" attuned neither to the American tradition nor to the new power realities that were bound to emerge under a federal system. Accordingly, they approached the problem along a quite different route.

Rejection of the "Congressional Negative"

From the outset of its deliberations the Convention's "working paper" was the so-called Virginia Plan submitted by Edmund Randolph on May 27.[2] The Virginia draft (historians assume it was mainly the work of James Madison) was a highly nationalistic scheme, and not surprisingly gave the legislative branch of the proposed national government the dominant role. In addition to the powers it had enjoyed under the Articles of Confederation, Congress was to have the broad and otherwise unqualified authority "to legislate in all cases in which the separate States [were] incompetent." Moreover, Congress would choose the Executive. The only check on Congress envisioned by the Virginia Plan was a "Council of Revision," composed of the Executive and some members of the national judiciary. The Council would have the power to veto legislation—i.e., the same quasi-legislative power that was ultimately given to the President alone, except that under the Virginia Plan the veto could not be overridden.* The draft also provided for a national judiciary that would consist of one or more "supreme courts" as well as inferior

---

some sense, the agents of the President and Senators who gave them their jobs. Or, looking at the matter the other way around, had the "Equalizing Court" been incorporated in the Constitution, we suspect a John Marshall would have been on it at an early date.

* As we saw earlier in assessing New York's Council of Revision, such a veto power is not to be confused with the power of judicial review. The Council's mandate was not to determine the *constitutionality* of legislation— though presumably it would take this factor into account, as, indeed, Congress would have done when it first enacted the legislation. Rather, the Council would have been at liberty to pass upon the wisdom and desirability of the legislation, and would thus have constituted, in effect, a third chamber of the legislature, lacking only the power of initiating legislation. Moreover, the Council was hardly an independent force under the Virginia scheme, since the legislature was to choose the executive directly and the participating judges indirectly.

courts—details as to the latter to be left for future determination by the Congress. The draft listed certain categories of cases to which the national judicial power would extend, but neither this provision, nor any others, implied a judicial power to pass upon the validity of legislation, either state or national.

The central feature of the Virginia Plan was, as we might expect, its approach to the problem of Union-State relations. And it was in that matter that the nationalistic tendencies of the Virginians, and those who supported their plan, were most plainly revealed. For Congress was to be given the further power to *"negative all laws passed by the several States, contravening, in the opinion of the National Legislature, the Articles of Union."* Moreover, should Congress' judgment be ignored or resisted, that body would be authorized "to call forth the force of the Union against any member of the Union failing to fulfill its duties under the Articles. . . ."

Here, then, in the Virginia Plan, was a straightforward answer to the problem of federalism. Who was to determine the boundary line between Union and state power? *Congress* was to do that, the Virginians said, and let there be no mistake about it. To be sure, Congress' mandate was theoretically subordinated to the "Articles of the Union" (that is, to the Constitution), for Congress was empowered to disallow state legislation only on the grounds the legislation "contravene[d] the Articles." However, the sweeping residuary grant mentioned above—Congress' power "to legislate in all cases" in which it deemed the States "incompetent"—plus the fact that no *other* body was authorized to construe the Articles, made Congress' power in this decisive area of constitutional interpretation, in effect, plenary. And the further provision for enforcing the Constitution by military means, coming as it did directly after the provision for the "congressional negative," served only to drive that point home.

Now we may assert flatly, without fear of serious dispute, that if the Constitution had embraced the "congressional negative," it would not have been ratified. As things worked out the framers were strongly pressed during the ratification campaign to defend the Constitution against the charge that it was a charter for obliterating the States. Plainly, the inclusion of the "congressional negative" would have clinched the argument for the Constitution's enemies. What the Virginia planners did not sufficiently understand, or so their arguments in the early weeks of the Convention suggest, is that the American community, at the deepest level of political consciousness, was searching for a *federal* solution to the crisis of Union impotency. Familiarity with that word was not essential. Inarticulate as well as articulate sentiment sensed an antagonism between coherence of the Union— one desideratum; and local autonomy—another; and so was looking for a synthesis that would, somehow, combine the two. In a word, Americans were determined to eat their cake and also to have it, and they expected the men at Philadelphia to devise a formula for doing so. Yet the Virginia planners, in order to escape one horn of the dilemma we mentioned earlier, had leaped onto the other: to cure Union impotency they had proposed Union omnipotency; and that remedy was doomed by the country's mood.

After the first flush of nationalist triumphs during May and June, the country's mood began to make itself felt at the Convention. The reaction came, as might be expected, from the weaker States, which stood to suffer most from a consolidation of power. It took the form, in the first instance, of a new draft-Constitution, submitted to the convention on June 15 by William Paterson of New Jersey.[3] The details of the New Jersey Plan need not detain us; we are concerned only with its key provision—the clause that sought to solve the problem of Union-State relations: the problem of how to enforce Union supremacy while at the same time safeguarding state integrity. That clause of the New Jersey Plan read:

> The legislative acts of the United States made by virtue and in pursuance of the articles of Union and all Treaties made and ratified under the authority of the United States shall be the supreme law of the respective States as far as those acts or Treaties shall relate to the said States, or their citizens and inhabitants, and the Judiciaries of the several States shall be bound thereby in their decisions, anything in the respective laws of the individual States to the contrary notwithstanding.

The reader will readily recognize this language as a primitive version of the Supremacy Clause of the present Constitution.

During the month that followed, the Convention devoted its attention to hammering out a series of compromises between—let us call them henceforth—the "nationalizers" and the "States'-righters" regarding representation in the legislature, the method of selecting the executive, and related matters concerning the make-up of the Union government; and thus postponed the critical issue of how the will of the Union government was to be enforced against the States. On July 17, however, the showdown came swiftly and decisively. The congressional negative, which had appeared to command overwhelming support in the early days of the Convention, was now brought under fire even by such nationalizers as Gouverneur Morris. Madison vigorously led the defenders of the "negative," but when the vote was called, the States'-righters won hands down, with only the Virginia, Massachusetts, and North Carolina delegations dissenting.[4] With the defeat of the congressional negative, Luther Martin of Maryland, on behalf of the States'-righters, moved the adoption of the New Jersey supremacy provision as a substitute. This motion was approved unanimously.[5] After several modifications in August and September by the Committees on Detail and Style, and one on August 23 by the Convention itself, the Supremacy Clause was finally adopted as it presently appears in Article VI of the Constitution:

> This Constitution and the Laws of the United States which shall be made in pursuance thereof; and all Treaties made, or which shall be made, under the Authority of the United States, shall be the Supreme Law of the Land, and the Judges in every State shall be bound thereby, any Thing in the Constitution or Laws of any State to the contrary notwithstanding.

Without prejudice to a detailed examination of the Supremacy Clause which follows in the next chapters, let us note carefully the historical fact that indisputably emerges from the sequence of events just related. *The Constitution's vaunted Supremacy Clause, so often cited as definitive authority for the federal government's exclusive right to determine the boundary line between federal and state power, was made the hub of the constitutional scheme—not by those framers, the nationalizers, who wished to entrust such a right to a national government and who had proposed a straightforward method for doing so—but at the behest of the champions of States' rights who, having defeated the nationalizers' proposal, thought themselves to be substituting a more "federal" solution to the problem of constitutional enforcement.* Whether this apparent paradox can be dismissed as merely a curious twist of history, or perhaps as a case of an author not fully appreciating the meaning of his own words, are questions we may hope to resolve by a closer look at the text of the Supremacy Clause and of related provisions. That is the task to which we now turn.

THE MEANING OF
THE SUPREMACY CLAUSE, I

The guardians of our present political Establishment, as we re-marked earlier, have managed to inhibit opposition to judicial law-making by reminding dissidents that a Supreme Court decision, what-ever one may think of it, is the "supreme law of the land." Any talk of *resisting* an alleged transgression by the Court, they insist, is es-sentially insurrectionary; and the dogma that a Supreme Court de-cision and the "supreme law of the land" are one and the same thing has been so successfully inculcated over the past decade—by the press, television, and radio, from lecture platforms and from pulpits, and by Presidents representing both political parties—that many, probably most, Americans are today fully convinced that no other reading of the Constitution is possible. Should a *New York Times* editorial writer one day remark in the course of scolding Southern interpositionists that "according to Article VI of the Constitution, '*the decisions of the Supreme Court . . . shall be regarded as the supreme Law of the Land,*'" it is a safe guess that most of the *Times*' learned clientele would pass over the purported quotation without blinking an eye.

We must, then, get one thing straight. According to the Supremacy Clause, "this Constitution"; "the laws of the United States" made "in pursuance" of the Constitution; and "Treaties"—*these* and only these are "the supreme Law of the Land." Nothing else. Not even by re-mote implication are the Supreme Court and its decisions included among the things that make up the supreme law.

More: the Supreme Court and its decisions are not mentioned *at all* in the Supremacy Clause. The Supreme Court, that is to say, is not named even as the agency charged with *enforcing* (much less with defining) the supreme law. More again: our point is not that the Supremacy Clause is merely declarative; it does have an explicit addressee, but that addressee is not the Supreme Court. The Clause reads: "*the Judges in every State* shall be bound [by the supreme Law of the Land], any Thing in the Constitution or Laws of any State to the Contrary notwithstanding." Nor is the right of appeal from a state court to the Supreme Court (a matter to which we shall turn momentarily) to be lightly assumed; for no such right is mentioned anywhere in the Constitution.

Now it may be objected that this is a curious way to organize a country's political system—to single out *local* officials as the executors, the enforcers, of the supremacy of the country's laws. But let us consider a tentative answer to that objection: the arrangement ceases to be quite so curious if we remind ourselves of the jurisprudential tradition that prevailed in the Anglo-Saxon world in 1787, and then ask, as suggested at the beginning of this section: In what particular did that tradition have to be broken in order to achieve the Convention's professed goal, the creation of an effective *federal* system?

The going tradition, as we know from the preceding chapters, recognized the *legislature* as the supreme branch of every government. Thus the judges of each American State were, by common consent if not by express provision, subordinate to their particular body of lawmakers. State judges were accustomed and obliged to *obey their own legislatures*—the claims of any other legislature, whether equal or superior in status, to the contrary notwithstanding. This rule, as we have seen, had been the cause of the difficulty in *Rutgers v. Waddington*: the Mayor's Court recognized that the State of New York was bound by the Peace Treaty that had been ratified by the legislature of the United States; but when confronted with a conflicting provision enacted by its *own* legislature, the court unhesitatingly proclaimed its obligation to comply with the latter. Experience under the Articles of Confederation had amply proved that mere assertion of the supremacy of the Union was not enough—that if Congress' supremacy was to be effectively established, its acts would have to be enforced in the state courts. And that necessity required, in turn, *that state judges be expressly relieved of the duty to obey their own legislatures*—that they be expressly charged with the duty of enforcing, if need be *against* their own legislatures, "the supreme Law of the Land."

This state of affairs was fully appreciated by the members of the Convention. Indeed, one of Madison's chief arguments on behalf of the "congressional negative" had been that, as matters in the country then stood, "the Judges of the State[s] must give the State laws their operation even if [it should] abridge the rights of the national government."[1] Madison's point, of course, was that because state judges were so bound, only a congressional power to nullify state legislation would be adequate to insure the States' subordination. Then, during the critical July 17 debate, he returned to the subject. With the States'-righters' Supremacy Clause now looming as the Convention's answer to the problem of upholding "the rights of the national government," Madison sought to bolster the wavering nationalizers by pointing out that a danger inhered in the prevailing relationship between judges and legislators that even the Supremacy Clause might not remove. "In Rhode Island," he said, alluding to the case of *Trevett v. Weeden*, "the judges who refused to execute an unconstitutional law were displaced, and others substituted, by the legislature, who would be the willing instruments of their masters."[2]

But while Madison had indeed put his finger on a potential weakness in the Supremacy Clause's solution—namely, that a state legislature might retaliate against a court that enforced "the supreme Law of the Land" against its own acts—*his objection was overruled.* For the larger danger, in the view of the Convention's majority, was to permit the Union government to determine the limits of its own power. Thus, while there were risks both ways, the framers concluded that the appropriate answer to the challenge of federalism was a) to assert unambiguously the supremacy of the law of the Union, and yet b) to charge state courts with the duty of enforcing it.

We may note here a striking dissymmetry in the Supremacy Clause. The framers saw fit to direct the state courts to enforce the Constitution, as well as the laws and treaties of the United States—"any Thing in the Constitution or Laws of any State to the Contrary notwithstanding." Why, then, did they fail to grant a *parallel* mandate to the *Supreme Court?* Why does the Clause not also say: "the Judges of the Supreme Court shall be bound by the Constitution—any Acts of Congress, or Treaties, to the Contrary notwithstanding?" (Before venturing an explanation, let us agree that apologists for the modern power of judicial review would have an enormously easier time of it had some such provision been included.)

The reason it was not included should be apparent if we have kept in mind a) the traditional relationship between courts and legislatures, and especially b) the framers' quite limited purpose in departing from the tradition to the extent they did. The tradition of legislative supremacy was breached in the Supremacy Clause, not for

the purpose of substituting judicial supremacy, but for the purpose
of establishing the Union's supremacy over the States. That purpose
required the release of state courts from the duty of obeying their
own legislatures, but it manifestly did not require the release of the
federal court from the duty to obey *its* legislature.

We may put this in a more positive vein. *The framers' failure to
instruct the federal judiciary to disregard unconstitutional federal
legislation—the dissymmetry we speak of—is prima facie evidence
that the framers did not intend to give the Supreme Court a general
power of passing upon the constitutionality of congressional acts.**
Congress, after all; would be the most conspicuous legatee under the
new government of the tradition of legislative supremacy. While the
state legislatures, in the very nature of the Union, might be expected
to submit to a higher authority—even in the absence of the Supremacy Clause's express instruction to state judges—Congress
could *not* be expected to. Unless something were said to the contrary, Congress would as a matter of course be the supreme organ
of government under the Constitution. If that had not been the framers' expectation—if the framers had intended the Supreme Court to
stand *between* Congress and the Constitution—the Supremacy Clause,
which is the only part of the Constitution that deals with such matters,
was the logical place to have made that clear.

The tradition of legislative supremacy applied, and could apply of
course, only to *coordinate* branches of government. While the framers'
failure to assert the Supreme Court's competence to sit in judgment
of Congress is presumptive evidence the tradition was to remain in
force with respect to federal laws, no such conclusion can be drawn
with respect to the Court's competence to pass on the constitutionality of state laws. Concretely, since the state legislatures would belong to a *subordinate* order of government under the new Constitution, the Court might gain control over state laws by asserting the
right to hear *appeals* from the state court judgments that dealt with
such laws. Moreover, if the framers had placed such a right beyond

---

* We shall see later on that this prima facie evidence is, to some extent,
rebutted by other considerations. The Supremacy Clause's formulation, that is
to say, permits certain inferences regarding a *limited* power of judicial
review of federal laws, and we shall draw them in due course. The argument
at this juncture is, simply, that the framers pointedly denied the Supreme
Court a general power to review federal legislation corresponding to the
state courts' power to review state legislation.

peradventure, the fact that state judges, rather than Supreme Court judges, were singled out as the enforcers of the Supremacy Clause might not loom so important after all.* But did they?

One approach to the problem would run as follows: The *absence* of a right to hear appeals from state courts would render unworkable an effective federal system, and place beyond reach the goal of Union supremacy which the framers indisputably embraced. Permit the country to be governed by as many interpretations of the Constitution as there are States? Permit state judges to dispense with the Constitution at will, with no recourse to the federal government? Surely, such a state of affairs could recommend itself only to anarchists or imbeciles. That, we repeat, is one view of the matter, and the one that present-day commentators deem indisputable.

Indisputable, however, it certainly is not. For in point of fact the framers, who to our knowledge did not include a single anarchist or imbecile, did *not* guarantee the right of appeal from state court judgment. *The* most *that can be said is that the framers* may *have provided that the right of appeal could be established at the future discretion of Congress.* Let us see why this is so, and then ask what inferences may be drawn from the framers' decision to handle the problem in this fashion.

---

* The Supreme Court might also have gained a measure of control over state laws if the framers had granted the inferior federal courts original jurisdiction over cases involving the constitutionality of state legislation. The framers did not do so, but left the matter, in Article III, to Congress' discretion. We have avoided systematic discussion of the possibility of challenging state legislation in the lower federal courts in order to simplify the presentation, and for two other reasons. First, if the Supreme Court does not have a constitutional prerogative to review *state court* judgments, its claim to supremacy is seriously compromised, no matter what success it might have in enforcing its will through cases brought in the federal courts. Second, we are mainly concerned with the argument that the *Supremacy Clause* made the Supreme Court the Constitution's special agent for interpreting and enforcing the document. The argument runs a) "the Judges of every State" are explicitly nominated as the enforcers of the Constitution; but b) state judges are subordinate to the Supreme Court; therefore c) the Supreme Court is the principal enforcer of the Constitution. And the validity of that argument, we are saying, is manifestly unaffected by the question of whether judicial review was anticipated in cases arising in the federal courts. We deal with this latter question generally in examining the implications of Article III ("Judicial Review Elsewhere in the Constitution," below); and the debates at the Constitutional Convention ("Judicial Review at the Constitutional Convention," also below).

Article III, Section 1 of the Constitution provides: "The judicial
Power of the United States shall be vested in one supreme Court. . . ."
But the relevant passages for our purposes are to be found in Section
2 of that article which proceeds to *define* the "judicial power," and
thus delineates the *jurisdiction* of the Supreme Court under the Constitution.

Clause 1 of Section 2 begins, *"The judicial power shall extend to
all Cases . . . arising under this Constitution, the Laws of the United
States and Treaties. . . ."*; then the balance of the clause enumerates
certain categories of cases that the framers chose to mention specifically, presumably to remove any doubt that they, too, fell within the
scope of the Supreme Court's jurisdiction. The scope of the Court's
jurisdiction, however, does not concern us as much as the *kind* of
grant the framers made in this instance. The language of Clause 1,
taken alone, suggests that the grant is "self-executing"—that is, automatic: that it was to come into being by force of the constitutional
provision itself, with the result that a litigant would have merely to
qualify his "case" as one encompassed by the grant in order to become entitled to a Supreme Court hearing. However, the next clause
of Section 2 promptly undermines that inference. For Clause 2 names
two categories of cases only—those "affecting [foreign diplomats] and
those in which a State shall be Party"—in which the Supreme Court's
jurisdiction is "original," and therefore, since nothing more is said,
presumably automatic. But *"in all the other cases before mentioned,"*
Clause 2 continues, "the supreme Court shall have *appellate* jurisdiction . . . *with such Exceptions, and under such Regulations as the
Congress shall make."*

Thus the Constitution's grant of appellate jurisdiction to the Supreme Court—the grant under which appeals from state courts might
be in order—is evidently *not* self-executing or automatic; but merely
potential, and contingent. The grant requires an implementing act
of Congress before it becomes actual—before the Supreme Court may
be said to possess it. Moreover, this scheme of things is rounded out
by the "necessary and proper" clause of Article I. That clause authorizes Congress "to make all Laws which shall be necessary and
proper *for carrying into Execution* the foregoing Powers [meaning,
the congressional powers enumerated in Article I] and *all other
Powers* vested by this Constitution in the Government of the United
States, or in any *Department* . . . thereof [meaning, for example, the
power to hear cases on appeal which the Constitution "vests" in the
Judiciary Department]."

Now if the Supreme Court's appellate jurisdiction is thus wholly dependent upon an act of Congress, it would seem to follow that such jurisdiction is a matter of congressional option—that Congress may withhold or grant the jurisdiction as it sees fit. For if the framers had meant to *require* Congress to confer jurisdiction, they were sufficiently articulate, surely, to say so. To be sure, a few commentators have disputed this inference, pointing to the use of the mandatory "shall" in Article III—"the Judicial Power *shall* be vested"; "the judicial Power *shall* extend"—and reading this language as an *order* to Congress to grant the Supreme Court appellate jurisdiction in the cases mentioned: an order to which Congress is bound to respond affirmatively in some way, only the details and form of the response being left to Congress' discretion.* But this view, which gives to the word "shall" a necessarily self-executing construction, demonstrably fails to

---

* See Mr. Justice Story's opinion in *Martin v. Hunter's Lessee,* 1 Wheaton, 304 (1816). Story upheld the appellate jurisdiction that Congress conferred on the Supreme Court in the Judiciary Act of 1789, and went on to argue, in dicta, that the grant was traceable to the Constitution itself. The Story doctrine, however, was abandoned in later Supreme Court opinions. Among modern writers, Professor Crosskey appears to be alone in urging textual reasons for supporting Story and for rejecting the view we are advancing. Crosskey's argument is that since Section 1 of Article III provides for "one supreme Court," and since that section further contemplates the possibility that Congress might decide *against* creating inferior federal courts, it follows "that the 'suprem[acy]' conferred upon the United States Supreme Court by the Constitution was a 'suprem[acy]' against the courts of the States, as well as against those of the nation. For, in the contingency contemplated, there would have been nothing else for the Supreme Court's 'suprem[acy]' to mean." (Op. cit., I, 613.) In other words, if the Supreme Court's power to hear appeals from state courts, as well as the creation of inferior federal courts, were contingent on congressional action, we are left with the contradictory proposition that there might be nothing for the Supreme Court to be supreme about.

The argument is ingenious, but, we submit, not much else. In the first place, by deftly affixing the bracketed [acy] to the word "supreme," Crosskey is guilty of precisely the kind of question-begging he excoriates with such profound effect in other portions of his work. The begged question in this instance is: Was the phrase "one supreme Court" intended merely to designate the national judicial tribunal? Or did it necessarily connote a supremacy over some other court, the existence of which Congress was obliged to guarantee? In the second place, even if Crosskey's reasoning is valid, once Congress created inferior federal courts, the "contingency contemplated" was removed—i.e., the Supreme Court now had something to be supreme about—and thereafter the state courts might be granted their independence.

take into account the stylistic preferences of the framers. Consider
the use of the same formula in another connection. According to Article I, Section 8, "The Congress *shall* have Power . . . to regulate
Commerce . . . among the several States." This grant, let us agree,
gives Congress authority to prescribe the size of paddle-wheels used
in interstate shipping. But it is certainly not an *order*—requiring Congress to do so. The phrase, clearly, confers on Congress only a potential jurisdiction, which will become an actual jurisdiction when and
as Congress sees fit to claim it—by passing a law prescribing the size
of paddle-wheels.

Now: the Supreme Court was evidently intended to acquire appellate jurisdiction the same way. The only difference is that the
Court's actual power was to come into existence, not at its own
pleasure, but at Congress'*—yet another illustration of the prevailing
doctrine of legislative supremacy.

We have seen so far that the Supreme Court's power to hear appeals from state courts is not a constitutional right, but a matter of
congressional pleasure. We must now go further, and ask the logically
prior question of whether even Congress' power in this area is free
from doubt. According to Section 2 of Article III, Congress may con-

---

* While there is considerable discomfort among constitutional lawyers and
others with the implications of this point, we do not mean to suggest that it
is under serious dispute. The Jenner-Butler bill, in 1958, sought to withdraw the Supreme Court's appellate jurisdiction in certain "Communist
cases," including some that would originate in state courts. The bill was
defeated, but even its enemies generally conceded Congress' power to eliminate the Court's appellate function. However, Mr. Joseph Rauh, testifying
on behalf of the Americans for Democratic Action, dissented. "I am aware,"
Rauh said, "that frequent statements can be found in Supreme Court
opinions that Congress has unlimited power to regulate . . . the appellate
jurisdiction of the Supreme Court." Yet Rauh preferred the authority of
Professor Henry W. Hart, Jr., of the Harvard Law School, who "has suggested that the Constitution must not be read as authorizing its own
destruction and that, therefore, Article III cannot reasonably be interpreted
to permit Congress to make such exceptions from the appellate jurisdiction
of the Supreme Court as will 'destroy the essential role of the Supreme
Court in the constitutional plan.' " (Hearings of the Senate Internal
Security Subcommittee, Feb. 19, 1958, pp. 44, 45.) We mention Rauh's
argument to acquaint the reader with the flimsy weaponry of the dissenters.
Who has granted, let alone justified, the assumption that the Constitution
would be "destroyed" under these circumstances? And how can one decry the
mayhem on the Court's "essential role . . . in the constitutional plan" without begging the question of what the constitutional plan is?

fer "appellate jurisdiction" on the Supreme Court in certain types of cases. But what does "appellate jurisdiction" mean in this context? One thing it certainly means is the power of a court to hear and dispose of a case that has originated elsewhere, assuming the originating court and the parties have no objection. But does the term also imply that the court in question has the power to reach into another court, or into another court system, and pluck out a case for its own consideration *against* the will of the originating court or of one of the parties? Is the power to *hear appeals*, in other words, synonymous with the power to *compel removal* of a case from another court?

Consider the case of the American traveling abroad who is haled into a Spanish court in a suit brought by a Spanish subject. Such a case would fall into one of the categories of cases mentioned by Section 2 of Article III—namely, "Controversies . . . between a State, or the Citizens thereof, and foreign States, Citizens or Subjects." It would therefore be a case, according to Clause 2 of that section, over which the United States Supreme Court "shall have appellate Jurisdiction." Now: Is it likely that the framers, by their grant of "appellate jurisdiction," meant to give Congress the power to *compel* the removal of our case from the Spanish courts to the United States Supreme Court? Obviously not; for this would have been an altogether vain grant. Such matters are controlled by treaty or by international comity, and are not subject to a unilateral assertion of right by one sovereignty over against another. But—and this is the point—if the framers' grant of "appellate jurisdiction" does not imply the power of removal in cases arising in foreign courts, how can it be maintained that the selfsame language *does* imply the power of removal in cases arising in *state* courts?

And of course we must not be put off by the objection that in the framers' contemplation the States, unlike Spain, were not "sovereign." For every attempt to resolve questions of this sort, either by affirming or denying that the States are "sovereign" under the Constitution, is question-begging. The real issue is always, as here: What *portion* of their sovereignty did the States surrender under the Constitution? The issue here, concretely, is whether the States surrendered the power to make final disposition of cases arising in their own court systems.

Consider the problem from a different angle. Section 2 of Article III gives Congress the power to grant appellate jurisdiction to the Supreme Court in "all Cases [save the two categories in which the

Court is given original jurisdiction] arising under this Constitution, the Laws of the United States, and Treaties." Now did the framers mean, once Congress had acted, that *only* the federal court system, headed by the Supreme Court, should have jurisdiction in the type of the case described? Again, obviously not. Suits answering that description would also be tried, as a matter of course, in state courts—under grants of jurisdiction by state legislatures or state constitutions. As it happens, moreover, the federal Constitution—in the Supremacy Clause—expressly anticipates state jurisdiction in just these cases: "the Judges in every State shall be bound" by "this Constitution and the Laws of the United States . . . and Treaties." Thus, on the face of the framers' scheme, the jurisdiction of the federal courts in cases involving conflicts between the federal and state governments is *not exclusive,* but merely *concurrent.* And since concurrent, the question arises: Which of the two jurisdictions was intended to be *superior,* and so have the power to compel the removal of a case from the other's court system to its own?

One way to handle the problem is to appeal to the "general tenor" of the Constitution: since the framers' manifest purpose was to establish the supremacy of the Union government, it would follow that the federal court system was to be superior to the state court system. But this argument is to some extent offset by another—namely, that state jurisdiction in these cases is fixed and permanent, and so acknowledged by the Supremacy Clause itself; while federal jurisdiction is merely contingent, in that it depends on Congress' power to give and to take away.

The better way to handle the problem, we suggest, is to recognize that it is question-begging. For to ask which jurisdiction was meant to be *superior* is to assume in advance the answer to the real question at issue: Was *either* jurisdiction meant to be superior? There is nothing in the language of the Constitution, after all, to exclude the possibility that the two jurisdictions would run in parallel, rather than in converging lines—a possibility that would leave neither with the power of removal over against the other.

Indeed, so real did the possibility appear to earlier generations of Americans that some thirty years after the Constitution was adopted the Union was jeopardized by a turbulent controversy over just this issue. The State of Virginia, though by no means alone, led the attack against the federal judiciary's claims of supremacy, and in the great case of *Cohens v. Virginia,* formally advanced the argument suggested above.[3]

The State's courts had found the Cohens guilty of selling a lottery ticket in Virginia in violation of a criminal statute. The Cohens maintained the lottery was authorized by an act of Congress. While the act had established the lottery in the District of Columbia, they said, it did not forbid the sale of tickets outside the District. But the Virginia Court of Appeals affirmed the Cohens' conviction, holding, in effect, that Congress had no power to authorize such sales in a State whose laws forbade them. The case was, thereupon taken to the United States Supreme Court on a writ of error, notwithstanding a resolution by the Virginia legislature voicing its "most solemn protest against the jurisdiction of that Court over the matter."[4] What is more, the legislature instructed Virginia's attorneys to refuse to argue the merits of the case before the Supreme Court (to have done so would have amounted to an admission of the Supreme Court's power to remove the case), but merely to state the reasons why Virginia was not prepared to have the judgments of its highest court questioned in another jurisdiction. Accordingly, Alexander Smyth, as Counsel for Virginia, placed before the Court the construction of the Constitution we have proposed: "[The] power of the Judiciary of the United States is either exclusive, or [as when federal and state laws are in conflict] concurrent," he said, but it is "not paramount. And where it is concurrent, whichever judiciary [state, or federal] gets possession of the case [first], should proceed to final judgment, from which there should be no appeal."[5]

Six years earlier, we may note, the Virginia Court of Appeals had advanced this same thesis when it refused to comply with a Supreme Court mandate in the equally celebrated case of Martin v. Hunter's Lessee.[6] The Virginia judges had ruled unanimously that "the appellate power of the Supreme Court of the United States does not extend to this Court under a sound construction of the Constitution of the United States; that so much of the [Judiciary Act of 1789] as extends the appellate jurisdiction of the Supreme Court to this Court, is not in pursuance of the Constitution of the United States; [and that therefore] obedience to its mandate [must] be declined by this court."[7] Moreover, one of the members of the Virginia court, Judge Roane, had ventured an answer to the charge that Virginia, by resisting the Supreme Court's claims, was encouraging "anarchical principles." Those who have levelled the charge, Roane had said, "ought to have remembered that . . . it is not [for this Court] to regard political consequences, in rendering its judgment. They should also have recollected that there is a Charybdis to be avoided, as well as a Scylla; that a centripetal, as well as a centrifugal, principle exists in the Government; and that no calamity would be more to be deplored by the American people, than a vortex in the General Government, which should engulf and sweep away every vestige of the state constitutions."[8]

As students of the period know, Virginia's position was flatly rejected by Chief Justice Marshall in the *Cohens* case—as it had been earlier by Justice Story in *Hunter's Lessee*. Yet the Supreme Court's victories were neither very impressive,* nor, in some quite exalted quarters, well received. Thomas Jefferson, for example, wrote a year later that he had been reading "with comfort everything which reprobates the apostatizing heresies of [the Supreme Court's decision in] the case of Cohens." "According to the doctrines of the Supreme Court in that case," he explained to his correspondent, "the States are provinces of the Empire, and [incidentally] a late pamphlet gives to that Court the infallibility of the Pope. Caesar then has only to send out his pro-consuls and with the *sanction of a Pope* all is settled;

---

* Story responded to the Virginia court's adamancy by re-issuing the Supreme Court's mandate, which the Virginia court had rejected, to a federal circuit court. The federal court, however, was never able to execute the judgment, and evidently did not try very hard. See Warren, *The Supreme Court in United States History*, I, 450. Thus Virginia's rebellion in *Martin v. Hunter's Lessee* was everywhere successful except on the pages of Story's opinion.

Marshall's was also a paper triumph, though he was more successful in salvaging the Court's prestige. After he had ruled against Virginia on the jurisdictional issue, and Virginia's attorneys had withdrawn from the case in protest, Marshall turned around and decided the substantive issue against the Cohens, in favor of Virginia. Marshall reasoned that Congress had not *intended* to authorize the ticket sale outside the District of Columbia, and therefore that Virginia was entitled to prosecute. Thus Marshall avoided a test of the Supreme Court's ability to enforce its decrees against an uncooperative state government, while simultaneously asserting the theoretical prerogatives of the Court, vis à vis the States, in the broadest terms. This was an instance, as we shall see in a subsequent volume, of Marshall's great rule of strategy in building the Court's power of review. *The rule, in short: first, stake out a claim to power in abstract terms and under conditions that will avoid a political showdown with rival branches of government; then, in a future case when a showdown can prudently be risked, cite the reasoning of the earlier case as authority for a "long-established principle."* Marshall's contemporaries were not unaware of the strategy, but its brilliance lay precisely in its denial to the Court's opponents of any retaliatory sanction beyond verbal recrimination. For an account of the bitter reaction to the *Cohens* démarche, see Warren, op. cit., I, 551-564.

but the battle of Bunker Hill," Jefferson thought, "was not fought to set up a Pope."*[9]

Now our point is not that the *Cohens* and *Hunter's Lessee* cases were decided incorrectly. Much less are we denying that—all things considered—the country, Virginia included, is probably better off for the cases having been decided the way they were. Our purpose, rather, has been to show that there is a tenable point of view about the Supreme Court's power to review state court judgments that is all but ignored by modern scholarship; that this point of view, the "Virginia position," is supported by a plausible logic drawn from the Constitution itself—a logic that, to some, fairly leaps out of the language of the document, and that in any event cannot be confuted by it; that this logic was fully appreciated by the Constitution's contemporaries, yet no more so, one would suppose, than by the men who drafted and adopted the language; and therefore—and this, finally, is the quite narrow point we wish to make—that it is intellectually irresponsible to maintain that the framers of the Constitution did, or even tried to, *settle* the problem *against* the Virginia position.

That conclusion, moreover, emerges unscathed, no matter how extensively one searches for further evidence that might bear on the problem. Such evidence would include what was said on the subject during the Convention debates (actually, almost nothing was said, itself a fact of large importance); what assumptions were encouraged during the ratification campaign, as influenced primarily by *The Federalist*; what Congress actually did in the premises in its first session in 1789. Suffice it to say that the results of that investigation furnish little occasion for quarrelling with the proposition we are urging: that the framers had every intention of leaving the problem of appeals from state court judgments in considerable doubt.

The question arises: Why? There are really two explanations, but both are covered by a suspicion that would occur, from the data we have seen, to schoolboys. *The problem was too hot to handle by constitutional prescription.* We are in the presence, in other words, of one of the Constitutional Convention's famous "compromises," in this instance a seldom noticed one, without which the Constitution most probably could not have been adopted. And as with the other, and better known compromises, this one was not simply a matter of the delegates, themselves, being unable to agree to one or the other of

---

* Emphasis in original.

polar positions. It was that too; but it was mainly a matter of their judgment as to what the country would accept. The States'-righters undoubtedly recognized that nationalist sentiment would balk at an explicit prohibition of appeals—partly because of the contention that greater juridical uniformity was a pre-condition of the Union's cohesion, and partly because of skepticism over whether the state courts would be *able* to be independent of their respective legislatures, as the Supremacy Clause contemplated and ordained. Similarly, the nationalizers understood that an explicit affirmation of the power to remove state cases would be regarded by important sections of the population as an avenue, or even an invitation, to national consolidation —to what the Jeffersonians would later deride as "Empire." Both sides, in other words, recognized that there is a time for drawing lines clear and fast, and a time for leaving them blurred; so that a tacit understanding was reached—to say nothing. And while later expounders of the Constitution might fault the framers for a notable imprecision, it is probably the sounder view that without the ambiguity there might have been no Constitution to expound.

But this is another way of saying, of course—and herein the second explanation—that the framers consciously *postponed* the issue, that they deliberately left it to the good sense of the constitution-makers, whether of the written or unwritten variety, of a later day. Whether the problem would be solved by constitutional amendment, or as actually happened, through the subtler processes of political competition between contending forces, the framers could not know; nor could they know the verdict that would be rendered. What they did know—and the moral may be profitably learned today—was that since nothing approaching a consensus on the issue existed in 1787, any attempt to establish a solution by constitutional fiat would be not only vain but mischievous. The moment might come when a relevant consensus would emerge; but that later moment, not 1787, would be the time to harden the verdict with the cement of a constitutional sanction.

Still: if all of this is true, are we not left with the objection that the framers, by refusing to settle the matter of appeals from state courts, also failed to accomplish what they had mainly come to Philadelphia to do—namely, to discover a means of enforcing Union supremacy within a framework of local autonomy? Could they have "ducked" the one problem, in other words, without by the same token having ducked the other? And may we then agree that if the objection is valid—if the two problems are the same—what we have said about the right of appeals is probably, though for reasons that would be hard to imagine on the textual evidence, wrong? Yet the two problems are not the same, and they could not be deemed so except, once again, on the question-begging assumption that the framers regarded the matter of appeals as marginally decisive in meeting the challenge of federalism. The alternative hypothesis, of course, is that the requirements of federalism could be met *with or without* the right of appeals. And that hypothesis, judging by what they did, was the one upon which the framers proceeded. According to the decision taken on July 17, and never thereafter successfully challenged,* the framers' chosen agents for enforcing the Constitution and Union laws, while avoiding the danger of national consolidation, were *"the Judges in every State."* The federal Supreme Court might be drawn into the enforcement scheme (in just what capacity we shall see in the next chapter); but regardless of that Court's eventual role, the *primary* responsibility for dispensing the chemistry of federalism would lie with the state courts. That is the conclusion to which all of the data point, and is the only one, we submit, that does not convict the framers of being so irresponsible and frivolous as to have turned over to the country a charter of government that recognizably fought shy of the country's transcendent preoccupation.

It is fashionable in our time to patronize the framers, to leaven admiration for their strengths with reminders about their limited vision and their naivete. Imagine entrusting the Constitution's future to the good faith of state judges! Very well; but it would be wise to withhold such judgments until we have come to the end of our story. For as we shall see the framers placed their bets rather more widely in assigning the broader responsibility for construing, enforcing, and perpetuating the constitutional plan as a whole. Thus far we have spoken only of their solution to the single problem, to be sure the major one before them, of ensuring the Union's supremacy over against the States. And with respect to that problem, it might be well to remember that good will was the principal resource, and good

---

* Late in August, Madison and some of his nationalist allies made a final bid for the "congressional negative"—not, on this occasion, as a substitute for the Supremacy Clause, but as a supplementary sanction. But the move was handily defeated. (See p. 295, "Judicial Review at the Constitutional Convention.") The incident furnishes still further evidence, of course, of the majority's belief that the Supremacy Clause, with its reliance on state judges, had provided adequate machinery for assuring the subordination of the States.

faith, in the last analysis, the only sanction at the framers' disposal. But for those basic civil virtues, there was no hope at all that serious disagreements between a State, or a combination of States, and the federal government could be resolved short of rebellion or civil war. The framers' function, as constitution-makers, was merely to devise a machinery for drawing forth such good will as there was in the country and spreading it evenly over the myriad fears, rivalries and tensions that were threatening to fragmentize a putatively united people. And if the judges of the States, in the main among the most esteemed men in every community, and those least vulnerable to the snares of personal ambition or factional interest—if they could not be presumed to possess enough good will and probity and wisdom to honor the solemn commands of the Supremacy Clause, who then?

THE MEANING OF
THE SUPREMACY CLAUSE, II

We have spoken up to this point about the "addressees" of the Supremacy Clause—about the parties that were assigned, by the terms of the Clause, the responsibility for enforcing its commands. We have seen that state judges were given that responsibility expressly, and have noted the possibility that the national Supreme Court was expected to share in the responsibility eventually, as Congress might provide.

Our next question, logically, is: What did the Supremacy Clause command? Or, more concretely: While judges clearly were to give "the supreme Law of the Land" preference over "the Constitution or Laws of any State," what, in fact, *was* the "supreme Law" the framers understood themselves to be defining in the Supremacy Clause?

Until very recently the mere asking of the question would have provoked much wonderment. Not only laymen, but most constitutional scholars would have replied that the Supremacy Clause's statement of the matter is remarkably straightforward and hardly worth a debate. *"This Constitution,"* the statement begins: that surely is an element of the "supreme Law." *"[The] Laws of the United States which shall be made in Pursuance thereof"* (i.e., those laws that do not themselves violate the Constitution): this surely is a further element—no problem there either. *"Treaties made . . . under the Authority of the United States"*: this is the third and final element—and while there *is* a slight problem there having to do, as proponents of the Bricker Amendment about that time (1953-54) were pointing out, with whether Treaties also must be made "pursuant to the Constitution," it happened that both sides in the Bricker controversy ended up by agreeing that legitimate treaties could not conflict with

other provisions of the Constitution.* But the treaty power aside
(for this is not a matter that need detain us), the meaning of the
Supremacy Clause's commands was plain enough: state laws or state
constitutions would have to give way in the event they clashed either with the Constitution, or with Acts of Congress that—in the
opinion of state judges—were in keeping with the Constitution. And
this meant, of course, that before judges could declare state measures
unconstitutional as contrary to an Act of Congress, they would first
have to examine the Act of Congress to see if *it* was constitutional.

All of this, as we say, was plain enough until 1953 when William
Crosskey came along with his two-volume work, *Politics and the Constitution*—undoubtedly the most impressive venture in iconoclasm in
the history of American legal scholarship. Professor Crosskey's challenge to received constitutional doctrine has worked considerable de-
vastation on many fronts, several of which we have already glimpsed;
while Crosskey does not always convince, his exceptional learning has
managed in most cases to shift the burden of proof onto the holders
of any received view he attacks—an achievement the legal fraternity

---

* The position of proponents of the Bricker Amendment was, in essence,
that the treaty power was traditionally understood to be subordinate to the
Constitution, but that in the light of a number of implicit challenges to this
understanding—notably, by the route of "executive agreements"—the prudent
course was to put the matter beyond doubt by means of a constitutional
amendment. Moreover, the proponents could point to a number of judicial
decisions that seemed to say that while the treaty power was theoretically
finite, as a practical matter the sky was the limit. For example, in the celebrated case of *Missouri v. Holland* the Supreme Court had held that a treaty
between the United States and Canada regulating migratory birds was valid,
although a previous Act of Congress that sought to accomplish the same
regulation had been declared invalid, as a violation of constitutionally
protected States' rights. The opponents of the proposal, for their part, argued
that an amendment would "tie the President's hands," and, anyway, that the
constitutional limitation was plain enough as it stood (how both of these
things could be true they never quite made clear), and therefore that the
amendment was not only undesirable, but unnecessary. In sum, although the
measure was defeated in the Senate, both sides came away from the scrap
committed in principle to the theory that no treaty could be valid that
conflicted with the Constitution. And although this understanding begged
all of the interesting questions about what kind of provision of the Constitution (just explicit ones, or also implicit ones) might limit the treaty
power, it was sufficient to establish the point we are making—namely, that
a broad consensus asserted that the only treaties entitled to the status of
"supreme Law" are those that have been made—as in the case of congressional
legislation—"in pursuance" of the Constitution.

has been regrettably slow to acknowledge and even slower to do something about. Such is the case here, where he contends that our understanding of the key passage of the Supremacy Clause has been, all along, root and branch wrong.

According to Crosskey, we have failed from a very early moment of the country's history to grasp what the framers meant by "Laws of the United States which shall be made in Pursuance [of the Constitution]." Everything hinges, he asserts, on the meaning of *"in Pursuance."* We have assumed the phrase means "in conformity with" or "consistent with"; and we have thus taken it for granted that, in the framers' contemplation, Congress is capable of passing not only valid laws, but also *invalid* laws—i.e., laws that are *not* consistent with the Constitution. And from this we have understandably regarded the former as part of "the supreme Law of the Land," but not the latter. Yet the fact of the matter on Crosskey's showing is that the eighteenth century was accustomed to a very different use of the word "pursuance": instead of meaning "consistent with," the phrase was normally synonymous with "in prosecution of"; "under the authority of"; "by virtue of"—so that what the framers really meant to describe by "Laws . . . made in Pursuance [of the Constitution]" were merely those laws that would be enacted by Congress after the Constitution had been adopted and had become operative. Thus Crosskey concludes that in the framers' view *every* Act of Congress was to be considered "valid." There was to be no distinction between "constitutional" acts and "unconstitutional" ones. The mere fact that Congress *passed* an Act was to be deemed sufficient evidence of its constitutionality. To be sure, Congress was to be "bound" by the Constitution, but Congress was to be the supreme judge of its own obligations in that matter. Under the new "national" government, Crosskey maintains, the principle of legislative supremacy was to have the same status it enjoyed in Great Britain and in the American States under the Articles of Confederation.

On the face of it, the implications of Crosskey's position are nothing short of breathtaking. If he is correct, the vaunted "States' rights" issue would never have arisen under a faithful execution of the framers' scheme. How could it have arisen if Congress, the body that represented the principal threat to those rights, was understood to be the sole judge of whether the rights existed, and if so, what they were? Moreover, the judiciary's power even to participate in the expounding of the Constitution could never have amounted to more than rubber-stamping. Federal laws could not have been challenged for unconstitutionality—because they were ipso facto constitutional. State laws might be found unconstitutional, but such verdicts would unavoidably be determined according to guide lines laid down by Congress. As for judges "arbitrating" between the state and national governments, such an umpire role for the courts—or for anyone else for that matter—would be out of the question, because state laws or constitutional provisions would have been deemed automatically liquidated upon a mere demonstration of a conflicting national law. In short, if Crosskey is correct, a country grew up—and did so from the moment of its birth—according to concepts that were diametrically opposed to those advanced by its founders. It thought, wrote, debated, legislated, adjudicated, and fought a savage civil war—all under a terrible misunderstanding. Moreover, the States' rights myth, as Crosskey deems it, still looms large in our affairs—so much so that numerous and influential parts of the population, as Little Rock and Oxford and Birmingham showed, are prepared to this day to sacrifice the country's peace on its behalf. For this reason, and because our own inquiry can hardly proceed with the issue in doubt, we ought to look closely at Professor Crosskey's evidence to see whether it warrants his conclusions.

Crosskey's first exhibit is Samuel Johnson's "famous dictionary of 1755." Johnson's then-authoritative work "defined 'pursuance' as meaning 'prosecution' or 'process;' and [it] defined 'pursuant' to mean 'done in consequence or prosecution of any thing.' These are the only definitions of these words that Johnson gave...." Crosskey adds that it "might possibly be wrong" to conclude this was the only sense in which these words were used in the eighteenth century, but that Johnson's definitions nonetheless "indicate what seem to him the general and usual meaning" of the words.

The second argument is that two opponents of the Constitution during the ratification campaign attacked the ambiguity of the phrase "in Pursuance of." A delegate to the North Carolina convention complained that it was "equivocal and ambiguous." "A writer in a New York newspaper" said it implied "little more than 'in consequence, etc.' "—with the result, the New York writer charged, that Acts of Congress and treaties would be on an equal footing with the Constitution itself.

Crosskey's third item is that James Wilson of Pennsylvania made a speech to the Constitutional Convention on July 21, 1787, in which he "seemed completely unaware" that the language of the Supremacy Clause, which had been approved just four days before, had exposed "all the legislation of Congress" to "judicial review"—though such exposure would have been an inescapable consequence, in Crosskey's view, of the modern interpretation of "pursuance." Wilson, Crosskey adds, was "one of the acutest lawyers" at the Convention.

Fourth, the words "in pursuance of" appear twice in the Articles of Confederation, and in both instances the sense intended is the one Crosskey is now urging. Article VI provided that no State should levy taxes that might "interfere with any stipulations in treaties [which might eventually be made] *in pursuance of* any treaties already proposed by Congress to the Courts of France and Spain." Now, according to Crosskey, since it was obviously the intention of this provision to "facilitate" treaty negotiations rather than obstruct them, it is unlikely the States were to be allowed to frustrate such future treaties as were not "in accord with" the proposals Congress was then making to France and Spain; hence "in pursuance of" must have had a meaning equivalent to "in consequence of" or "in further prosecution of." And then Article XII provided that all debts incurred "by, or under the authority of Congress, before the assembling of the United States, in pursuance of the present Confederation, shall be deemed . . . a charge against the United States. . . ." Crosskey comments: "[again] the sense of 'in pursuance of' seems to be 'in prosecution of,' 'in consequence of' or 'under'; for the intention of the provision manifestly was to validate all the commitments of the United States, both those *antecedently* made by Congress 'under' the original informal confederation, and those *subsequently* made by it—that is, by 'the United States assembled'—'under,' or 'in pursuance of, the present confederation'—that is, the Articles. It cannot certainly be supposed there was any intention to set up, by this provision, a basis for state quibbling over whether 'the United States,' in connection with future commitments, was or was not 'assembled' in strict conformity to the Articles. The intention was to prevent state quibbling, not to promote it."

Fifth, Crosskey tries to anticipate an objection—namely, the rejoinder that if he is right about all of this, the framers' use of "in pursuance" in the Supremacy Clause was mere surplusage. Why—the rejoinder might run—if the words "in Pursuance [of this Constitution] "were not meant to *qualify* the expression "the Laws of the United States" so as to distinguish between constitutional laws and unconstitutional ones, why were they used at all? That is a much less formidable difficulty, Crosskey replies, than it seems: the framers did not want to give "supreme law" status to those "Laws of the United States" that had been in effect *prior* to the Constitution—either the laws that had been enacted by the Congress established by the Articles of Confederation, or those that owed their sanction to the Common Law of England; the latter, on Crosskey's showing, was assumed at that time to be a part of "the Laws of the United States." Accordingly, the framers needed a form of words that would distinguish between those previous "laws" on the one hand, and statutes that would be enacted *after* the adoption of the Constitution, on the other —for only the latter were to have "supreme law" status. That explanation, Crosskey maintains, fully accounts for the use of the phrase "in Pursuance thereof."

Sixth—and this final item by way of circumstantial reasoning—Crosskey deems it absurd to suppose that the framers "deliberately conferred the right" of judging the constitutionality of acts of Congress "primarily, upon every petty 'Judge in every State' in the Union." Since "state recalcitrance and state delays had been the bane of the Articles of Confederation," it is unlikely the framers wished to perpetuate these evils—which would be the inevitable effect of using the words "in Pursuance thereof" to mean "consistent with."

Such then, is Crosskey's case.[1] We venture the following comments:

First, we may agree that Samuel Johnson's definition of "pursuant" demonstrates "what seemed to him" the word's "usual meaning" in the general usage of England in 1755. But of course we are concerned with discovering the word's meaning not so much in general usage, as in politico-legal composition; not in England, but in America; not in 1755, but 1787. Moreover, we may take it for a fact—for no evidence has ever been adduced to the contrary—that from the moment the business of Constitution-expounding got under way in the United States, American lawyers, judges, and statesmen uniformly read "pursuant," as used in the Supremacy Clause, in a different sense from the one certified by Johnson. Concretely: 1) a judicial power to review acts of Congress was asserted as early as 1792; 2) from that moment forward (though let us speak only of the first decades of the Constitution when the framers and their contemporaries lived and acted) such a power was challenged from many quarters and on many grounds; yet 3) no one whose views are recorded challenged the power on the grounds that by their use of the word "pursuant" the framers intended to legitimize automatically any act Congress might pass—i.e., on the grounds of Johnson's definition. Many arguments against judicial review, we repeat, were summoned—but never *that* one; and this is an altogether improbable oversight if, as Crosskey argues, Johnson's definitions governed late eighteenth-century American usage. Granted, our reasoning here, like Crosskey's, is inferential; yet these early American pronouncements and debates, occurring much closer in time and circumstance to the framing of the Constitution than did the publication of Johnson's English Dictionary, are surely the better evidence of the sense in which the framers used the word.

Second, the fact that certain opponents of the Constitution made a futile attempt to discredit the document during the ratification campaign on the grounds that "pursuant" was an ambiguous word and for that reason invited the dangerous possibility that Congress would be the sole judge of its own powers—the fact that such an argument was made in isolated instances, *and rejected,* is pretty clearly evidence that on balance weighs *against* the position Professor Crosskey is contending for. What we have here, recognizably, is the following political situation: a) certain eighteenth-century "States'-righters" were seeking to alert their compatriots to the dangerous centralizing tendencies that, in their view, inhered in the proposed Constitution; and, understandably for this purpose, they had gone over the document with a fine-toothed comb for every scrap of evidence that might help make their point; b) the search had uncovered the word "pursuant" which demonstrably had (as, indeed, it still does in the twentieth century) two possible meanings; and a few of the States'-righters—Professor Crosskey has been able to find two who did so—proceeded to add this arguable ambiguity to their list of complaints; c) their adversaries—the proponents of the Constitution—took the cavil in stride, preferring to concentrate their energies on more serious objections; d) the proponents' general answer of course, which runs all the way through *The Federalist* and is the dominant theme of the whole ratification campaign, was that the new national government would be *limited* by the Constitution—a claim they could not possibly have made if they understood "pursuance" to mean, merely, "in consequence of." The point may be put otherwise. If Crosskey were right about the contemporary meaning of "pursuance"—if the framers and their contemporaries were all under the impression that its use in the Supremacy Clause made Congress the supreme judge of its own powers—would not this provision of the Constitution have been the central issue of the ratification campaign? Would not the States'-righters have zeroed in their Big Berthas on precisely that target? And would not the proponents of the Constitution, in turn, have been forced to *concede* the States'-righters' interpretation of the provision, and have proceeded to *defend* the virtual elimination of state power which is implied? The fact that none of these things happened sets up the strongest kind of presumption that just about everybody was under precisely the opposite impression as to the meaning of the word—a presumption that was to be corroborated, as we have seen, by the way in which the provision was interpreted in the years directly following the adoption of the Constitution.

Third, with reference to James Wilson's remarks to the Convention on July 21, we should note at the outset that Wilson made no reference to the Supremacy Clause, let alone to its use of the word "pursuance." In that speech he was urging the Convention to incorporate into the Constitution a "Council of Revision," composed in part of judges, having the power to veto Acts of Congress on policy grounds. A close examination of Wilson's argument, moreover, shows that the Supremacy Clause probably did not figure in his reasoning at all—and that if it did, his understanding of "pursuance" was certainly not the one Crosskey imputes to him.

The key passage of the speech, on Crosskey's showing, argued that judges of the Supreme Court ought to participate in the proposed "Council" so that they might "remonstrate" against "projected encroachments on the people *as well as themselves.*" Crosskey reads this passage—the italics are his—as proving that Wilson believed a) that judges *already* had power to protect "themselves" (i.e., the B1 power of resisting invasions of judicial prerogatives), and b) that they should now be given some additional power in order to protect the general public. But since the Convention had just adopted the Supremacy Clause, Crosskey reasons, Wilson could not have regarded the Supremacy Clause as having conferred the *additional* power he was now seeking—i.e., as having already conferred, in Crosskey's words, "a *general* right of judicial review." And since Wilson thought the judiciary did not have this "general right" under the Supremacy Clause, Crosskey concludes that Wilson did not read "in Pursuance thereof" in the modern sense which alone would authorize judicial review of general congressional legislation.[1]

Our first answer is that Crosskey's "general right of judicial review" is manifestly *not* the additional power Wilson wished to confer on judges in the Council of Revision. The additional power Wilson was seeking, as the balance of the July 21 speech makes clear, was not the power to declare general congressional legislation *unconstitutional*

—i.e., Crosskey's "general right of judicial review"; but, rather, the power to join with the Executive in deciding whether such legislation was *"unjust," "unwise,"* or *"dangerous"*—i.e., what we call today the *veto* power. Thus Wilson was recommending a far broader power for judges than the Supremacy Clause, under *either* interpretation of "in Pursuance thereof," could have conferred; obviously, then, the recommendation is neither here nor there on the question as to *which* interpretation Wilson endorsed.

Our further answer is that Crosskey has evidently not thought through Wilson's observation that judges already had the right to defend *"themselves"* against congressional usurpations. Whence might this right have come? One possibility is that Wilson believed such a right was to be *inherent* in the judicial power and that it was thus implicitly recognized by the Convention's intention to establish a national judiciary—an intention that was to be embodied eventually in Article III. This theory, as we know, had very little support in the American legal tradition; yet Wilson may have espoused it, and if he did, we may agree his observation sheds no light at all on his understanding of "in Pursuance thereof." The second, and more likely, explanation (it does not seem there is a third) is that Wilson based his observation on the Supremacy Clause; he believed, that is to say, that the qualifying phrase "in Pursuance thereof" meant that judges would not be expected to enforce congressional acts relating to the judiciary that were not "consistent with" the Constitution. But if that was Wilson's reasoning, Crosskey's case obviously collapses. If "in Pursuance thereof" meant "consistent with" in respect of usurpations of judicial prerogatives, why not in respect of *all* congressional usurpations? The framers stated this qualification of Congress' authority— if qualification it was—in all-inclusive terms, a fact that could not have been lost on "one of the acutest lawyers" at the Convention.

Fourth, regarding the provision in the Articles of Confederation (Article VI) that sought to prevent state tax levies from obstructing treaty negotiations, it seems clear that Professor Crosskey has once again tried to push the evidence further than it will go. Granted, the provision was designed to "facilitate" treaty negotiations with powers like France and Spain that might give aid to the Revolutionary cause. Does this mean, however, that the States were prepared to give congressional negotiators a blank check in this matter—that the negotiators were to be allowed to annul the States' taxing power by entering into any agreement whatever that might colorably be termed "a treaty in prosecution of" certain earlier proposals to France and

Spain? To suppose any State would concede Congress such latitude
is to ignore the spirit of the times, and to ignore, specifically, the
States' jealous concern for their taxing power, as evinced elsewhere
in the Articles. For example, Article IX expressly forbade Congress
to make treaties that would exempt foreigners from the normal operation of state tax laws. Article VI was a qualified exception to this
prohibition: the States were to defer to congressional policy *"in accord with,"* or *"in keeping with"* certain proposals that had already
been drawn up for securing foreign assistance in the war effort. Now
we may agree that Professor Crosskey's interpretation—"in prosecution of"—is also legitimate; this is an instance where *both* meanings
are tolerated by the context. Our point is simply that to rule out
the former meaning, as Crosskey would have us do, is to cast an unreasonable construction on the Articles as a whole.

Regarding Article XII, we concede that Professor Crosskey has correctly read "in Pursuance of" in the Johnsonian sense.*

---

* However, the careful reader may feel, as we do, that Crosskey misconstrued Article XII in his discussion of it, and by doing so, made his
argument more complicated than it needed to have been. Article XII provided: "All bills of credit emitted, monies borrowed, and debts contracted
by, or under the authority of Congress, before the assembling of the United
States, in pursuance of the present confederation, shall be deemed and
considered as a charge against the United States, for payment and satis-
faction whereof the said United States, and the public faith are hereby
solemnly pledged." Thus Article XII plainly does not purport, as Crosskey
maintains it does, to guarantee both those commitments *"antecedently"* made
by Congress [before the Confederation went into effect] and those *subsequently* made by it." If the drafters of the Articles had wanted to bring
subsequent commitments into the scope of the provision, they obviously would
have had to insert an "or" before the phrase "in pursuance of"—and in that
case, paradoxically for the purposes of Crosskey's argument, the meaning of
"pursuance" would have shifted to the *non-*Johnsonian sense. The phrase
would no longer, that is to say, modify "the assembling of the United
States," but would refer back to the subject of the sentence—thus indicating,
by a natural reading, that only those commitments were to be honored that
would be contracted *"in accord with"* the "present Confederation." (We do
not suggest, of course, that the drafters of the Articles expected the Confederacy to dishonor its future commitments; on the contrary, they undoubtedly believed a pledge of future financial integrity to be *implicit* in
the formation of a new state, that an express guarantee in this particular
would hardly befit the dignity of a sovereign nation.) If, then, Article XII
was designed merely to reassure existing creditors that debts contracted by
the Continental Congress *prior* to the Articles would be honored, it is clear
from the context that the phrase "in pursuance of the present Confed-

Crosskey's fifth argument, we may recall, is a defense of his thesis—an explanation of why "in Pursuance thereof" was used at all in the Supremacy Clause if the phrase meant merely "in virtue thereof." Let us agree he has given a plausible reason why the framers might have used *"in virtue thereof."* Yet the fact of the matter is that the framers chose a different phrase—and they appear to have done so, as we shall see momentarily, for reasons easily adducible that quite effectively dispose of Crosskey's "explanation."

Finally, the rhetorical play that constitutes Crosskey's sixth argument plainly proves too much. If it is absurd, as he says, to suppose that the framers gave "primary" responsibility for judging the constitutionality of acts of Congress to "every petty [state] judge," is it not also absurd to suppose that these same petty jurists were given the primary responsibility for construing and enforcing the Constitution in the case of an alleged conflict with *state* laws? Yet Crosskey has no doubt that the Supremacy Clause gave the latter function to state judges, in the first instance to the petty ones. The issue, then—in either case—is whether state judges were deemed competent to expound the Constitution. "State recalcitrance and . . . delays" may indeed, as Crosskey complains, have been the "bane" of the Confederation; and we might add that lack of uniformity in state judicial decisions contributed to the "bane." But the architects of American federalism, as we have seen, did not seek to *eliminate* the possibilities of state obstructionism—for that would have ushered in the even more fearsome ravages of unleavened centralism; but rather to *minimize* those possibilities by formally obliging state judges, in the Supremacy Clause, to give the federal Constitution and valid federal laws preference over state laws—an obligation that necessarily presupposed the competence of state judges to construe and apply the Constitution faithfully. But since the Constitution those judges would have to construe in assessing the validity of state laws is the same Constitution they would have to construe in assessing the validity of

---

eration" was designed merely to clarify the meaning of the previous phrase, "the assembling of the United States," and was thus, indeed, equivalent to "in consequence of" or "under." The "pursuance" phrase, in other words, cannot reasonably be read as referring to prior debts—suggesting that those that had been contracted "in pursuance of [i.e., in accordance with] the present Confederation" would be honored and others would not; for, manifestly, *no* debts contracted *prior* to the "present Confederation" could be deemed to have been made "in pursuance of" that Confederation, and this quite irrespective of which interpretation is given to "pursuance."

congressional laws, why should the framers have imputed to them a greater competence for the one job than for the other?

Such is the case Professor Crosskey has made—and we may take it to be the best case available—for the proposition that the framers' use of "in Pursuance thereof" demonstrated their intention to make Congress the sole judge of its constitutional powers.

We may now examine some evidence on the other side of the question, which Professor Crosskey has overlooked.

First, there is the fact that *in every instance in which the word "pursuance"* (or, as the case might be, *"pursuant"* or *"pursue"*) *was used by the framers during the debates at the Constitutional Convention, the speakers' manifest meaning was compatible with some equivalent of "in accord with" or "in keeping with."* The word does not appear often in the Convention records, but when it does, the sense intended is invariably the *non*-Johnsonian one. We may take as an illustration the July 23 debate during which Elbridge Gerry and Gouverneur Morris commented on the issue of how the new Constitution was to be ratified. Both men took the position that the Constitution amounted to an "alteration" of the old Articles of Confederation, and thus, by the express terms of the Articles, that it should be submitted for ratification to the "Legislatures of every State." Gerry said this method would give the Constitution sufficient authority because "everything done *in pursuance of*" the Articles would be "paramount to any State Constitution"—his obvious point being that things *not* done in pursuance of the Articles, that is not "in accord with" them, would not have this paramount status. And Morris said: "if the Confederation be *pursued,* no alteration can be made without the unanimous consent of the legislatures." Again, the obvious meaning of "pursued" is "observed," rather than "prosecuted"; for Morris was clearly warning against a solution under which the Articles would *not* be observed.

And now, a far more decisive point. The original version of the Supremacy Clause, as introduced by Luther Martin on behalf of the States'-rights faction and adopted by the Convention on July 17, contained the double-barreled phrase "by virtue *and* in pursuance of." The original version read: "Resolved that the legislative Acts of the United States made by virtue and in pursuance of [the Constitution, etc.] shall be the supreme law. . . ." Now, unless we wish to accuse the draftsmen of a quite pointless tautology, it is clear that "in pursuance of" meant something *different* from "by virtue of." The draftsmen, that is to say, obviously had *two* thoughts in mind: in or-

der for congressional acts to be the "supreme law" they would have
to be enacted *both* "in prosecution of" the Constitution (Professor
Crosskey's idea) *and* "in accordance with" the Constitution. For the
former idea they chose the phrase "by virtue of"; for the latter, "in
pursuance of"—which would seem to put their understanding of "pursuance" beyond peradventure. But that is not all. For the Convention
eventually *dropped* the words "by virtue": as we know, they do not
appear in the final version of the Supremacy Clause. Why was this
done? We may be sure it was not because the framers wished to
eliminate the "in accordance with" requirement, for if that had been
their intention, they surely would have *preserved* the "by virtue"
phrase, and dropped the other! The only reasonable inference is
that the Convention's stylists, recognizing that "in pursuance thereof"
had two meanings, chose to employ that single phrase to communicate
both of the purposes they had in mind. This, then, is why Crosskey's
"explanation" of the framers' decision, as set forth in his fifth argument, does not wash.

Finally, Professor Crosskey's understanding of "pursuance"—convenient though it may be to his general thesis about congressional
supremacy—reduces the parliamentary situation at Philadelphia, as
we know it from the Convention's records, to chaos and incompre-
hensibility. We have seen that on July 17, at the insistence of the
States'-righters, the Convention rejected the idea of a "congressional
negative" on the grounds that such a provision would leave the States
at the mercy of the Union government. Under the circumstances, is
it credible that the Convention, the same day, turned around and
adopted a new plan that everyone concerned understood would contain the same potential for congressional despotism as the one just
rejected? We must not suppose the States'-righters—for it was they,
after all who proposed the new plan—were so dull. Moreover, is it
likely—if Crosskey is correct in believing that the Supremacy Clause
assured congressional supremacy over the States—that proponents of
the "Congressional negative" would have renewed their campaign on
its behalf long after the Supremacy Clause had been accepted as a
permanent ingredient of the Convention's scheme? Yet Charles
Pinckney, supported by Madison and others, did urge reconsideration of the "negative" on August 23, and a substantial debate ensued.
The Pinckney-Madison forces lost by a vote of only six states to
five,[3] which shows that nationalist sentiment was far from subdued.
But the main teaching of that episode is that neither the nationalizers,
nor their victorious opponents, thought that a congressional right to

define the limits between the federal and state governments *had already been asserted*—thanks to a Johnsonian usage of "in Pursuance of"—*in the Supremacy Clause.* Or, to put all of this in a word: Professor Crosskey's understanding of *"pursuance" could* not have been the one held by the framers unless we suppose that all of those at Philadelphia who from July 17 on thought they were winning the debate about congressional supremacy were in fact losing it, and all of those who thought they were losing the debate were in fact winning it.

To sum up, we may agree with Professor Crosskey that eighteenth-century legal draftsmen could correctly use "in Pursuance thereof" as an equivalent to "in virtue of" or "in consequence of"—which will hardly come as a surprise to lawyers in the twentieth century who occasionally use the phrase in just that sense. Our point has not been that this use of the phrase was malapropistic in the eighteenth century, but that it had, then as now, two meanings; that the more usual meaning, then as now, was "in accordance with" or some equivalent; and that, in any event, the meaning actually intended must be inferred, then as now, from the surrounding context. And we conclude from the context here that the traditional understanding of "in Pursuance of," as used in the Supremacy Clause, is quite correct: the framers did *not* intend to give Congress an unlimited right to define its own powers, and thus did not intend that state judges should be obliged, automatically, to enforce every act Congress might see fit to enact. As Mr. Brinton Coxe felicitously put it many years ago, this provision of the Supremacy Clause *"liberates* [state judges] from the rule of [national supremacy] whenever U.S. laws are not made in pursuance of the U.S. Constitution."[4]

THE MEANING OF
THE SUPREMACY CLAUSE, III

I

The operational significance of the "liberation" we have just
spoken of was that under the new Constitution state judges were expected to rule upon the constitutionality, not only of state laws, but
of *federal* laws. Yet the moment we add that expectation to the conclusions previously reached about the addressees of the Supremacy
Clause, we are in the presence of an apparent anomaly of quite
startling proportions. For if it is true 1) that the enforcement of "the
supreme Law of the Land" was expressly entrusted to state judges—
with the right of appeal to federal judges being, as best, problemat-
ical; and if it is true 2) that state judges, as part of this trust, were
to have the power to invalidate such federal legislation as they
deemed contrary to "supreme law"; it would seem to follow 3) that
the real seat of power, under the framers' plan, was to have been
the state courts. Congress and the President might *attempt* to enact
"supreme laws," but state judges would decide, in the final analysis,
whether such attempts had been successful. And that being the case,
the "Supremacy Clause" might more appropriately have been nick-
named the "Subordination Clause," and the American Constitution
from the beginning should have been recognized as the charter, not of
a federal government, but of a league of states that would be governed
in the last instance by the several state judiciaries.

Now since all of this is pretty clearly not the case, we must re-
examine the premises of the reasoning just set forth to see where the
argument went wrong. It went wrong, in the first place, because in
Premise 1 we failed to make clear that the state judges' special re-

257

sponsibility for *enforcing* the supreme law did not necessarily entail a special responsibility—let alone, an exclusive responsibility—to *define* and *interpret* the supreme law. And the argument went still further awry in Premise 2 because we airily assumed—as most modern commentators do—that the power to *rule on a law's constitutionality*, as part of the judicial enforcement process, is equivalent to the power to *invalidate a law*. In Premise 2, in other words, we came face-to-face with the central problem of this inquiry—What *effect* was a judicial determination of unconstitutionality to have had, under the framers' scheme, on *other branches of government?*—and then failed to make the relevant distinctions. So let us probe a little further to see if the framers' scheme still seems anomalous once their ideas on these two matters have been properly understood.

Consider Premise 1. While the Supremacy Clause states who shall be "bound" by the supreme law, it says nothing at all about who shall define or interpret that law. It says nothing expressly, that is, and therefore leaves the matter open to inference. What is the reasonable inference? The first part of the Clause proclaims in the most general terms possible that three kinds of enactments shall have the status of "the supreme Law of the Land." Now no one is exempted from that sweeping command; therefore we may conclude that *everyone is obliged to observe it*: Congress, the President, the Supreme Court, state governors, state legislators, state courts, sheriffs, private citizens—everyone. The first part of the clause, then, made observation of "the supreme Law" a civic duty for all the people, and where official bodies might be concerned, an official duty. Yet, clearly, nobody could observe the supreme law without first making a judgment as to what it was he was observing—i.e., without first defining and interpreting the supreme law. Congress could not be expected to pass laws "in pursuance [of the Constitution]" without first making a determination as to what the Constitution permitted. The President would have to make a similar judgment in the performance of his duties. So would the courts. So would state legislatures. So, even, would private citizens. This much would seem to go without saying.

Yet there remains a further dimension of the problem. It is possible that these mutual duties are, so to speak, "structured," that the framers intended A's duty of defining and interpreting to have a *higher standing* than B's, with the result that B is expected to abandon his own judgment, and accept A's, should the two come into conflict. And let us agree that such structuring as the framers had in mind might be deduced from any of three sources—from common sense, from the historical context, or from what the framers actually said in the balance of the Clause. For instance, common sense tells us that private citizens were expected to defer to the judgments of official bodies, for this is an obvious condition for maintaining the public order. Again, the historical context discloses that judgments of *legislatures*, failing clear evidence that a contrary rule was intended, were to take precedence over those of other, co-ordinate branches of government. And finally, as an illustration of the third source, the balance of the Supremacy Clause reveals that the framers made one exception to the rule of legislative supremacy: state courts were to be released from the obligation to follow their own legislatures in the matter of defining and interpreting the "supreme Law." (Note, however, that the exception does not appear to have turned the state court-state legislature relationship upside down, thus obliging state legislatures to *follow* their respective courts. This is a more difficult matter than the others, but the correct conclusion, apparently, is that while state courts were put at liberty to cast their own construction on the Constitution in ordinary litigation, and while the Supremacy Clause, certainly in its spirit, envisioned the judiciary's construction being treated with great respect in the State concerned, nothing, withal, in the Clause would make the court's decision *binding* on the rest of the state government, thus formally barring the state legislature from subsequently insisting on its own construction of the Constitution.)

Turning to the problem at hand, what do these three sources disclose regarding the obligation of a *Union legislature* to defer to the judgments of *state courts*? The answer from the first two is easy: neither common sense nor the historical context suggests that a nominally, and by every other standard, *superior* body was expected to subordinate itself to an *inferior* body; indeed, both common sense and history compellingly affirm the opposite. What of the third source? Does the balance of the Supremacy Clause in any way detract from this presumption? It is true that the Clause singles out state judges as *enforcers* of the supreme law. Yet we have seen there was good and sufficient reason—nay, an essential reason—for the framers to have marked out that special role: state courts had to be released from their traditional obligation to accede to the judgments of their own legislatures. And consequently there is no need to search for a further motivation—in this case the palpably unlikely one of making the state judges' *interpretation* of the Constitution binding on Congress. We conclude, then, that a) the framers imposed on every element of the body politic an obligation to *observe*—and thus

to define and interpret—the supreme law; and b) while certain inferences may be drawn regarding who was expected to bow to whom
in the matter of defining and interpreting, the possibility that Congress was supposed to subordinate itself to the state courts is certainly
not among them.

Consider Premise 2. We saw in the previous chapter that the
phrase "in Pursuance thereof" gave state courts authority to rule
upon the constitutionality of acts of Congress as incident to their
role of enforcing the supreme law. We now must ask whether the
framers expected that a state court judgment that Congress had *not*
acted in pursuance of the Constitution would *invalidate* the law in
question. Was Congress, that is to say, expected to regard the law
as having been "repealed"—the C2 view of the effect of judicial review? Or, a still more drastic possibility—was Congress expected to
take the C3 view that the court had rendered a "final" determination
of the Constitution's meaning, thus barring Congress from reenacting
the law? From what we have seen of the pre-Convention tradition,
either of these expectations would be altogether astonishing. For we
know there was not a single instance in Anglo-American legal history
down to the summer of 1787 in which a judicial decision was regarded as binding on the legislature concerned—much less binding
on a *superior* legislature. We did indeed come across several instances in which state courts, prior to the Constitutional Convention,
declined to *enforce* laws, but nobody—least of all the judges concerned (remember *Trevett v. Weeden!*)—supposed the law in question was thereby liquidated. The judges understood themselves to be
saying simply—and were so understood by everyone else—that *as
far as the courts were concerned the law was invalid and could not
be executed*; that is, the C1 theory as to the *effect* of judicial review.
By the same token the legislators involved understood themselves—
and were so understood by everyone else—to be free to accept or reject the judges' verdict as they saw fit. Now if we may agree that
legal traditions are presumed to be in force in the absence of evidence
of an intention to depart from them, and that the presumption is
particularly strong when departing from them entails some utterly
incongruous result such as the subordination of an otherwise superior
legislature to an otherwise inferior court—to say nothing of the further incongruity, present here, of inviting as many "final" interpretations of the Constitution as there were States of the Union—must we
not conclude that the framers believed the traditional (C1) view of
the effect of judicial review would, as a matter of course, govern relations between the state courts and Congress?

But we need not rely entirely on presumptions. For this view of the framers' expectations is repeatedly set forth in their remarks at the Constitutional Convention. We shall have occasion in a later chapter to examine the Convention debates in detail insofar as they relate to judicial review, but it is relevant to note here that the framers invariably employed language that either unmistakably endorsed the Cl theory, or is easily interpretable in that sense. Judges will have the opportunity of *"deciding on the constitutionality"* of certain kinds of laws (Elbridge Gerry), and will refuse to enforce those they *"consider"* invalid (Madison, Gouverneur Morris). And since the courts will thus *"impede the operation"* of unconstitutional laws (George Mason), they *"may do good"* (Hugh Williamson). *"May,"* that is, because the legislature concerned may be persuaded by such *"remonstrances"* (James Wilson) to repeal the offensive legislation. In any event, a court's refusal to *"say [an unconstitutional measure] is law"* (Morris) will operate as a temporary check on the legislature inasmuch as that court will be denying the law makers the use of its particular enforcement machinery. And whether the legislature will eventually change its mind in the light of the court's opposition, or the judges change theirs—the recent experience of the *Trevett, Rutgers* and perhaps the Newbern cases is implicitly acknowledged in the delegates' remarks—will depend on which of the two views has the support of community sentiment.

The absence of any reference at all in the Convention debates to a judicial power of *"invalidating"* legislation is especially revealing for our purposes here; for the delegates were speaking in every instance of the relationship between *coordinate* branches of government—in most cases between the proposed Congress and the proposed Supreme Court; moreover, they were speaking in most instances merely of a judiciary's right *to defend its own prerogatives* against a coordinate legislature. If these were the framers' views with regard to the effect of a Supreme Court decision on Congress (or a state court's decision on a state legislature), how much more emphatically they apply to the effect of an *inferior* court's decision on a *superior* legislature! Plainly, the idea that state judges could invalidate an act of Congress—let alone forbid Congress to re-enact the legislation the judges disapproved of—could not have been further from the framers' minds.

In sum, the apparent anomaly does disappear on a closer examination of the framers' reasoning, and we find ourselves looking at an altogether coherent and plausible arrangement: a) state judges were to enforce the "supreme Law of the Land" whenever that law clashed with state legislation; b) that responsibility might occasionally oblige the judges to hold that an act of Congress did not qualify as supreme law and thus did not take precedence over state legislation; yet c) the fundamental objective of Union supremacy would be carried out through the understanding that Congress, being a legislature—and a superior legislature at that—might, after due consideration, ignore the state court's ruling and continue to regard its legislation as valid; and finally d)—the more difficult matter mentioned previously—while state legislatures would perhaps have a moral obbligation, sounding in the spirit of the Supremacy Clause, to adopt the construction of the Constitution cast by their respective state courts, they would ultimately have the same right and duty as all other public authorities to support the Constitution according to their own lights.

II

We have undoubtedly given more attention to the state courts than has seemed justified to modern commentators accustomed to wishing away the evidence that the framers made those courts the keystone of their scheme for enforcing Union supremacy. We have not, however, forgotten the Supreme Court. On the contrary, since the Supreme Court's role in the enforcement plan is at best implicit, a reliable assessment of that role required preliminary scrutiny of the *explicit* parts of the plan, as well as of the theory and reasoning that apparently underlay the plan as a whole. If the general picture could be brought into focus we have assumed, the individual parts would probably fall into the pattern intended for them.

It should be clear by now that there are only two routes by which the Supreme Court, on the strength of the Supremacy Clause, can enter the picture at all. One is via the questionable, and in any case contingent (on Congress), right of appeal from state court judgments. The other proceeds from the implication in the first part of the Supremacy Clause that all public authorities, including, naturally, the Supreme Court, are obliged to observe "the supreme Law of the Land" in the course of performing their official duties. Thus, by tracking down these two possibilities, we will have discovered all the Supremacy Clause can teach us about the effect a judicial determination of unconstitutionality was to have had on other branches of government when handed down by the highest court of the land.

Regarding the first, let us put aside all quarrels about the *right* of appeal, and assume arguendo that the framers anticipated that some of the controversies originating in state courts which involved the constitutionality of state or federal legislation would be taken to the Supreme Court on a writ of error—as Congress indeed provided in the Judiciary Act of 1789. And with all of our earlier doubts thus resolved in the Supreme Court's favor, we may ask what the transfer of such a case to Supreme Court might imply with regard to that Court's authority over the parties to the controversy. Now: *it is among the most fundamental precepts of our jurisprudence that a grant of appellate jurisdiction does not confer upon the appellate court any authority vis à vis the litigants that was not held by the court of original jurisdiction.* The appellate court's jurisdiction is "superior" to that of the original court only in the sense that it can decide whether the original court's judgment was right or wrong. It can "re-examine" the judgment, and "reverse or affirm" it, in the words of the first Judiciary Act; but that is all. If the appellate court affirms, the original court proceeds to execute its own judgment as though there had been no appeal; if the appellate court reverses, the original court proceeds to deal with the litigants as though its own judgment had gone the other way. In short, the original judgment does not acquire any *additional* status, or dignity, by virtue of its having been appealed.*

Yet if this is true with respect to the litigants—to the parties formally and directly affected by the suit—how much more emphatically is it true with respect to persons or governmental bodies *not* formally party to the suit and only *indirectly* affected by it. If the original court's judgment does not acquire a different status vis à vis the litigants by virtue of having been appealed, how can it take on a different status vis à vis some branch of government whose rights and duties were only collaterally at issue?† Therefore, *a state court judgment denying the constitutionality of an act of Congress—or of a state*

---

* In saying that an original judgment does not gain additional dignity after review, we do not refer to the status of the judgment in the internal affairs of the judicial system concerned. Thus a federal district court decision, once it has been affirmed by the Supreme Court, becomes the rule for all federal courts until such time as the Supreme Court changes its mind. And while there is no such automatic obedience demanded of state courts, they too, as a practical expedient for avoiding reversals, will usually follow the Supreme Court's lead regardless of the jurisdiction in which the issue in question originally arose.

† Occasionally, of course, a state government or the United States government is formally party to a suit; in such a case the government's rights after appeal are the same as any other litigant's.

legislature—must possess exactly the same capacity to bind Congress or the state legislature after *the Supreme Court has spoken that it enjoyed* before *the appeal was taken.* And since we have agreed that a state court judgment is *not* finally determinative of the rights of other branches of government, it follows that a Supreme Court judgment in such a case is not either.

*The Supreme Court's appellate powers, in other words, are strictly derivative. To the extent the Court's claims to the power of judicial review rest on an implied extension of the Supremacy Clause's mandate to state judges, then the common-sense conclusions reached earlier regarding the effect of state court decisions on other branches of government must apply—*though admittedly they inconvenience the doctrine of judicial supremacy—*to Supreme Court decisions as well.*

It remains to see whether the doctrine fares any better when the Court's claims are asserted via the second route. We agreed earlier that the first part of the Supremacy Clause implicitly charges the Supreme Court—along with Congress, the President, and everyone else with a general duty of defining and interpreting the "supreme Law of the Land"—a duty that exists over and beyond the Constitution's specific mandates. The first question, then, is whether the Supreme Court's duty (and therefore its rights) in this nebulous area is of a higher or a lower standing than that of *Congress.* The language of the Constitution itself provides no guidance; hence we are forced once again to summon the historical context for clues to the framers' intentions. The obvious and controlling clue is, of course, the nigh-universal acknowledgment that was accorded the principle of legislative supremacy in the going political tradition. When legislators and judges fell out, according to the tradition and contemporary practice, the latter were expected to give way or suffer the consequences; the idea that judges should prevail as a matter of right was altogether strange to the age. We must conclude, then, that Congress' authority, as an expounder of the Constitution, was certainly not meant to be *subordinate* to that of the Supreme Court—that, at the very least, Congress was to have an opportunity to *reassert* its own interpretation of the Constitution should the Supreme Court refuse to execute a congressional enactment on grounds of unconstitutionality.

This construction of the Clause's first section, moreover, coincides entirely with the conclusions just reached regarding the Supreme Court's authority as an appellate court for state judgments. It also coincides with the external evidence we shall be weighing later on—

with the framers' remarks during the Convention debate, and with the contentions of *The Federalist. Federalist* No. 81, to reach ahead just once, is illustrative. In that paper Alexander Hamilton expressly addressed himself to the charge (attributed to the Constitution's enemies) that "the authority of the proposed Supreme Court of the United States, which is to be a separate and independent body, will be superior to that of the Legislature." The charge had been advanced, Hamilton explained, by the argument that "the Parliament of Great Britain, and the Legislatures of the several States, can at any time rectify, by law, the exceptionable decisions of their respective courts, but the errors and usurpations of the Supreme Court of the United States will be uncontrollable and remediless." To which Hamilton made the following answer: "[Neither] the Parliament of Great Britain [nor] the Legislatures of the particular States, can rectify the exceptional decisions of their respective courts *in any other sense than might be done by a future Legislature of the United States—*[i.e., *by Congress*]. A Legislature, without exceeding its province, cannot reverse a determination once made in a particular case; *though it may prescribe a new rule for future cases. This is the principle, and it applies in all its consequences, exactly in the same manner and extent, to the State governments, as to the national government now under consideration. Not the least difference can be pointed out in any view of the subject.*"

Whether a *state* legislature was obliged to defer to the Supreme Court's construction of the Constitution is, to be sure, a somewhat different matter. The two would not be, like Congress and the Court, coordinate branches of the same government: as against a state legislature the Court would belong to a *superior* order of government. And therefore, comparing their roles as Constitution-expounders in the abstract, we may agree the Court's construction would have a "higher" standing—would be entitled to greater deference and respect by the rest of the government and by the country at large. But from what we know of the *raison d'être* of the Supremacy Clause, it would obviously be wrong to conclude from this that a state legislature that found itself in conflict with the Court would be bound categorically to accept the Court's construction of its rights and powers. For the Constitutional Convention's rejection of the "congressional negative" was motivated precisely by the majority's unwillingness to permit the definition of the boundary lines between federal and state power to be the unilateral prerogative of the federal government. And while the framers may conceivably have felt the Supreme Court would be a more dispassionate, a safer, arbiter between Congress and the

States than Congress itself, it remains that the Supreme Court would be part of the federal government. Is it not reasonable to conclude that is why the Supremacy Clause pointedly omits *any* reference to *any* branch of the federal government, and thus pointedly declines to place the state legislatures—as the congressional negative would have done—wholly at the mercy of federal whim and federal power?

Such, then, appears to be the teaching of the Supremacy Clause on the subject of judicial review. We may summarize:

1. The purpose of the provision in the framers' contemplation was to secure the supremacy of the Union government over the state governments. It was inserted in the Constitution on the initiative of the "States' rights," or "federalist" faction, as an alternative to the nationalist-supported congressional negative. The latter solution, many feared, might achieve Union supremacy at the expense of legitimate state powers. Thus the main function of the Supremacy Clause, as the framers saw it, was not to designate an interpreter of the supreme law, but to make clear that when otherwise legitimate state laws clashed with legitimate federal laws, or with the Constitution itself, the state laws should give way.

2. The command of Union supremacy was implicitly addressed to every person and public authority that might be affected by the kind of enactments defined as "the supreme Law of the Land." The only parties expressly named to *enforce* the command were—state judges.

3. The reason state judges were singled out is that their ability to enforce Union supremacy required a release from their traditional and well understood obligation to enforce the enactments of their own legislatures. The tradition of legislative supremacy was so strong that this sharp departure from the tradition could not be left to inference. Arguably, a further reason for the express designation is that state courts were the place where clashes between Union and state authority were most likely to occur.

4. The modern assumption that the express designation of state judges confers a special authority on the Supreme Court runs afoul of the fact that a right of appeal from state court judgments is not conferred by the Constitution, and of the evidence that such a right may even have been contrary to the framers' intentions. In any event, the framers' failure to mention the Supreme Court, and the doubt that surrounds the matter of appeals, would seem to preclude the possibility that the Supreme Court was expected—on the strength of

the Supremacy Clause—to be the chief custodian of the Constitution.

5. Since state judges were not intended to be rubber stamps for a potentially despotic federal legislature, they were obliged to enforce only those federal laws that were "made in pursuance" of the Constitution. Therefore, the power of ruling upon the constitutionality of acts of Congress was recognized as a necessary incident to the judges' duty of enforcing Union supremacy. And this is the second great departure, clearly affirmed by the Clause, from the principle of legislative supremacy.

6. The state courts' right to refuse to enforce unconstitutional legislation did not, however, make them the "final arbiters" of the Constitution's meaning. Should the legislature concerned disagree with the judges' view, it would be at liberty to conduct its affairs in the future in accord with its own understanding of the Constitution. Thus, the C1, or at most the C2 theory of the *effect* of judicial review emerges from the Supremacy Clause's reference to state judges.

7. The Supreme Court's power of review, whether regarded as derivative from the power of state courts, or as implied by the general command of the Supremacy Clause's first section, is likewise a C1, or at most a C2 power.

In short, the Supreme Court's claim to be the final arbiter of the Constitution is a total stranger to the surroundings that are most frequently alleged to have begot it, the famous Supremacy Clause; and one wonders how the myth of its origins there has survived. A chance duplication in nomenclature—"the supreme law," "the supreme court"—may help explain why the ordinary citizen links the two and supposes the one must be simply what the other expounds. But what of more attentive commentators—and especially of students of the subject—who can read and who know very well that the two phrases never appear together in the Constitution—that where the "supreme law" is discussed and defined, the "supreme court" is conspicuous only by its absence, an absence that is only partially cured by the most determined efforts to force an entrance through the back door?

To be sure, judicial review apologists have another contrivance or two in their textual tool chest. The back door, they confidently assure us, springs wide open once the Supremacy Clause is viewed "in context" of the other provisions of the Constitution that deal with the Judiciary. Very well; we shall oblige and give that contention the run it is worth.

JUDICIAL REVIEW ELSEWHERE
IN THE CONSTITUTION

The place in the Constitution we are normally told to go for further information about judicial review is Article III, the Judiciary Article. The allegedly relevant passages are Sections 1 and 2:

> The judicial Power of the United States *shall be vested* in one Supreme Court, and in such inferior Courts as the Congress may from time to time establish. . . .

> The judicial Power *shall extend* to all Cases, in Law and Equity, arising under this Constitution, the Laws of the United States, and Treaties [plus certain categories of cases specifically enumerated].

The difficulty with these supposedly illuminating passages is suggested by the verbs which manifestly add up to a *grant of jurisdiction*, and nothing more. The passages tell us who is to *possess* "the judicial power of the United States," and the *types* of cases the possessors of the power are entitled to deal with. They do not tell us, however, what "the judicial power" *is*. Article III is distinctive in this regard. Article I begins, "All legislative Powers herein granted shall be vested in a Congress" and then goes on to specify, in Section 8, what those powers are. Article II begins, "The executive Power shall be vested in a President" and then proceeds to itemize the elements of that power in Sections 2 and 3. Article III, however, contains no comparable passages describing the judicial power. This means, so far as the text is concerned, that we are left altogether in the dark on the question at issue here—namely, whether "the judicial Power," as the term was used by the framers, *included* the power of judicial review. It means we can read judicial review neither into the text, nor out of it, without assuming ex hypothesi the answer to the very question we are asking.

Another way of stating the difficulty presented by Article III is that a mere grant of jurisdiction—an instruction to a court that its power "shall extend" to a certain kind of case—tells the court nothing at all about what it should *do* with the case once it has taken jurisdiction. The power of a municipal court may "extend" under the terms of a local ordinance to jewel-filching by John Jones, but what the court will do with Jones once it has him in the court room will depend on the principles of larceny law that exist quite independently of the court's grant of jurisdiction. Similarly, when judges are called upon to hear cases "arising under this Constitution," they will not know *how* to decide those cases until they have consulted the established principles of constitutional construction and application. And those principles, we are saying, must be sought, either from auxiliary provisions of the Constitution, or from sources outside the document.

Does it follow that the drafters of Article III were obscurantists? Not at all. There is a plausible explanation why they did not spell out the elements of "the judicial Power"—perhaps two plausible explanations. The more likely is that they regarded the meaning of the term as self-evident—as encompassing the traditional, inherent authority courts were generally understood to possess under the existing jurisprudence. And if that is the case, of course, Article III turns out to be a better argument *against* judicial review than for it; for we know that the "tradition," as established by state jurisprudence prior to the Convention, and by colonial and English courts before that, embraced the rule of legislative supremacy, and by clear implication excluded anything even resembling judicial review, except possibly as a means of protecting judicial prerogatives. To be sure, as we have seen in the preceding chapters, the Supremacy Clause was designed to modify that rule to the extent necessary to achieve the supremacy of the Union government—and it may be argued that to *that* extent the framers intended "the judicial power" to include the power of review. Thus, while Article III may be read as encompassing the limited review role contemplated by Article VI, there appears to be no justification for thinking Article III went *beyond* Article VI.

The other possibility is that the framers purposely left to Congress the task of amplifying the meaning of the national "judicial power." We must remember that even the grant of jurisdiction set forth in Article III (except for the Supreme Court's original jurisdiction in two types of cases) was merely *potential*, that it required an implementing act of Congress to bring it into actual existence. Thus the framers may have expected Congress—when and if it established inferior federal courts of original jurisdiction, and when and if it provided for the Supreme Court's appellate jurisdiction—also to instruct the courts on the scope of their power relative to judicial review. It is certainly relevant to ask what the drafters of Article III expected Congress' instructions to be—a matter on which the Convention debates, as we shall see, shed some light—but the point once again is that the answer cannot be gathered from the *text* of Article III.

And of course these considerations apply with even greater force to the problem of the framers' intentions about the *effect* of a judicial determination of unconstitutionality. If Article III's grant of jurisdiction, by itself, does not enlighten us as to how a federal court was expected to decide a case, much less does it tell us how other branches of government were expected to react to the court's decision. Once again, "the judicial power" must be *assumed* to include the power to cast a final and definitive interpretation on the Constitution before the provisions of Article III can be taken as authority for such a power.

Understandably, then, even the most avid apologists for judicial review do not cite Article III, by itself, as proof-positive of the framers' intentions. The advice, rather, is to read Article III *in connection with the Supremacy Clause*; whereupon, the argument runs, the framers' design will emerge in a clear light. We have no objection to this procedure. Our point is simply that Article III *adds nothing* to the picture: reading the two provisions together leads to exactly the same conclusions about judicial review as the Supremacy Clause leads to independently.

The other provision typically cited as authority for judicial review is the third paragraph of Article VI which requires judges to take an "Oath . . . to support this Constitution." Thus Chief Justice Marshall asked in *Marbury v. Madison*: "Why, [unless the Constitution contemplated judicial review] does it direct the judges to take an oath to support it? This oath certainly applies in an especial manner to [the judges'] conduct in their official character. How immoral to impose [the oath] on them, if they were to be used as the instruments, and the knowing instruments, for violating what they swear to support!"[1] The argument is recognizably foolish. The selfsame provision of the Constitution requires many people—including state legislators and "all executive and judicial Officers . . . of the several States"—to take a similar oath. If Supreme Court judges are authorized, in virtue of this oath, to pass upon the constitutionality of the acts of state legislatures, are not state legislators, by the same token, authorized to pass on the constitutionality of Supreme Court decisions? The question begged here, of course, is: What duties does "this Constitution" impose on each of the several parties who must swear to uphold it? And the question is not going to be answered by homilies on the immorality of oath-breaking.

A better textual argument for some kind of judicial review is found in certain provisions of the Constitution that appear to have been addressed directly to the courts. Therefore it is arguable, under the (B1) theory, that judges are entitled to defend their own prerogatives, that the courts were expected to refuse to enforce legislation that violated these special instructions to the judicial department. But there are only a handful of such provisions. Article III, Section 2, provides that "the Trial of all Crimes . . . shall be by Jury," and adds that the trial must be held in the State in which the crime was committed. Section 3 of the same Article provides: "No person shall be convicted of Treason unless on the Testimony of two Witnesses to the same overt Act, or on Confession in open court."* Article I, Section 3, provides that the Chief Justice of the Supreme Court "shall preside" over a Senate trial of a Presidential impeachment. Finally, the jurisdictional provisions of Article III, Section 2, specify that the Supreme Court "shall have original jurisdiction" in two types of cases, and unlike the Court's appellate jurisdiction, this grant is not subordinated to the regulatory power of Congress. Thus, the original Constitution. The Amendments, however, furnish several additional items. The Fourth concerns the issuance of warrants; the Fifth, Sixth, and Seventh relate to trial procedures; the Eighth deals with bail and criminal punishments; and the Eleventh denies the federal courts jurisdiction over suits brought against States by citizens of foreign States. (Note that the great "human rights" Amendments, the First and the Fourteenth, which today provide the major occasions for judicial law-making, have no place on this list.)

We must be wary, however, of concluding too much from the mere *existence* of provisions pertaining peculiarly to the judicial department. For state constitutions had such provisions too; and yet the

---

* Section 3 also imposes certain restrictions on the punishment for treason. Since Congress is expressly given the power "to declare the Punishment of Treason," this provision appears to have been addressed to Congress, not to the Courts.

instances in the pre-Constitutional period when the courts rushed to their defense against legislative attack, and so used them as a handle for judicial review, were few and recognizably aberrational. The fact the framers included such judicial provisions in *their* document hardly establishes, by itself, an intention to elevate the (B1) doctrine of those isolated state cases into a constitutional principle. Such an intention would have to be established by external evidence— notably by what the framers *said* on the subject during the course of the Convention debates. And we may now plunge into those debates for evidence, not only on this point, but on every aspect of judicial review.

JUDICIAL REVIEW AT
THE CONSTITUTIONAL CONVENTION

The typical inquiry into whether the framers of the Constitution authorized judicial review centers on the data we are about to ex amine. Most scholars, that is to say, have given a wide berth to the kind of analysis of the Constitution's text we have just labored through—a methodological lapse in itself worth remarking. Close textual analysis, after all, is the exegete's primary tool on most points of constitutional doctrine. Perhaps, scholars have felt—on this subject— that even the most painstaking examination of the text would prove too inconclusive to be rewarding. But the reader of the foregoing pages may be forgiven the suspicion that some writers have viewed the wide berth as simply the more commodious way of living with material uncongenial to the doctrine of judicial supremacy.

Whatever the reason, the preferred method of inquiry has been to ask how the individual members of the Constitutional Convention *felt* about judicial review, as may be adduced from their remarks during the Philadelphia proceedings and elsewhere. This approach normally produces a kind of box-score verdict revealing a certain number of framers "in favor" of the institution and a certain number "opposed." Thus Professor Charles Beard has discovered 25 in favor of judicial review, 3 opposed; Professor Edward Corwin lists 8 in favor, 4 opposed; Horace Davis, 8 in favor, 8 opposed; and so on.[7] Some of these writers, it is fair to add, have tried to make their score-sheets more realistic by giving the opinions of the Convention's "influential" members—a Madison say, or a James Wilson—extra weight.

Now, clearly, an examination of the delegates' views as expressed at the Convention has a place in our study. But equally clearly the value of such an inquiry is limited, and may be lost altogether unless some of the more important limitations are kept in mind.

We should note, first of all, that not once during its deliberations did the Convention undertake a systematic, let alone a formal, consideration of judicial review. Whenever a delegate's speech touched on that subject, the remark was addressed primarily to some other issue. In every case, then, we are dealing with an "aside"—an explanation or justification of the position the delegate was taking on an arguably related matter that was then formally before the house. For instance, Charles Pinckney's comment on the Supreme Court's jurisdiction was advanced as an argument for imposing property qualifications on judges. This does not mean we can dismiss such remarks as *merely* argumentative, and thus as tendentious or ill-considered; it does warn us, however, against regarding them a priori as carefully-chiselled statements of political theory, or of the law, designed to illuminate the judiciary's role in the new governmental system. The best we can do is to take each remark on its own and judge from the context its quality and seriousness. (Here one may be tempted to ask: *Why* was judicial review dealt with so haphazardly by the Convention? But since the record we are about to consider may itself throw some light on that problem, let us postpone it until all of the evidence is in hand.)

Second and more important, we should be aware of the difficulties of arguing from the proposition that certain framers "favored" judicial review to the further proposition that they believed judicial review was to be a feature of the governmental system they were establishing. This mode of reasoning is doubly dangerous, moreover, where the opinions have been expressed before the document has taken final shape, and, in the majority of cases, at a quite early stage in the drafting proceedings. By way of analogy, it is easy enough to prove by citing their recorded remarks that a number of the delegates to the United Nations' founding conference at San Francisco favored the principle of subordinating the sovereignty of individual nations to the collective will of an international organization; yet it is doubtful that any of those delegates went away from San Francisco believing they had been successful in effectively incorporating such a principle into the U.N. Charter. The problem is further complicated in the case of the Constitutional Convention by the fact that the delegates' observations have come down to us in a highly abbreviated form. The entire record, let us remember, is derived from unofficial and recognizably sketchy note-taking. The result is that in nearly every case it is impossible to say with certainty whether the delegate is merely expressing a personal preference, or is purporting to describe (correctly or incorrectly) the state of the Convention's mind at that moment of the drafting proceedings. And since no general guidelines are available for handling the problem, the best we can do, once again, is to judge each observation on its own with the existence of the problem clearly in mind.

Third, and more important still, any meaningful review of this record must take into account the *kind* of judicial review the delegate appears to have had in mind. *Against what branch of government* did he suppose the power would be exercised? What *scope* did he envision for judicial review? What *effect*? It obviously does no legitimate service to the cause of adducing historical authority for the Supreme Court's modern activities to cite remarks that recognizably envisioned a far more limited review role than is now claimed for the Court. Such remarks constitute "con" evidence on the question of judicial supremacy, not "pro." Yet almost without exception those who have undertaken the box-score approach have listed as "favoring" judicial review those delegates who expressed opinions favorable to *any* version of judicial review. In our own examination of the record,* we shall try to be more discriminating.

Finally, there is the possibility, advanced quite bluntly by Professor Crosskey, that the record we shall be dealing with has been doctored. Crosskey points out that with one exception every remark during the proceedings that touched on judicial review is attested to exclusively by the Notes of James Madison. And since the Notes were published posthumously, and were edited quite late in Madison's career at a time he had come to take a relatively favorable view of the judiciary's claims, Crosskey suggests that both opportunity and motive were present for a stunning instance of one-man "revisionism."[1] We need not take the possibility too seriously. The sufficient answer to Crosskey is not that the noble Madison was above counterfeiting, or that the interests of the national morale now require us to assume he was; but that if Madison had been of a mind to falsify history in order to bolster the claims of judicial supremacy, he would have done a more effective job of it than appears from the record to which we now turn.†

---

* We urge the reader, for the purpose of this chapter, to glance back at the analysis set forth in "The Faces of Judicial Review," pp. 116-118.

† The further answer to Crosskey is that the emendations to Madison's account are evidently easy to spot, and that such as can be recognized have little bearing on the judiciary's role. On the former point, Professor Max Farrand relates in his Introduction to the Convention's Records: "The ink

We take up the relevant testimony in chronological order.

June 4

The question before the house was whether the federal judiciary should be included in the "Council of Revision" which, according to the Virginia Plan then before the Convention, would have the power to veto congressional legislation. *Elbridge Gerry* of Massachusetts opposed judges sitting on the Council inasmuch as

> they will have a sufficient check against encroachments of their own department by their exposition of the laws, which involved a power of deciding on their Constitutionality. In some States the Judges had actually set aside laws as being against the Constitution. This was done too with general approbation. It was quite foreign from the nature of the office to make them judges of the policy of public measures.[3]

Gerry was the first of several delegates who would be mentioning judicial "exposition of the Laws" as an *alternative* (whether desirable or not, whether adequate or not, would depend on the speaker's viewpoint) to the oft-proposed idea of giving the Supreme Court a role in *making* the laws. We should keep in mind, therefore, that remarks in this context were not concerned with state legislation, but apparently envisioned some kind of review of *congressional* laws (in our schema, the A2 power as to the branch of government subject to review).

Regarding the *scope* of review, Gerry spoke solely of the (B1) power of judicial self-protection: since the Supreme Court would possess *that* power incident to its regular duties, he was saying, judicial participation on the Council would be superfluous. There is no suggestion, in other words, that Gerry expected the judges to weigh the constitutionality of *all* congressional legislation that might come before them in the course of ordinary litigation.

As for the *effect* of that purely defensive power, note that Gerry appears to have been remarking, as an afterthought, the *difference*

---

which was used at the later date [apparently 1821] has faded quite differently from that of the original notes, so that most of the later revisions stand out from that page almost as clearly as if they had been written in red ink." Moreover, Farrand is satisfied that for the most part Madison made the changes in order to bring his own record into line with previously published accounts of the proceedings where the latter appeared to him to have a better claim to accuracy. (1 Farrand xvii, xviii.)

between merely "deciding on [a law's] Constitutionality," and "set [ting] aside" the law. He seems to have assumed that the former understanding of the power's effect (the C1 view that a judicial verdict against a law's constitutionality governs only the rights of the litigants in the particular case) *would prevail under the new federal Constitution*—even though the latter (the C2 view that such a verdict strikes the law from the books, and thus, failing legislative re-enactment, also governs future cases) had "actually" been recognized in the previous experience of "some States." (Indeed, Gerry's further assertion that such state verdicts had received "general approbation" might suggest they had been accepted as permanently binding on other branches of government, as "final"—the C3 view.) Now: the important point for our purposes is that Gerry apparently appreciated at least two of the possible "effects" a judicial determination of unconstitutionality might have, and declared as his own opinion that such a decision by the new national judiciary would amount merely to *a refusal to enforce a law that attacked judicial prerogatives*. Beyond this we should note that his brief account of what had "actually" occurred in the States' experience is simply incorrect and must be attributed either to misinformation or to a garbling of his remarks by Madison.* For, as we know, the single instance in which state judges may be said to have "set aside" a law was the North Carolina case of *Bayard v. Singleton* which came to the Convention's attention, at the earliest, in July, 1787—a month *after* Gerry's remark is reported to have been made. And of course it is even more astonishing to learn that such judicial activism in the States was received with "general approbation."

Finally, we must not overlook, as other commentators invariably do, the last sentence of the speech here attributed to Gerry. True, it does not bear directly on his estimate of judicial review, but rather emphasizes the inappropriateness of judicial participation in the

---

* The possibility of a deliberate misrepresentation by Madison—recalling Professor Crosskey's charge—is remote. True, Madison's Notes are the only authority for this passage. Moreover, Farrand has concluded from his analysis of the original manuscript that the word "actually" was inserted in the passage by Madison in a subsequent editing. Yet that addition, in our view, does not affect, except to clarify, the meaning of the passage. What is more, it is difficult to imagine what Madison, as a putative champion of judicial review, might have hoped to gain by falsely attributing to Gerry a speech depicting a pre-Convention atmosphere favorable to judicial review—when, elsewhere in his Notes, he records himself as portraying in a colorful reference to *Trevett v. Weeden*, just the opposite state of affairs. See p. 280.

Council of Revision. Nonetheless, Gerry's sharp disapproval of allowing courts to be the "judges of the policy of public measures" is certainly relevant to our subject, for the Supreme Court today is generally understood to be doing just that, not as a co-wielder of the
veto power—a role explicitly rejected by the framers—but as part and
parcel of judicial review.

Rufus King, also of Massachusetts, seconded Gerry's motion to bar
the judiciary from the Council of Revision. King reasoned, according to Madison's account, that the judges might have a "bias" in expounding a law if they had earlier "participated in its formation."[4]
Robert Yates' account is to the same effect.[5] King's own notes of this
day make no mention of a speech by him.[6] William Pierce's account,
however, contains the following passage:

> Mr. King was of opinion that the Judicial ought not to join in the
> negative of a Law, because the Judges will have the expounding of
> those laws when they come before them; and they will no doubt stop
> the operation of such as shall appear repugnant to the Constitution.[7]

King, then, is represented as having expected *all* laws of Congress
to come before the courts for a judgment of their constitutionality.
Thus, taking Pierce's notes at face value, King must be recorded as
anticipating a judicial review power of unlimited (B3) *scope*, as distinct from the (B1) power of judicial self-protection. Regarding the
effect of the power, King's formulation is closer to what we might
have expected. For he spoke not of "setting aside" laws, or of declaring them "void," but merely of "*stop[ping] the operation*" of unconstitutional laws. The phrase is equivalent to "not enforcing" such
laws, and is distinctly C1 language.

That having been said, we may question whether King made *any*
of the remarks Pierce attributed to him. For Pierce is not only alone
among the note-takers in attributing to King an opinion about judicial review; he is also alone in failing to make any reference at all
to *Gerry's* role in the matter. Under the circumstances, there is a
strong possibility that Pierce mistakenly put in King's mouth Gerry's
sentiments about judicial review (instead of the remark King actually
made about "bias"), and in the course of doing so failed to catch
Gerry's qualifying reference to encroachments on the judicial department. This construction of the episode has the advantage of assuming that the maker and seconder of the motion advanced com-
plementary rather than substantially identical arguments in the mo-

tion's support. And if the construction is valid we are dealing, on June 4, with a *single* speech relating to judicial review, rather than two: a speech that anticipated a power merely of the A2, B1, C1 character.

July 17

The issue under discussion is the "congressional negative" which, as we know, the Convention rejected this day, in favor of the Supremacy Clause. *Roger Sherman* of Connecticut was among those attacking the negative.

> [He] thought it unnecessary, as the Courts of the States would not consider as valid any law contravening the Authority of the Union, and which [Congress] would wish to be negatived.[8]

Sherman as well as the others who would participate in this colloquy were referring, of course, to *state* laws, for it was these laws alone that the congressional negative was supposed to subordinate to "the Authority of the Union." Let us therefore keep in mind in this and later debates over the "negative" (the proposal was to be revived in August) that the delegates were necessarily concerned with the (A1) power of reviewing state legislation. Regarding *scope*, Sherman spoke of "any" law—any state law, that is—and must thus be credited with a B3 view as to the judiciary's authority over state legislation. As to the power's *effect*, he thought the courts simply "would not consider as valid" unconstitutional laws—which is the C1 view.

A further point. Sherman spoke only of the *"Courts of the States."* The parliamentary situation suggests, moreover, that he did so mindful of the provisions of the Supremacy Clause which Luther Martin was about to introduce as a substitute for the "negative." Does this not indicate that Sherman took the Clause's explicit reference to "the Judiciaries of the several States" (and its failure to make any mention at all of the federal judiciary) at face value? and thus that he did not anticipate an *appeal* of these state cases to the Supreme Court?

James Madison, a staunch partisan of the congressional negative, now replies, denying that the Supremacy Clause solution will assure the subordination of state laws:

> [These] laws . . . will accomplish their injurious objects before they can be repealed by the General Legislature or be set aside by the National Tribunals. [Nor can] confidence . . . be put in the State

Tribunals as guardians of the National authority and interests. In all
the States these are more or less dependent on the Legislatures. In
Rhode Island the Judges who refused to execute an unconstitutional
law were displaced, and others substituted by the Legislature who
would be willing instruments of the wicked and arbitrary plans of
their masters.[9]

The Rhode Island episode Madison summoned to illustrate his argument was, of course, the case of *Trevett v. Weeden*, which involved
an attempted invasion of judicial prerogatives. It is therefore arguable that Madison envisioned judicial intervention only in B1 cases;
yet the better view, taking the passage as a whole, is that Madison,
like Sherman, assumed *all* state laws would be subject to review—the
B3 theory. The passage is also ambiguous regarding the *effect* of review. Having first remarked the possibility of a law being "set aside"
(a typical C2 formulation), Madison then cited the experience of
the *Trevett* judges who had merely "refused to execute" a law—the
C1 theory.

Note that Madison, unlike Sherman, did not restrict his speculation concerning the judiciary's response to the "Courts of the States."
He spoke of "National" as well as "State Tribunals," and so must be
read as expecting the Supreme Court to be drawn into the enforcement of the Supremacy Clause.

Gouverneur Morris of Pennsylvania sharply disputed Madison.

He was more and more opposed to the negative. The proposal of it
would disgust all the States. A law that ought to be negatived will be
set aside in the Judiciary Department; and if that security should
fail, may be repealed by a National law.[10]

Since Morris advanced no qualifications as to *scope*, let us credit
him with anticipating an unlimited (B3) power of reviewing state
laws. And his use of the phrase "set aside" seems to indicate the C2
view as to *effect*. Yet at this point we must take account of a dimension of the situation not previously noticed—one that should remind
us of the danger of supposing that the framers viewed the problem
of enforcing the Constitution through the same lenses we wear today.

Note that Morris spoke of the possibility of Congress *repealing* a
state law in the event the judicial check should prove ineffective.
(Madison, we may recall, allowed for the same possibility in the
speech just preceding.) Now the "repeal" remedy obviously differed
in the Convention's mind from the "negative" since the two were ad-

vanced as *alternative* solutions: the negative apparently envisioned the automatic submission of all state laws to Congress for its approval, while repeal would await an initiative by Congress and be addressed to a specific piece of offensive state legislation. What is more, both Morris and Madison seem to have assumed Congress would possess the repeal power *without an express constitutional provision to that effect.* For the alternative to the negative then under consideration was the Supremacy Clause which affirmed, simply— i.e., with no provision for congressional enforcement—that acts of Congress "shall be the supreme law."

All of this plainly suggests that these delegates looked not only to the judiciary, state and federal, to enforce the Supremacy Clause; but also to *Congress.* To be sure, Congress has never in fact exercised that mandate by enacting legislation expressly repealing a state law. Yet the Constitution's framers evidently intended Congress to have that authority, but chose to leave it to inference and thus placed it on the same textual footing as the Supreme Court's own authority.

Nor, to take the problem a step further, do Morris and Madison appear to have recognized any *priorities* in the matter. As Madison saw it, should a state legislature become obstreperous, both the "General Legislature" and the "National Tribunals" would have a try at closing the barn door (albeit, he feared, after the horse had got out), and either the one or the other might do the job. But what would happen should the one see fit to close the door and the other not, Madison did not say. Similarly, Morris: "if [the judicial] security should *fail,*" he observed, then congressional repeal legislation would be in order. But since the contingency in question might include a judicial decree *upholding* the state law, Morris must have contemplated a repeal law *disputing* the judicial verdict. And he ventured no suggestion as to how that latter dispute might be resolved.

Thus neither of the speakers reached the question of *ultimate* authority to interpret the Constitution. And this may be the place for a more general observation. The delegates we have heard so far have been content to speak of the *response* one branch of the federal system might be expected to make to a transgression by another. The responses they envision, moreover, seem to be in the nature of "checks"—mere counterweights to the transgression. The delegates do not appear, in other words, to be proposing means for *settling* constitutional disputes. Of course we shall be on the lookout for evidence of a different tendency as we proceed, but in the meantime we may begin to ponder the implications of an approach to the problem of

constitutional enforcement that does not seem to share our modern
preoccupation with "final authority."

Before the vote was taken that would discard the congressional
negative, *Roger Sherman* rose once again, this time to attack the
sheer incongruity of the device:

> Such a power involves a wrong principle, to wit, that a law of a
> State contrary to the articles of the Union, would if not negatived, be
> valid and operative:[11]

Thus to his earlier objection that the negative was "unnecessary"
Sherman now adds, simply, that it is based on "a wrong principle."
And that wrong principle is the assumption that the *"Courts of the
States"*—to recall his earlier language—will go ahead and enforce unconstitutional state laws in the absence of the negative. The two
Sherman passages, in other words, advance fundamentally the same
assessment of the judiciary's role—though the first contains some significant emphases that are slid over in the second. And so it is not
without interest that the Supreme Court's modern apologists typically
cite Sherman's second remark with no mention at all of the first! They
thus suppress not only the corroborating evidence in the first of his
preference for the Cl view as to the *effect* of judicial intervention—
but also his view as to *which* courts would be intervening.

July 21

The Convention has returned to the question of whether Supreme
Court judges should be included on the Council of Revision. *James
Wilson* of Pennsylvania conceded that the "proposition had been before made, and failed; but . . . thought it incumbent on him to make
another effort"—

> The Judiciary ought to have an opportunity of remonstrating against
> projected encroachments on the people as well as on themselves. It
> had been said that the Judges, as expositors of the Laws would have
> an opportunity of defending their Constitutional rights. There was
> weight in this observation; but this power of the Judges did not go
> far enough. Laws may be unjust, may be unwise, may be dangerous,
> may be destructive; and yet not be so unconstitutional as to justify
> the Judges in refusing to give them effect.[12]

Note that while Wilson was taking issue with the argument Elbridge Gerry had advanced in the June 4 debate, his premises regarding the scope and effect of judicial review were the same as had

been entertained on that earlier occasion. Granted, Wilson said, affirming the B1 view of *scope*, that in their strictly judicial capacity, judges would have a forum for "defending *their* constitutional rights," for speaking out against "projected encroachments . . . on *themselves*"; but since judicial review could not afford "the people" protection against legislative encroachments—here was his point of difference with Gerry—it "did not go far enough."

As to *effect*, Wilson thought that the manner in which the courts would resist laws that invaded judicial prerogatives—and such laws, be it noted, were the only kind he seems to have regarded as "unconstitutional" for review purposes—would be by "*remonstrating*" against them; or, as he put it, a moment later, by "*refusing to give them effect.*" These, of course, are clearly C1 formulations.

Wilson, to be sure, was not content with this state of things. But what he advocated as a remedy was *not* an extension of the scope and effect of *judicial review*. His recommendation, rather, was that judges, presumably because of their superior sobriety and learning, be given a role in the *legislative* function; that, jointly with the President, they be granted power to veto proposed legislation before it should become law because it was "unjust," "unwise," or "dangerous" —i.e., because it was *bad* legislation. As we know, this recommendation, though frequently advanced, was rejected by the Convention.

There is a further point to note about Wilson's comments, and about all those we shall be seeing from now on. On July 17, four days before Wilson spoke of this matter, the Convention adopted the Supremacy Clause in its primitive version. This means that while Gerry and others who discussed the judicial power before that date were necessarily drawing on pre-Convention experience—or pure surmise— as to the course the Convention would take, those who spoke afterwards had the benefit of a more-or-less "hard" Convention decision on the judiciary's role as a constitutional arbiter. This does not mean that Wilson and the others who declared themselves after July 17 always spoke as conscious exegetes of the Supremacy Clause, but that factor undoubtedly influenced their thinking, and so adds extra significance to their remarks.

Nathaniel Gorham of Massachusetts "did not see the advantage" of Wilson's proposal:

> As Judges they are not to be presumed to possess any peculiar knowledge of the mere policy of public measures. Nor can [their inclusion on the Council] be necessary as a security for their constitutional

rights. The Judges in England have no such additional provision for their defense, yet their jurisdiction is not invaded.[13]

Thus Gorham held, at most, the Bl view of *scope*: the judges' exposition of the laws would be a sufficient "security for *their* constitutional rights," for *"their* defense," for *"their* jurisdiction." We say at most, however, because it is not at all certain from this passage that Gorham anticipated *any* kind of judicial review. Note that he argued, by analogy, from the English practice which, as we know, did not recognize a judicial right *to refuse to enforce* legislative acts in the course of expounding them. The security of English judges depended, rather, on a certain leeway in judicial construction, vide Blackstone— plus parliamentary restraint; and this speech suggests that Gorham expected a similar practice to evolve under the new American Constitution. As to *effect*, the speech is silent altogether, which may be a further reason to doubt that Gorham had any kind of "review" in mind.

James Madison supported Wilson's motion. He listed a number of reasons why judicial participation on the Council would be advantageous, one of which is relevant here:

> It would be useful to the Judiciary department by giving it an additional oportunity of defending itself against legislative encroachments.[14]

Again we may glimpse judicial review through the back door, and again it is the Bl theory of *scope* that emerges. The Council would give the judiciary an "additional opportunity"—i.e., in addition to the one it would have anyway through expounding the laws—"of defending *itself.*" The remark sheds no light on the power's *effect.*

Elbridge Gerry was not happy that "this point which had undergone full discussion [was] again revived." But the new Wilson argument (which Madison had endorsed) that "the people" would benefit from judicial participation on the Council deserved a reply:

> It was making Statesmen of the Judges; and setting them up as the guardians of the Rights of the people. He relied for his part on the Representatives of the people as the guardians of their Rights and interests. It was making the Expositors of the Laws, the Legislators, which ought never to be done.[15]

To be sure, this comment by Gerry does not bear directly on judicial review; yet it is illustrative of the thinking of the Convention majority that turned down the idea of giving Supreme Court judges a role in the veto power. Let us recall the two principal arguments that were being advanced on behalf of the judicial veto: a) the judiciary needed extra protection, and b) judges would contribute an element of stability and wisdom to the legislative process, and thus benefit "the people." The reply to the first, as we know, was that the courts had an adequate weapon of self-defense in their role of "expositors" of the laws. And now Gerry states the objection to the second—namely, that since judges were not qualified to be "legislators," it was improper to try to mix the two functions. While the second reply is not strictly applicable to judicial review, neither is it totally unrelated. For manifestly, the further judges drew away from the restrictive B1, C1 concepts of judicial review, the closer they would edge up to a "legislative" role; and it is that state of affairs that Gerry and the others who spoke for the majority on this issue were warning against. The debate of July 21, however, was not yet over; before the vote was taken that would reject Wilson's motion, one further colloquy occurred that requires attention.

Luther Martin of Maryland, after associating himself with Gerry's sentiments—"A knowledge of mankind and of Legislative affairs cannot be presumed to belong in a higher degree to the Judges than to the Legislature"—said:

> And as to the Constitutionality of laws, that point will come before the Judges in their proper official character. In this character they have a negative on the laws. Join them with the Executive in the Revision, and they will have a double negative.[16]

The comment, as it relates to *scope*, can be taken in two ways. Martin may be read as saying that should the judges be granted the dual role in question, "they will have a double negative *on all laws involving Constitutional issues*"—in which case he meant that in their ordinary judicial capacity judges would be challenging not only encroachments on "themselves" (B1), but encroachments on other departments as well (B2 or B3). Or he may be read as saying "Judges will have a double negative *on such laws involving Constitutional issues as would reach them in their proper official character*"—in which case the comment was in line with the understanding expressed by previous speakers that in "their proper official character" judges might challenge the constitutionality only of those laws that intruded on judicial prerogatives (B1). The first interpretation is perhaps the natural one for twentieth-century readers, unaccustomed to the distinction between the judiciary defending its own boundaries, and also defending everyone else's; but the second would have been more natural in the eighteenth century when the latter practice was simply unknown. In either view, Martin's objection to a "double negative" makes perfectly good sense.

As to *effect*, Martin's word "negative" seems to imply a *mere* negative—that is, a mere refusal to give the law effect; the C1 view. For if he thought that in their ordinary capacity judges could definitively nullify a law—could remove it from the books—then his objection would not have been that a share in the Council's veto power would give judges *too many* opportunities to block a law (a "double negative"), but that the veto role would be *superfluous* inasmuch as the judges could kill the law outright when it came before them in their judicial capacity. But let us not press the point. Recognizably, we have here an instance in which it is the better part of wisdom not to attribute to the speaker an attempt to formulate a precise statement of the judicial role: Martin, in all likelihood, was simply expressing a general aversion to the principle of giving one branch of government two cracks at a law, while other branches get only one, and we should perhaps try to get out of him nothing more than that.

George Mason of Virginia spotted the hole in Martin's argument:

> It had been said (by Mr. L. Martin) that if the Judges were joined in this check on the laws, they would have a double negative, since in their expository capacity of Judges they would have one negative. [Mason] would reply that in this capacity they could impede in one case only, the operation of laws. They could declare an unconstitutional law void. But with regard to every law however unjust, oppressive or pernicious, which did not come plainly under this description, they would be under the necessity as Judges to give it a free course.[17]

Mason correctly observed, in other words, that the two "negatives" were not of the same *genre*: the veto-negative could be exercised against merely undesirable laws as well as unconstitutional ones, while the judicial negative would be relevant to the latter category only. But while the point was well taken, Mason's statement suffers

from the same ambiguity as to the *scope* of the strict judicial-negative
that we saw in Martin's remark. Did *all* laws that violated the Constitution come, for judicial review purposes, "plainly under [the] description" of "unconstitutional"? Or was Mason's "one case only" the
case of an invasion of judicial prerogatives as the previous speakers
had maintained? As to the *effect* of the judicial-negative, Mason's
language is more illuminating. He thought that judges, on finding a
law unconstitutional, could *"impede . . . the operation"* of it—they
could *"declare* [it] *void"*; or, alternatively, they could *"give it a free
course."* These formulations, taken together, are highly suggestive of
the CI theory that a judicial determination of unconstitutionality
amounts simply to a refusal by the court to enforce the law in the
case before it.

July 23

The Convention has taken up the question of how the Constitution
is to be ratified. The possibilities under consideration are a) submitting the draft to the state legislatures, as a proposed amendment to the
Articles of Confederation, and b) submitting it to popular conventions in each of the States, specially convoked for that purpose.
Gouverneur Morris opposed treating the Constitution as an amendment to the Articles:

> If the Confederation is to be pursued,* no alteration can be made
> without the unanimous consent of the Legislatures: Legislative alter-
> ations not conformable to the federal compact would clearly not be
> valid. The Judges would consider them as null and void.[18]

Thus Morris anticipated the possibility the new Constitution would
not win the favor of every state legislature, and recommended popular conventions as a way out of the Confederation's unanimity rule.
He predicted, concretely, that if the Constitution were treated as
simply a series of "alterations" to "the federal compact" (to the Articles, that is), and if a single state legislature should dissent, then
the judges in all of the States would be forced to regard the whole
Constitution as illegal for having been adopted in violation of the
Articles' amendment procedures. Manifestly, then, Morris was not attempting in this instance to describe how judicial review would operate under the *new* Constitution: he was purporting to describe

---

* Note the usage of "pursued."

how it worked, or would work, under *the Articles of Confederation.*
Here is a case where "context" is of some importance. Students of our
subject are frequently exposed to a truncated version of this passage,
without allusion to its context, rendered thusly: "Legislative alterations not conformable to the federal compact would clearly not be
valid. The Judges would consider them as null and void."—which to
the contemporary reader suggests, of course, *federal* judges. Morris
has thus been understood to have expected the Supreme Court, under
the Constitution, to exercise the broadest power of review over acts
of Congress as well as of the States, and so has become for many commentators a leading early advocate of judicial supremacy!

   James Madison also favored the popular convention approach:

> He considered the difference between a system founded on the legis-
> latures only, and one founded on the people, to be the true difference
> between a *league* or *treaty*, and a *Constitution.**

Then, to show how the two types of systems would operate differently as a practical matter, he added:

> A law violating a treaty ratified by a preexisting law might be re-
> spected by the Judges as a law, though an unwise or perfidious one.
> A law violating a constitution established by the people themselves,
> would be considered by the Judges as null and void.[19]

The last sentence of this passage, unadorned by reference to its context, is also a favorite with judicial supremacists. As well it might be,
for taken alone it seems to commit Madison, just as the cropped version of the preceding passage apparently commits Morris, to the view
that the Supreme Court is superior to Congress. However, the context
refutes that inference, as clearly in this case as in the former. Madison
was demonstrating how the *States* would be affected—on the one
hand by a "treaty" ratified by the state legislatures, and on the other,
by a "constitution" adopted by popular convention. The "laws" he
spoke of were thus *state* laws, and the "judges," *state* judges. Madison, in other words, had in mind the Al power of judicial review;
moreover, what he said about that power in the passage's famous last
sentence is exactly what we might have expected from our earlier
analysis of the Supremacy Clause. State judges would be expected to
enforce the Constitution against "any" state law, and thus would not

---

* The emphases are Madison's.

recognize limitations as to *scope*—the B3 view. As to *effect*, an unconstitutional state law *"would be considered . . . null and void"*—the C1 view.

August 10

Four days earlier the Convention was presented with a draft of the Constitution from the Committee on Detail. *Charles Pinckney* of South Carolina now complains that the Committee, contrary to its instructions, failed to stipulate property qualifications for federal officials. Pinckney held this to be a mistake, arguing that the country's leaders ought to possess "competent property to make them independent and respectable" if they were to be granted "such great powers":

> The Legislature would have the fate of the Nation put into their hands. The President would also have a very great influence on it. The Judges would not only have important causes between Citizen and Citizen but also where foreigners are concerned. They will even be the Umpires between the United States and individual States, as well as between one State and another.[20]

We may agree, considering the passage as a whole, that Pinckney was not in this instance embarked on a fastidious delineation of the powers distributed by the Constitution. The rhetoric, with its several figures of speech, was plainly designed to serve the single point that all of the officials named would have sufficiently grave responsibilities to warrant the property qualification. There are thus no textual grounds for attaching importance to his characterization of "The Judges" as "Umpires" between the federal and state governments—notwithstanding that the literature has exploited it as "proof" that Pinckney embraced the (C3) theory that the Supreme Court was to be the "final arbiter" of the Constitution's meaning. It is enough to see why Pinckney's figure is equally well adapted to the interpretation of the Supremacy Clause we have been advancing—that is, to the C1 theory of *effect*. Note that Pinckney almost certainly did not have in mind *direct* litigation between a State and the United States, for the sovereign immunity of both was taken for granted by all during the "Convention's deliberations. Therefore—assuming he had judicial review in mind at all*—he must have been thinking of private litiga-

---

* Professor Crosskey doubts that Pinckney, in this remark, was referring to *any* kind of judicial review. The Supreme Court's "umpire" role, he points out, could be performed in the course of exercising its "strictly

tion that involved conflicting state and national legislation. Now in
that situation the courts would, of course, have to "umpire" between
the rival pieces of legislation before the litigants could get a decision.
And since that responsibility would be weighty enough for the purposes of the point Pinckney was making, we are hardly warranted in
attributing to him—alone among the framers—the modern view that
"the umpires'" verdict would be binding on the respective governments involved, as well as on the litigants.

August 15

It will be recalled that on July 21 the Convention rejected for the
second time the idea of joining Supreme Court judges with the Executive on a Council of Revision. That decision—duly reflected in the
draft prepared by the Committee on Detail—left the "revisionary," or
"veto," power solely in the hands of the President, subject to a two-
thirds vote by both houses of Congress to override. Heavy doubts,
however, still hung over the Convention as to the sufficiency of this
"check," for the President was still slated to be elected by the very
legislature he was expected to restrain. Accordingly, Madison and
Wilson made one more attempt to bring the judiciary into the act—
though this time under a somewhat different formula. The Supreme
Court and the Executive, according to the motion Madison made
this day, would each have an *independent* veto, the exercise of either
of which would require two-thirds vote by Congress to override. *John
Mercer* of Maryland, one of the very late-comers to the Convention,
"heartily approved the motion":

> It is an axiom that the Judiciary ought to be separate from the Legis-
> lative: but equally so that it ought to be independent of that depart-
> ment. The true policy of the axiom is that legislative usurpation and
> oppression may be obviated. He disapproved of the Doctrine that
> the Judges as expositors of the Constitution should have authority
> to declare a law void. He thought laws ought to be well and cautiously
> made, and then to be uncontrollable.[21]

From the last part of his statement it is clear that Mercer opposed
any kind of judicial review—at least by the Supreme Court; and this
much is normally conceded by constitutional scholars. But many go
further, professing to see in the statement a grudging acknowledg-

---

judicial jurisdiction"—e.g., in the course of arbitrating between state and
national versions of the common law—and that function, Crosskey suggests,
is a sufficient explanation of the remark. Op. cit., II, 1024-25.

ment—a lament—by Mercer that the institution he personally disapproved had been, in fact, incorporated into the Constitution. A second glance, however, shows that his language encourages no such inference, and the context plainly discourages it. Mercer spoke disapprovingly, not of a "provision" of the Convention's working draft, not even of an implied one, but of the "doctrine" of judicial review—a theory he feared the Convention might be driven to embrace unless some other means were found to "obviate" the danger of "legislative usurpation and oppression." Mercer's understanding of the parliamentary situation appears to have been 1) the Convention had not yet devised an adequate check on the national legislative power; 2) the Convention now had before it a proposal that would meet this need in the way it ought to be met—the double-veto; 3) by failing to grasp this opportunity, the delegates would be inviting recourse—either by the Convention itself or through subsequent developments —to the undesirable "Doctrine" of judicial review.

Mercer, however, was not to have his way. Elbridge Gerry grumpily observed that the new Madison-Wilson scheme came "to the same thing with what has already been negatived." The Convention evidently agreed, and promptly voted down the motion, eight States to three.

Shortly, thereafter, *John Dickinson* of Delaware ventured a postmortem. He

> was strongly impressed with the remark of Mr. Mercer as to the power of the Judges to set aside the law. He thought no such power ought to exist. He was at the same time at a loss what expedient to substitute. The Justiciary of Aragon, he observed, became by degrees the law-giver.[22]

Thus Dickinson associated himself with Mercer's opposition to giving the Court any power of judicial review. He thought the tendency of the power, in words that may appear prophetic to us, was to make judges "law-givers," as witness his understanding of developments in fifteenth-century Spain. However, he seems to have been depressed at the course events were taking at Philadelphia: unless some other "expedient" could be found that would reliably curb legislative excesses, the Convention might be forced by circumstances to grant the federal judiciary a role he did not think "ought to exist."

Let it be noted, parenthetically, that our reading of Mercer and Dickinson does not deny to them an awareness of the presence of the Supremacy Clause in the Convention's working draft. Both men were addressing themselves to review of congressional legislation by the *Supreme Court*, as an alternative to the veto power. Yet the Supremacy Clause, as we know, made no express reference to that Court. While the Clause might be read as *implying* a role for the federal courts, it *said*, merely, that *state* judges would have the (C1) power and (C1) duty not to enforce unconstitutional laws. Hence Mercer and Dickinson appear to have interpreted the Clause literally, and thus to have been unaware that a right of appeal would run from the state courts to the Supreme Court. This, as we have seen earlier, was, and is, an altogether plausible construction of the framers' scheme. What Mercer and Dickinson evidently feared was that in the absence of another "expedient," the delegates would decide to broaden the Supremacy Clause's present approach into a full-blown authorization for review by the Supreme Court—possibly along the extreme lines being urged during this period (note Dickinson's phrase, "set aside the law") in the letters of Mr. James Iredell.*

At this difficult moment, according to Madison's account, *Gouverneur Morris* came forward and

> suggested the expedient of an absolute negative in the Executive. He could not agree that the Judiciary which was part of the Executive, should be bound to say that a direct violation of the Constitution was law.[23]

Morris' contribution here is, to say the least, crabbed. Not only do his two thoughts, as recorded, lack logical sequence; the second seems to have no bearing at all, after close reading, on this phase of the proceedings. Still, we must do with them what we can, keeping in mind that the Convention was in a restless mood and that Madison's note-taking may not have been at its best on what may have been an uncomfortably hot August afternoon.

The first part of the statement seems perfectly straightforward: since the Convention was dissatisfied with every other formula for "revision"—the Council veto, the overridable Executive vote, the double-veto—Morris proposed an *absolute* veto in the Executive as the adequate "expedient" for keeping Congress in line. And the balance of the speech Madison attributed to him (following the passage we have quoted) is devoted to justifying this solution.

The second part of the passage thus emerges as an "aside." But to

---

* Cf. "Bayard *v.* Singleton," p. 209 et seq.

what purpose? At first blush it appears to be a thought Morris has interjected in order to register his disagreement with Mercer's and Dickinson's opposition to judicial review. Such, in any event, is the interpretation advanced by most scholars. Now: *if* this interpretation is correct, it is clear that Morris was announcing a position favorable to judicial review—though it is less clear whether he believed the institution had actually been incorporated into the Constitution. Moreover, he seems to have envisioned a wider *scope* for the power than mere judicial self-defense. On the other hand, he limited its scope to "*direct violation[s]* of the Constitution"—language that seems far closer to the (B2) theory that judges may review violations of express prohibitions of the Constitution than to the (B3) theory that they may construe the document as a whole. As to *effect*, Morris' formulation—the judges were not "*bound to say* [the violation] was law"—is perhaps the clearest expression we have yet seen of the (C1) theory that the power is a kind of "release" by which courts may avoid enforcing a law they deem unconstitutional.

That having been said, let us look more closely at Morris' curious phrase, "the Judiciary *which was part of the Executive.*" The scholars we speak of have treated those six qualifying words, either as though they were not there, or as though they meant the judicial function was *something like* the executive function and therefore could be subsumed in the general category, "Executive." But how can we attribute to Morris a fuzzy notion like that when we know that all of the political thinkers of the time, none less than he, were concerned to the point of fetish with the *differences* among the three classical governmental functions? Surely the more natural reading of the phrase is "the Judiciary, *when it participated in the Executive function*, should [not] be bound to say," etc.—in which case Morris was referring to the judges' special role as co-wielders of the executive veto power, the role that had just been rejected by the defeat of the Madison-Wilson double-veto proposal. All things considered,* we think this reading of the passage cannot be avoided; and if it cannot, then of course Morris was not speaking about judicial review at all.

---

* To be sure, this interpretation presents difficulties of its own: in order to establish a dialogue between Morris, on the one hand, and Dickinson or Mercer on the other, we must assume either that Morris misunderstood one of the previous speakers to be criticizing the judicial veto, or that one of them actually did so but was misreported by Madison; otherwise, how explain Morris' statement that he "could not agree" with what had gone before?

It remains to see what "expedient" the Convention eventually resorted to in order to prevent legislative usurpation. Morris did not press his idea of an absolute executive veto, but rather moved to postpone the problem to another day. This provoked angry complaints about the "tediousness of the proceedings," as one delegate put it; another "saw no end to these difficulties"; a third predicted: "If we do not decide soon, we shall be unable to come to any decision." Postponement, accordingly, was voted down. Then, after quickly tacking on three amendments which need not detain us beyond noting Madison's report of a "rather confused conversation," the Convention agreed to adopt the draft section containing the overridable executive veto, and adjourned.[24] Yet this was not to be the end of the matter, for as we all know the Convention ultimately decided (on September 6) that the President should be chosen, not by Congress, but by independent Electors. That decision obviously gave the President, as wielder of the veto, a freedom he would not otherwise have had, and so made the veto far more meaningful. This, then, was the "expedient" the framers had been seeking on August 15. This, *not* judicial review, appears to have been their answer to the fear that had plagued the Convention all summer—that the new federal legislature would prove to be an uncontrollable monster.

August 22

A double-motion has been made to prohibit a) bills of attainder and b) ex post facto laws. The first half went through without trouble, but the second stirred opposition on several grounds. It was said, on the one hand, that since every "lawyer" and "civilian" recognized ex post facto laws to be invalid, an express ban was "unnecessary" and would imply "an improper suspicion of the National Legislature." On the other hand, it was argued that such prohibitions were "useless" since they were present in many state constitutions and had had "no effect." To this latter objection, *Hugh Williamson* of North Carolina replied:

> Such a prohibitory clause is in the Constitution of North Carolina, and though it has been violated, it has done good there and may do good here, because the judges can take hold of it.[24]

Let us note, first, that it is unclear whether Williamson was claiming the clause had "done good" in North Carolina because the state legislature had occasionally heeded it, or because—as he said "may" happen "here"—the "Judges [had taken] hold of it": all we know is that the North Carolina records do not disclose any instance of judicial interference with ex post facto laws. But what of Williamson's wistful hope that the clause, with the judges' help, "may do good" in the federal Constitution? On first impression, to be sure, Williamson seems to have been advancing the (B2) view that the Supreme Court would reject laws that violated an express provision of the Constitution. But note that this particular prohibition was one that arguably concerned the special jurisdiction of the judiciary: an ex post facto law asks the courts to convict a man for an act that was not illegal when he committed it and so violates one of the most fundamental *substantive* tenets of our criminal jurisprudence. That this was Williamson's understanding of the situation, moreover, is strongly corroborated by the surrounding discussion—as witness the record of it set forth in James McHenry's notes:* "G. Morris, Wilson, Dr. Johnson, etc. thought the [ban on ex post facto laws] an unnecessary guard [since] the principles of justice, law, etc. were a perpetual bar to such. To say that the legislature shall not pass an *ex post facto* law is the same as to declare they shall not do a thing contrary to common sense—that they shall not cause that to be a crime which is no crime."[26] Thus Williamson probably expected the courts to balk at ex post facto laws, anyway, as part of their defense of judicial prerogatives—which would be a recognition of the (B1) power of judicial self-protection as to *scope*; and he was saying in the passage Madison attributes to him that an express prohibition would make the job easier since the judges could "take hold of it" as a further justification for their resistance. As to *effect*, Williamson could not have had in mind more than the limited (C1) power of non-enforcement, for it would have been redundancy for the courts to "invalidate" laws that by constitutional definition were void to begin with.

August 23
The Madison-Wilson forces made one last effort, this time with Charles Pinckney making the motion, to include the "congressional negative" in the constitutional scheme. Earlier in the day the Convention had peremptorily amended the draft Supremacy Clause to make "This Constitution" the third element, along with laws and treaties, of the "supreme law."† It was with this earlier decision in

---

* Williamson's remark is not recorded by McHenry.

† Although this amendment was adopted without discussion, the framers' probable motive, as Professor Crosskey points out, was to make clear that

mind, evidently, that *James Wilson*, arguing in favor of Pinckney's motion, described the "negative" as

> the keystone wanted to complete the wide arch of Government we are raising. The power of self-defense had been urged as necessary for the State Governments—it was equally necessary for the General Government. The firmness of Judges is not of itself sufficient. Something further is requisite—It will be better to prevent the passage of an improper law, than to declare it void when passed.[27]

Thus Wilson, at this very late date in the proceedings, still doubted the adequacy of the Supremacy Clause as an instrument for keeping the States within their constitutional boundaries. But note that his construction of the clause was entirely consistent with what we have been saying about it. His "improper" laws were of course *state* laws, and thus he was describing the (A1) power to review state legislation, which would be either B2 or B3 as to its *scope*. His "Judges" may have been only state judges, though he may well have had the Supreme Court in mind also. As for *effect*, mark well that Wilson did not question whether the judges would be firm, but whether their "firmness" would be *"sufficient."* What does this suggest but the (C1) theory that an "improper" law might be kept on the books by a recalcitrant state legislature even should judges, as required by the Supremacy Clause, *"declare* it void" for the purposes of the case before them?

Wilson's misgivings, however, did not win over the Convention's majority. Some of the delegates undoubtedly agreed with John Rutledge, who answered him, that the States would be unwilling "to be bound hand and foot." Others may have been more sanguine as to the disposition of state legislatures to honor the Constitution on their own initiative, or on their constituents'. Whatever the reason, the Convention voted down Madison's motion to send the problem to committee for further study; Pinckney's motion was then withdrawn, and the matter never again arose.

August 27

Dickinson and Gerry have introduced a motion providing for the removal of Supreme Court judges by the President upon the request

---

the express restraints on state action they had added to the draft constitution since they last discussed the Supremacy Clause on July 17 were to be directly binding on state judges. See Crosskey II, 989.

of both houses of Congress. *John Rutledge* of South Carolina commented:

> If the Supreme Court is to judge between the United States and particular States, this alone is an insuperable objection to the motion.[28]

We shall not labor the passage, for what we said in connection with Charles Pinckney's comment on August 10 applies equally well here. Recall, first, Crosskey's point that "judging" or "umpiring" between the States and the federal government could take place as well through the Court's strictly juridical office as through judicial review. And recall, second—assuming Rutledge had judicial review in mind —that "judging" or "umpiring" would be required equally under the C1 theory of *effect* as under the C2 or C3 theories: Rutledge could have meant that the Court was to be the *final* "judge" between the state and national governments—the modern (C3) theory; but he could just as well have meant that in the course of any private litigation involving a contest between state and national laws the Court would have to "judge" between the two laws in order to render a decision. In either case the Court's role would raise the "insuperable objection" he spoke of to giving a removal power to the President and Congress; for the federal lawmakers could obviously point the power at the judges' heads as an inducement to settle the dispute their way. That Rutledge actually held the C1 view is of course suggested by the surrounding context. The idea that federal judges would be the "final arbiters" in federal-state disputes is inconsonant with the whole tenor of the debates, not least of all with the warning Rutledge himself issued four days earlier against binding the States "hand and foot."

August 28

King has moved to forbid the States "to interfere in private contracts," the proposal that would eventually be adopted as the Constitution's "Obligation of Contracts" clause. *James Madison* first said that, on balance, he favored the motion. A moment later, apparently having some second thoughts, he asked:

> Is that not already done by the prohibition of *ex post facto* laws, which will oblige the Judges to declare such interferences null and void?[29]

Madison's idea was that violations of contracts might fall into the general category of retroactive laws, which the Convention had decided to forbid six days before. But note that he said the prohibitory clause *itself* would "oblige" the courts to block such laws. This appears to be a different view from the (C1) theory entertained on August 22 that the provision would be a useful handle the judges "could take hold of" in justifying their defense of judicial prerogatives; and we should obviously be reluctant to attribute to Madison a considered position on judicial review, at variance with this earlier understanding, on the strength of a single sentence pensively addressed to another point. Still, the sentence as it stands is authority, on the matter of *scope*, for the (B2) view that a violation of any express prohibition in the Constitution demands judicial intervention. As to *effect*, the remark is also ambiguous. Although his choice of words—the judges would be obliged *"to declare,"* etc.—is C1 language, Madison's question seems to ponder the possibility that the judicial check would be an effective substitute for a direct ban on state legislatures—that it would have, in other words, the (C2) effect of killing retroactive laws.

With this desultory episode, our review—fittingly—comes to an end. In summarizing the Convention debates, let us forgo depth analyses: it is probably better to save the underlying "why" questions until we have before us all of the material that bears on the constitutional period. We may be content with the following observations:

1. At no point during its proceedings did the Convention undertake a systematic examination of judicial review, either of its nature and extent, or even of whether there was to be such a power under the Constitution. A number of opinions and ad hoc assumptions were expressed, but nothing that came close to a serious exposition of the role judicial review would play in the new federal system. The explanation might be offered that the framers felt such an exposition to be unnecessary since the Supremacy Clause had made the courts' role as the Constitution's interpreters and enforcers sufficiently clear; but the difficulty with the explanation is—

2. Nowhere do the debates reveal an explicit reference to the Supremacy Clause's bearing on the courts' role. When we remember that the Supremacy Clause was incorporated into the Convention's working plan as early as July 17, and that nearly all of the framers' comments relating to judicial review were made subsequent to that date, this fact is singularly remarkable. There was considerable disagreement, as we have seen, on the role judges would play; yet

none of the disputants saw fit to bolster his position by reminding his colleagues that certain things had been already settled by the Supremacy Clause. This is hard to explain if there was, in fact, any sort of consensus on the subject. Which leads to the further observation that—

3. The dominant mood of the framers was one of *speculation* as to how the Constitution was to be interpreted and enforced, and as to the role the courts would play in the process. Just as there is no textual authority for definitively resolving the problem, just so there was no recognizable consensus at the Convention as to the full implications of the problem. There are only two conclusions for which anything approaching a consensus might be claimed:

4. The framers, for the most part, seem to have understood that the *scope* of judicial review of congressional acts—to the extent such a power would exist at all—would be limited, as it had been prior to the Constitution, to defense of judicial prerogatives; that is, to the B1 view. As for state acts, the framers seem to have understood (though the evidence is largely circumstantial) that every variety of state legislation that challenged the supremacy of Congress would be subject to review (whether only by the state courts, or also by the Supreme Court, is a question that can *not* be answered out of the documents).

5. The framers, for the most part, seem to have understood that the *effect* of judicial review—assuming the power to exist at all—would be limited, as it had been prior to the Constitution, to a refusal to enforce unconstitutional laws in the case at hand: the C1 view. Or, to recapitulate from another angle—

6. The Convention debates do not furnish a particle of evidence in support of the modern doctrine of judicial supremacy. They do not reveal the smallest hint of either the modern (B3) view of *scope*—that the Supreme Court was expected to construe and enforce the Constitution as a whole, e.g., as a guarantor of the people's rights against government excesses or neglect; or of the modern (C3) view of *effect*—that the Supreme Court's word as a constitutional arbitrator would be "final" with respect to the powers of sister branches of government.

THE FEDERALIST

The Federalist occupies a prominent place in this phase of our story, for several reasons. For one thing, these papers constitute the only systematic exposition of the Constitution written more or less contemporaneously with it. For another, they have become an *independent* source of the American tradition, speaking through the years with an authority second only to the language of the Constitution itself. Finally, the papers have substantially more to say about our particular concern, judicial review, than does the Constitution proper.

There has been considerable speculation as to what the authors of *The Federalist*—James Madison, Alexander Hamilton, and (for his much smaller contribution to the subject of foreign relations) John Jay—were really up to when they set their pens in late 1787 and early 1788 to a series of essays about the Constitution addressed "to the People of New York." We need not join this debate beyond observing that the authors plainly had a variety of purposes in mind, three of which are usually noted in the literature—plus a fourth that has received considerably less attention than it deserves.

First, there is no denying the authors wrote to some extent as *propagandists*. Their avowed objective, after all, was to persuade "the people of New York" to ratify the proposed Constitution; and for this purpose, presumably, they also had their eyes on the much larger national audience the essays in fact reached. Moreover, the presentation in a large number of the papers expressly took the form of "answers" to "objections" that detractors of the Constitution had advanced. But while the essays thus qualify as campaign literature, the authors did very little in the execution of that role to compromise *The Federalist's* future value. There was, that is to say, precious little misrepresentation of the Constitution for the purpose of appeasing its critics. Admittedly, there was tendentious argument, usually designed to show that the alleged dangers of national consolidation were unreal, or that they had to be risked in the interests of national safety; but of textual distortion there was almost none. Indeed, one of the remarkable aspects of *The Federalist*, given the nature of the fears entertained by the target audience, is how much the decentralization features of the Constitution were played down, and how much its centralization features were played up.

Second, precisely because they approached their task conscientiously, the authors must also be viewed as authentic *expositors* of the Constitution. The framers, by the time they were through, had reduced the charter for the new form of government they were proposing to six thousand-odd words—hardly enough to answer the myriad questions that were bound to arise back home as to how the charter would work in practice. The framers had furnished the form—a skeleton; but others would have to supply the gloss—the flesh and blood of concrete application that would make the Constitution an intelligible instrument of government. That job required, of course, a large measure of prediction, as well as mere explication; and it is another remarkable feature of *The Federalist* that the authors' predictions have turned out, in the main, so well.

Third, the authors of *The Federalist* wrote, and quite consciously so, as *theorists*. The framers had built, to some extent, upon the ideas of previous political thinkers, as well as on the experience of other commonwealths; but much of what they did was original, the fruit of their own keen minds and those of their American contemporaries. It thus remained for somebody, and nobody had ever done it better than the authors of *The Federalist*, to elaborate the doctrinal basis—the relevant principles, assumptions, and inferences, in the manner of political theory—for the new adventure in government on which the American people were about to embark. George Washington put it this way: "When the transient circumstances and fugitive performances which attended this Crisis shall have disappeared, That Work [*The Federalist*] will merit the Notice of Posterity; because in it are candidly and ably discussed the principles of freedom and the topics of government, which will be always interesting to mankind so long as they shall be connected in Civil Society."[1]

Each of these functions or purposes, we repeat, certainly figured in the shaping of *The Federalist*. Yet the authors manifestly entertained still another purpose, one that probably overshadows all of the rest in its impact on subsequent generations. Professor Willmoore Kendall, one of the astutest students of *The Federalist*, has suggested that the authors of the essays wrote, above all, as "founders" of a new

nation. They regarded themselves not only as expositors and polemical champions and theorists for the framers' Constitution, but also,
like the framers themselves, as *creators*: along with the framers, they
would help determine the shape of the new Republic and the course
it would take with regard to matters the framers had left unsaid or
undone, or with regard to which, in the authors' judgment, the
framers might have said or done better. And while the assumption of
this role by two men with no official standing in the premises, who
chose moreover to conceal their authorship of the essays from the
contemporary reading public, might seem presumptuous, in fact the
American people have never questioned their credentials.

Both Madison and Hamilton, it must be remembered, had reason
to want to improve on the work of the framers. As a result of all of the
"compromises" of Philadelphia, the Constitution had turned out to be
a document considerably less nationalistic than these two men had
originally favored. Madison had lost his battle not only for the congressional negative, but for many of the other consolidating tendencies that had been embodied in the Virginia Plan. And Hamilton had
entertained even stronger centralist views. It was well known at the
time that Hamilton personally admired British monarchical forms,
and had, in fact, brought forward a plan of his own under which both
the Senate and the President would hold office for life. Indeed, so
far out of sympathy was Hamilton with the Convention's work that
he stayed away from Philadelphia during most of the summer of 1787
and took practically no part in the actual framing of the document.

The framers' Constitution—at this moment a mere framework unadorned by usage or authoritative interpretation—provided a number
of opportunities for improvisation and expansion. Two such openings,
in particular, were seized upon by Madison and Hamilton. The first
was that all-important question about which the framers had maintained a resounding silence—namely, how, in the last analysis, the
Constitution's provisions were to be *enforced*. What would happen in
the case of disputes—whether in good faith or bad—among the various
departments of the federal system as to what their several rights and
obligations were? What would be the procedures for resolving such
disagreements? What was there in the framers' system—or *was* there
anything short of recourse to the sword?—that might be expected to
prevent a falling out, to hold together the rival power centers in the
face of disintegrating controversy? *The Federalist's* answers to these
questions, while by no means free of difficulty, are undoubtedly the
paper's most valuable contribution. They constitute a part of what

Professor Kendall calls the "constitutional morality" that *The Federalist* sought to infuse into the document as a guide to those who would inherit the job of making the Constitution "work."

The other contribution we speak of bears directly on judicial review. Madison's views are comparatively difficult to nail down, in part because he dealt with the subject *en passant* and thus perhaps carelessly, but mostly because his one apparent clear-cut allusion to the matter in *The Federalist* utterly contradicts what he was saying elsewhere at the time, and would be saying later on. Hamilton, on the other hand, left no doubt as to where he stood, or where, on his showing, the Constitution stood on judicial review. As we shall see, Hamilton fell considerably short of espousing a doctrine of judicial supremacy that would be familiar to modern ears, yet he went much further in that direction than anyone had before him.* He did so, moreover, with breathtaking boldness, summoning neither tradition, nor contemporary practice, nor the text of the Constitution itself to support his position. Hamilton's motivations, or what we may guess to have been his motivations, are not uninteresting; let us, however, postpone speculation of that kind until we have seen what the authors of *The Federalist* actually wrote about the matters that concern us.

First Madison. In *Federalist* No. 39 Madison advanced his well-known proposition that the Constitution was "neither wholly federal nor wholly national," and undertook to explain wherein it partook of the one character, and wherein the other. He had just made the point that the scheme was certainly "federal" in that Congress' power "extends to certain enumerated objects only"—whereupon he interjected the following parenthetical comment:

> It is true that in controversies relating to the boundary between the [local and federal governments], the tribunal which is ultimately to decide is to be established under the general government. . . . Some such tribunal is clearly essential to prevent an appeal to the sword and a dissolution of the compact; and that it ought to be established under the general rather than under the local governments . . . is a position not likely to be combated.

On the face of it, this appears to be conclusive evidence that Madison regarded judicial review as an integral element of the constitu-

---

* Excepting possibly James Iredell in his letter to Richard Spaight. See "Bayard *v.* Singleton," p. 209-212.

tional scheme. To be sure, the comment was not supported by argument; it was in the nature of an aside, apparently an afterthought to his main thesis. Still, the words are plain enough: not only was the Supreme Court to "decide" disputes between the federal and state governments, it was to decide them "ultimately"—that is, one is tempted to conclude, finally, supremely, without recourse. Consequently, if Madison had let it go at that, we would have to regard him not only as a supporter of judicial review, but as a supporter of the broadest version of that power. Madison, however, did not let it go at that. Shortly thereafter, in No. 44, he approached the subject less obliquely and with quite different results. In that paper Madison sought to explain and defend the "necessary and proper" clause of Section 8, Article I; in the course of the argument he anticipated an objection:

> If it be asked what is to be the consequence, in case the Congress shall misconstrue this part of the Constitution, and exercise powers not warranted by its true meaning, I answer: *the same as if they should misconstrue or enlarge any other power vested in them. . . . In the first instance, the success of the usurpation will depend on the executive and judiciary departments, which are to expound and give effect to the legislative acts; and in the last resort a remedy must be obtained from the people, who can, by the election of more faithful representatives, annul the acts of the usurpers.*

Madison added that "this *ultimate* redress" of going to the people could be "confided in" because the "state legislatures . . . will be ever ready to mark . . . an invasion of [their] rights . . . to sound the alarm to the people, and to exert their local influence in effecting a change of federal representatives."

All of which suggests a very different procedure for deciding constitutional issues "ultimately" from the one Madison had intimated in No. 39. In No. 44 Madison recognized a judicial *role* in enforcing the Constitution, but this role was to be exercised only "in the first instance." Moreover, it would evidently have the same standing as the role the executive was to exercise: both departments, Madison implied, would have an equal right to refuse to "give effect" to unconstitutional legislation. With what consequences? Let us suppose—as one of the two hypotheses Madison could have had in mind—that the judiciary or the executive were *not* to "give effect" to the legislation in question, i.e., did not enforce it. In that case Madison plainly doubted that the judicial or executive refusal to enforce the law would necessarily have the effect of getting rid of it—that is, of *nullifying* the law in such fashion as to be binding on Congress. For he promptly spoke of a "last resort" whereby newly elected Congressmen might "annul"—and why "annul" if the law was already a nullity?—"the acts of the usurpers." Let us consider the other possibility—namely that Madison was thinking of a case where the judiciary and executive departments, perhaps because they had been cowed by Congress, *did* "give effect" to an unconstitutional law. In that case the enforcement of the law by the judiciary or the executive would amount to a perverse judgment by those departments *in favor of* the law's constitutionality; yet Madison assures us that far from being bound by such a ruling, the next Congress, guided by a new mandate from the people, would proceed to annul the law.

Federalist No. 44, in other words, depicts the business of interpreting and enforcing the Constitution in terms that tally very closely with the conclusions we drew from the text of the Constitution and from the Convention debates: everyone was to have a hand in it, and if there was to be a "last say," it would be heard from the people on election day.

Is it possible, however, to reconcile No. 44 with No. 39? (These two papers, be it noted, contain the only direct references by Madison to judicial review to be found in *The Federalist*.) It is, provided we are willing to give the benefit of doubts and apparent conflicts to No. 44 on the theory that of the two No. 44 better conforms on its face with the primary evidence. If we treat No. 44 as probably the more careful statement of Madison's position, we may then read the word "ultimately," as used in No. 39, to apply to a single set of circumstances: in the case of a clash between a federal law and a state law, the Supreme Court was "ultimately to decide"—"ultimately," that is, between the two parties in the courtroom. That is what would happen "in the first instance," to recall the language of No. 44. Whereupon Congress (or the state legislature concerned) would, as guided by "the people," have the "ultimate redress" in deciding what the Constitution really meant.

That this was Madison's true position regarding the effect of judicial review is difficult to dispute in the light of what he was writing and saying on other occasions during this period. In the fall of 1788, several months after the publication of *The Federalist*, yet prior to the adoption of the federal Constitution, he wrote to a friend in Kentucky, commenting on a proposed constitution that Thomas Jefferson had drafted for the State of Virginia:

In the [proposed] state constitution and indeed in the federal one
also, no provision is made for the case of a disagreement in expounding them; and as the courts are generally the last in making the
decision, it results to them by refusing or not refusing to execute
a law, to stamp it with its final character. This makes the Judiciary
Department parallel in fact to the legislature, which was never
intended and can never be proper.[1]

Madison was thus criticizing Jefferson's draft for failing to specify a
procedure for settling inter-department disputes about the Constitution's meaning; he felt the omission might be interpreted—in the light
of the time sequence involved between the enactment of a law and
the enforcement of it—as placing the courts on a footing equal (or
even superior) to that of the legislature. The same omission, moreover, was present in the proposed federal Constitution. Now: it is
not clear from the passage whether Madison at this writing regarded
the omission as a serious defect in the federal Constitution; he may
have felt the Philadelphia draft had compensating safeguards—a possibility we shall be exploring toward the end of this chapter. What is
crystal clear, however, is that Madison was opposed to any *construction* of the federal Constitution that would make the Supreme Court
"parallel in fact" to Congress, much less one that would allow the
Court to "stamp [a law] with its final character." *This "was never
intended and can never be proper."*

In June of the following year, now as a United States Congressman
from Virginia, Madison had two further occasions to comment on the
method by which the Constitution was to be interpreted. The first,
because the remark is recognizably argumentative, is the less instructive of the two. It is nonetheless a favorite with modern partisans of
judicial supremacy.

The setting was the historic House debate on the group of State-
proposed constitutional amendments that Madison had consolidated
into a "declaration of rights," and that was destined to become the
Bill of Rights. Replying to the objection that such declarations had
proved of little practical value in the States' past experience, Madison
said:

Independent tribunals of justice will consider themselves in a peculiar
manner the guardians of those rights; they will be an impenetrable
bulwark against every assumption of power in the Legislature or
Executive. . . .[3]

The reference here to "an impenetrable bulwark" is often cited as proof that Madison expected Congress and the President, as a matter of course, to regard judicial decisions as final and binding, even on themselves. That Madison himself, however, intended a far less literal reading of the phrase is amply demonstrated by the words he immediately added:

> Besides this [judicial] security there is a great probability that such a declaration in the federal system would be enforced: because the state legislature would jealously and closely watch the operation of this government, and be able to resist with more effect every assumption of power than any other power on earth can do.[4]

Now it would hardly be necessary for the state legislatures to interpose their power, which was greater than "any . . . on earth," in defense of such a judicial declaration if the courts were really expected to be an "impenetrable bulwark"—if, that is, Congress and the President were expected to abide in every case by the Supreme Court's construction. Thus, once again, we see Madison regarding the federal judiciary as but *one obstacle among several others* to putative violations of the Constitution. The idea that one branch of government would presume to sit in judgment on all of the others, and that the others would dutifully acquiesce, was quite foreign to Madison's experience,* and the passage we have just seen provides scant evidence that he suddenly decided to embrace it in the summer of 1789.

The second occasion occurred several weeks later when the House was considering a bill Madison had introduced to establish the executive departments of State, Treasury, and War. The question at hand was whether the Constitution permitted the President to remove the

---

* As an illustration of the way he expected such matters to work out in practice, take Madison's report to Congress later on in the summer of 1789 regarding the condition of religious freedom in his own State of Virginia: "Notwithstanding the explicit provision contained [in the Virginia Declaration of Rights] for the rights of conscience, it is well known that a religious establishment would have taken place in that State if the legislative majority had found, as they expected, a majority of the people in favor of the [establishment] measure; and I am persuaded that if a majority of the people were now of one sect, the measure would still take place and on a narrower ground than was then proposed, notwithstanding the additional obstacle which the law [the Statue of Religious Liberty] has since created." Thus, as Madison saw it, Virginia's Declaration, her even more explicit Statute of Religious Liberty, and her courts—all of these—were "obstacles" to a religious establishment; but none would prove insuperable if the current legislature were of a mind to establish a religion.

Secretaries of these departments at will, or required the consent of
two-thirds of the Senate as in the case of appointments. In the course
of the debate, Madison said:

> The decision that is at this time made will become the *permanent
> exposition of the Constitution. . . .*[5]

The significance of the observation lies of course in who was to make
this "permanent exposition of the Constitution." For the "decision"
Madison had in mind would not be a judicial one, but a *legislative*
one: it would be made by the House, the Senate and the President,
as enactors of the statute in question. And Madison was predicting
that the legislative determination would endure—meaning, apparently, that in the future the courts, along with everyone else, would
regard the issue as settled.

The observation did not go unchallenged. William Smith of South
Carolina wondered whether this expository function might not be the
province of the Supreme Court. Madison's reply should be carefully
noted:

> I acknowledge, in the ordinary course of government, that the ex-
> position of the laws and Constitution devolves upon the judiciary.
> *But I beg to know, upon what principle it can be contended that
> any one department draws from the Constitution greater powers
> than another, in marking out the limits of the powers of the several
> departments. . . . If the Constitutional boundary of either be brought
> into question, I do not see that any one of those independent depart-
> ments has more right than another to declare their sentiments on
> that point.*[6]

Taking the two statements together, Madison appears to have been
saying a) that constitutional construction is equally the affair of all
the departments of government—none having "more right than another" to participate, but b) that, in practice, the department directly
affected by the dispute is likely to have the occasion to make a construction—which the other, indirectly affected, departments may be
expected to follow.

Ten years later Madison composed what his leading modern biographer* has described as "the last major constitutional utterance by
the man who was to be called 'the father of the Constitution.' "[7] The
previous year Madison had played a prominent role in drafting the

---

* Irving Brant.

celebrated Virginia Resolutions supporting Kentucky's call for state resistance to the Alien and Sedition Acts. Now, in 1799, he was ready with a "Report" to the Virginia legislature defending the Resolutions against their critics throughout the nation. The Report is typically disparaged by modern scholars—as politically motivated, as incompatible with Madison's previous views, as an unhappy States'-rights interlude in an otherwise nationalistic career. Such judgments are unduly harsh. Some of the Report's emphases were undoubtedly tailored to the political object at hand, but the main thrust of the argument was altogether in keeping with what Madison had been saying ever since the Constitution was drafted about constitutional interpretation and enforcement. Indeed, the Report may be regarded as the most careful statement we have—ranking only after *The Federalist*—of the Madison Doctrine of constitutional enforcement.

". . . it is objected,"* Madison wrote, "that the judicial authority is to be regarded as the sole expositor of the Constitution in the last resort."[8] But that contention, he argued, was defective on a number of counts. For one, usurpations might occur "which the forms of the Constitution would never draw within the control of the judicial department."[9] For another, the judiciary itself might "exercise or sanction dangerous powers beyond the grant of the Constitution"[10]—as, indeed, Madison thought the federal courts had done in agreeing to enforce the Alien and Sedition Acts. But the main answer to the objection was the logical error of supposing there could be any tribunal superior to the *creators* of the federal compact—namely, the States themselves:

> The States . . . being the parties to the constitutional compact, and in their sovereign capacity, it follows of necessity that there can be no tribunal, above their authority, to decide, in the last resort, whether the compact made by them be violated.[11]

---

* The particular Resolution Madison was defending in these pages read: "That this Assembly doth explicitly and peremptorily declare that it views the power of the federal government, as resulting from the compact to which the States are parties, as limited by the plain sense and intention of the instrument constituting that compact—as no further valid than they are authorized by the grants enumerated in that compact; and that, in case of a deliberate, palpable, and dangerous exercise of other powers, not granted by the said compact, the States who are parties thereto have the right, and are in duty bound, to interpose, for arresting the progress of the evil, and for maintaining, within their respective limits, the authorities, rights, and liberties appertaining to them."

While "it may be . . . true," he added—and note that the preliminary
concession here may have been a bone thrown to the Court's supporters—

> . . . that the [federal] judicial department is, in all questions sub-
> mitted to it by the forms of the Constitution, to decide in the last
> resort, this resort must necessarily be deemed the last in relation to
> the authorities of the other departments of the [federal] government;
> not in relation to the rights of the [States], from which the judicial,
> as well as the other departments hold their delegated trusts.[12]

Did this mean, then, that the state *legislatures* were to have the
"final say" in interpreting the Constitution? By no means. We must
not read more into the expression "last resort" than Madison, as he
shortly went on to explain, intended it to have in this connection:

> *The declarations [by state legislatures] in such cases are expressions*
> *of opinion, unaccompanied with any other effect than what they may*
> *produce on opinion, by exciting reflection.* The expositions of the
> judiciary, on the other hand, are carried into immediate effect by
> force. The former [i.e., state declarations] *may lead to a change in*
> *the legislative expression of the general will—possibly to a change*
> *in the opinion of the judiciary*; the latter [i.e., the judiciary] *enforces*
> *the general will, whilst that will and that opinion continue*
> *unchanged.*[13]

The right of the States "to decide in the last resort," in other words,
was merely a right not to obey in the event the federal government
should perpetrate "a deliberate, palpable, and dangerous breach of
the Constitution;"* but this did not mean the federal government
had to obey the States. A State could hope that its dissent, especially
if joined by other States as contemplated in the Kentucky and Virginia Resolutions, would persuade Congress, or as the case might be,
the Supreme Court, to change its mind; and the issue would be resolved *ultimately*—as Madison's overall approach to the problem
makes abundantly clear—by a statesmanlike effort on all sides to ascertain, and then to follow "the general will." As for the judiciary, it
would be expected to enforce the general will—that is: either Congress' "expression" of the general will, or the courts' "opinion" of it—
until such time as Congress, or the judiciary itself, were brought
around to a different view of the Constitution's meaning. And if we

---

* In the words of the Resolution that Madison was defending. See p. 309,
note.

translate Madison's "general will" as equivalent to what we would call today a "national consensus" about the Constitution's meaning, it becomes clear that his much maligned Report, far from being an aberration in American political theory, is a remarkably accurate blueprint for the consensus machinery that has in fact determined the course of our constitutional growth.

Such then is the record of contemporary commentaries on the subject of judicial review by the "father of the Constitution." Most legal historians, we should note now, have found little sympathy with this record. As Professor Charles Beard saw it, Madison "was in no little confusion."[14] "Characteristically erratic," wrote Professor Corwin.[15] A "checkered" career, Professor Crosskey concludes: "Madison was guilty . . . of about as complete inconsistency upon this subject as was possible."[16]

Yet these judgments by Madison's critics, justly provoked though they are by this and that detail, miss sight of the two main threads of argument that run with undeviating consistency through every opinion Madison uttered on the subject. First, Madison believed, whether or not the Constitution supported him, in judicial review—that is, that the courts could refuse to enforce legislation they deemed unconstitutional. And we may set it down that he came to this view after the Constitution was written—after, that is to say, the final defeat of his pet projects, the congressional negative and the Council of Revision, which together, in his view, would in many ways have accomplished the same objectives as judicial review. Second, he believed that a judicial determination of unconstitutionality was *not* binding on other branches of government. Constitutional interpretation and enforcement was a common obligation and a common right, shared by all public authorities, each of which was expected to show a proper respect for the duties and the rights of the others. If Madison seems to have moved from opinion to opinion as to how, precisely, those interrelated rights and duties were to be exercised, we can sympathize with the enormous difficulties of laying down broad, immutable rules in this matter; and perhaps applaud the wisdom of a man who expected events, and allowed his own judgments, to be shaped not only by theory, but by the developing experience of the country.

Returning to *The Federalist*, let us view the references to judicial review that can be attributed to Alexander Hamilton. In No. 16 Hamilton touched on the subject briefly but significantly. In that paper

he advanced the familiar argument that the country's recent experience had proved the need for a national government that would
operate directly on individuals—that would "carry its agency to the
persons of the citizens without having to rely on "intermediate legis-
lations." "The majesty of the national authority must be manifested
through the courts of justice." Under the old Confederation, he explained, Congress had frequently required "the interposition of the
state legislatures" to enforce a law of the Confederacy. Consequently,
the state legislatures had "only not to act, or to act evasively, and the
measure [was] defeated." Moreover, the "state leaders" could proceed without fear of reprisal since their passive resistance did not
"excite any alarm in the people for the safety of the constitution." It
would be otherwise, however, under the new Constitution because
obstructionism by state legislatures would have to take the form of
"direct and active resistance." Hamilton then ventured a prediction
as to what would happen should a state legislature, under the new
system, undertake "an open and violent assertion of an unconstitutional power":

> The success of it would require not merely a factious majority in the
> legislature, but the concurrence of the courts of justice and of the
> body of the people. If the judges were not embarked in a conspiracy
> with the legislature, they would pronounce the resolutions of such
> a majority to be contrary to the supreme law of the land, uncon-
> stitutional and void. If the people were not tainted with the spirit
> of their state representatives, they, as the natural guardians of the
> Constitution, would throw their weight into the national scale and
> give it a decided preponderancy in the contest.

The Supreme Court, be it noted, is not mentioned in this passage,
or anywhere else in the argument. Thus the "courts of justice" that
Hamilton expected to uphold "the majesty of the national authority"
turn out to be *state* courts! These tribunals, he hoped, would not be
in a "conspiracy" with their own legislatures, but would dutifully
carry out the Supremacy Clause's command to strike down unconstitutional state legislation. True, he seems to have doubted that the
judges, alone, would be a match for the legislative branch—that a
legislature would be persuaded to mend its ways merely by a demonstration of judicial displeasure. The legislature could be expected
to back down, Hamilton implied, only after *"the natural guardians of
the Constitution"*—the people of the State in question—had backed
up their judges by joining the national opposition to the legislature's

illegal conduct. We have, then, still further testimony that the founders of the Republic looked to the federal system's built-in consensus
machinery as the ultimate means of enforcing the Constitution, rather than to any single branch of government such as the Supreme
Court. It is worth remembering, moreover, that the argument was
advanced in this instance as a derivative of the proposition, so familiar to American History classrooms, that the crowning achievement of
the framers was to have created a "national" government that would
operate directly on individuals. The tendency of the typical classroom
teaching is, of course, that an all-powerful Supreme Court was the
essential ingredient of the achievement; yet that conclusion apparently did not occur to Alexander Hamilton when he wrote *Federalist*
No. 16.

In Nos. 21 and 22, Hamilton systematically catalogued the "defects" of the old Confederation; in 22, he cited "the want of a judiciary power" as the one that "crowns" them all. Significantly, however, the want of a judicial power of *review*—except as it would contribute to the uniform enforcement of treaties—does not figure in the
discussion as one of the weaknesses of the Confederation. (What
hurt the Confederation, Hamilton contended, was the absence of a
"uniform rule of civil justice." And the cure for that "defect"—which
of course we have never cured, Hamilton's efforts to the contrary
notwithstanding—would entail a national tribunal capable of defining
and enforcing throughout the country a national version of the common law. But such a role would not involve constitutional interpretation, and would not require the power even to review congressional
legislation.) Nor—again significantly for our purposes—did Hamilton
include in his list of the Confederation's defects the Articles' failure to
designate a "final arbiter."

In No. 33, as part of a general examination of the tax power begun
several papers earlier, Hamilton discussed the effect of the "necessary
and proper" clause on Congress' taxing authority. It might be asked,
he wrote—anticipating an objection to the clause—"who is to judge of
the *necessity* and the *propriety* of the laws to be passed for executing
the powers of the union?"* Some today might answer: the Supreme
Court. But not Hamilton:

> I answer, first, that this question arises as well and as fully upon the
> simple grant of those powers, as upon the ["necessary and proper"]

---

* Emphases in the original.

clause: and I answer, in the second place, that the national government, like every other, must judge, in the first instance, of the proper
exercise of its powers; and its constituents in the last. If the federal
government should overpass the just bounds of its authority and make
a tyrannical use of its powers, the people, whose creature it is, must
appeal to the standard they have formed, and take such measures to
redress the injury to the Constitution as the exigency may suggest and
prudence justify.

Note that in the first part of his answer Hamilton made clear that
the rule he was laying down applied to all grants of power—not just
to the "necessary and proper" clause. The rule was that "in the first
instance" the *possessor* of the power would be the judge of its "proper
exercise." And while Hamilton spoke of "the national government" as
the possessor of the power in this instance, we may assume he meant,
concretely, the Congress (together with the President in his veto
capacity), for neither the executive department proper nor the judiciary had been granted the power "to make all laws which shall
be necessary and proper. . . ." By analogy, the Supreme Court would
be the judge of the proper exercise of grants of power that the
Constitution had addressed to the judiciary, and the executive of
those that had been addressed to the executive. That would be the
procedure in "the first instance." In the "last"—note that he envisioned
no intermediary stage—Hamilton, like Madison, would have recourse
to "the people."

Thus in the early numbers of *The Federalist* Hamilton's views
seem to have been even less inclined toward the modern power of
judicial review than Madison's. In No. 16 he recognized the obligation of state judges, under the Supremacy Clause, to enforce the
Constitution against their own legislatures. In No. 33, and obliquely
elsewhere,* he asserted the right of each department of government
to judge the extent of its own powers, which, let us agree, implied
that the courts would have the (B1) power of judicial review to defend judicial prerogatives against attacks from other departments.
But nowhere in these early papers did Hamilton claim for the Supreme Court any special power to interpret and enforce the Constitution, and to impose its will on other branches of government.

It was otherwise, however, when Hamilton set his pen to No. 78.
In that number Hamilton boldly blazed a new theoretical trail,
along which he took huge strides toward the modern view of the ju-

---

* For example, in No. 73.

dicial power. Let us, then, examine this famous paper with some care.

The rubric under which the argument proceeded was the question of judicial tenure. The Constitution had provided that federal judges would "hold their Offices during good Behaviour," and the entire paper was ostensibly designed to show the "propriety" of giving judges that degree of security. Hamilton began by drawing attention to what he called "the natural feebleness of the judiciary":

> Whoever attentively considers the different departments of power must perceive that . . . the judiciary, from the nature of its functions, will always be the least dangerous to the political rights of the Constitution; because it will be least in a capacity to annoy or injure them. The executive not only dispenses the honors, but holds the sword of the community. The legislature not only commands the purse, but prescribes the rules by which the duties and rights of every citizen are to be regulated. The judiciary, on the contrary, has no influence over either the sword or the purse, no direction either of the strength or the wealth of the society; and can take no active resolution whatever. It may be truly said to have neither FORCE nor WILL, but merely judgment. . . .

The argument to this point seems very much in order. The idea that the legislature would "prescribe the rules" for regulating constitutional "duties and rights," and that the judiciary would exercise "merely judgment" not only reflected pre-constitutional experience, but was altogether in keeping with the text of the Constitution and with the sentiments expressed by the framers at the Convention. The assurance that judges *"can take no active resolution whatever"* might be unconvincing in the era of the Warren Court, but to Americans in the eighteenth century that view of the judicial role was axiomatic.

> This simple view of the matter [Hamilton went on] proves incontestably that the judiciary is beyond comparison the weakest of the three departments of power; that it can never attack with success either of the other two; and that all possible care is requisite to enable it to defend itself against their attacks. It equally proves that though individual oppression may now and then proceed from the courts of justice, the general liberty of the people can never be in danger from that quarter. . . .

The real danger, in a word, was not that the judiciary would be too strong, but that it would be too weak—that it would be "in continual jeopardy of being overpowered, awed or influenced by its coordinate branches." And that was the reason, Hamilton concluded, why the framers had decided to give the judges tenure:

> . . . nothing can contribute so much to [their] firmness and independence as PERMANENCY IN OFFICE.

Note that so far nothing had been said about judicial review. Still, contemporary readers of No. 78 may have begun to suspect the argument was moving in that direction. Since Hamilton was so concerned with equipping the judiciary "to defend itself against . . . attacks," it would have been reasonable to assume that he was implicitly endorsing a second weapon of self-defense—namely, the (B1) power to resist legislation that encroached on the judiciary's special constitutional prerogatives. This theory of judicial review was, as we know, increasingly in the air—as witness the remarks of some of the framers at the Convention—and might thus have been associated with a plea to give the judiciary adequate means to protect itself against potential aggressions by the other, stronger departments of government.

In fact, however, these preliminary probings had prepared the ground for a much more ambitious démarche. Having demonstrated at considerable length the judiciary's pitiable incapacity to harm a flea —let alone a States' right, or a power of Congress—Hamilton now proceeded to march out a series of propositions that, if generally accepted by the country, could not fail to convert this weakest of lambs into the strongest of lions.

The initial advance began as an apparent afterthought, and seemed to have quite modest objectives. Permanent tenure, Hamilton had just shown, would help insure the "complete independence of the courts." This independence, he now added blandly, "is peculiarly essential in a limited constitution." Why? Because such a constitution "contains certain specified exceptions to the legislative authority such for instance, as that it shall pass no bills of attainder, no *ex post facto* laws, and the like." Then:

> Limitations of this kind can be preserved in practice no other way than through the medium of courts of justice, whose duty it must be to declare all acts contrary to the manifest tenor of the Constitution void.

We said this was a modest thrust, for while Hamilton had moved forward from the (B1) position that the courts might protect themselves, he had pulled up short at the (B2) position that the courts might enforce the express prohibitions of the Constitution. "Limitations *of this kind*," he said, might be declared "void." Moreover, the argument to this point implied nothing one way or the other about the *effect* of such a declaration, and thus Hamilton's readers were entitled to assume he had nothing more in mind than a judicial refusal to enforce the kind of legislation in question. They would soon discover, however, that he had now gained the necessary footing for a far more sweeping advance.

Once again Hamilton sallied from a previous position disarmingly, still clinging to the defender's role: "Some perplexity . . . has arisen," he observed, "from an imagination [that the power to declare legislative acts void] would imply a superiority of the judiciary to the legislative power." The issue, moreover, "is of great importance in all the American constitutions"; therefore "a brief discussion [of it] cannot be unacceptable." To wit:

> There is no position which depends on clearer principles, than that every act of a delegated authority, contrary to the tenor of the commission under which it is exercised, is void. No legislative act, therefore, contrary to the Constitution, can be valid. To deny this, would be to affirm that the deputy is greater than his principal; that the servant is above his master. . . .

Which everyone would grant; but while those legal truisms raised, they did not answer the question of *who was to decide* whether a legislative act was valid or invalid—as Hamilton, at last ready to loose his coup de main, quickly acknowledged: "If it be said that the legislative body are themselves the constitutional judges of their own powers," the answer is that such a view would "enable the representatives of the people to substitute their *will* to that of their constituents,* [and] it is not . . . to be supposed [that the Constitution condoned such incongruities]. *It is far more rational to suppose that the courts were designed to be an intermediate body between the people and the legislature, in order, among other things, to keep the latter within the limits assigned to their authority.*" And then the famous syllogism that was to be repeated fifteen years later by John Marshall in *Marbury v. Madison* (though by no means acted upon in the decision), and has survived as the cornerstone of the doctrine of judicial supremacy down to the present day:

> *The interpretation of the laws is the proper and peculiar province of the courts. A Constitution is, in fact, and must be regarded by*

---

* Emphasis in the original.

the judges, as a fundamental law. It therefore belongs to them [and to them peculiarly, we must conclude from the context] to ascertain its meaning, as well as the meaning of any particular act proceeding from the legislative body.

Thus—to drain the last from our metaphor—an action that had ostensibly begun as a defensive maneuver had now carried all the way to the enemy's home cities. We suggest, moreover, that there is little to be gained by straining against the plain import of this passage— by trying to force out of it a meaning that is, somehow, compatible with the conclusions reached elsewhere in this study. In these particular lines Hamilton endorsed all of the essential components of the doctrine of judicial supremacy, and on the strength of the language he used there is no hauling him back from them. With respect to the authorities that would be subject to the Supreme Court's power of review he recognized no limitations: the States were covered by implication, and Congress was the "legislative body" to which he expressly referred; he thus adopted the A3 view. As for the scope of the Court's power, there was no longer any talk of the express prohibitions of a "limited Constitution": rather, he spoke of the judges' right "to ascertain [the Constitution's] meaning"—which the context requires us to read as the *"whole* Constitution's meaning"; and he spoke also of "any particular act" the legislature might pass. This of course is the B3 theory as to scope. With respect to the effect of judicial review, Hamilton, in No. 78, underwrote the C3 theory: "The interpretation of the laws"—and of the Constitution, too, since it also was a "law"—was the *"peculiar* province of the courts.... It therefore belong[ed] to *them* to ascertain [the Constitution's] meaning." That formulation certainly seems to rule out the possibility that Congress might disregard the Court's view and register a different interpretation of the Constitution in subsequent legislation.

But while there is no denying the far-reaching implications of Hamilton's dialectic, neither—we may note parenthetically—is there any need to be swept away with admiration for it. A syllogism's conclusion, after all, can be no more persuasive than its more suspect premise; this being so, a pause over Hamilton's premise No. 2 will prove rewarding. The second premise took it as a "given" that the Constitution was within that class of laws which it was the "peculiar province of the courts" to interpret. But what was, and is, the basic question at issue if not precisely that one? The writer and readers of this book, for instance, are trying to discover whether the business of interpreting the Constitution is, like the business of interpreting ordinary statutes, the "peculiar province of the courts." Hamilton, at this point in *The Federalist*, had embarked on the same inquiry. Yet, obviously, he was no more likely than we to produce a convincing solution by postulating the answer as part of the argument. In a subsequent volume, in reviewing the case of *Marbury v. Madison*, we will have occasion to examine the substance of the syllogism; our purpose here, before passing on to the balance of Hamilton's argument in No. 78, has been simply to note its question-begging character.

Having endorsed the essential tenets of the doctrine of judicial supremacy, Hamilton hastened, in a passage hardly distinguished for its candor, to soften the blow. Harking back to the apprehensive "imagination" he had originally set out to assuage, he purred:

> Nor does this conclusion [as to the peculiar province of the courts to interpret the Constitution] by any means suppose a superiority of the judicial to the legislative power. It only supposes that the power of the people is superior to both[!]; and that where the will of the legislature, declared in its statutes, stands in opposition to that of the people, declared in the Constitution, the judges ought to be governed by the latter rather than the former.

That Hamilton here was playing with words seems clear. Nobody doubted that the people were theoretically "superior" to the government they had created when they adopted the Constitution. The question was which branch of government—the legislature or the judiciary—had the superior right *to speak for the people* in the critical matter of construing the Constitution. If the judiciary had that superior right, it followed that the judiciary, as the people's ultimate spokesman, was the superior branch of government. Hamilton's earlier remark that "the courts were designed to be an intermediate body between the people and the legislature"—a formulation frequently advanced in our own day—reveals the same sleight of hand. Since the people, in reality, have no way of communicating their "will" to appointed judges, the courts perforce must rely on their own will (a faculty Hamilton had denied they possessed) in construing the Constitution. And if constitutional construction is the courts' "peculiar province," it follows that the judiciary, far from being "an *intermediate* body between the people and the legislature," is in practice superior to both.

So much for Hamilton's celebrated discussion of judicial review in *Federalist* No. 78. It was not, however, his last word on the subject. In No. 80 he affirmed the right of the federal judiciary to "overrule" unconstitutional state laws—a point, it will be recalled, that he conspicuously failed to make in No. 16. In No. 82 he said flatly that appeals "would certainly lie" from the state courts to the Supreme Court—thus attempting to settle ex cathedra a matter the framers had left ambiguous. It is No. 81, however, that bears most heavily on our inquiry. *For in that paper Hamilton so far retreated from the teaching of No. 78 as to leave him, at the end of* The Federalist, *an opponent of the doctrine of judicial supremacy.*

We have already seen the key passages of No. 81 in another connection, but it will be useful to review them here in the light of the argument of No. 78. Once again Hamilton addressed himself to the "charge" that "the authority of the Supreme Court of the United States . . . will be superior to that of the legislature"—a charge that was founded, he said, on the contention that while the British parliament and the American state legislatures can at any time rectify, by law, the exceptionable decisions of their respective courts . . . the errors and usurpations of the Supreme Court of the United States will be uncontrollable and remediless." But where, in No. 78, Hamilton had tried to evade the charge by the ingenuous suggestion that it was not the judges who would be "superior," but "the people" on whose behalf the judges would act, in No. 81 he came to grips with the real problem—namely: Which of the two departments, *in the normal operations of government,* would have the last say in the event of a conflict between them? Nor, in facing that problem in No. 81, was there any further talk of constitutional interpretation being the "peculiar province of the courts": rather, Hamilton now said, such conflicts would be resolved according to the following principle: "*A legislature, without exceeding its province, cannot reverse a determination once made, in a particular case; though it may prescribe a new rule for future cases.*" "*This . . . principle,*" he went on, "*applies in all its consequences, exactly in the same manner and extent to the* [present] *state governments, as to the national government now under consideration. Not the least difference can be pointed out in any view of the subject.*"

The "consequences" of applying this principle to the practice of judicial review seem plain. The courts might be obliged to give the Constitution preference over ordinary laws should they find the two in conflict; yet this obligation would not be their "peculiar province": it would not preclude Congress from taking issue with the courts by passing new legislation at variance with the judges' opinion. But neither—for we must not wrench from Hamilton a greater concession than he in fact made—would the judges, for their part, necessarily be required to bow to Congress the next time a case involving the "new rule" came before them. Hamilton, rather, seems to have visualized a fluid contest: a disagreement between the two departments had been registered, a tension had been established, and one department or the other would give way once community sentiment had made itself felt. This, of course, is the C-2 theory of the effect of judicial review, and it was Hamilton's *last* word on the subject in *The Federalist*.

How, then, explain the zigzag course of Hamilton's commentary in *The Federalist* on the effect of judicial review? While it is impossible to speak confidently about this—Hamilton himself never attempted to reconcile the diverse emphases—we may venture the following hypothesis. When Hamilton touched on the subject in the earlier papers (Nos. 16 and 33), either because he thought ratification of the Constitution was in jeopardy, or because he had not yet made up his own mind as to the best method of "improving" on what he deemed a fundamentally bad job, Hamilton was content to endorse the approach that emerged from the text of the document and from the framers' discussion of it during the Convention. Then, in No. 78— perhaps confident now that anti-nationalist opposition to ratification was under control—he saw an opportunity to remedy what he regarded as the chief weakness of the Constitution, and proceeded to play the role, not of an expounder of the framers' approach, but as a founder in his own right. It is well known that Hamilton's great bête noire was mass democracy—a danger that would most likely materialize through the legislative branch of government. Hamilton's own remedy for potential legislative excesses had been a strong executive, elected for life. The framers, however, had rejected that idea: while they had gone to some pains, through the device of the electoral college, to make the executive "independent" of the legislature and to free him from direct control by the people, they had nonetheless failed to give the office that element of stability—i.e., permanent tenure—which Hamilton thought necessary to resist legislative encroachment. The Supreme Court judges, on the other hand, *were* given tenure, and were therefore in a position—provided their power to curb the legislature was recognized—to turn the governmental balance against the threat of democratic excesses. With all of this in mind (according to our hypothesis), Hamilton sought in No. 78 to lay the foundations for the judicial power that the Marshall Court was to assert several decades later when, as Hamilton probably foresaw, the other two branches of government had fallen under Republican control. These foundations, moreover, were honed in the most extreme terms, the better to support whatever edifice might later have to be built. Thus constitutional interpretation was to be "the peculiar province of the courts," language that might prove serviceable should the Supreme Court one day decide to challenge congressional legislation. With this rhetorical armament the Court might feel strong enough to resist the operation of an offensive law; and if the circumstances were right—as they were in *Marbury v. Madison*—the Court might even make its resistance stick. At the same time, we must not suppose Hamilton was under any illusions about the possibility of creating, through his offerings in *The Federalist*, an *automatic* obligation on the part of the legislature to heed judicial decrees. In No. 81, accordingly (and there may also have been some prudential reasons for backing down), he acknowledged the legislature's right to "prescribe a new rule for future cases." In sum, Hamilton's strategy seems to have been to furnish "the naturally feeble judiciary" with an additional weapon to offset the enormous power of Congress; he tried to give balance to what he feared would otherwise be an unequal contest. And he was able to make this attempt precisely because he recognized that the framers themselves had *not* provided for a final authority to interpret the Constitution, but had left that matter to the natural processes of tension and competition among the various public authorities.

One way of discovering whether the authors of *The Federalist* believed the courts would have the last say in interpreting the Constitution is to seek out the references in the essays to the judicial branch to see if that role was assigned to the courts—the task we have just completed. Another approach—one that would impute to the authors a more orderly scheme of argument—is, surely, to consult that section of the essays that was addressed to the problem of final authority. For this is a problem the authors did confront squarely and systematically, and it is surprising that so many constitutional scholars have passed over these passages without, evidently, learning from them. To be sure, the authors did not come up with neat formulas for solving the problem; but it is precisely their rejection, after due consideration, of mechanistic solutions that provides the true key to an understanding both of the Constitution as a framework of government and of the constitutional morality envisioned by *The Federalist*.

The discussion opened in No. 46; there Madison ventured a prediction as to who, in the nature of things, was likely to "win" in the event of a conflict between the federal and state governments. The first part of the prediction underscored *The Federalist's* basic proposition that constitutional interpretation would depend, in the last analysis, on some manifestation of popular consensus. He said that those who regard the federal and state governments, "as mutual rivals and enemies . . . uncontrolled by any common superior in their efforts to usurp the authorities of each other . . . must here be reminded of their error":

> They must be told that the *ultimate authority, wherever the derivative may be found, resides in the people alone,* and that it will not depend merely on the comparative ambition or address of the different governments, whether either, or which of them, will be able to enlarge its sphere of jurisdiction at the expense of the other.

The second point was that "the ultimate authority" of the people would ordinarily be thrown *against* the federal government inasmuch as "the first and most natural attachment of the people will be to the governments of their respective States." And this "natural attachment," Madison thought, was bound to be decisive: "should an unwarrantable measure of the federal government be unpopular in particular States . . . or even a warrantable measure be so . . ."— without deciding which it is, let us take, as an example, the federal attempt to secure James Meredith's admission to the University of Mississippi in 1962—"the means of opposition to it are powerful and at hand."

> The disquietude of the people; their repugnance and perhaps refusal to cooperate with the officers of the Union; the frowns of the executive magistracy of the State; the embarrassments created by legislative devices, which would often be added on such occasions, would oppose, in any State, difficulties not to be despised . . . and where the sentiments of several adjoining States happen to be in unison, would present obstructions which the federal government would hardly be willing to encounter. [Moreover, such] encroachments . . . would be signals of general alarm. Every [state] government would espouse the common cause. A correspondence would be opened. Plans of resistance would be concerted [etc.]

What should interest us here is not the accuracy of Madison's prediction (it was not too far off with respect to the Constitution's first seventy years), but that he should have advanced it without the slightest suggestion that such measures of resistance would be *wrong*, either legally or morally. There was no hint of an automatic obligation, under such circumstances, to obey the federal government, much less its judicial arm; on the contrary, Madison seems to have regarded recourse to various state weapons of defiance as an altogether legitimate way for the people to assert their "ultimate authority."

The five succeeding papers dealt with the possibility of conflicts within the federal government. No. 47 made the preliminary point, which need not detain us, that Montesquieu's doctrine of the "separation of powers" did not require that the various departments of government be "absolutely separate and distinct"—that they "have no *partial agency* in, or no *control* over the acts of each other."* It nonetheless remained true, Madison went on in No. 48, "that power is of an encroaching nature, and [therefore] that it ought to be effectually restrained from passing the limits assigned to it." No. 48, accordingly, weighed the adequacy of one such restraint: "Will it be sufficient to mark, with precision, the boundaries of these departments, in the constitution of the government. . . ?" No, Madison answered in a famous phrase—"these parchment barriers [that] have been principally relied on [in] most of the [state] constitutions [have] been greatly overrated. . . ." Whereupon he cited the case of Virginia—which "expressly declared in its constitution that the three great departments ought not to be intermixed"—and that of Pennsylvania—where a Council of Censors had been entrusted with the preservation of the state constitution—as instances in which the most precise constitutional provisions had proved utterly incapable of thwarting legislative encroachments.

No. 49 examined a second possibility. Thomas Jefferson had proposed in his draft constitution for the state of Virginia, Madison related, "that whenever any two of the three branches of government shall concur . . . that a convention is necessary for altering the constitution, or *correcting breaches of it*, a convention shall be called for the purpose."* "There is certainly great force in this reasoning," Madison conceded: since "it is evident [that none of the three departments] *can pretend to an exclusive or superior right of settling the boundaries between their respective powers* . . . how are the encroachments of the stronger to be prevented, or the wrongs of the weaker to be redressed without an appeal to the people themselves . . . ?" Yet, in the end, Madison rejected this solution as well,

---

* Emphasis in the original.

principally on the grounds that the legislature, which could be counted on to be the most frequent usurper, would have a disproportionate influence on a popular convention.

A third possible restraint—that of fixed, "periodical" appeals to the people, instead of the "occasional" ones proposed by Jefferson—was weighed and rejected in No. 50.

In No. 51, Madison was ready, at last, with *The Federalist's* solution. At the outset of that paper he restated the subject of the inquiry—in a form that could serve very well as the topic question of the present book.

> *To what expedient, then, shall we finally resort, for maintaining in practice the necessary partition of power among the several departments, as laid down in the Constitution?*

We may agree that today the typical answer to the question—the one taught in most of our colleges and high schools—is that the Constitution's partitions of power are authoritatively defined by the Supreme Court, and are maintained by the willingness of the other departments and of the community at large to abide by the Court's determinations. Let us compare that answer with the one *The Federalist* gave:

> *The only answer that can be given is, that as all these exterior provisions are bound to be inadequate, the defect must be supplied by so contriving the interior structure of the government as that its several constituent parts may, by their mutual relations, be the means of keeping each other in their proper places . . . the great security against a gradual concentration of the several powers in the same department consists in giving those who administer each department the necessary constitutional means, and personal motives to resist encroachments of all the others.*

The arresting aspect of *The Federalist's* answer, the reader will appreciate, is not its failure to mention a "final authority"—for instance, the Supreme Court—but that it *precludes* such an authority. Suppose the Supreme Court were, in fact, to "encroach" on the powers of Congress; and suppose further that the Court's modern claim to be the final arbiter of the Constitution's meaning were universally accepted. Would Congress be likely under such conditions to "prescribe a new rule for future cases" (to recall Hamilton's phrase), or to retaliate against the Court—say by limiting its appellate jurisdiction? Obviously Congress would do neither of these things, because Con-

gress would then feel legally and morally obliged to submit to the
Court's authority. The modern view of the judicial power, in other
words, flatly repudiates the teaching of *The Federalist* inasmuch as
it denies to Congress—and to every other branch of government—
"the necessary constitutional means and personal motives to resist encroachments" of the Supreme Court.

It is impossible, we are saying, to reconcile *The Federalist* doctrine
of checks and balances with the modern doctrine of judicial supremacy
—or, for that matter, with any other theory that lodges "an exclusive or superior right" of defining constitutional boundary lines
with any one branch of government. No doubt political systems can
operate by granting such a right to a single department, as the British system has granted it to the legislature, the Spanish to the executive, and the American, in very recent years, to the judiciary; but the
authors of *The Federalist*, with their consuming preoccupation with
the "encroaching spirit of power," went to considerable pains to point
out that the new Republic they were helping to found would place
its bets for order and liberty on a quite different set of arrangements.

Having laid down the rule for preventing aggressions by one branch
of government against another, Madison then turned, in the second
part of No. 51, to a different problem, equally vital to our inquiry:

> It is of great importance in a republic, not only to guard the society
> against the oppression of its rulers, but to guard one part of the
> society against the injustices of the other part. Different interests
> necessarily exist in different classes of citizens. If a majority be united
> by a common interest, the rights of the minority will be insecure.

The second problem, then, was to protect "minority rights"—and
the relevance of that problem to the problem of judicial supremacy
could not be plainer. Today the Supreme Court is regarded not only
as the final arbiter among the various branches of government, but
also as the special guardian of certain "rights"—notably those enumerated in the Bill of Rights and the Fourteenth Amendment—which
are asserted by individuals over against society as a whole. *The Federalist* proposed a rather different solution for securing such rights
against oppressive majorities:

> There are but two methods of providing against this evil: the one
> by creating a will in the community independent of the majority—
> that is [independent] of the society itself; the other, by comprehend-
> ing in the society so many separate descriptions of citizens as will

render an unjust combination of a majority of the whole very improbable, if not impracticable.

What did Madison mean by an "independent" will? The example
he cited was "an hereditary or self-appointed authority"—in other
words, a king or dictator. He could as well have mentioned the
Church, having in mind the theocratic arrangements of a medieval
or Calvinist society. Or—had he anticipated the modern tendency to
regard judges as the special custodians of individual rights—he might
have mentioned the Supreme Court. Whatever form it might take,
Madison rejected this first method:

> A power independent of the society may as well espouse the unjust
> views of the major, as the rightful interests of the minor party, and
> may possibly be turned against both parties.

And then the flat affirmation:

> The second method will be exemplified in the federal republic of the
> United States. Whilst all authority in it will be derived from and
> dependent on the society, the society itself will be broken into so
> many parts, interests, and classes of citizens, that the rights of in-
> dividuals, or of the minority, will be in little danger from interest
> combinations of the majority.

This, then, is the true *Federalist* doctrine. *The Federalist* was not
silent or equivocal on the question of how disputes under the Constitution—whether they should arise within government or out in the
society—were to be "settled." A "final" decision would not come down
from on high, from a source outside of and superior to the society's
organic processes; rather, the decision would *emerge*—from the
stresses, strains, tensions, rivalries and competitions of the consensus
society.

1789: THE STATUS QUO ANTE

The American commonwealth was now ready to set sail on the course the new federal Constitution had charted. It is a fitting juncture to recapitulate: to remark where, exactly, the commonwealth was on the matter of judicial review at that moment of launching; and how it got there; and also, where, in the light of what had gone before, it seemed likely to be going.

1. The American people, whether under state governments or British colonial administration, had no experience with any kind of judicial review down to 1787, except for three occasions (perhaps only two) on which a state court in one way or another had balked at enforcing a flagrant intrusion on the judicial sphere. On each of these occasions a state legislature had passed a law containing certain summary judgment provisions that shortcircuited the established judicial process—New Hampshire's Ten-Pound Act (Professor Crosskey's "occurrences"?), Rhode Island's paper money legislation (*Trevett v. Weeden*), a North Carolina wartime-confiscation law (*Bayard v. Singleton*). The country had thus been exposed to three isolated experiments with the theory* that judges might decline to be parties to an attack on their own department; and the country had seen to it that those experiments were, as far as the courts were concerned, exceedingly stormy. The Constitutional Convention, however, generated some further developments:

2. State judges were directed by the Supremacy Clause of the new federal Constitution to enforce "the supreme law" of the Union, notwithstanding any contrary provisions of the laws or constitutions of their own States. This amounted to an explicit assignment to state courts of a limited power of judicial review—a command to state judges *not to enforce* state laws of any character that conflicted

---

* Bl, Cl.

either with acts of Congress, or with treaties, or with the Constitution itself.* This was the Convention's solution to the problem of federalism. But beyond this, since an act of Congress (or a treaty) that conflicted with a state law might itself be unconstitutional, state judges would also be expected, as an unavoidable corollary to their explicit assignment, to pass judgment on the *federal* law in question; and should they decide the state law was valid, and the federal law was not, they would be expected to enforce the state law and to decline to enforce the federal law. Actually, then, *for the purpose of adjudicating state disputes with Congress, state judges were assigned the power and duty to refuse to enforce legislation of whatever kind, federal or state, they deemed unconstitutional.*† As for whether the Supreme Court would share this assignment to enforce the Union's supremacy, all of the external evidence, as well as the text of the Constitution, leaves the framers' intentions very much in doubt. The truth appears to be, in part, that the framers disagreed among themselves; in part that they had not thought the matter through; but mostly that they wished to leave that possibility "open"—a contingency to be resolved in the future through the discretionary power granted to Congress in Article III, Section 2, to establish and regulate the Supreme Court's appellate jurisdiction.

3. Over and beyond the implications of the Supremacy Clause, it seems clear that a number of the delegates to the Constitutional Convention, but by no means all of them, hoped, or expected, that the Supreme Court would feel free, by means of judicial review, to defend its own prerogatives against encroachments by Congress, or for that matter by the States. In other words, quite apart from any review power the Court might derive from the Supremacy Clause, or from congressional expansion of the Supremacy Clause via Article III, some of the framers evidently hoped, or expected, that the Supreme Court would exercise an *independent* power to look after its own interests. Such a power was by and large understood, however, to mean that the Court would merely refuse to heed—that it would *decline to enforce*—attempted usurpations of the judicial role, thus defending the boundaries of the judicial department.‡

4. The possibility that other departments of government would accede automatically to judicial interpretations of the Constitution—

---

* A1, B3, C1.
† A3, B3, C1.
‡ A3, B1, C1.

that they would recognize, as a necessary consequence of a court's ruling, an obligation to *obey* the judicial department—does not seem to have occurred seriously to anyone connected with the framing of the federal Constitution. There is some evidence that the other departments were expected to defer to the judiciary in matters peculiarly affecting the judicial department; but there is no evidence of an expectation that any department of government, in any matter, ever, would be relieved of its own obligation to interpret and enforce the constitution according to its own lights.

5. This latter problem of who was to interpret and enforce the Constitution—the key issue on which the success of the framers' plan would seem to have depended—was not dealt with, as such, in the Constitution itself, and was never mentioned in the delegates' recorded remarks at the Constitutional Convention. The framers' solution to the problem must therefore be gathered from the general sense of the document, notably the Supremacy Clause, and from the tenor and tendency of the delegates' overall approach to the situation that had brought them to Philadelphia. The *articulation* of the framers' solution to the problem—to put this somewhat differently—was left to future expounders of the Constitution. The first of these—who was then and ever since has been regarded as an authoritative spokesman on such matters—was James Madison, whose explanation of the solution in *The Federalist* we have just seen. Now: in spite of the framers' failure to deal with it explicitly, the possibility they had not thought *this* problem through, at least in the back of their minds, is not really plausible. *There is little doubt the framers expected the job of interpreting and enforcing the Constitution—as The Federalist explained—to devolve, in the first instance, severally, upon each and every duly constituted authority in the commonwealth that might be affected; and, ultimately, upon the people themselves.*

6. Nevertheless, a new, and for those times, quite revolutionary approach to the problem of final authority was being booted about by two persons we know of, James Iredell and Alexander Hamilton, who were, moreover, influential. And because of certain factors not yet mentioned, the idea insinuated by these men that the judiciary might sit astride the appointed operations of government, as the Constitution's special custodian, would bear watching.

How account for these developments? The explanations are, of course, several, and some of them lie outside the scope of this inquiry. Still, the material we have examined supplies important clues and permits at least these conclusions:

1. The received view about the origins of judicial review and of the doctrine of judicial supremacy is false. The seeds of judicial review were *not* sown during the colonial era in America, or before that in England, either by the Bonham doctrine, or by related theories about the implications of the natural law, or by any other agent. That institution did *not* grow into a sturdy sapling during the eleven years of the American Confederacy preceding the Philadelphia Convention. The framers of the federal Constitution did *not* receive the institution as part of the going American tradition, as a "given" which they could assume would be a component of the new system they were creating without some deliberate provision for it. The Constitution therefore was *not* simply a catalyst for an institution that was predestined to mature, anyway, into the mighty oak it has become in the Warren Era: the Constitution played no part at all in giving birth to the doctrine of judicial *supremacy*. All of this may be set down flatly, notwithstanding the contrary legends first invented and then promoted over many decades by historians, legal scholars, and political scientists—by the giants of these disciplines no less than by their epigones—and that, therefore, understandably, have become part of the stock in trade of American education. It is thus the teachers of the American commonwealth, rather than its ancestors or founders, who deserve credit for midwifing the doctrine of judicial supremacy, for it is they who built the doctrine's mythical foundations.

2. The framers themselves built the foundations for the institution of judicial review (as distinct from judicial supremacy), and in a quite deliberate fashion. The overarching challenge at Philadelphia had been to devise a formula for enforcing Union supremacy while preserving a fixed measure of local autonomy for the States. The nationalizing forces at the Convention had favored giving Congress a veto over all state legislation, the "congressional negative": they were beaten. The States'-rights forces favored a federal solution that would entrust the enforcement of the Union's "supreme law" to the state courts: they were successful. The result was Article VI of the Constitution, the Supremacy Clause, which released state judges from their traditional obligation to obey their own legislatures, and gave them in these matters the limited power of judicial review described above. Thus, in this one particular, the framers deliberately breached the prevailing tradition of legislative supremacy, not for the purpose of substituting judicial supremacy, but for the purpose of enforcing the Union's supremacy over its component States. And it may be set down now, also flatly, that the principal inspiration and cause of the American institution of judicial review was the problem of federalism

that confronted the framers of the American Constitution, together with their strikingly original, and down to the present moment in history, unique solution to that problem.

3. The idea that governments should contain three distinct branches, and that each should be clothed with sufficient armor to maintain the integrity of its separate powers, had become a strong current in the mainstream of American political thought in the late eighteenth century. This tripartite conception of government, which Americans drew principally from the Frenchman Montesquieu, was the one serious contemporary rival of the doctrine of legislative supremacy that America had inherited from the England of Blackstone. This competitor did not oppose, as an alternative to legislative supremacy—judicial supremacy; it did, however, imply judicial *independence*. As a result, the phrase "independent judges" gained considerable currency in the latter part of the century, if not as the description of a reality, at least as the hopeful statement of an aspiration and an ideal. Many of the delegates to the Constitutional Convention evidently shared this vision, and hoped it would become a reality in the new federal government. This is the explanation both for the aberrational exercise of the power of judicial self-protection in the state courts prior to 1787, and for the framers' occasional allusions at Philadelphia to the prospect of "independent judges" resisting legislative attacks on their own department. This second departure from the tradition of legislative supremacy was considerably more tentative than the one dictated by the requirements of federalism, but it appears to have had support in depth—sufficient to have adumbrated the event (if not the rationale) of John Marshall's defense of judicial prerogatives in *Marbury v. Madison*, the only challenge the Supreme Court dared to level at an act of Congress prior to the gestations of the Civil War.

4. Two other currents were running in the formative years of the American Union that left no immediate imprint on the role assigned to the judiciary by the framers, but that in retrospect seem to have been destined to cut important channels for the judiciary's future evolution. One was the essentially anti-democratic fear of legislative excesses that is popularly associated today with the name of Alexander Hamilton, but that every serious historian knows was shared in one degree or another by the great majority of the leadership of the early American commonwealth in all of its strata, political, economic, and social. The cause of the wise, the rich, and the well-born, moreover, was earnestly and ably represented at Philadelphia. A num-

ber of devices for frustrating the democratic tendency were proposed, such as property qualifications for voters; and once the problem of federalism had beeen solved, no subject occupied so much of the time and attention of the Convention as the nigh-universally recognized need to construct some durable obstacle to hasty, extremist legislation generated by demagogic agitation or popular fancy. One remedy, frequently and powerfully advanced, but just as frequently rejected, was a "Council of Revision," an executive-judicial group that would be expected to veto rash laws prior to their final enactment. The "expedient" (to recall Gouverneur Morris' phrase) the Convention finally settled upon, however, was the overridable presidential veto, coupled with a decision to select the President, not by congressional or popular election, but by a special group of Electors appointed for that purpose by the States. Now this latter was an ingenious as well as an original solution, but whether it would prove practical, or durable, or adequate to the ends for which it was designed, was something else again. Hamilton seems to have confessed in *Federalist* No. 78 that he, for one, entertained considerable doubts. What recourse, then, would remain should the framers' visions of the Electoral College fail to pan out? What new refuge would be sought by the wise, the rich, and the well-born if the Presidency, as well as one branch of the Congress, should fall under popular control? It is just possible that thoughts would begin to turn, as Hamilton's had in that celebrated passage of No. 78, to the opportunities present in the judicial office of "expounding" the laws. These opportunities were not particularly promising in the experience of the eighteenth century, since "exposition" of the laws had always been understood to mean the power of declaring what laws meant, not the power of deciding whether they were valid. Nevertheless a new phenomenon had recently made an appearance in the political experience of the West that could affect this previous understanding, namely—

5. The *written* constitution. The development of this mode of recording a country's underlying political commitments is traceable in part to the theoretical prescriptions of writers like Vattel, but it was mostly a matter of the newly independent commonwealths of the West needing a fresh articulation of their political assumptions. The need would not be felt by older commonwealths whose constitutions had evolved from tradition and custom, still less by barbarian communities to whom the articulation of a political system seldom occurs. But since the comparatively sophisticated new commonwealths in America, as well as those later on in Europe and South

America, were shedding at least a part of their traditions—in the case
of the American States, their dependence on the British Crown—they
were forced to reach an agreement about a substitute; and the best
way of avoiding a misunderstanding about the terms of the new
agreement seemed, to the extent this was feasible, to write them
down. These verbalized understandings were expected to take their
place alongside such of the commonwealth's basic cultural commitments as did not lend themselves to codification; and together, the
written and the unwritten terms of the agreement, would be recognized as the commonwealth's "fundamental law."

But here we must recall the relation between "fundamental law"
—a term used more or less indiscriminately in the eighteenth century
and before as an equivalent to "the law of God," or "the law of na-
ure," or the amalgam of beliefs, traditions, and customs that made
up a commonwealth's "constitution"—and ordinary laws. In the
eighteenth century's experience fundamental law had the character of
"admonitory law," in the phrase of Professor Hyneman,[1] as opposed
to the body of law enacted by legislative assemblies, which Hyneman
calls "effective law." The latter was the law that actually governed
the commonwealth; the former, so to speak, the law under which the
commonwealth was supposed to be governed. In the event of a dis-
crepancy, legislators were expected to correct the discord by bringing effective law into line with the admonitions of the fundamental
law, because fundamental law was superior. Judges, for their part,
were expected to enforce effective law as it stood, notwithstanding
the admonitory norms of the fundamental law.

Very well; but why should this relation be disturbed by the appearance of written constitutions?

Let us say simply that it *might* be disturbed by the possibility that
the commands of a formal document would acquire a peculiarly
vivid and formidable status in virtue of their having been reduced to
the rigid formulations of the written word. These particular commands, unlike the unwritten portions of the fundamental law, might
take on the appearance of "laws" comparable to those other "effective
laws" that had been enacted in the ordinary course of the commonwealth's affairs by its duly constituted lawmaking authorities—but
with this difference: that this new body of effective law would also
be superior law. Now, plainly, the operational consequences of these
impressionistic deductions would be of a very high order for the judicial department; for now, in their role of "expounding" the laws,
the judges could have two conflicting sets of effective laws in front

of them, a situation that might seem to require a choice between them, a preference for one at the expense of the other. Indeed, we know this line of thought was pursued to that very conclusion by a contemplative citizen of North Carolina in the summer of 1787. Recall the letter of James Iredell to Richard Spaight: "[W]hen we were at liberty to form a government as we thought best," we North Carolinians created a legislature with powers "limited and defined [by a written] Constitution"; by this act "the Constitution [became] a *law of the State*"; but since judges are expected "to decide [cases] according to the *laws of the State*," they must choose between the Constitution's "superior" law and the legislature's "inferior" law; this does not mean that "the judges are appointed arbiters . . . as it were [to decide] whether the Assembly have or have not violated the Constitution, "but merely that when the two sets of "laws" are "necessarily brought in judgment before them, they must, unavoidably, determine one way or another."*

But recall also that this argument made but one other appearance in our study, Hamilton's famous démarche in *Federalist* No. 78. The reasoning does not, that is to say, appear to have been particularly compelling to a generation accustomed to distinguishing sharply between "admonitory" and "effective" law, and to respecting that distinction, even after the emergence of written constitutions, as the cornerstone of an orderly jurisprudence. And why, really, *should* written constitutions have made a difference? One can imagine Iredell's and Hamilton's contemporaries scornfully asking them to explain what magic was present in merely writing words down that could metamorphose the judicial role in government. Why not, with another waft of the wand, decree that the unwritten elements of a constitution—for instance, the commonwealth's uncodifiable cultural commitments—were also "effective law" against which judges would be expected to weigh the legitimacy of all legislative acts? (Indeed, that further step has been taken, in our own time, by the Warren Court and its apologists. The Supreme Court, to recall Dean Rostow's defense of "sociological jurisprudence," "should be the proponent and protector of the values which are the premises, goals, needs, and ambitions of our culture, as they have been expressed in its living constitution.")

The fact is, that question was not asked. On the record, the Iredell-Hamilton argument was not taken seriously enough by their contem-

---

* Emphases in the original. See "Bayard *v.* Singleton," above.

poraries to generate a rejoinder of any kind. The argument has nonetheless seemed worth remarking, both because it anticipated, and
may even have inspired, John Marshall's opinion in *Marbury v. Madison*, and because it reveals the impoverished genesis of a position
about the judiciary's role in the enforcement of a constitution that
seems to modern minds to command the support of an overpowering,
ineluctable logic. It is enough to notice that the logic is, at best, superficial—that it certainly does not command adherence sub specie
aeternitatis, and that it was disdainfully dismissed by the founders
of the Republic. In fine, if the logic was to have a future, the explanation would not lie in its interstices, but in its serviceability to men
with substantive interests and causes to promote—for instance, those
of the wise, the rich, and the well-born, or, more topically, those who
are intoxicated with the wine of equalitarianism.

6. The foregoing is of no help at all in accounting for the doctrine of judicial *supremacy*. The power of judicial review could be
enlarged along the lines just suggested so as to give the Supreme
Court a somewhat larger role in interpreting and enforcing the Constitution than the framers contemplated—as indeed happened during
the reign of John Marshall; but even the blanket prerogative asserted
by Marshall of refusing to enforce any legislation the Court deemed
unconstitutional would not establish the Supreme Court as the "final
arbiter" of the Constitution—in the sense that its decisions would determine not only the rights of litigants, but also of sister departments
of government. The claim to that role was not laid by the Court of
John Marshall, drawing, however tenuously, upon eighteenth-century
antecedents; but by the Court of Earl Warren, drawing upon factors
that came into play many years beyond the scope of this volume.

We are able, however, to venture an accounting of another sort.
We can suggest why the framers handled the problem of interpreting
and enforcing the Constitution the way they did: why they did *not*
designate a "final arbiter"; why they placed their bets instead on the
intricate consensus machinery they had gone to such pains to con-
trive. A moment's reflection on the various possibilities open to them
will explain a great deal; the rest requires an appreciation of the
framers' quite striking insights into the nature of political man and
his capacity to fashion, with some sanction other than brute force, enduring political arrangements.

Any thought of designating a "final arbiter" naturally raised the
question: Who?

The States? It is true that very soon Jeffersonian Republicans, and somewhat later spokesmen for the South, would be hinting at this solution as a consequence of their contention that the Constitution was essentially a "compact" of sovereign States. But for the framers this solution would have metaphysical as well as practical difficulties: while the States could be "final" authorities unto themselves, they could not very well be, severally, *the* final authority of the Union. Besides, the Philadelphia Convention had been called precisely to remedy the common inconvenience caused by the Confederacy's reserving to each of the States its ultimate autonomy.

Congress? The idea could not be rejected entirely out of hand in the light of the going tradition of legislative supremacy—and indeed it was not, as witness the dogged struggle by some of the delegates on behalf of the "congressional negative." Still, there was also much against that solution. For one thing, the American commonwealth, for all of its experience with legislative supremacy, was not altogether happy with it: as witness the widespread apprehension of democratic excesses; as witness also that a war had just been fought against parliamentary oppression. For another, the claims of local self-government, and the survival of the States as partially sovereign entities, were at stake, and as we know the framers explicitly refused to override those claims when they turned down the congressional negative in favor of the Supremacy Clause.

The executive? That solution the framers *would* reject out of hand. If Parliament had been the actual oppressor in the country's experience, the symbol of oppression was the King. And it was not only hereditary monarchy that bore the country's animus: one proposition on which the American people were indisputably united was that supreme authority over their affairs was not to be entrusted to an autocrat.

What was left? Only the judiciary; but that department was, for different reasons, as unlikely a candidate as autocracy. Enough has been said to the point that a judicial solution was altogether alien to the commonwealth's disposition and experience: that it would strike the framers as artificial and gimmicky, a device totally unprecedented in the political theory and practice, not only of the Anglo-Saxon race, but of all of the West. It remains to remark why—a priori—this was so.

Enduring political authority needs the sanction either of physical force, or of some mode of legitimacy. Of force, and the judicial department's want of it, no elaboration is required. As for legitimacy, history has observed three ways in which it is conferred: by custom and tradition; by a tolerated assertion of divine right; by the deliberate choice of the governed. Obviously the judges of the early American commonwealth could look neither to tradition nor to the divinity to support an assignment to rule the country. But what of the third possibility? Was there anything that excluded the crowning of the courts, ex nihilo, by the commonwealth's deliberate choice? In a world of abstractions, nothing at all. Theoretically, there was nothing to prevent the American people from suddenly deciding in a moment of collective afflatus to entrust their ultimate destiny to a small group of judicial potentates who would be appointed to their stations by some intermediary officials over whose selection the people had only indirect control; and who, themselves, would never thereafter be answerable to the people. The difficulty is that men do not live in a world of abstractions. In the real world of late eighteenth-century America, the possibility that a people passionately and notoriously committed to the idea of *representative self-government* would deliberately embrace such a proposal is in a class, not with Hollywood fantasy, but with science-fiction.

To put it otherwise: according to the framers' lights, the idea of the judiciary acting as the final arbiter of the American political system was not grounded in political reality. The Supreme Court, acting in this role, would possess neither force nor legitimacy. The Court might display "will," should the judges decide to try their hand at governing; but who would indulge the charade, except in amusement? Who would *obey*? This is why Hamilton's suggestion in *Federalist* No. 78 that constitutional construction would be acknowledged as the "peculiar province" of the judiciary was, on the face of it, absurd. He could have advanced the idea seriously only by assuming—or fearing?—that future events would so unfold. . . .

By contrast, the framers' actual approach to the problem of final authority, as set forth by Madison in *Federalist* No. 51, was grounded solidly in the political realities. There were to be, in the framers' conception of the new constitutional system, not one, but several power centers, each with an appointed authority appropriate to its competence. In operation, each authority would be endowed with rights and duties so contrived as to permit the defense of its own sphere, yet so interwoven with all of the others' as to discourage aggressions, either against one another, or against the people. This solution avoided, on the one hand, reliance on artificial mechanisms that would have no roots in the country's underlying power structure, and on the other, the ever present danger of evolution toward tyranny. The framers anticipated tensions between the various authorities; indeed they did. The success of their plan *depended* on the tensions. They could hope the plan would ignite and command the support of the nobler impulses of man, but they would have been mischievous utopians to have confided the country's future to such hopes. Their approach, rather, was to anticipate the frailities of man, and to try to channel the ignoble impulses such frailities produce into purposes that might nourish the common good. Let the human impulse of self-aggrandizement, in its corporate as well as its individual expression, be acknowledged; let every department of government be equipped with means both for promoting its own interests and for jealously defending them against attack; let the rivalries so contrived generate tensions, and, on occasion, discord; but count on those same rivalries and tensions, guided by the interposition of community sentiment, to fashion a consensus solution—and so restore harmony. This paradox is better known as a system of "checks and balances." Their brilliant orchestration of that system was the supreme achievement of the framers of the American Constitution.

In sum, the success of the framers' plan would not depend solely, or even primarily, on the virtues of self-denial and restraint, on public-spirited sacrifices for the common good. The country would be expected to display a measure of these virtues, and the larger the measure the better: a realistic appraisal of human nature did not lead the framers to cynicism, nor should it us. But the key to success was the skill and devotion and stamina that every department of government was expected to bring to bear on the discharge of its own assignments. The constitutional morality envisioned by *The Federalist* was not a pietistic exhortation to the several departments to behave themselves, but a summons to every department to exercise energetically and resolutely the rights and duties the Constitution had confided to it. The system would break down, the founders of the Republic seem to have been warning us, should ever the components of the system lie down and permit one department to overpower the others by a superior assertion of will.

A subsequent volume will relate how the founders' successors responded to that admonition. As might be expected during the near century and three-quarters between 1789 and the beginning of the Warren Era in 1954, the country's consensus machinery was subjected to stresses and pressures and historical currents that the founders' experience, even their extraordinarily perspicacious vision, did not anticipate. Not surprisingly either, the experience of living under the Constitution vitally affected the operation of the machinery, including the practice of judicial review: it established new modes of handling the country's affairs that in time became traditions in their own right, and were thus added to the country's fixed, or as the case might be, its fluid constitution.

Still—in spite of all that—we may discover that the founders' admonition, in most instances, *was* heeded; that the essential parts of the consensus machinery were kept in working order; that from the country's first major constitutional crisis, the challenge of the Alien and Sedition Acts in the 1790's, to its last prior to the Warren Era, the Roosevelt court-packing episode of the 1930's, the several departments resisted intimidation and, within the limits of prudence, sought to guard their respective domains; that the all-important tensions thus remained intact and operative: *that the business of interpreting and enforcing the Constitution remained a joint enterprise.* And if that is the way the story actually unfolds, the question that has lain at the bottom of this inquiry—whether the Supreme Court, from whatever source, owns a prescriptive claim to the role of the Constitution's final arbiter—will have to be answered in the negative. We shall have to conclude that the Warren Era inaugurated a *revolution* in American jurisprudence. Whereupon the moment will have arrived when we may ask whether the Warren Revolution is, on its merits, in the best interests of the American commonwealth, and if not, what weapons are available for the Counter-Revolution.

APPENDIX

Herewith the balance of Justice Black's treatment, in *Wesberry*, of the "historical context" of Art. 1, Sec. 2. (See p. 109.) Black's statements are set forth in the lefthand column; the relevant passages of the original records, together with what commentary is required for clarity, appear at the right.

JUSTICE BLACK

1. "Madison in *The Federalist* [No. 57] described the system of division of States into congressional districts, the method which he and others assumed States probably would adopt: 'The city of Philadelphia is supposed to contain between fifty and sixty thousand souls. It will therefore form nearly two districts for the choice of Federal Representatives.'"

THE RECORD

1. Madison was replying to the argument that the numerical ratio between the people and their representatives stipulated by the Constitution (a minimum of 30,000 to 1) was too large for good government. The essence of the argument was that electorates so large would facilitate the intrigues of aristocratic factions, and Madison's rebuttal at this point was designed to show that comparable ratios governed the elections of local and state officials in many of the States. Having discussed New Hampshire, Massachusetts, and New York, he said: "Pennsylvania is an additional example. Some of her counties, which elect her state representatives, are almost as large as her districts will be by which her federal representatives will be elected. The city of Philadelphia is supposed to contain between fifty and sixty thousand souls. It will, therefore, form nearly two districts for the choice of federal representatives. It forms, however, but one county, in which every elector votes for each of his representatives in the state legislature.

341

JUSTICE BLACK

THE RECORD

And what may appear to be still more directly to our purpose, the whole city actually elects a *single member* for the executive council."*

2. " '[N]umbers,' he said [in No. 54], not only are a suitable way to represent wealth but in any event 'are the only proper scale of representation.' "

2. (This item directly follows No. 1 in the opinion; hence the reader of an "un-footnoted" version of the *Wesberry* analysis, such as appeared in the newspapers, would suppose that Madison was still talking about Philadelphia.) In point of fact No. 54 reads as follows: "It is agreed on all sides that numbers are the best scale of wealth and taxation, as they are the only proper scale of representation. Would the Convention have been impartial or consistent if they had rejected the *slaves* from the list of inhabitants, when the shares of representation were to be calculated; and inserted them on the lists when the tariff of contributions was to be adjusted?" The provision for representing slaves was one proof, of course, that numbers were *not* to be the "only . . . scale of representation." And it will be recalled that No. 54 is the very paper in which Madison laid down the "fundamental principle of the proposed constitution that . . . the right of choosing [the] allotted number [of representatives] in each State is to be exercised by such part of the inhabitants as the State itself may designate."

3. "In the state conventions, speakers urging ratification of the Constitution emphasized the theme of equal representation in the House which had permeated the debates in Philadelphia."*

3. Ames said: "I consider biennial elections as a security that the sober, second thought of the people shall be law. [Remember also that] the representatives are the grand inquisition of the Union. They are, by impeachment, to bring great offenders to

---

* "See, e.g., . . . Fisher Ames, in the Massachusetts Convention . . . Oliver

---

* Emphasis in the original.

JUSTICE BLACK   THE RECORD

justice. One year will not suffice to
detect guilt, and to pursue it to conviction; therefore they will escape,
and the balance of the two branches
will be destroyed, and the people
oppressed with impunity. The senators will represent the sovereignty of
the States. The representatives are to
represent the people. The offices
ought to bear some proportion in
point of importance. This will be
impossible if they are chosen for one
year only."[42]

Wolcott said: "I have given [the
proposed Constitution] all the consideration in my power, and I have
. . . made up my mind . . . in favor
of adopting it. It is founded upon
the election of the people. If it varies
from the former system, or if it is to
be altered hereafter, it must be with
the consent of the people. . . . The
Senate, a constituent branch of the
general legislature, without whose
assent no public act can be made, are
appointed by the States, and will
secure the rights of the several States.
The other branch of the legislature,
the Representatives, are to be elected
by the people at large. They will
therefore be the guardians of the
rights of the great body of the
citizens. So well guarded is this Constitution throughout, that it seems
impossible that the rights either of
the States or of the people should be
destroyed."[43]

Davie said: "The [old] Confederation derived its sole support from the
state legislature. This rendered it
weak and ineffectual. It was therefore
necessary that the foundations of
[the new] government should be
laid on the broad basis of the people.
Yet the state governments are the
pillars upon which [the federal]
government is [to be] extended over
such an immense territory, and are

Wolcott, Connecticut . . . William
Richard Davie, North Carolina . . .
Charles Pinckney, South Carolina."

JUSTICE BLACK

THE RECORD

essential to its existence. The House of Representatives are elected immediately by the people. The Senators represent the sovereignty of the States; they are directly chosen by the state legislatures, and no legislative act can be done without their concurrence."[44]

Pinckney said: "After much anxious discussion [at the Constitutional Convention] a compromise was effected, by which it was determined that the first branch be so chosen as to represent in due proportion the people of the Union; that the Senate should be the representative of the States, where each should have an equal weight."[45]

4. "Charles Cotesworth Pinckney told the South Carolina Convention, 'the House of Representatives will be elected immediately by the people, and represent them and their personal rights individually. . . .' "

4. Pinckney was defending the Great Compromise by remarking that it solved a problem South Carolina had experienced under her original constitution. The passage, in toto, reads: "The reason why our present state constitution, made in 1788, changed the mode of electing senators from the mode prescribed by our first constitution, passed in 1776, was because, by the first, the senators were elected by [the lower] house, and therefore, being their mere creatures, they could not be supposed to have that freedom of will as to form a proper check on its proceedings; whereas, in the general [federal] Constitution, the House of Representatives will be elected immediately by the people, and represent them and their personal rights individually; the Senate will be elected by the state legislatures, and represent the States in their political capacity; and thus each branch will form a proper and independent check on the other, and the legislative powers will be advantageously balanced."[46] As for how Pinckney expected abuses of "the people's" election "rights"—e.g., rot-

JUSTICE BLACK

THE RECORD

ten boroughs—remedied, he had addressed himself to just that question a few moments earlier. In reply to Rawlins Lowndes' charge that Congress' supervisory power over "The Times, Places and Manner of holding Elections" gave too much power to the federal government, Pinckney said: ". . . it is absolutely necessary that Congress should have this superintending power, lest, by the intrigues of a ruling faction in a State, the members of the House of Representatives should not really represent the people of the State. . . ."[47]

5. "Speakers at the ratifying conventions emphasized that the House of Representatives was meant to be free of the malapportionment then existing in some of the state legislatures—such as those of Connecticut, Rhode Island, and South Carolina—and argued that the power given Congress in Art. I, Sec. 4, was meant to be used to vindicate the people's right to equality of representation in the House."*

5. Dana said: "It is apparent [from Article I, Section 4, that] the intention of the Convention was to set Congress on a different ground [from that of the Confederacy]; that a part should proceed directly from the people, and not from their substitutes, the [state] legislatures; therefore [a state] legislature ought not to *control* [congressional] elections. The legislature of Rhode Island has lately formed a plan to alter their representation to corporations, [whereas representation] ought to be by numbers. Look at Great Britain, where the injustice of this mode is apparent. The legislature of Rhode Island are about [to adopt] this plan in order to deprive the towns of Newport and Providence of their weight, and [in order that] the legislature may have a power to counteract the will of a majority of the people."[48]

King commented directly thereafter, using Virginia as an illustration, that one of the reasons for Section 4 was that it was not "practicable" to have a "fixed place" for holding elections: "a district that may now be fully settled, may in time be scarcely inhabited; and the back country, now scarcely inhabited, may

---

* "See . . . Francis Dana, in the Massachusetts Convention . . . Rufus King, Massachusetts . . . James Madison, Virginia."

JUSTICE BLACK

THE RECORD

be fully settled. Suppose [Virginia were] thrown into eight *districts,* and a member apportioned to each; if the numbers increase, the representatives and districts will be increased. The matter, therefore, must be left subject to the regulation of the state legislature, or to the general government. . . . In Connecticut they do not choose by numbers, but by corporations. . . . The same rule is about to be adopted in Rhode Island. The inequality of such representation, where every corporation would have an equal right to send an equal number of representatives, was apparent. In the Southern States, the inequality is greater. . . . The back parts of [South] Carolina have increased greatly since the adoption of their constitution [which allowed Charleston 30 of the General Assembly's 200 members], and have frequently attempted an alternation of this unequal mode [to which] the members from Charleston . . . will not consent. [Moreover], the delegates from Carolina [to the present] Congress have always been chosen by the delegates of that city. The representatives, therefore, from that State, will not be chosen *by the people,* but will be the representatives of a faction of that State. If the general government cannot control in this case, how are the people secure?"*49

James Monroe had asked "why Congress had an ultimate control over the time, place, and manner of elections of representatives. . . ."

Madison replied: ". . . it was thought that the regulation of time, place and manner of electing the representatives should be uniform throughout the continent. Some States might regulate the elections on the principles of equality, and others

---

* Emphasis in original.

JUSTICE BLACK

might regulate them otherwise. This diversity would be obviously unjust. Elections are regulated now unequally in some States, particularly South Carolina, with respect to Charleston, which is represented by thirty members. Should the people of any State by any means be deprived of the right of suffrage, it was judged proper that it should be remedied by the general government. *It was found impossible to fix the time, place, and manner, of the election of representatives, in the Constitution. It was found necessary to leave the regulation of these, in the first place, to the state governments, as being best acquainted with the situation of the people, subject to the control of the general government, in order to enable it to produce uniformity, and prevent its own dissolution.* And, considering the state governments and general government as distinct bodies, acting in different and independent capacities for the people, it was thought the particular regulations should be submitted to the former, and the general regulations to the latter. Were they exclusively under the control of the state governments, the general government might easily be dissolved. But if they be regulated properly by the state legislatures, the *congressional* control will very probably never be exercised. *The power appears to me satisfactory, and as unlikely to be abused as any part of the Constitution.*"50

6. "Congress' power, said John Steele at the North Carolina convention, was not to be used to allow Congress to create rotten boroughs; in answer to another delegate's suggestion that Congress might use its power to favor people living near the seacoast, Steele said that Congress [*sic*] 'most

6. The "[other] delegate" Steele answered was James Galloway, who had asked: "What have the state governments left for them if the general government is to be possessed of such extensive powers, without control or limitation, without any responsibility to the States? He [W.

probably' would 'lay the State off
into districts,' and if it made laws
'inconsistent with the Constitution,
independent judges will not uphold
them, nor will the people obey
them.' "

R. Davie, a few moments earlier]
asks, 'How is it possible for the members [of Congress] to perpetuate
themselves?' I think I can show how
they can do it. [Suppose Congress
accepts representatives chosen under]
the government [of North Carolina]
as it now stands organized. We [will]
send five members to the House of
Representatives in the general
government. They will go, no doubt,
from or near the seaports. In other
States, also, those near the sea will
have more interest, and will go forward to Congress; and they can,
without violating the Constitution,
make a law continuing themselves, as
they have control over the place,
time, and manner of elections. This
may happen. . . ."[51]

To which Steele replied: "What
reason has [Galloway] to say [our
five representatives] will go from the
seashore? The time, place, and manner of holding elections are to be
prescribed by the [state] legislatures.
Our legislature is to regulate the
first election, at any event. They will
regulate it as they think proper.
They may, and most probably will,
lay the State off into districts. Who
are to vote for them? Every man who
has a right to vote for a representative to our legislature will have a
right to vote for a representative to
the general government. Does [the
Constitution] not expressly provide
that the electors in each State shall
have the qualifications requisite for
the most numerous branch of the
state legislature? Can [Congress],
without a most manifest violation of
the Constitution, alter the qualifications of the electors? The power
over the manner of elections does not
include that of saying who shall
vote: [thus the suggestion that repre-
sentatives] shall go from the seashore,
and be able to perpetuate themselves,

JUSTICE BLACK

is a most extravagant idea. Will the members of Congress deviate from their duty without any prospect of advantage to themselves? What interest can they have to make the place of elections inconvenient? The judicial power of [the federal] government is so well constructed as to be a check. There was no check in the old Confederation. The [old Congress'] power was, in principle and theory, transcendent. If the [new] Congress make laws inconsistent with the Constitution, independent judges will not uphold them, nor will the people obey them. A universal resistance will ensue."[52] Justice Harlan commented in his dissent: "The particular possibilities that Steele had in mind were apparently that Congress might attempt to prescribe the qualifications for electors or 'to make the place of elections inconvenient.' . . . Steele was concerned with the danger of *congressional* usurpation, under the authority of Section 4, of power belonging to the States."[*53] It should be added that the "independent judges" Steele had in mind may have been the *state* judges of North Carolina. (See our discussion of the meaning of the Supremacy Clause.)

7. "Soon after the Constitution was adopted, James Wilson of Pennsylvania, by then an Associate Justice of this Court, gave a series of lectures at Philadelphia in which, drawing on his experience as one of the most active members of the Constitutional Convention, he said: '[A]ll elections ought to equal. Elections are equal, when a given number of citizens, in one part of the state, choose as many representatives,

7. Black's presentation implies that "the state" Wilson spoke of in this post-Convention lecture was a State of the American Union, e.g., Pennsylvania, and that his notion that such a state ought to be divided into equal election districts was something he had learned from "his experience [at] the Constitutional Convention." Actually, in this passage, Wilson was speaking of the genus "state," in the abstract, and his prescription for

---

* The emphases are Harlan's.

JUSTICE BLACK

as are chosen by the same number of citizens, in any other part of the state. In this manner, the proportion of the representatives and of the constituents will remain invariably the same.' "

8. "In urging the people to adopt the Constitution, Madison said in No. 57 of *The Federalist*: 'Who are to be the electors of the Federal Representatives? Not the rich more than the poor; not the learned more than the ignorant; not the haughty heirs of distinguished names, more than the humble sons of obscure and unpropitious fortune. The electors are to be the great body of the people of the United States. . . .' Readers surely could have fairly taken this to mean, 'one person, one vote.' "

THE RECORD

equal election districts was part of a paradigm for his conception of the ideal polity.[54] In an earlier paragraph, he had taken pains to identify the sense in which he was using the word: "To this moral person, we assign, by way of eminence, the dignified appellation of *state*."*[55]

8. "Readers," of No. 57, presumably, would have read its opening paragraph, and so would have understood what Madison was driving at. "The *third* charge against the House of Representatives," that paper began, "is that it will be taken from that class of citizens which will have least sympathy with the mass of the people; and be most likely to aim at an ambitious sacrifice of the many, to the aggrandizement of the few."* The substance of the complaint, Madison went on to explain (see item 1), was that the numerical ratio of the people to their representatives would be so large as to encourage corruption. The rhetorical flourish here quoted by Black was the way Madison introduced his reply to the complaint. And the last sentence of that paragraph which Black omitted, read: "They [the electors] are to be the same who exercise the right in every State of electing the correspondent branch of the legislature of the State."

---

* Emphasis in the original.

NOTES

CRISIS IN THE CONSENSUS SOCIETY

1. 358 U.S. 1, 18 (1958).
2. *Supreme Court on Trial* (New York, 1963), p. 79.
3. Hearings of the Senate Internal Security Subcommittee, Feb. 19, 1958.

BROWN *v.* BOARD OF EDUCATION

1. 347 U.S. 483, 489 (1954).
2. Ibid., 489.
3. Ibid., 489-90.
4. Cong. Globe, 39th Cong., 1st Sess., 129 (1866).
5. Ibid., 475.
6. Ibid., 1117.
7. 14 Stat. 27 (1866).
8. 14 Stat. 343 (1866).
9. Message of the Governor of Indiana to the Legislature, Jan. 11, 1867, p. 21.
10. Alabama: Acts of Ala. 1868, 148; Arkansas: Stat. 1868, No. LII, Sec. 107; Georgia: Ga. Pub. Laws (1870), 49; Kansas: Chap. 49, Sec. 7, Laws of Kansas, 1867; Kentucky: Ky. Acts 1867, 94; Mississippi: Ann. Rep. of Supt. of Pub. Instr. of Miss. (1871) 66, 124-7; App. 4-5, 11; Nevada: Rev. Stat (1867), 95; North Carolina: N.C. Laws of 1868-9, Chap. 184; Tennessee: Tenn. Stat. 1866-7, Chap. XXVII, Sec. 17; Texas: Const. of 1866, Art. 10, Sec. 7; Virginia: Va. Acts (1869) 70, Chap. 259, Sec. 47; West Virginia: W. Va. Acts (1867) Chap. 98.
11. California: Calif. Stat. 1866, No. CCCXLII, Sec. 57-59; Indiana: Ind. Laws 1869, 41; Maryland: Md. Laws 1868, Chap. 407; Missouri: Mo. Const. of 1865, Art. IX, Sec. 2; Pennsylvania: Pa. Laws (1854), 623.
12. See Rep. of Supt. of Pub. Inst. of Ill. (1867-8), 18-21; N.J. Laws (1894) 536; N.Y. Laws 1864, Chap. 555, Title X, Sec. 1; *Garnes v. McCann*, 21 Ohio Stat. 198.
13. Del. Laws 1901, Chap. 235.
14. Iowa Laws, 1858, Chap. 52, Sec. 30; Mass. Acts and Resolves, 1855, Chap. 256; Rhode Island never legally sanctioned segregated schools.

15. Conn. Pub. Acts (1866) No. CVIII; 1 Mich. Laws (1867) 43; Nebraska, admitted to the Union in 1867, ratified the Fourteenth Amendment in the same year; it never legally sanctioned segregated schools.
16. 347 U.S. 483, 490-92.
17. 163 U.S. 537, 544.
18. Ibid., 544.
19. Ibid., 551.
20. 175 U.S. 528, 545 (1899).
21. 275 U.S. 78, 85 (1927).
22. 305 U.S. 337, 349 (1938).
23. 347 U.S. 483, 492-3.
24. Ibid., 493.
25. Ibid., 493-5.
26. *The Sovereign Prerogative* (New Haven & London, 1962), p. xxxiv.

PENNSYLVANIA *v.* NELSON

1. *Pennsylvania v. Nelson*, 350 U.S. 497, 499 (1956).
2. Ibid., 500.
3. Ibid., 502-4.
4. The letter is on file in the Congressman's office.
5. 350 U.S. 497, 519.
6. Ibid., 505.
7. 312 U.S. 52 (1941).
8. 254 U.S. 325 (1920).
9. Ibid., 329-31.
10. 350 U.S. 497, 501.
11. 254 U.S. 325, 331.
12. 350 U.S. 497, 517.
13. Ibid., 516-7.
14. Ibid., 508.
15. Ibid.
16. Ibid., 518-19.
17. *Nelson v. United States*, 352 U.S. 1.
18. *Yates v. United States*, 354 U.S. 298 (1957).

THE SCHEMPP—MURRAY CASES

1. Cf. *Engel v. Vitale*, 370 U.S. 421, 422 (1962).
2. *School District of Abington Township, Pennsylvania v. Schempp* and *Murray v. Curlett*, 374 U.S. 203 (1963).
3. 24 Pa. Stat., Sec. 15—1516, as amended, Pub. Law 1928 (Supp. 1960) Dec. 17, 1959: "Any child shall be excused . . . upon the written request of his parent or guardian." Rule of the Board of School Commissioners of Baltimore City (1905), pursuant to Art. 77, Sec. 202, Annotated Code of Maryland, uses identical language.
4. 374 U.S. 203, 208 [n. 3].
5. Ibid., 215.

6. Ibid., 216.

7. Ibid., 217.

8. Ibid., 225.

9. Jonathan Elliot, *The Debates in the Several State Conventions* (Philadelphia, 1836), 2nd. ed., III, 659.

10. IV Elliot 244.

11. *Documentary History of the Constitution* (Department of State, Washington, D.C., 1894), II, 143.

12. David K. Watson, *The Constitution of the United States* (Chicago, 1910), II, 1372.

13. Ibid.

14. *Annals of the Congress of the United States*, Gales ed. (Washington, D.C., 1834), Vol. I, August 15, 1789 (p. 730).

15. Joseph Story, *Commentaries on the Constitution of the United States*, 3rd. ed. (Boston, 1858), II, 667.

16. Eleventh edition, IX, 787.

17. 374 U.S. 203, 233.

18. Ibid., 233-4.

19. Ibid., 236.

20. Ibid., 237.

21. Cf. Proposed Amendments to the Constitution, H.R. Doc. No. 551 (70th Cong., 2nd Sess.), 182.

22. 374 U.S. 203, 222.

23. Charles E. Rice, *The Supreme Court and Public Prayer* (New York, 1964), pp. 79, 81.

WESBERRY *v.* SANDERS

1. 369 U.S. 186 (1962).

2. 376 U.S. 1 (1964).

3. 5 Stat. 491 (1842).

4. 17 Stat. 28 (1872).

5. 46 Stat. 21 (1929).

6. Max Farrand, *The Records of the Federal Convention of 1787*, Rev. ed. (New Haven, 1937), I, 20. [May 29]

7. I Farrand 242-5. [June 15]

8. I Farrand 177-8. [June 9]

9. I Farrand 179-80. [June 9]

10. I Farrand 464. [June 29]

11. I Farrand 460. [June 29]

12. I Farrand 541. [July 6]

13. I Farrand 457. [June 28]

14. I Farrand 196. [June 11]

15. I Farrand 197-8. [June 11]

16. I Farrand 467. [June 29]

17. I Farrand 286-7. [June 18]

18. I Farrand 465-6. [June 29]

19. I Farrand 322. [June 19]

20. I Farrand 446. [June 28]

21. I Farrand 447. [June 28]
22. I Farrand 486. [June 30]
23. I Farrand 527-8. [July 5]
24. I Farrand 180. [June 9]
25. I Farrand 456-7. [June 28]
26. I Farrand 459. [June 28]
27. I Farrand 253-4. [June 16]
28. I Farrand 406. [June 25]
29. I Farrand 482-3. [June 30]
30. I Farrand 406. [June 25]
31. II Farrand 523. [Sept. 6]
32. II Farrand 240. [Aug. 9]
33. II Farrand 240. [Aug. 9]
34. II Farrand 241. [Aug. 9]
35. II Farrand 241. [Aug. 9]
36. II Farrand 241. [Aug. 9]
37. *The Federalist* (Glazier ed., 1842), 253.
38. Ibid., 272.
39. 377 U.S. 533 (1964).
40. 377 U.S. 713 (1964).
41. *Washington Post*, Sept. 10, 1964.
42. II Elliot 11.
43. II Elliot 202.
44. IV Elliot 21.
45. IV Elliot 257.
46. IV Elliot 304.
47. IV Elliot 303.
48. II Elliot 49.
49. II Elliot 50-1.
50. III Elliot 366-7.
51. III Elliot 70.
52. III Elliot 71.
53. 376 U.S. 1, 39.
54. *The Works of James Wilson* (Andrews ed., 1896), II, 15.
55. Ibid., 10.

THE FACES OF JUDICIAL REVIEW

1. *Collected Legal Papers* (New York, 1920), 295-6.
2. *Martin v. Hunter's Lessee*, 1 Wheaton 304 (1816); *Cohens v. Virginia,* 6 Wheaton 264 (1821).

FROM COKE TO BLACKSTONE

1. a) Humphry W. Woolrych, *The Life of Sir Edward Coke* (London, 1826). b) Cuthbert W. Johnson, *The Life of Sir Edward Coke* (London, 1845). See I, 302.

2. See, e.g., E. S. Corwin, *The "Higher Law" Background of American Constitutional Law* (Ithaca, N.Y., 1955), p. 54.

3. *Dr. Bonham's Case*, 8 Co. 107 (a) (1610).

4. Ibid., 118 (a).

5. Ibid.

6. Ibid., 119 (a).

7. See Louis B. Boudin, *Government by Judiciary* (New York, 1932) I, 506.

8. 4 Co. Inst. 36

9. Hobart 85, 87.

10. 12 Mod. 669, 687.

11. Ibid., 678.

12. Ibid., 687-8.

13. *Captain Streater's Case*, 5 How. St. Tr. 365, 386.

14. 2 Show. K. B. 475.

15. *The History of England*, 2nd ed. (London, 1849), II, 84.

16. 2 Show. K. B. 475-8.

17. Bill of Rights, 1688 (1 Will. & Mary Sess. 2, c. 2), s. 12.

18. Blackstone's *Commentaries*, Book I, Section 3, [91]. (I Chitty's Blackstone 63.)

ACROSS THE ATLANTIC

1. Op. cit., p. 53.

2. "Bonham's Case and Judicial Review," 40 *Harv. L. Rev.* 64-5 (1926).

3. *The American Doctrine of Judicial Supremacy*, 2nd ed. (Berkeley, 1932), p. 73.

4. 40 *Harv. L. Rev.* 62.

5. Op. cit., p. 57.

6. See Bondin, op. cit., I, 519-526.

7. See Andrew M. Davis, "The Case of *Frost v. Leighton*," 2 *Am. Hist. Rev.* 229-240 (1897) for source of the case.

8. Op. cit., p. 56.

9. McMaster, op. cit. (New York, 1900), V, 394.

10. He was the Reporter of the volume which contains the case; see 1 Jeff. (Va.) 109.

11. *American Doctrine of Judicial Supremacy*, 1st ed. (New York, 1914), p. 52.

12. James Bradley Thayer, *Cases on Constitutional Law* (Cambridge, 1895), I, p. 49.

13. J. T. Morse, *John Adams—American Statesmen Series* (Boston and New York, 1898), p. 23.

14. *The Works of John Adams* (Boston, 1856), X, 248.

15. I Thayer's *Cases* 50.

16. I Thayer's *Cases* 51.

17. Plucknett, op. cit., p. 63, quoting 26 MS. Archives of Massachusetts, 153-4 ff.

18. Ibid.

19. Ibid., p. 64.
20. Ibid.
21. Op. cit., p. 78.
22. IX, 390-91.
23. Op. cit., p. 74.
24. 40 *Harv. L. Rev.* 41, n.
25. See Corwin, op. cit., p. 74.

THE "HIGHER LAW"

1. *Nicomachean Ethics* (Ross tr., 1925), V, 7, Sec. 1-2.
2. Lactantius, *Div. Inst.* (Roberts and Donaldson tr., 1871), VI, 8, 370.
3. Ibid.
4. See *John Locke and the Doctrine of Majority Rule* (Urbana, 1940) by Willmoore Kendall; *Natural Right and History* (Chicago, 1953) by Leo Strauss.
5. John Locke, *Second Treatise of Civil Government*, Sec. 134.
6. Ibid.
7. Ibid., Sec. 149.
8. Ibid., Secs. 149, 150.
9. *The Law of Nations*, (London, 1811), pp. 11, 12, 77.

INDEPENDENCE: THE BEGINNING OF AN "IRRESISTIBLE PROCESS"?

1. 1st edition (New York, 1914), p. 73.
2. Op. cit., p. 62.
3. Haines, op. cit., 2nd ed., p. 69.
4. See Haines, ibid., pp. 67-87.
5. Pennsylvania Constitution of 1776, Sec. 47, 5 Thorpe, Charters and Constitutions 3091.
6. New York Constitution of 1777, Sec. 3, 5 Thorpe 2628-9.

THE CASE OF JOSIAH PHILIPS

1. I Tucker's Blackstone, App. 293.
2. Hening, Va. Stat. at L. LX 463. Such bills were not forbidden, however, by the Virginia Constitution.
3. See Jesse Turner, "A Phantom Precedent," 48 *Am. Law Rev.* 321 (1914).
4. Op. cit., p. 91.
5. III Elliot 66-7.
6. III Elliot 66-7 et seq.

HOLMES *v.* WALTON

1. Alfred H. Kelly and Winfred A. Harbison, *The American Constitution, Its Origins and Development* (New York, 1955), Rev. ed., p. 99.
2. *Holmes v. Walton: The New Jersey Precedent,* 4 *Am. Hist. Rev.* 456 (1899).

3. Op. cit., p. 99.

4. See Articles XXII and XXIII, New Jersey Constitution of 1776.

5. See W. W. Crosskey, *Politics and the Constitution in the History of the United States* (Chicago, 1953), II, 949.

6. Acts of New Jersey, 1775, Chap. IX, Sec. 5.

7. Cf. Art. XXII, N.J. Const. of 1776.

8. Acts of New Jersey, 1778, Chap. XLV, Sec. 6.

9. Votes of New Jersey Assembly, December 8, 1780.

10. II Crosskey 950.

11. Cf. II Crosskey 951, n. 28.

COMMONWEALTH v. CATON

1. 4 Call 5, 20; 8 Va. 5, 20.

2. Preface to 4 Call (8 Va.).

3. Cf. II Crosskey 952.

4. Cf. 1 Call, Dedication.

RUTGERS v. WADDINGTON

1. *Cases on Constitutional Law*, James Bradley Thayer (Cambridge, 1895), I, 63.

2. I Thayer's *Cases* 69.

3. I Thayer's *Cases* 70.

4. I Thayer's *Cases* 71.

5. See pamphlet, "An account of the Case . . . Rutgers v. Waddington," by Henry B. Dawson (Morrisania, 1866), quoted in Haines, op. cit., 101-2.

6. Ibid., p. 103.

7. *Judicial Power and Unconstitutional Legislation* (Phila., 1893), p. 230.

TREVETT v. WEEDEN

1. (New York, 1959), p. 23.

2. James M. Varnum, pamphlet: *The Case, Trevett v. Weeden* (Providence, 1787), reprinted in I Thayer's *Cases* 74-5.

3. I Thayer's *Cases* 75.

4. I Thayer's *Cases* 73.

5. Rhode Island Acts & Resolves, October (1st Session), 1786, p. 3.

6. I Thayer's *Cases* 76.

7. I Thayer's *Cases* 77.

8. I Thayer's *Cases* 78.

9. Op. cit., p. 99.

10. Varnum, op. cit., quoted in Coxe, p. 242.

11. Ibid., 243-4.

THE SYMSBURY CASE

1. Kirby (Conn.) 444 (1785).

2. Kirby (Conn.) 444, 447.
3. II Crosskey 961.

THE "LOST" MASSACHUSETTS PRECEDENT

1. See Bancroft, *History of the Formation of the Constitution of the United States* (New York, 1882) II, 472-3.
2. A. C. Goodell, Jr., "An Early Constitutional Case in Massachusetts," 7 *Harv. L. Rev.* 415 (1894).
3. Op. cit., 1st ed., p. 120-1.

SOME NEW HAMPSHIRE "OCCURRENCES"

1. II Crosskey 970.
2. II Crosskey 969.
3. II Crosskey 970.
4. II Crosskey 969-70.
5. II Crosskey 970.
6. II Crosskey 970.
7. II Crosskey 971.

BAYARD *v.* SINGLETON

1. Cf. I Thayer's *Cases* 78.
2. I Thayer's *Cases* 79.
3. I Thayer's *Cases* 79.
4. North Carolina State Records, XVIII, pp. 42, 215-17, 428-29.
5. Ibid.
6. I Thayer's *Cases* 79.
7. I Thayer's *Cases* 79-80.
8. II Crosskey 972.
9. See, e.g., Boudin, op. cit., I, 63-5; Crosskey, op. cit., II, 971-3; Coxe, op. cit., pp. 266-7.
10. McRee, *Life and Correspondence of James Iredell* (New York, 1858), II, 168-9.
11. I Thayer's *Cases* 79.
12. I Thayer's *Cases* 79.
13. See Coxe, op. cit., pp. 251-52.

THE PROBLEM AT PHILADELPHIA

1. See II Crosskey 976.
2. See I Farrand 18-23.
3. See I Farrand 240-41.

4. See II Farrand 28.
5. See II Farrand 32.

THE MEANING OF THE SUPREMACY CLAUSE, I

1. I Farrand 169.
2. II Farrand 28.
3. 6 Wheaton 264 (1824).
4. *Journal of the House of Delegates, Virginia*, 1820, p. 108.
5. 6 Wheaton 264, 320.
6. 1 Wheaton 304 (1816).
7. 4 Mumford (18 Va.) 1, 58-9 (1814).
8. 4 Mumford 1, 26.
9. Quoted from *Jefferson Papers MSS* by Charles Warren, *The Supreme Court in United States History*, Revised ed. (Boston, 1935), I, 564.

THE MEANING OF THE SUPREMACY CLAUSE, II

1. See II Crosskey 990-1000.
2. II Crosskey 1015.
3. See Coxe, op. cit., p. 335.
4. Op. cit., p. 326.

JUDICIAL REVIEW ELSEWHERE IN THE CONSTITUTION

1. 1 Cranch 137, 180 (1803).

JUDICIAL REVIEW AT THE CONSTITUTIONAL CONVENTION

1. Beard: *The Supreme Court and the Constitution* (New York, 1912), pp. 50-51; Corwin: 1913 *American Political Science Review* 330; Davis: *The Judicial Veto* (Boston & New York, 1914), p. 49.
2. II Crosskey 1009, et seq.
3. Max Farrand, *The Records of the Federal Convention* (New Haven, 1937), I, 97-8.
4. I Farrand 98.
5. I Farrand 105.
6. I Farrand 107.
7. I Farrand 109.
8. II Farrand 27.
9. II Farrand 27-8.
10. II Farrand 28.

11. II Farrand 28.
12. II Farrand 73.
13. II Farrand 73.
14. II Farrand 74.
15. II Farrand 75.
16. II Farrand 76.
17. II Farrand 78.
18. II Farrand 92.
19. II Farrand 93.
20. II Farrand 248.
21. II Farrand 298.
22. II Farrand 299.
23. II Farrand 299.
24. II Farrand 300-02.
25. II Farrand 376.
26. II Farrand 378-9.
27. II Farrand 391.
28. II Farrand 428.
29. II Farrand 440.

THE FEDERALIST

1. *The Writings of George Washington* (Washington, 1939), XXX, 66.
2. *The Writings of James Madison* (Philadelphia, 1865), I, 194.
3. I *Annals*, June 8, 1789 (p. 439).
4. Ibid.
5. Ibid., June 17 (p. 495).
6. Ibid., (p. 500).
7. Irving Brant, *James Madison* (Indianapolis and New York, 1941), III, 470.
8. *Letters and Other Writings of James Madison* (Philadelphia, 1865), IV, 519.
9. Ibid.
10. Ibid.
11. Ibid., p. 517.
12. Ibid., p. 519.
13. Ibid., p. 553.
14. Op. cit., p. 55.
15. *Constitution of the United States* [Annotated] (Washington, D.C., Government Printing Office, 1953), p. 55.
16. II Crosskey 1011.

1789: THE STATUS QUO ANTE

1. Hyneman, op. cit., pp. 96-7.

INDEX

AAA (Agricultural Adjustment Acts of 1933, 1938), 22

Abington Township v. Schempp—see Schempp-Murray Cases

Adams, John, 138, 143, 144-45

Albertus Magnus, 149

Alexander of Hales, 149

Alien Registration (Smith) Act of 1940, 58-59, 62, 63n, 64, 68, 69

Alien and Sedition Acts, 18, 309, 340

American Constitution, The, 185

American Constitution, Its Origins and Development, The, 124n

American Doctrine of Judicial Supremacy, 124n, 142n, 159

Americans for Democratic Action, 234n

Ames, Fisher, 342

Annuitie 41, 129n

Apportionment Act of 1929, 84, 84n

Aristotle, 148

Article I, 59, 82-85, 87-88, 93n, 104, 108, 232, 234, 268, 304, 341, 345

Article II, 268

Article III, 110, 231n, 232-35, 251, 268-71, 329

Article IV, 81, 269, 270, 331

Article V, 20, 30, 46, 93n

Article VI, 33, 226, 227

Article VII, 20

Articles of Confederation, 88n-89n, 91n, 96, 116, 179, 221-23, 228, 245, 247-48, 251-52, 252n, 254, 287-88, 312, 313, 337, 343

Baker v. Carr, 82, 83, 85, 109

Bayard v. Singleton (Newbern case), 203-12, 213-14, 261, 277, 303n, 328, 335n

Beard, Charles, 273, 311

Bill of Rights, 17, 25, 77, 306, 326

Black, Hugo, 70n, 85-109, 341-50

Blackstone, Sir William, 134-36, 146, 147, 152-54, 181, 182, 184, 192, 193, 284, 332

"Blaine Amendment," 78

Bonham—*see Dr. Bonham's Case*

Boudin, Louis B., 126n, 167, 167n, 168n, 198n

Bracton, Henry de, 150

Brandeis, Louis D., 52

Brant, Irving, 308n

Brattle v. Hinckley, 198n

Brearly, David, 171-72

Brennan, William J., Jr., 76, 82, 85

Bricker Amendment, 243, 244n

British Privy Council, 124n-125n

Browder, Earl, 58

Brown v. Board of Education of Topeka, 20, 27n-28n, 32-33, 35, 41-57, 184

Burke, Edmund, 146n

Burton, Harold H., 63n

Butler, Pierce, 52, 53

"Call's Reports," 173-78

Canon Law, 150n

Cantwell v. Connecticut, 72

Case of the Judges, 178n, 197, 197n

Case de Libellis Famosis, 126n

Case of the Seals, The, 129n, 134

Caton—*see Commonwealth v. Caton*
Cessavit 42, 128, 129n
Charleston and Western Carolina R.
    Co. v. Varnville Furniture Co., 61n
Cicero, Marcus Tullius, 149, 153
City of London v. Wood, 131
Civil Rights Act of 1866, 20n, 28n,
    44-45
Civil War, 25, 26, 27, 31; *see also*
    Reconstruction
Clark, Tom, 67n-68n, 72-73, 78-79,
    85n
Cohens v. Virginia, 116, 236-39
Coke, Sir Edward, 123-36, 139-40, 142-
    48, 209
Colden, Mr., 145
Commentaries, 134, 146, 146n, 153
Commentaries on the Constitution of
    the United States, 75
Commonwealth v. Caton, 173-78, 213
Commonwealth v. Nelson, 58, 62-63,
    63n, 69
Communist Control Act of 1954, 62
Communist Party of the U.S., 58, 67
Constitutional Convention, 86-108,
    116, 124n, 171, 185, 200-201, 203-8,
    220-26, 239, 246, 250-51, 254-55, 260,
    261, 265, 269, 270, 272-99, 302, 316,
    321, 328-33, 337, 342
Continental Congress, 88n, 179, 252n
Cooper v. Aaron, 32-33
Corwin, Edward S., 77, 116n, 123,
    130n, 137, 137n, 144, 145, 160, 273,
    311
Council of Censors, 160, 324
Council of Revision, 161, 223, 223n,
    250, 276, 278, 290, 311, 333
Court Over Constitution, 116n
Coxe, Brinton, 125n, 150n, 154n, 183,
    209, 256
Crosskey, William W., 146n, 168n,
    170, 175n, 178, 193n, 196, 198n,
    199-203, 206, 233n, 244-56, 275,
    275n, 277n, 289n-290n, 295n-296n,
    297, 311, 328
Cumming v. Richmond (Ga.) County
    Board of Education, 51-53
Cushing, William, 138, 144, 145
Cutting, J. B., 197, 197n, 198

Dana, Francis, 345
Dandridge, Bartholomew, 175n
Davie, William R., 207n, 343, 347
Davis, Horace, 273
Dawson, Henry B., 183n
Day v. Savadge, 130, 142
Declaration of Independence, 79
Devol, Judge, 187, 192, 193
Dickinson, John, 291-93, 293n, 296
Dirksen, Everett M., 111
Dr. Bonham's Case; Bonham Doc-
    trine, 124, 126, 127, 128n, 130, 131,
    137, 142-48, 331
Dred Scott v. Sanford, 117, 137n

Eighteenth Amendment, 25, 28
Eighth Amendment, 271
Electoral College, 333
Eleventh Amendment, 26, 271
Elizabeth Rutgers v. Joshua Wad-
    dington, 183n
Ellsworth, Oliver, 105n
Encyclopedists (France), 154
Engel v. Vitale, 70n, 72, 75
"Equalizing Court," 222-23
Everson v. Board of Education, 72,
    75, 78

Farrand, Max, 89n, 275n-276n, 277n
Federal Bureau of Investigation, 66
Federalist, The, 108, 109n, 239, 249,
    265, 300-327, 330, 339; No. 16, 311-
    14, 320, 321; No. 21, 313; No. 22,
    313; No. 32, 60n; No. 33, 313-14,
    321; No. 39, 303-5; No. 44, 304-5;
    No. 46, 322; No. 47, 324; No. 48,
    324; No. 49, 324; No. 50, 325; No.
    51, 325-26, 338; No. 54, 108, 342;
    No. 57, 341, 350; No. 59, 108; No.
    73, 314n; No. 78, 314-21, 333, 335,
    338; No. 80, 319; No. 81, 265, 320-
    22; No. 82, 320
Fifteenth Amendment, 26, 27
Fifth Amendment, 19, 271
Finch, Heneage, 133
First Amendment, 18-20, 24, 29, 71-
    79, 271
"Footnote 11," 55
Fortescue, Sir John, 150

Fourteenth Amendment, 19, 20n, 27, 27n-28n, 31, 33, 42-57, 72, 77-78, 82, 271, 326
Fourth Amendment, 271
"Fragments on the Confederation of the American States," 222
Frankfurter, Felix, 82n
Franklin, Benjamin, 93n, 96, 96n, 103
Freeman's Journal, 222
Frost v. Leighton, 125n, 138, 139-40

Gaines—see Missouri ex rel Gaines v. Canada
Galloway, James, 347-48
Gerry, Elbridge, 93n, 96-97, 208, 254, 261, 276-78, 282-85, 291, 296
Giddings v. Brown, 138-39
Gilbert v. Minnesota, 64-66
Godden v. Hales, 132, 134
Gong Lum v. Rice, 52, 53
Goodell, A. C., Jr., 198n
Gorham, Nathaniel, 105, 105n, 283-84
Government by Judiciary, 126n
Grant, Ulysses S., 78
Gratian, 149
Great Compromise (Constitutional Convention), 86-87, 92-94, 98, 100, 103, 344
Gridley, Jeremiah, 144
Guaranty Clause—*see* Article IV

Haines, Charles G., 124n, 125n, 137-40, 142, 142n, 154n, 159, 164-66, 198, 198n, 199, 204
Hales, Sir Edward, 133
Hamilton, Alexander, 60n-61n, 97, 102, 108-9, 180, 183, 183n, 184, 265, 300-325 *passim*, 330, 332, 333, 335, 338
Harbison, Winfred, 124n, 166, 190
Harlan, John Marshall, 51, 69, 82n, 84n, 85n, 86, 88, 349
Harrison, Benjamin, 165
Hart, Henry W., Jr., 234n
Harvard Law Review, 197
Harvard Law School, 234n
Hazard, Judge, 193
Henry, Patrick, 163-65

Herle, Judge, 128, 128n
"Higher Law" Background of American Constitutional Law, The, 123, 130n
Hines v. Davidowitz, 64
History of the People of the United States, 141
Hobart, Lord, 130-32
Holmes, Oliver Wendell, 19, 52, 116
Holmes v. Walton, 166-72, 191n, 213, 214
Holt, Lord, 131, 132
Hoover, J. Edgar, 66
Howell, Judge, 187-93
Hughes, Charles Evans, 37, 118
Hunter's Lessee—see Martin v. Hunter's Lessee
Hutchinson, Thomas, 143-44
Hyneman, Charles, 33, 334

Institutes, 127, 130
Iredell, James, 207, 209-12, 214, 292, 303n, 330, 335

Jackson, Robert H., 72
Jacobins, 154n
Jay, John, 300
Jefferson, Thomas, 73, 75-76, 76n, 142, 163, 197, 238-39, 305-6, 324-25
Jenner-Butler bill, 234n
John of Salisbury, 149
Johnson, Samuel, 246, 248-49, 252, 254, 256, 295
Johnson, William Samuel, 93n
Jones, Sir Thomas, 133
Judicial Power and Unconstitutional Legislation, 125n
Judiciary Act of 1789, 263
Judiciary Article—*see* Article III

Kelly, Alfred H., 124n, 166, 190
Kendall, Willmoore, 301, 303
King, Rufus, 91, 92, 92n, 97, 100n, 106, 278, 297, 345

Lardner, Mr., 76
Law of Nations, 153
League of Women Voters, 80
Life and Works (John Adams), 145

Lincoln, Abraham, 31
Locke, John, 148, 150-55, 160-61
Lowndes, Rawlins, 345
Lucas v. Forty-Fourth General Assembly, 110
Lyons, Peter, 176n

Machiavelli, Niccolo, 149
Macaulay, Thomas Babington, 133
Madison, James, 73-76, 85n, 89-92, 94, 94n, 95n, 97-99, 100n, 102, 105-6, 107, 107n, 108, 124n, 175n, 221, 223, 226, 228-29, 241n, 255, 261, 275-81, 284, 288, 290-98, 300-327, 330, 338, 341-42, 345n, 346, 350
Marbury v. Madison, 33, 37, 212, 270, 317, 319, 322, 332, 336
Marshall, John, 37, 165, 177, 212, 223n, 238, 238n, 270, 317, 321, 332, 336
Martin, Luther, 94, 98, 226, 254, 279, 285-87
Martin v. Hunter's Lessee, 116, 233n, 237-39
Mason, George, 89, 89n, 93n, 95n, 261, 286-87
McCarran Act of 1950, 62, 63n
McCollum v. Board of Education, 72, 75, 78
McHenry, James, 295, 295n
McKenna, Joseph, 65-66
McMaster, John, 141
McReynolds, James C., 52, 53
Mercer, James, 175n, 176n
Mercer, John F., 175n, 290-93, 293n
Mercury (Newport, R.I.), 187, 192, 193
Meredith, James, 323
Metternich, Clemens, 24n
Minton, Sherman, 63n
Missouri ex rel Gaines v. Canada, 52-53
Missouri v. Holland, 244n
"Monmouth Petition," 191n
Monroe, James, 346
Montesquieu, Charles, 324, 332
Morris, Gouverneur, 106, 171, 226, 254, 261, 280-81, 287-88, 292-95, 333
Mumford, Paul, 187, 190

Murray v. Curlett—see Schempp-Murray Cases

National Lenin Institute of Moscow, 58
Nelson, Steve—*see Commonwealth v. Nelson; Pennsylvania v. Nelson*
Newbern case—*see Bayard v. Singleton*
New Deal, 22-23
New Hampshire Spy, 199-201
New Jersey Plan (Constitutional Convention), 86-87, 96n, 97, 100, 225
Nicholas, George, 165
Nineteenth Amendment, 26-27
Ninth Amendment, 17n
Notes (James Madison), 275, 275n, 277n, 278

"Obligation of Contracts" clause, 18, 297
Otis, James, 138, 142, 142n, 143

Paterson, William, 90, 91n, 99, 100, 225
Pendleton, Edmund, 175n, 176n, 178
Pennsylvania v. Nelson, 35, 58-69
Pennsylvania Sedition Act, 58-62, 63n
Petition of Right, 127
Philips, Josiah, 162-65, 213
Pierce, William, 278
Pinckney, Charles, 105, 106, 255, 274, 289, 289n, 290, 295-97, 343n, 344
Pinckney, Charles Cotesworth, 344
Plato, 148
Plessy v. Ferguson, 48, 50-51, 54
Plucknett, Theodore, 128n, 129n, 137, 138, 144-45
Politics and the Constitution in the History of the United States, 146n, 244
Powis, Thomas, 133
Preamble, 22, 57
Pritchett, Herman, 185
Privy Council—*see* British Privy Council
Prohibition Era, 25; *see also* Eighteenth Amendment

Raleigh, Sir Walter, 126n
Randolph, Edmund, 89n, 93n, 105n, 163, 164-65, 223
Rauh, Joseph, 35, 234n
Read, George, 106n
Reconstruction; Reconstruction Acts, 26, 46-48; see also Civil War
Records of the Federal Convention of 1787, The (Farrand), 89n, 275n-276n
Reed, Stanley F., 63n, 66
Reynolds v. Sims, 109, 110
Rice, Charles E., 79
Rice v. Santa Fe Elevator Corp., 61n, 64n
Rice—see Gong Lum v. Rice
Rights of the British Colonies Asserted and Proved, The, 143
Roane, Judge Spencer, 237
Roberts, Owen J., 52, 72
Robin v. Hardaway, 138, 142
Roosevelt, Franklin D., 23, 24, 52, 66
Rostow, Eugene, 57, 335
Rousseau, Jean Jacques, 154
Rutgers, Elizabeth, 180
Rutgers v. Waddington, 174n, 179-84, 191n, 201, 208, 213, 214, 228, 261
Rutledge, John, 105, 105n, 107, 296, 297
Rutledge, Wiley Blount, 72

St. Isidore of Seville, 149
St. Thomas Aquinas, 149
Sawyer, Sir Robert, 133
Schempp-Murray Cases, 35, 70-79
Scott, Austin, 166, 171
Second Amendment, 60
Second Treatise on Civil Government, 150
Seventeenth Amendment, 26
Seventh Amendment, 271
Sexton v. California, 63n
Sherman, Roger, 93n, 106, 279-80, 282
Sherman Anti-Trust Act, 41
Sixteenth Amendment, 20, 26
Sixth Amendment, 271
Small Causes Act, 167, 168, 172n
Smith, Howard W., 58n, 62
Smith, William, 308

Smith Act—see Alien Registration Act
Smyth, Alexander, 237
Spaight, Richard Dobbs, 206-9, 303n, 335
Stamp Act, 138, 141-42, 143
Steele, John, 347-49
Stevens, Thaddeus, 45
Stewart, Potter, 78
Stone, Harlan F., 52
Story, Joseph, 75, 233n, 238, 238n
Streater, Captain, 131-32
Supremacy Clause, 208, 225-67, 269, 270, 279-83, 288, 289, 291-92, 295, 296, 296n, 298-99, 312, 314, 328-31, 337, 349
Supreme Court in United States History, The, 238n
Sutherland, George, 52
Sweezy v. New Hampshire (1957), 67n-68n
Symonds, Magistrate, 138-39
Symsbury Case, 174n, 195-96, 213

Taft, William Howard, 52
Ten-Pound Act, 199-202, 328
Tenth Amendment, 17n, 22, 42-43, 46, 59, 60, 77, 83, 117
Tenth Rule (for construing English statutes), 134, 181
Test Oath Act of 1673, 132
Thirteenth Amendment, 27, 31
Tillinghast, Judge, 187, 193, 193n
Tregor's Case, 128, 128n, 129n
Trevett, John, 187
Trevett v. Weeden, 179, 185-94, 201, 206, 208, 213, 229, 260, 261, 277n, 280, 328
Trumbull, Lyman, 44, 56
Truscott, Frank, 62
Tuck bill, 110-11
Tucker, St. George, 162-63
Twelfth Amendment, 25
Twentieth Amendment, 25
Twenty-first Amendment, 25, 28
Twenty-second Amendment, 24, 25
Twenty-third Amendment, 26-27
Twenty-fourth Amendment, 26-27, 31

United Nations, 274
University of Mississippi, 323

Van Devanter, Willis, 52
Varnum, James M., 185-93, 206
*Varnville—see Charleston and West-
ern Carolina R. Co. v. Varnville
Furniture Co.*
Vattel, Emmerich de, 148, 153, 154,
160-61, 333
"Virginia county court case," 141
Virginia Plan (Constitutional Con-
vention), 86-87, 97, 102, 223-24,
276, 302
Virginia Resolutions, 309, 310
Voegelin, Eric, 149
Voltaire, François, 154

Waddington, Joshua—*see Rutgers v.
Waddington*
Walton, Elisha—*see Holmes v. Walton*
Warren, Charles, 238n
Warren, Earl, 43-44, 48-57, 58, 60-69,
336
Washington, George, 301
Washington Post, 111

Weeden, John—*see Trevett v. Weeden*
Weinberg, Joseph, 58
Wesberry v. Sanders, 35, 80-112, 341-
42
William of Occam, 149
Williamson, Hugh, 99-100, 261, 294-
95
Wilson, James, 90-91, 94, 94n, 95n,
98-104, 105n, 107, 109n, 246-47,
250-51, 261, 282-85, 290, 291, 293,
295, 295n, 296, 349
Wilson, James F., 45
Winthrop v. Lechmere, 125n
Wolcott, Oliver, 343
Wood v. Broom, 84n
Writs of Assistance, 138, 142
Wythe, George, 173-77, 178n

Yale Law School, 57
Yates, Robert, 90n, 94n, 99, 278
Yick Wo v. Hopkins, 51n

Zorach v. Clauson, 72